Social Indicators and
Social Theory

THE WILEY SERIES IN URBAN RESEARCH

TERRY N. CLARK, Editor

Resources for Social Change: Race in the United States
by James S. Coleman

City Classification Handbook: Methods and Applications
Brian J. L. Berry, Editor

Bonds of Pluralism: The Form and Substance of Urban Social Networks
by Edward O. Laumann

Nonpartisan Elections and the Case for Party Politics
by Willis D. Hawley

Politics and Poverty: Modernization and Response in Five Poor Neighborhoods
by Stanley B. Greenberg

Education, Opportunity, and Social Inequality: Changing Prospects in Western Society
by Raymond Boudon

Guerrillas in the Bureaucracy: The Community Planning Experiment in the United States
by Martin L. Needleman and Carolyn Emerson Needleman

The Roots of Urban Discontent: Public Policy, Municipal Institutions, and the Ghetto
by Peter H. Rossi, Richard A. Berk, and Bettye K. Eidson

Human Activity Patterns in the City: Things People Do in Time and in Space
by F. Stuart Chapin, Jr.

Ethnicity in the United States: A Preliminary Reconnaissance
by Andrew M. Greeley

Mayors in Action: Five Approaches to Urban Governance
by John P. Kotter and Paul R. Lawrence

Leadership and Power in the Bos-Wash Megalopolis: Environment, Ecology,
and Urban Organization
by Delbert C. Miller

Social Indicators and Social Theory: Elements of an Operational System
by Karl A. Fox

Social Indicators and Social Theory

ELEMENTS OF AN OPERATIONAL SYSTEM

KARL A. FOX

A WILEY-INTERSCIENCE PUBLICATION

JOHN WILEY & SONS, New York · London · Sydney · Toronto

To

MORDECAI EZEKIEL and FREDERICK V. WAUGH

*Pioneers in combining
measurement with theory*

Library of Congress Cataloging in Publication Data

Fox, Karl August, 1917–
    Social indicators and social theory.

    (The Wiley series in urban research)
    "A Wiley-Interscience publication."
    Includes bibliographical references.
    1. Social sciences—Methodology.   2. Social
indicators.   3. System theory.   I. Title.

H61.F62   300′.1′8   74-16255
ISBN 0-471-27060-1

Printed in the United States of America

10 9 8 7 6 5 4 3 2 1

The Wiley Series in Urban Research

Cities, especially American cities, are attracting more public attention and scholarly concern than at perhaps any other time in history. Traditional structures have been seriously questioned and sweeping changes proposed; simultaneously, efforts are being made to penetrate the fundamental processes by which cities operate. This effort calls for marshaling knowledge from a number of substantive areas. Sociologists, political scientists, economists, geographers, planners, historians, anthropologists, and others have turned to urban questions; interdisciplinary projects involving scholars and activists are groping with fundamental issues.

The Wiley Series in Urban Research has been created to encourage the publication of works bearing on urban questions. It seeks to publish studies from different fields that help to illuminate urban processes. It is addressed to scholars as well as to planners, administrators, and others concerned with a more analytical understanding of things urban.

TERRY N. CLARK

Preface

The literature on social indicators is expanding rapidly, and outstanding social scientists are contributing to it. The time is not ripe for a definitive work by a single scholar. However, I hope that this book will facilitate convergence toward an operational system or systems of social accounts and indicators.

What is called for, I believe, is an integration of theory, methods, and data across the "social" parts of the social and behavioral sciences. The horizontal integration of theory across this domain has been accomplished to varying degrees by able scholars from Plato to Pareto. The vertical integration of theory, methods, and data was not seriously contemplated even in economics until Henry L. Moore announced such an intention in his 1908 article, "The Statistical Complement of Pure Economics." Moore made the first major attempts to combine economic theory and statistical techniques in the empirical estimation of economic relationships. He applied multiple regression analysis to time series data on crop prices and production that were routinely published by the U.S. Department of Agriculture and obtained useful estimates of demand and supply curves. In effect, he converted economic indicators into econometric models.

Since the 1940s, increasing numbers of social scientists have learned to operate in two or more disciplines and to work effectively on multidisciplinary teams. Others have achieved partial syntheses of social science concepts around such fields as regional science, quantitative geography, urban planning, industrial relations, organization theory, policy sciences, public choice, management science, and business, public, and educational administration.

This book is addressed to scholars, practitioners, and students in the social sciences and in applied or professional fields with (in part) a social science base. I believe it will also be of interest to statisticians, operations researchers, systems analysts, and others working on social indicators for particular areas of concern such as health and air pollution.

I view the book as a monograph, and I have written the best monograph I could in the time available. Nevertheless, I hope it will also serve some of the functions for which texts are intended in more settled fields. Social indicators are expected to be numerical, practical, and operational. Many of them will be published by government agencies, discussed by legislative committees, and interpreted by journalists. A useful monograph in this field will not be as esoteric or advanced as a monograph on relativistic quantum mechanics.

From a technical standpoint, the book should be quite accessible to advanced undergraduates in the social sciences and related fields, with the usual help from their instructors. The principal awkwardness in using the book as an undergraduate text is its multidisciplinary character—I have juxtaposed (and to some extent integrated) concepts from sociology, economics, and ecological psychology in the core of my proposed system of social accounts and indicators. I have also given considerable emphasis to the delineation of appropriate regions for social indicators, using concepts that appear under different names in geography, regional science, and other fields. I have also made extensive use of Tinbergen's "theory of economic policy," which can readily be extended to models of social systems.

The book is not mathematically difficult. Several chapters contain no mathematics at all; some make limited use of matrix algebra, differential calculus, and mathematical programming. Chapter 3 contains several pages of mathematical proofs that are somewhat advanced, but their practical implications are clearly stated in words and (in Chapters 5 and 6) profusely illustrated with numerical examples.

I have tried to avoid drawing lines between disciplines, since I see more similarities than differences in their data system problems. As of 1967, some major objectives of the social indicators movement were based on economic prototypes (a Council of Social Advisers, a President's Social Report), and some sociologists may have felt that the economists had their data problems solved. In 1970 the president of the American Economic Association expressed the opinion that the economists had not solved their data problems but the agricultural economists had. In 1972 a committee of the American Agricultural Economics Association (AAEA) accepted this compliment on behalf of "an earlier generation," remarking, however, that the conceptual foundation of their present data system "is crumbling—and has been for some time." Edgar Dunn complimented the AAEA committee for recognizing that data problems were "bigger than we thought" and expressed his own view that data problems are, for the time being, "bigger than we are." The data problems of the social sciences will not be solved within conventional disciplinary boundaries.

In Section 1.2 I have presented the plan of the book and commented briefly on each chapter. I will use the rest of the preface to describe some aspects of my training and experience that have influenced my approach.

The first is an early interest in sociology, stimulated by Arthur L. Beeley. In my M.A. thesis I had hoped to make a substantive analysis of factors responsible for the unusually low crude death rate reported by a religious denomination that proscribed the use of tea, coffee, alcohol, and tobacco. I learned quite a bit about demography and a great deal more about underreporting, classification errors, and the difficulties of casual interpretation in complex social and biological systems. My objectives were 35 years ahead of the data, and the final title of my thesis was *A Critique of Mortality Statistics* (1938).

The second aspect is an early and somewhat eclectic introduction to econometrics, just after the Keynsian revolution in macroeconomics and just before the Haavelmo revolution in estimation techniques. In 1941 I took two courses based on Ezekiel's *Methods of Correlation Analysis* (1930), one from a psychometrician and the other from an actuary, and a business cycle seminar in which I gave reports on Schultz's *Theory and Measurement of Demand* (1938) and Tinbergen's *Statistical Testing of Business Cycle Theories* (1939). Directly and indirectly, the same courses introduced me to Sewall Wright's article on "Correlation and Causation" (1921), Frisch's *Statistical Confluence Analysis by Means of Complete Regression Systems* (1934), Koopmans's *Linear Regression Analysis of Economic Time Series* (1937), and Wold's *A Study in the Analysis of Stationary Time Series* (1938).

The third aspect is an intensive exposure to the field in which econometrics achieved its first practical successes. During 1942–1954 I read a substantial proportion of the published literature on statistical demand analysis, met many of the people who had contributed to it, and examined many unpublished studies in the files of the U.S. Bureau of Agricultural Economics. The dominant characteristic of this literature was a close integration of theory, methods, and data. The most visible contributors to its methodology were Mordecai Ezekiel, who became Vice-President of the American Statistical Association at age 30, and Frederick V. Waugh, one of the first American economists to make practical use of matrix methods (1935a), canonical correlation (1942), and linear programming (1951); Waugh also made empirical estimates of the marginal utility of money (1935b) and partial indifference surfaces (1956).

The fourth aspect is an opportunity during 1942–1954 to work with the data systems of the U.S. Department of Agriculture as they were approaching a peak of completeness, accuracy, and relevance to economic analysis and policy. As associate head (1947–1951) and head (1951–1954) of the Division of Statistical and Historical Research of the U.S. Bureau of Agricultural Economics, I had the pleasure of testing these data against the requirements of new methods and models (simultaneous equation techniques, input–output analysis, linear programming, spatial price equilibrium, optimal inventory policy, economic stabilization theory) and a wide range of policy problems in collaboration with one of the best-balanced research groups in the public serivice. The group had a continuous tradition dating from 1922 under the able leadership of O. C. Stine and (later) James P. Cavin. The nature of my own contributions is reflected in my book, *Econometric Analysis for Public Policy* (1958).

The fifth aspect is an interest, dating from the late 1950s, in Tinbergen's "theory of economic policy" (1952, 1954, 1956) and its extensions by Theil (1958). This interest took the form of a graduate workshop in economic policy developed jointly with Erik Thorbecke in 1959, a series of research grants from the National Science Foundation (jointly with Erik Thorbecke) during 1962–1971, and coauthorship of a book, *The Theory of Quantitative Economic Policy* (Fox, Sengupta, and Thorbecke, 1966).

The sixth is an interest in problems of resource allocation and output measurement for nonmarket organizations stemming from my 16 years (1955–1972) as head of a large and complex university department. This interest is reflected in a number of joint articles with Jati K. Sengupta and others and a book, *Economic Analysis for Educational Planning* (Fox, ed., 1972, with contributions by Fox, Sengupta, Kumar, and Sanyal).

The seventh is an interest in the spatial organization and location of economic and social activities, which goes back as far as 1941 and was extended in an ad hoc fashion as I encountered specific research and policy problems, ranging from industrial location prospects for the Central Valley of California to spatial equilibrium models of the livestock-feed economy of the United States (1953). This interest cumulated after 1956 as I participated in various studies of economic and institutional readjustment in Iowa and became familiar (through personal contact or reading) with the work of Leven, Tiebout, Isard, Garrison, and Berry. It also led me to the functional economic area (FEA) concept, which I first formulated in a 1961 paper, "The Concept of Community Development."

The eighth is my service during 1963–1967 as a member of the board of directors of the Social Science Research Council. This experience increased my awareness of research problems in disciplines other than economics and my admiration for some outstanding scholars who were working across disciplinary lines.

Since 1967, and particularly during 1972–1973, I have tried to read quite widely in the social sciences and to achieve a fairly uniform understanding of them at the level of the *International Encyclopedia of the Social Sciences*. In this book I have tried to juxtapose concepts from several disciplines in a rough and preliminary fashion: time budgets, behavior settings, generalized media of social exchange, total income, transactional analysis, life cycle stages, social readjustment rating scales, functional economic areas, occupational structures, and others. These concepts *could* be integrated into a formal mathematical system, but the result would be a notational morass—subscripts, like hypotheses, should not be multiplied unduly.

At this stage it is not clear that some of the concepts *should* be integrated, or that some of the variables could be measured with sufficient accuracy at a reasonable cost. "Experience," said Ambrose Bierce, "shows us the way that we should not have gone." I will not be disappointed if my numerical illustrations show us quickly and cheaply some ways we should not go—as well as some we should.

I have drawn on the published works of many scholars; I have stated my indebtedness to them at appropriate places in the text. I have had access to unpublished manuscripts by Nestor E. Terleckyj, by Kenneth C. Land, and by John P. Robinson and Philip E. Converse, whose courtesy has greatly expedited my own efforts; I believe these manuscripts will all be published before this book goes to press.

Chapter 3 was written jointly with Paul Van Moeseke, whose mathematical prowess far exceeds my own. Nearly all the research that underlies this book was supported by the National Science Foundation under Grant GS-2363 to Iowa State University.

Special thanks go to Ellen D. McGibbon, who did a magnificent job of typing the original manuscript and raising questions of an editorial nature on tables and references. Later she typed the bodies of all the tables in camera-ready form. My thanks also to Rita Bauman, who typed my redrafts of several sections with accuracy and dispatch.

KARL A. FOX

*Distinguished Professor
in Sciences and Humanities
and Professor of Economics*

*Iowa State University
Ames, Iowa
May 1974*

Acknowledgments

Permission to reprint the following material is gratefully acknowledged:

Quotation, p. 2: Reprinted from Raymond A. Bauer, "Detection and Anticipation of Impact: The Nature of the Task," p. 20, in *Social Indicators*, Raymond A. Bauer, editor, by permission of the M.I.T. Press, Cambridge, Massachusetts. Copyright 1966 by The American Academy of Arts and Sciences.

Quotation, p. 3: Reprinted from Bertram M. Gross, "The State of the Nation: Social Systems Accounting," pp. 270–271, in *Social Indicators*, Raymond A. Bauer, editor, by permission of the M.I.T. Press, Cambridge, Massachusetts. Copyright 1966 by The American Academy of Arts and Sciences.

Quotation, p. 4: from Social Science Research Council, *Social Indicators Newsletter*, No. 1, March 1973, p. 1.

Quotation, p. 5: from Kenneth C. Land, "Social Indicator Models: An Overview," in *Social Indicator Models*, Kenneth C. Land and Seymour Spilerman, editors. New York: Russell Sage Foundation, 1974, p. 17. Copyright © 1974 by Russell Sage Foundation. Reprinted by permission.

Quotation, pp. 10–11: from Erik H. Erikson, "Life Cycle," in *International Encyclopedia of the Social Sciences*, Volume 9. New York: The Macmillan Company and The Free Press, pp. 288–292. Copyright 1968 by Crowell Collier & Macmillan, Inc.

Quotation, pp. 10–12: from Henry A. Murray, "Personality: Contemporary Viewpoints. II. Components of an Evolving Personological System," in *International Encyclopedia of the Social Sciences*, Volume 12. New York: The Macmillan Company and The Free Press, p. 7. Copyright 1968 by Crowell Collier & Macmillan, Inc.

XII   ACKNOWLEDGMENTS

Quotation, p. 13: from Wilder Penfield, "Memory Mechanisms," *American Medical Association Archives of Neurology and Psychiatry*, **67** (1952), pp. 178–198. Copyright 1952, American Medical Association.

Quotation, pp. 13–14: from Thomas A. Harris, *I'm O.K.—You're O.K.: A Practical Guide to Transactional Analysis*. New York: Harper and Row, Publishers, 1969, pp. 18–29. Copyright 1967, 1968, 1969 by Thomas A. Harris, M.D.

Quotation, pp. 14–15: from Talcott Parsons, "Systems Analysis: Social Systems," in *International Encyclopedia of the Social Sciences*, Volume 15, pp. 461–469. New York: The Macmillan Company and The Free Press. Copyright 1968 by Crowell Collier & Macmillan, Inc.

Quotation, p. 15: from "Evolution of Human Behavior" by S. L. Washburn and Virginia Avis, in *Behavior and Evolution*, edited by Anne Roe and George Gaylord Simpson. New Haven: Yale University Press, 1958, p. 435.

Quotation, p. 16: from Peter M. Blau and Otis Dudley Duncan, *The American Occupational Structure*. New York: John Wiley & Sons, 1967, pp. 6–7.

Quotation, p. 17: from "The Churches of Midwest, Kansas and Yoredale, Yorkshire: Their Contributions to the Environments of the Towns," by Roger G. Barker, Louise S. Barker, and Dan D. M. Ragle, in *Change in the Small Community*, William J. Gore and Leroy C. Hodapp, editors, pp. 158–159. Copyright 1967, Friendship Press, New York. Used by permission.

Quotations, pp. 18–19 and 196–203, and Figure 11.1: Reprinted with permission of the publisher from *Ecological Psychology: Concepts and Methods for Studying the Environment of Human Behavior* by Roger G. Barker. Stanford: Stanford University Press, 1968, pp. 80–81, 83, 90, 161–163, 215, 217, 225, 45–46, 128, and 92, and Figure 5.1 (p. 99).

Chapter 3, pp. 29–42, is reprinted with minor alterations from Karl A. Fox and Paul Van Moeseke, "Derivation and Implications of a Scalar Measure of Social Income," in *Economic Structure and Development: Essays in Honour of Jan Tinbergen*, H. C. Bos, H. Linnemann, and P. de Wolff, editors. Amsterdam: North-Holland Publishing Company and New York: American Elsevier, 1973, pp. 21–40. Reprinted with permission of the publisher and of Paul Van Moeseke.

Quotation, p. 43–44: from Kenneth R. Andrews, "Introduction," p. x, in *The Functions of the Executive*, by Chester I. Barnard, 30th Anniversary Edition. Cambridge, Massachusetts: Harvard University Press, 1968. Copyright 1938, 1968 by the President and Fellows of Harvard College. Copyright 1966, by Grace F. Noera Barnard.

Quotations, pp. 46–48: from Gary S. Becker, "A Theory of the Allocation of Time," *Economic Journal*, **75** (1965), pp. 493–494, 497, 498–499, 517. By permission of Gary S. Becker and the Royal Economic Society.

Quotations, pp. 49–50: from Ismail Abdel-Hamid Sirageldin, *Non-Market Components of National Income*, Survey Research Center, University of Michigan, Ann Arbor, 1969, pp. 2, 55, 13 and 14. Copyright 1969 by the University of Michigan; reprinted by permission of the publisher, Survey Research Center of the Institute for Social Research.

Quotations, pp. 52–53: from Philip E. Converse, "Time Budgets," in *International Encyclopedia of the Social Sciences*, Volume 16. New York: The Macmillan Company and The Free Press, pp. 42–43 and 46–47. Copyright 1968 by Crowell Collier & Macmillan, Inc.

Tables 5.1, 5.2, 5.3, 5.4, 6.1, 6.2, 6.3A and 6.3B: data from John P. Robinson and Philip E. Converse, *Sixty-six Basic Tables of Time Budget Data for the United States*, Survey Research Center, University of Michigan, Ann Arbor, May 30, 1966 (xeroxed), Tables 1, 17, 33, and 45. Reprinted by permission of John P. Robinson.

Tables 6.10 and 6.11 and Figure 6.1: from Emanuel Melichar, "Factors Affecting 1966 Basic Salaries in the National Register Professions," in Supplement to *American Economic Review*, **58** (December 1968), pp. 62, 66, and 63 respectively. Reprinted by permission of Emanuel Melichar and the American Economic Association.

Quotations, pp. 98–99 and 291–292: Reproduced, with permission, from "Communications Stress," by Richard L. Meier, *Annual Review of Ecology and Systematics*, Volume III (1972). Palo Alto, California: Annual Reviews, Inc., pp. 299, 289, 292, and 311. Copyright © 1972 by Annual Reviews, Inc. All rights reserved.

Table 6.13: Reprinted with permission from Thomas H. Holmes and Richard H. Rahe, "The Social Readjustment Rating Scale," *Journal of Psychosomatic Research*, Vol. II (1967). New York: Pergamon Press, pp. 213–218, Table 3 (p. 216).

Quotations, pp. 105–109, Table 7.1, and format and data underlying Table 7.2: from Nestor E. Terleckyj, "Estimating Possibilities for Improvement in the Quality of Life in the United States, 1972–1981," *Looking Ahead*, **20** (January 1973). Washington, D. C.: National Planning Association, pp. 1–12.

Table 8.1: from Martin V. Jones and Michael I. Flax, *The Quality of Life in Metropolitan Washington, D.C.: Some Statistical Benchmarks*. Washington, D. C.: Urban Institute, 1970, p. 6.

Quotations, p. 135–136: from Brian J. L. Berry, "Latent Structure of the American Urban System, with International Comparisons," in *City Classification Handbook*, Brian J. L. Berry, editor. New York: John Wiley & Sons, 1972, pp. 44–47.

Quotation, p. 136: from Jesse Burkhead, "Public Finance as an Integral Part of Regional Accounts," in *Elements of Regional Accounts*, Werner Z. Hirsch, editor. Baltimore: Johns Hopkins University Press, 1964, p. 51. Copyright 1964, Johns Hopkins University Press. Published for Resources for the Future by the Johns Hopkins University Press.

Pages 146–151 and 217–226 are reprinted with minor alterations from Jati K. Sengupta and Karl A. Fox, *Economic Analysis and Operations Research: Optimization Techniques in Quantitative Economic Models*. Amsterdam: North-Holland Publishing Company, 1969, pp. 441–447 and 429–441 respectively.

Figure 8.5 and quotation, pp. 151–152: from Herbert H. Fullerton and James R. Prescott, *An Economic Simulation Model for Regional Development Planning*. Ann Arbor, Mich.: Ann Arbor Science Publishers Inc., forthcoming 1975, Figure II.5 in 1973 manuscript version. Reprinted by permission of James R. Prescott.

Quotation, pp. 153–154: from Richard M. Cyert, book review of Karl A. Fox, editor, *Economic Analysis for Educational Planning: Resource Allocation in Nonmarket Systems*, in *Journal of Economic Literature*, 11 (June 1973), 592–593. By permission of Richard M. Cyert and The American Economic Association.

Figures 9.1 and 9.2: Reprinted by permission from Allan M. Cartter, *An Assessment of Quality in Graduate Education*. Washington: American Council on Education, 1966, pp. 80, 85.

Figure 10.1 and quotation, p. 178: from Gary S. Becker, *Human Capital: A Theoretical and Empirical Analysis, with Special Reference to Education*. New York: Columbia University Press, 1964, Chart 1 (p. 15) and p. 38 respectively. Published by the National Bureau of Economic Research. Copyright © 1964 by the National Bureau of Economic Research. Reprinted by permission of Gary S. Becker and the National Bureau of Economic Research.

Tables 10.2 and 10.3, and Figure 10.3: from Peter M. Blau and Otis Dudley Duncan, *The American Occupational Structure*, John Wiley & Sons, New York, 1967, Table 4.1 (pp. 122–123), Table 5.1 (p. 169), and Figure 5.1 (p. 170) respectively.

Tables 10.4 and 10.5: from Richard Stone, *Demographic Accounting and Model-Building*. Paris: Organization for Economic Cooperation and Development, 1971, Tables III.11 (p. 34) and III.13 (p. 38) respectively.

Figure 12.3: from John R. Borchert and Russell B. Adams, *Trade Centers and Trade Areas of the Upper Midwest*, Upper Midwest Economic Study, Urban Report No. 3. Minneapolis: University of Minnesota, September 1963, p. 4.

Quotation, pp. 236–237: from Carnegie Commission on Higher Education, *The Open-Door Colleges: Policies for Community Colleges*, pp. 1–2. Copyright © 1970 by Carnegie Commission on Higher Education. Used with permission of Mc-Graw-Hill Book Company.

Quotation, pp. 278–279: from Robert H. Strotz, "The Utility Tree—A Correction and Further Appraisal," *Econometrica*, 27 (July 1959), p. 482. By permission of Robert H. Strotz and the Econometric Society.

Quotation, pp. 286–287: from Lotfi A. Zadeh, "Fuzzy Sets," *Information and Control*, 8 (June 1965), 339. By permission of Lotfi A. Zadeh and Academic Press.

Quotation, p. 287: from Lotfi A. Zadeh, "Outline of a New Approach to the Analysis of Complex Systems and Decision Processes." Reprinted from *Multiple Criteria Decision Making*, p. 688, edited by James L. Cochrane and Milan Zeleny, by permission of the University of South Carolina Press. Copyright © 1973 by the University of South Carolina Press.

Quotation, p. 296: Reprinted from *Science and Economic Development: New Patterns of Living*, by Richard L. Meier (second edition, 1966, pp. ix–xiii) by permission of The MIT Press, Cambridge, Massachusetts.

Quotation, p. 297: from Wassily W. Leontief, "Theoretical Assumptions and Non-observed Facts," *American Economic Review*, 61 (March 1971), p. 5. By permission of Wassily W. Leontief and the American Economic Association.

Quotations, pp. 297–298: from American Agricultural Economics Association Committee on Economic Statistics, "Our Obsolete Data Systems: New Directions and Opportunities," *American Journal of Agricultural Economics*, **54** (December 1972), pp. 867–868 and 874. By permission of the American Agricultural Economics Association.

Quotation, p. 298: from Edgar S. Dunn, Jr., "Discussion," *American Journal of Agricultural Economics*, **54** (December 1972), p. 878. By permission of Edgar S. Dunn, Jr. and the American Agricultural Economics Association.

Contents

* Written jointly with Paul Van Moeseke, Professor Ordinarius of Mathematical Economics, University of Louvain.

Tables

Figures

I

Introduction

IT SEEMS SAFE TO ASSUME that readers of this book will have had at least a casual exposure to the literature on social indicators. I therefore devote little space to a history of the field. However, I will refer briefly to some classic works that helped initiate and shape the social indicators movement, and to some recent survey articles. These will serve as an introduction to the major themes of the book.

1.1 The Present State of the Field

Ralph M. Brooks (1972) gives an excellent review of the history and development of the social indicators movement. An important forerunner was the Report of the President's Research Committee on Social Trends (1933), commissioned in 1929 by President Hoover. Among the topics investigated in the 29 chapters of *Recent Social Trends* were changing social attitudes and interests; rural life; the family; recreation and leisure time activities; crime and punishment; population, government, and society; and health and medical practice. The committee was chaired by Wesley C. Mitchell, and its Director of Research was William F. Ogburn. In its introduction, the committee stated that "the primary value of this report is to be found in the effort to interrelate the disjointed factors and elements in the social life of America, in the attempt to view the situation as a whole rather than a cluster of parts" (pp. xii–xiii).

Another forerunner was the report of President Eisenhower's Commission on National Goals, *Goals for Americans* (1960). Under "goals at home," the commission discussed eleven topics: the individual, equality, the democratic process, education, the arts and sciences, the democratic economy, economic growth, technological change, agriculture, living conditions, and health and welfare. Under "goals abroad," the commission included four more topics: helping to build an open and peaceful world, the defense of the free world, disarmament, and the United Nations.

The commission evidently viewed its recommendations as operational and sufficiently concrete to justify the following statement: "If these [tax] reforms are made and the minimum growth rate we postulate is achieved, it is this Commission's conclusion that the levels of public spending we would need to realize the recommendations of this Report are attainable" (p. 22). This lead was pursued in a National Planning Association study by Leonard Lecht (1966), *Goals, Priorities, and Dollars*, which was an attempt to determine the economic cost of achieving the commission's goals by 1975.

In 1966 the National Commission on Technology, Automation, and Economic Progress (1966), chaired by Howard R. Bowen, recommended that a system of social accounts be established to supply systematic information about the nation's "social health" and its needs, and to provide a firm basis for policy decisions on social welfare (Bowen, 1967).

About the same time, the National Aeronautics and Space Administration became concerned with assessing the possible social effects of the space exploration program. Raymond A. Bauer suggested that a comprehensive system of social indicators was needed for this and other purposes, and he brought together some well-known social scientists to consider the problem. The outcome was the often-quoted book, *Social Indicators* (Bauer, ed., 1966); its basic assumption, according to Bauer, was this: *"For many of the important topics on which social critics blithely pass judgment, and on which policies are made, there are no yardsticks by which to know if things are getting better or worse"* (p. 20).

Other major contributions to the social indicators movement followed rapidly. In 1966 President Johnson directed the Department of Health, Education, and Welfare to explore the possibility of developing a set of social statistics and indicators that would supplement the economic indicators prepared by the Bureau of Labor Statistics and the Council of Economic Advisers. The publication, *Toward a Social Report* (U.S. Department of Health, Education, and Welfare, 1969), was released on the last day of the Johnson administration. It included one of the first attempts to define such terms as "social accounts," "social indicators," and "social reports." According to William Gorham (1967), more than a score of first-rate scholars served as consultants to the department in connection with this effort.

In February 1967 Senator Walter Mondale introduced a bill (S.843) entitled "The Full Opportunity and Social Accounting Act of 1967." It provided for an annual social report of the president, a council of social advisers to aid in preparing the report, and a joint committee (of Congress) on the social report to review the recommendations contained in the president's report and to issue its own findings and recommendations as a guide to the several committees of Congress dealing with matters relating to the report. The hearings on this bill (U.S. Senate, Full Opportunity and Social Accounting Act, Hearings, 1967) contain some prepared statements of continuing reference interest (see especially Hauser, 1967) and some excellent informal discussion. Senator Mondale (1969) reintroduced the bill, with some modifications, in 1969.

Major contributions to the social indicators movement were made by Raymond A. Bauer (1966), Bertram M. Gross (1966), Albert D. Biderman (1966), Otis Dudley Duncan (1968, 1969), Wilbert E. Moore and Eleanor Bernert Sheldon (1965, 1968), Daniel Bell (1969), Mancur Olson (1969), Abbott Ferriss (1969, 1970, 1971), Daniel Tunstall (1971), and Bauer and Fenn (1972). The American Academy of Political and Social Science (1967a, 1967b) published two volumes of papers on social goals and indicators by some of the authors just named (and others). A much fuller list of important contributions and contributors appears in the article by Brooks (1972) previously cited and in the annotated bibliography by Wilcox, Brooks, Beal, and Klonglan (1972). The report of the National Goals Research Staff (1970) should also be mentioned.

In my estimation, Bertram Gross's (1966) article, "The State of the Nation: Social Systems Accounting" (in Bauer, ed., 1966), is the classic statement of the potentialities of *social accounts* as distinct from social indicators. The "article" is comprehensive enough (118 pages) to have formed a separate book. It is a fundamental conceptual contribution.

In his concluding paragraphs, Gross stressed the importance of a long-range perspective:

> No matter what may be done in the immediate future, a long-range perspective is necessary. Thus, the pioneering work in national economic accounting in the United States was undertaken through a series of annual conferences under the sponsorship of the National Bureau of Economic Research. A similar series of conferences—both on a national and international basis—could likewise be sponsored on the broader subject of social accounting. Private and public foundations and national academies of arts and sciences could play a significant role in the promotion of this intellectual pioneering. Over a period of ten years regular conferences of this type would make considerable progress in grappling with the conceptual difficulties and getting a few preliminary compilations underway.
>
> In any case, *progress in the collection of social indicators will be slow and uneven.* It would be utopian to expect that any government would set itself to the task of moving from economic to social indicators in one comprehensive operation. The first social system reports of presidents and prime ministers will be fragmentary and exploratory.
>
> Above all, *the maturation of social accounting concepts will take many decades.* Let us remember that it took centuries for Quesnay's economic tables to mature into national income accounting. In most countries of the world, national income accounting is still at a rudimentary stage. In countries where it is highly developed, national income experts recognize that they face many conceptual problems that still require years of dedicated attention. By contrast, the formulation of national social accounts is a much more complex undertaking. It requires the participation of social scientists from many disciplines and the breaking down of many language barriers among them. The ideas set forth in this chapter provide little more than an initial staking out of the territory upon which vast debates must take place (pp. 270–271).

The current state of the field owes much to the influential article by Eleanor Bernert Sheldon (1971), with the collaboration of Kenneth C. Land and Raymond A. Bauer, "Social Reporting for the 1970s," pages 407 to 435 in Volume 2 of *Federal Statistics*, the report of the President's Commission on Federal Statistics. Pursuant to their recommendations, the Social Science Research Council in September 1972 appointed an Advisory and Planning Committee on Social Indicators under the chairmanship of Otis Dudley Duncan. At the same time, the Social Science Research Council (SSRC) established a Center for Coordination of Research on Social Indicators, located in Washington, D.C., to disseminate information to, and facilitate communication among, the many research workers involved in some aspects of the field.

The SSRC Center issued its first *Social Indicators Newsletter* in March 1973. The Center's role, as perceived at that time, is indicated by the following paragraphs:

> What are social indicators? We take them to be statistical time series that measure changes in significant aspects of a society. This is a minimal definition but for present purposes we think it is a realistic one, in light of the variety of meanings currently imputed to the term. Our purpose is communication and we would rather start by including too much than by excluding prematurely. Thus, a social indicator described in the newsletter may be a time series which at present contains very few points. The aspect of society it measures may not be deemed "significant" by all observers. And the "society" involved may be no larger than the population of a census tract. But the social indicator expresses something about the composition, structure, or functioning of that society, and expresses it in quantitative terms that can be compared with similar measures in the past or future.
>
> We will cover current research on social indicators—books, articles, and unpublished writings—and research-related activities such as conferences and sessions at professional meetings. Reports will be included on ongoing work and research plans of individuals, organizations, and institutions active in the field, and on problems in indicators research and plans for their resolution (p. 1).

In the present state of the field, many useful insights can be obtained by applying simple models to existing data—for example, models involving relationships among groups of two or three variables. Workers directly concerned with particular data sets have much to contribute here. At the same time, workers primarily interested in theory and methods will be designing more complex models that run ahead of the currently available data.

High levels of communication and interaction between workers with these different orientations will be essential. The possibilities of misunderstanding are suggested by a once-famous interchange among economists, in which the charge of "measurement without theory" was met by a countercharge of "theory without measurement." Within a few years, measurement *without* theory had been drummed out of the economic journals, but measurement *with* theory was painfully slow to come forward. Much time was lost before effective communication and a new synthesis of theoretical and empirical expertise were achieved.

A recent paper by Kenneth C. Land (1974) (in Land and Spilerman, eds., 1974) suggests that this kind of controversy may be minimized. Land points out that three rationales, each involving a different emphasis, have been put forward in the social indicators literature, namely, (1) the analysis of social policy, (2) the measurement of social change, and (3) social reporting.

In the short run, the social reporting rationale probably makes the most effective use of existing data and imposes the least demands on our present theoretical and conceptual capacities. The measurement of social change offers an intermediate degree of difficulty. The social policy rationale would require us not only to measure social change but to place values on it and to predict the consequences of alternative policy interventions.

Land distinguishes between three kinds of social indicators: *output descriptive, other descriptive,* and *analytic*. He refers to an article by Sheldon and Land (1972) wherein it is specified that each of the three types of indicators

> shares the attributes of being capable of collection in time series form and the possibility of aggregation or disaggregation to whatever level appropriate for a particular analysis. Moreover, both [the other descriptive and the analytic indicators] might be viewed as indirectly policy related, for in the long run it will be these measurements and models that will provide guidance for social intervention.
>
> Although the descriptive and output categories have been identified in the social indicators literature from the outset, the analytic indicator category was only implicit until it was identified and emphasized by Land (1971). In brief, Land proposed that, in addition to the disaggregation and time series criteria, social indicators are identified as components in a social system model (possibly including sociopsychological, economic, demographic, and ecological aspects) or some particular segment or process thereof. Thus, *for any particular social condition, social indicators are specified when some conception of the relevant social process is stated* (p. 17).

Land illustrates the relationships between the three types of indicators in a figure (Figure 2.1) which is logically equivalent to my own diagram of Tinbergen's theory of economic policy (Figure 7.1, this volume), except that Land does not include an explicit objective function. The important point is that Land's illustration incorporates the logical structure of Jan Tinbergen's (1952) classic formulation of the theory of economic policy and therefore converges perfectly with one of the most fruitful developments in modern economics.

1.2 The Plan of the Book

The primary object of the pioneers of the social indicators movement was to secure he establishment of *national* data systems, reports, and institutions. However, much of this information would relate to changes in the average levels and distributions of attributes of individuals and households (health, education, skills, income, etc.), and theories of the individual's development, values, and concerns are at least implicit in the choice of things to be measured.

Chapter 2 juxtaposes ideas from several prominent scholars (Rawls, Cantril, Erikson, Murray, Berne, Parsons, Barker, and others) on aspects of personality formation, values, and behavior. It also presents a tentative integration of some of these ideas, notably Talcott Parsons's theory of generalized media of social interchange and Roger Barker's theory of behavior settings, to provide (under certain assumptions) an estimate of an individual's "total income"—an equivalent dollar figure, based on his own perception of values, for all rewards he receives from his participation in the social system in a given year. Chapter 3 (coauthored with Paul Van Moeseke) states my conjectured model of an individual allocating his resources among behavior settings in a more rigorous form that connects it with mathematical programming and utility theory. Sections 3.6 and 3.7 point out some implications of our approach for data systems and models.

Chapter 4 cites a number of works by others (Barnard, Williamson, Isard, Becker, Linder, Sirageldin) which combine economic and noneconomic variables in theoretical models similar to or compatible with those put forward in Chapters 2 and 3.

Chapters 5 and 6 resume the line of development initiated in Chapters 2 and 3. Chapter 5, with the help of data from a 1966 time use study conducted by the Survey Research Center of the University of Michigan (Robinson and Converse, 1966), illustrates the kinds of numerical estimate that would be required to implement the "total income" approach, including the allocation of total income among an individual's resources (health, skills, and other categories) and among various groups of behavior settings or activities (paid employment, housework and family tasks, personal care, education, organizations, mass media, and leisure). Chapter 6 extends this approach to families of two or more persons and introduces the problem of quantifying (and perhaps discounting) streams of total income and its components extending over several or many years. The Holmes and Rahe method of rating the stresses associated with various life events is also discussed.

Chapter 7 jumps directly to the national level. It draws extensively on Nestor Terleckyj's (1973a) study of national goal output indicators and activities (1) to illustrate the structure of a national policy model and (2) to relate his variables as far as possible to groups of resources and behavior settings at the levels of individuals and households. Chapter 7 also discusses Jan Tinbergen's theory of economic policy, which should be as fruitful in social system models as it has been since 1952 in models of national economies.

Chapter 8 moves to the level of metropolitan areas and functional economic areas. For illustration, it draws on the list of urban indicators presented by Jones and Flax (1970) and raises the possibility of urban or regional indicators based on the total income approach. It also discusses the advantages of functional economic areas (1) for regional disaggregation of national accounts and indicators and (2) as territorially based societal communities with a greater degree of "closure" and internal cohesiveness than other regions of similar geographic extent.

Chapter 9 presents a framework for organizing data and models of the higher education sector from university departments on up to the national level. It also contains some quantitative analyses relating to perceived quality, visibility, and prestige of university departments.

Chapter 10 gives a skeletal account of the theoretical derivation of earnings in specific occupations, using a sequence that runs from final GNP demand through sectoral production and employment levels to demands for occupational skills, training, and retraining. It then outlines human capital theory (based on the ideas of Schultz and Becker), some aspects of the Blau and Duncan study of the American occupational structure, and some features of Richard Stone's demographic accounts and models emphasizing earning and learning activities. All these approaches are concerned with fundamental aspects of occupations and earnings.

Chapter 11 goes more deeply into Roger Barker's system for exhaustively classifying and partitioning the public environment of a small town. It seeks to extend the total income approach (with numerical illustrations based partly on Barker's data) to time budgets and accounts for such a community, also considering some problems of multiplier analysis associated with exogenously induced increases in the skills, health, and other resources of individual residents. It suggests that the effects of sets of national goals and programs might well be simulated in a generalized model of a

small community, in which particular programs might apply directly to only a few persons or households and common-sense interpretations can be given to the computer inputs and results.

Chapter 12, building on Chapter 8, discusses quite thoroughly the internal structures of functional economic areas (FEAs) with respect to (1) interactions between firms, shopping centers, and communities; (2) gradients of education, income, and occupational status from smaller to larger communities; and (3) gradients in width of product line, relative "closure," and multiplier values with increasing community size up to the regional capital (hence FEA) level. Recommendations of the Carnegie Commission on Higher Education concerning numbers, sizes, and locations of community colleges are examined and are found to fit perfectly into the FEA pattern. The commission's *suggestions* concerning the numbers and locations of area health education centers are checked against a detailed study of the 1971 distribution of medical specialists in Iowa; the great majority are located in the regional capitals of Iowa's 11 FEAs, indicating (along with other evidence) that health service areas coincide with the established trade areas and commuting fields. The community college is of central importance in the formation and maintenance of skills which, in turn, are the primary bases of income and occupational prestige. The health care delivery system is crucial in the formation and maintenance of another major resource category.

Chapter 13 presents some simple illustrative models of a world economy and the manner in which economic policies adopted by one nation affect prices and incomes in others. It discusses the need for, and recent progress toward, operational models of the world economy and its major sectors. It then considers some problems of interstate and international comparisons based on political and social (as well as economic) indicators. Also described are recent applications of factor analysis and econometric modeling techniques (by Adelman and Morris) to sets of social, political, and economic variables for 74 less-developed countries. Finally, there are the possibilities presented by Szalai's recent publication of time use surveys for 12 countries in 1966, one of them being the Robinson and Converse survey for the United States on which we drew extensively in Chapters 5 and 6.

Chapter 14 concludes the text with a summary and a bit of history about the development of econometrics which offers a constructive parallel to the current situation in social indicators and models.

Supplementing the text, an appendix introduces many references that are not directly *about* social indicators but may (1) prove basic to the full development of the field or (2) provide examples of rapid and turbulent social change that our data systems should be designed to measure. Many of the appendix references are very recent and have extensive bibliographies; they are listed by number under major topics on pages 299 to 309 and should not be confused with the alphabetical list of references (pp. 266–276) associated with Chapters 1 through 14.

I have not attempted to combine my models and suggestions at different levels (individual, region, nation, and world) into a tight mathematical system. I believe the links between the successive levels of organization are fairly obvious. Models of particular organizations or regions are best made by, or in close collaboration with, the people who are going to use them. The world I hope to live in will have standardized data systems for things that must add up to national and world totals but a good deal of creative improvisation in the models used by organizations for their own purposes.

II

Social Science Concepts Relevant to a System of Social Accounts

THIS CHAPTER IS CONCERNED with the problem of what ought to be measured. It describes concepts developed or emphasized by a number of leading social scientists. Some of these concepts relate to the development of the individual, his personality, and his values. Others relate to interactions between individuals and society.

In the concluding section, we suggest the integration of several of these concepts to measure an individual's total income, including noneconomic as well as economic components. Other integrations are, of course, possible; however, if semantic differences are resolved and problems of measurement faced squarely, the number of distinct operational possibilities may be small.

2.1 Concepts of a Good Life (Rawls) and of the Individual's Basic Demands on Society (Cantril)

To a biographer, the relevant unit for evaluation is the complete life experience of an individual. The success of a society in promoting human well-being must be reflected in the life experiences of its members. The title of a volume of essays in honor of Henry A. Murray, *The Study of Lives* (White, ed., 1963), at least suggests the issues involved.

For perspective here, we draw on the work of the philosopher, John Rawls. In *A Theory of Justice* (1971), Rawls discusses the concept of a "good life" as follows:

> The rational plan for a person determines his good. Here I adapt Royce's
> thought that a person may be regarded as a human life lived according to

a plan. For Royce an individual says who he is by describing his purposes and causes, what he intends to do in his life. If this plan is a rational one, then I shall say that the person's conception of his good is likewise rational. In his case the real and the apparent good coincide (p. 408).

What is a rational plan? According to Rawls, a person's plan of life is rational if, and only if, it is consistent with the principles of rational choice when these are applied to all the relevant features of his situation and is the plan (among the set of plans meeting the first condition) he would have chosen with full awareness of the relevant facts and after careful consideration of the consequences.

Happiness is closely connected with rationality. A person is happy if he is successfully carrying out a rational life plan under more or less favorable conditions and is reasonably sure that success will continue. His happiness may, of course, be limited by harsh natural conditions and oppressive demands from others.

A rational person is to act at each moment of his life in such a way that he need never blame himself, no matter how things turn out. Viewing himself as one being continuing over time, the person at one time cannot complain about the actions of the same person at an earlier date.

Rawls asserts that the most important primary good for an individual is *self-respect:*

> We may define self-respect (or self-esteem) as having two aspects. First of all . . . it includes a person's sense of his own value, his secure conviction that his conception of his good, his plan of life, is worth carrying out. And second, self-respect implies a confidence in one's ability, so far as it is within one's power, to fulfill one's intentions. When we feel that our plans are of little value, we cannot pursue them with pleasure or take delight in their execution. Nor plagued by failures and self-doubt can we continue in our endeavors (p. 440).

Hadley Cantril (1965) and his associates studied the aspirations and concerns of adults in many walks of life in many contemporary societies. Toward the end of *The Pattern of Human Concerns*, Cantril summarizes "the demands human beings everywhere impose on any society or political culture because of their very nature. . . ." He lists these demands as follows:

1.   The satisfaction of survival needs. . . .

2.   Man needs a sense of both physical and psychological security to protect gains already made and to assure a beachhead from which further advances can be staged. . . .

3.   Man craves sufficient order and certainty in his life to enable him to judge with fair accuracy what will or will not occur if he does or does not act in certain ways. . . .

4.   Human beings continuously seek to enlarge the range and to enrich the quality of their satisfactions. . . .

5.   Human beings are creatures of hope and are not genetically designed to resign themselves. . . .

6.   Human beings have the capacity to make choices and the desire to exercise this capacity. . . .

7.   Human beings require freedom to exercise the choices they are capable of making. . . .

8.   Human beings want to experience their own identity and integrity, more popularly referred to as the need for personal dignity. . . .

9.   People want to experience a sense of their own worthwhileness. . . .

10.   Human beings seek some value or system of beliefs to which they can commit themselves. . . .

11.   Human beings want a sense of surety and confidence that the society of which they are a part holds out a fair degree of hope that their aspirations will be fulfilled . . . (pp. 315–322).

Abraham Maslow (1954, 1970) formulated a hierarchy of basic human needs that has been frequently cited. These needs are "prepotent" in the following order: physiological needs, safety needs, belongingness and love needs, esteem needs, and the need for self-actualization.

2.2   Life Stages (Erikson)

Some social programs are designed for specific age groups, and the corresponding social indicators will also be age-specific. However, the continuity of the individual life from birth to death is undeniable, and the success of a society is reflected in the quality of the entire life. Can we find a construct that reconciles the continuity of the individual life with the tendency of social institutions to break the life experience up into distinct phases?

Erik Erikson (1968) examines the life cycle from the viewpoint of his experience in clinical psychoanalysis. He organizes his discussion around eight stages: infancy, early childhood, play age, school age, adolescence, young adulthood, adulthood, and old age. Each stage has its own developmental crisis—"crisis" here connoting "not a threat of catastrophe but a turning point, a crucial period of increased vulnerability and heightened potential, and, therefore, the ontogenetic source of generational strength and maladjustment" (p. 286).

The alternative directions that may be taken at these respective crises Erikson lists as basic trust versus basic mistrust, autonomy versus shame and doubt, initiative versus guilt, industry versus inferiority, identity versus confusion, intimacy versus isolation, generativity versus stagnation, and integrity versus despair. He offers alternative words for the good qualities that are acquired at each stage if the crisis is successfully negotiated. The favorable outcome in infancy is hope; in early childhood, will power; in play age, purpose; in school age, competence; in adolescence, fidelity; in young adulthood, love; in maturity, care; and in old age, wisdom.

At the end of his discussion of each of the eight crises, Erikson gives a succinct summary of his meanings, as follows:

Hope, then, is the first psychosocial strength. It is the enduring belief in the attainability of primal wishes in spite of the anarchic urges and rages of dependency. . . .

Will power is the unbroken determination to exercise free choice as well as self-restraint in spite of the unavoidable experience of shame, doubt, and a

certain rage over being controlled by others. Good will is rooted in the judiciousness of parents guided by their respect for the spirit of the law. . . .

Purpose . . . is the courage to envisage and pursue valued and tangible goals guided by conscience but not paralyzed by guilt and by the fear of punishment. . . .

Competence . . . is the free exercise (unimpaired by an infantile sense of inferiority) of dexterity and intelligence in the completion of serious tasks. It is the basis for cooperative participation in some segment of the culture. . . .

Fidelity . . . is the ability to sustain loyalties freely pledged in spite of the inevitable contradictions of value systems. It is the cornerstone of identity and receives inspiration from confirming ideologies and "ways of life." . . .

Love . . . is a mutuality of devotion greater than the antagonisms inherent in divided function. . . .

Care is the broadening concern for what has been generated by love, necessity, or accident—a concern which must consistently overcome the ambivalence adhering to irreversible obligation and the narrowness of self-concern. . . .

Wisdom . . . is a detached and yet active concern with life in the face of death (pp. 288–292).

In summary, Erikson writes:

> From the cycle of life such dispositions as faith, will power, purposefulness, efficiency, devotion, affection, responsibility, and sagacity (all of which are also criteria of ego strength) flow into the life of institutions. Without them, institutions wilt; but without the spirit of institutions pervading the patterns of care and love, instruction and training, no enduring strength could emerge from the sequence of generations. . . .
>
> Psychosocial strength, we conclude, depends on a total process which regulates individual life cycles, the sequence of generations, and the structure of society simultaneously, for all three have evolved together (p. 292).

2.3   Hierarchical Constitution of the Personality (Murray)

Murray (1968) gives a compact statement of his conception of three "vertical" divisions of a personality, which in childhood are quite comparable with the Freudian id, ego, and superego:

> In this PS [personological system] the adult id embraces the entire stratified population of instinctual (genetically given, viscerogenic, subcortical, unbidden and involuntary) affective dispositions (hedonic, wishful, emotional, evaluative) with their engendered orienting fantasies, some forms of which have been repressed for years and may or may not be operating influentially "below" the boundary of the ego, but others of which have access to consciousness. The adult ego is the more or less fact-perceptive, knowledgeable, rational, articulate, future-oriented regnant system of the personality with energies of its own (during waking hours) to fulfill its role as both governor and servant of the id. As the self-conscious "I," who leaves most things to habit (dynamic mechanisms), the adult ego will, on signal

occasions, try as far as possible to function as the autonomous (uncoerced) and self-sufficient (unaided) determiner of his destiny—especially as "I" the decision maker (the identifier, interpreter, evaluator, rejector of the "worse" and chooser of the "better" pressing id components) and as "I" the plan-composer for the "better" ones, the executor and adjuster of the plans, and, finally, the achiever of effects which are sufficiently satisfying to self-respect and to the destructive and constructive id, greedy for pleasure, companionship, love, possessions, parenthood, power, and prestige. The adult superego (superregnant system of the personality) consists of stratified imaginal representors of the rulers (parent, king, god) and verbal representors of the ruling culture (moral precepts, laws, beliefs, sentiments, principles) of the world (family, group, nation, mankind) of which each ego is a member. Its function is to commit the individual to the support and service of these values (p. 7).

Levinson (1968) uses Freud's model of personality structure in terms of id, ego, and superego and gives considerable emphasis to what he calls the *ego ideal* in connection with personal growth and motivation:

> The ego ideal is an internalized image of oneself at his future best. This image is constructed from the expectations which parents and others hold of the child, from the aspirations the child develops for himself out of his recognition of his capacities and abilities, and from his identification with important figures in his environment (p. 13).
>
> In the course of its development, the ego ideal ultimately incorporates norms, ethics, and social ideals which become part of the person's aspirations. . . . When a person meets some of the expectations of his ego ideal, he experiences the applause of the ego ideal with relief, satisfaction, and increased self-respect. The consciousness of deserving this love is felt as pride (pp. 214–215).

2.4   Other Aspects of Personality Formation (Berne, Harris)

Eric Berne's (1961, 1964) work on transactional analysis is well known. His concept of the structure of personality is similar to Murray's (and, of course, to Freud's), but his colloquial terminology has gained wide acceptance. Thomas A. Harris (1969), a close associate of Berne, has also done much to popularize and apply Berne's approach.

Berne and Harris were greatly impressed by Wilder Penfield's (1952) findings concerning the nature of human "memory mechanisms." Harris (1969) describes Penfield's experiments and quotes a number of excerpts from his 1952 article. Harris states:

> During the course of brain surgery, in treating patients suffering from focal epilepsy, Penfield conducted a series of experiments during which he touched the temporal cortex of the brain of the patient with a weak electric current transmitted through a galvanic probe. . . . In each case, the patient under local anesthesia was fully conscious during the exploration of the cerebral cortex and was able to talk with Penfield (p. 5).

Penfield (quoted in Harris, pp. 5–11) found that the stimulating electrode could force recollections clearly derived from the patient's memory:

> The physical experience, thus produced, stops when the electrode is withdrawn and may repeat itself when the electrode is reapplied. . . .
>
> The subject feels again the emotion which the situation originally produced in him, and he is aware of the same interpretations, true or false, which he himself gave to the experience in the first place. Thus, evoked recollection is not the exact photographic or phonographic reproduction of past scenes or events. It is reproduction of what the patient saw and heard and felt and understood. . . .
>
> Whenever a normal person is paying conscious attention to something, he simultaneously is recording it in the temporal cortex of each hemisphere. . . .
>
> The thread of temporal succession seems to link the elements of evoked recollection together. It also appears that only those sensory elements to which the individual was paying attention are recorded, not all the sensory impulses that are forever bombarding the central nervous system.
>
> The demonstration of the existence of cortical "patterns" that preserve the detail of current experience, as though in a library of many volumes, is one of the first steps toward a physiology of the mind. The nature of the pattern, the mechanism of its formation, the mechanism of its subsequent utilization, and the integrative processes that form the substratum of consciousness— these will one day be translated into physiological formulas.

Berne used this insight in describing the origin and content of the three components of human personality, which he refers to as Parent, Adult, and Child. These correspond approximately to the superego, ego, and id of Freudian theory.

Harris (1969) describes Berne's construct as follows:

> The Parent is a huge collection of recordings in the brain of unquestioned or imposed external events perceived by a person in his early years, a period which we have designated roughly as the first five years of life. . . . The name Parent is most descriptive of these data inasmuch as the most significant "tapes" are those provided by the example and pronouncements of his own real parents or parent substitutes. . . . Parent is specific for every person, being the recording of that set of early experiences unique to him (pp. 18–19).
>
> While external events are being recorded as the body of data we call the Parent, there is another recording being made simultaneously. This is the recording of *internal* events, the responses of the little person to what he sees and hears. . . . It is this "seeing and hearing and feeling and understanding" body of data which we define as the Child. Since the little person has no vocabulary during the most critical of his early experiences, most of his reactions are *feelings* (pp. 24–25).
>
> At about 10 months of age a remarkable thing begins to happen to the child . . . he begins to experience the power of locomotion. He can manipulate objects and begins to move out, freeing himself from the prison of immobility. . . .
>
> The ten-month old has found he is able to do something which grows from his own awareness and original thought. This self-actualization is the be-

> ginning of the Adult. . . . Adult data accumulates as a result of the child's
> ability to find out for himself what is different about life from the "taught
> concept" of life in his Parent and the "felt concept" of life in his Child. The
> Adult develops a "thought concept" of life based on data gathering and
> data processing (pp. 28–29).

2.5   Talcott Parsons's "Human Action System"

Talcott Parsons (1968) has presented a summary statement of some of his theories.
We shall make use of his concepts of organism, personality, society, culture, and
generalized media of interchange.

Parsons includes in his conceptualization of the "human action system" (1) the
organism, (2) the personality, (3) the social system, and (4) the cultural system
(including beliefs, ideas, and symbols that give the action system its primary "sense
of direction"). Our interest here centers on the social system, with which we begin.

> I shall define society as the category of social systems embodying . . . the
> greatest self-sufficiency of any type of social system. . . .
>
> The core structure of a society I will call the societal community. More
> specifically, at different levels of evolution, it is called tribe, or "the people,"
> or, for classical Greece, *polis*, or, for the modern world, *nation*. It is the col-
> lective structure in which members are united or . . . associated (p. 461). . . .

The nature of this association is reflected partly in the patterns of citizenship
(civil-legal, political and social).

The other three primary subsystems of a society are the economy, the polity, and
the cultural (or pattern-maintenance) subsystem. Each of the four subsystems of a
society is characterized by its own medium of exchange: the societal community by
influence; the economy by *money*; the polity by political *power*; and the cultural or
pattern-maintenance subsystem by *value commitments* or "generalized commitments to
the implementation of cultural values. . . ." Influence is interchangeable for power,
money, and value commitments.

Personality, Social System, and Roles.   Parsons has written:

> The personality as analytically distinguished from the organism, consti-
> tutes the third primary environment of a social system. It interpenetrates
> with the organism in the obvious and fundamental sense that the storage
> facilities of learned content must be organic, as must the physical mech-
> anisms of perception and cognition, of the control of learned behavior,
> and of the bases of motivation.
>
> . . . *the primary goal output of social systems is to the personalities of their members.*
> Although they interpenetrate crucially with social systems, the personali-
> ties of individuals are not core constituents of social systems (nor vice versa)
> but precisely environments of them. . . .
>
> The unit of interpenetration between a personality and a social system is
> not the individual but a *role* or complex of *roles*. The *same* personality may
> participate in *several* social systems in different roles.

> From the viewpoint of the psychology of the personality, the positive out-
> puts from the social system are rewards. Indeed, I would even say that . . .
> except for intermediate cases specially involved at the crux of differentiation
> between organism and personality (notably, erotic pleasure), all rewards
> are social system outputs. Conversely, outputs from the personality to the
> social system are personal goal achievements which, from the viewpoint
> of the receiving social system, are *contributions* to its functioning . . . (p. 469).

Generalized Media of Interchange.   We have already mentioned the four media of exchange (influence, money, power, and value commitments) which, according to
Parsons, are used within the social system proper. In addition, Parsons (1968) indicates that "other generalized media seem to operate in the zones of interpenetration
between the social system and the other primary subsystems of action" (p. 471).
These media evidently include erotic pleasure, affect (including recognition and
response), technological know-how and skill, ideology, conscience, reputation, and
faith.

The concept of media of exchange (in addition to money) "circulating" in particular subsystems of the social system as a whole is a fruitful one, and we shall make
use of it in subsequent sections.

The Organism.   Parsons (1968) is careful to distinguish between the organism and
the personality:

> It should be emphasized that all relations between the social system and
> the *physical* environment are mediated through the behavioral organism.
> The perceptual processes of the organism are the source of information
> about the physical environment. . . . The organism is also the source of the
> "instinctual" components of the motivation of individuals' personalities
> (p. 466).

Evidently, the health of the organism places some limits on the behavioral contributions of the associated personality. Barker (1968) speaks of five behavior mechanisms—gross muscular activity, affective behavior, manipulation, talking, and thinking—all of which draw on capacities of the organism. Gross muscular activity and
affective behavior have a very long evolutionary history; manipulation, talking, and
thinking are closely interrelated in the most recent phase of human organic evolution
which, according to Washburn and Avis (1958), was dominated by the use of tools:

> Increase in brain size resulted from the new selection pressures stemming
> from tool use. Speech, made possible by the larger brain, was correlated
> with a complicated technological tradition; and the larger and more com-
> plicated society was made possible by the larger food supply. Human hunt-
> ing depended on tools, and hunting brought about greater mobility. . . .
> Increase in brain size was associated with a slowing of the growth rate and
> a much greater period of dependency. This changed the social life, estab-
> lishing long-term social relations. Thus the hunting life changed man's psy-
> chology and the way of life of the human group (p. 435).

These factors have also determined the general nature of human personality and
the process of its development. Personalities, in Parsons's sense, receive the various

outputs of the social system and attach values to them as rewards, which serve as justifications and incentives for their contributions to the social system.

To what extent can people recognize and respond to Parsons's media of social interchange? There is a great deal of evidence that people recognize and respond to noneconomic media (as well as money) in choosing jobs. For example, Zytowski (1970) surveyed some 72 references dealing with the concept of "work values," "work needs," or "work satisfactions." He cites with approval Eli Ginzberg's trichotomization of work values into intrinsic, extrinsic, and concomitant types. Comparing lists used by several different authors, including from 7 to 20 "values" each, Zytowski found that they cluster rather well into Ginzberg's three categories.

Extrinsic factors, which represent "the outcomes of work, as contrasted with the means," include security, prestige, economic return, achievement, advancement, and recognition.

Intrinsic factors, which are "part of the job itself," include independence, altruism, creativity, way of life, intellectual stimulation, variety, and similar terms.

Concomitant factors include surroundings, working conditions, company policy and administration, interpersonal relations (with peers, subordinates, and superiors), dominance, dependence, leadership, authority, and similar terms.

The extrinsic factors can be identified with some of Parsons's media of exchange (money, prestige, recognition, and perhaps influence and political power), plus a survival need, security.

The concomitant factors appear to center on interpersonal relations. They evidently relate in part to affect (including recognition and response) and to Berne's "procurement of stroking" (1964, p. 19).

Some of the intrinsic factors reflect the use of behavior mechanisms (thinking, talking, manipulation, gross motor activity, affective behavior) in line with special abilities and preferences. However, since "altruism," "moral values," "social welfare," "helpful to others," and "responsibility" are also classified among the intrinsic factors, it appears that media such as ideology, conscience, faith, and "generalized commitment to the implementation of cultural values" are involved here, as well.

In any event, it is clear that many if not all Parsons's reward media may be involved in the total satisfactions associated with jobs. Blau and Duncan (1967) also point out the close relationship between occupation and social stratification, stating that "the American occupational structure . . . [is] the major foundation of the stratification system in our society" (p. 1). Furthermore, they believe that

> The occupational structure in modern industrial society not only constitutes an important foundation for the main dimensions of social stratification but also serves as the connecting link between different institutions and spheres of social life, and therein lies its great significance. The hierarchy of prestige strata and the hierarchy of economic classes have their roots in the occupational structure; so does the hierarchy of political power and authority, for political authority in modern society is largely exercised as a full-time occupation. . . . The occupational structure also is the link between the economy and the family, through which the economy affects the family's status and the family supplies manpower to the economy. The hierarchy of occupational strata reveals the relationship between the social contributions men make by furnishing various services and the rewards they receive in return, whether or not this relationship expresses some equitable functional adjustment (pp. 6–7).

2.6   Roger Barker's Theory of Behavior Settings

According to Parsons, "the unit of interpenetration between a personality and a social system is not the individual but a *role* or complex of *roles. . . . The primary goal output of social systems is to the personalities of their members* (p. 469)." Outputs from the social system to personalities are rewards; inputs from personalities to the social system are contributions.

Can we find appropriate units for observing the performance of roles and estimating the rewards and contributions associated with their performance? A highly promising approach to these questions has been pioneered by the psychologist Roger Barker (1963, 1967, 1968).

The Concept of a Behavior Setting.   Roger Barker spent a good many years observing the behavior of residents of a small midwestern community of about 830 people. He early addressed himself to the question of how the environment of human behavior was to be identified, described, and measured. Concluding that the community environment could be divided into parts or units, which he called behavior settings, he wrote (1967):

> Behavior settings are units of the environment that have relevance for behavior. They provide the primary data of the study to be reported here. We have dealt only with the settings that occur outside the homes of the community, that is, the public behavior settings. The number of public behavior settings in the town is a measure of the size of the town's public environment.
>
> We must emphasize that a behavior setting coerces people and things to conform to its temporal-spatial pattern. This is not an incidental or accidental characteristic. The person or persons who maintain and control the setting (the performers) make a deliberate effort to insure that this is so, and that the setting therefore fulfills its function. This aspect of a setting we call its program. Two settings are said to have the same program when their parts and processes are interchangeable. When this is true, two or more settings belong to the same genotype. Two grocery stores, for example, could exchange stock, personnel, bookkeeping systems, shelving, and so forth, with little interruption in their operation. They belong to the same genotype. A Methodist and a Presbyterian minister could, and sometimes do, exchange pulpits. The number of behavior setting genotypes in a town is a measure of the variety of the town's environment (pp. 158–159).

Barker identified 198 genotype settings in his town of 830 people. Examples include grocery stores, hardware stores, ice cream socials, kindergarten classes, business meetings, religion classes, hallways, and bus stops.

When individual grocery stores, churches, and the like were recognized as separate or specific behavior settings, Barker found 884 public behavior settings in his town during 1963–1964. He was able to record that the number of daily occurrences of behavior settings during 1963–1964 was 53,258 and that the hours of duration of public behavior settings in the same period totaled 286,909. Multiplying the hours of duration of each behavior setting by the number of persons participating in it, Barker obtained a record of "hours of occupancy" of behavior settings, totaling 1,129,295 in 1963–1964. Since there are 8760 hours in a year, the total hours of "life lived" during the year by the town's 830 residents was 7,270,800. About 15 percent of these hours were spent in public behavior settings; the remaining "hours of living" were presumably passed in private homes and in transit from one behavior setting to another.

An Outline of Barker's System.   In 1968 Barker published a comprehensive statement of his approach in *Ecological Psychology: Concepts and Methods for Studying the Environment of Human Behavior.* We will summarize the main features of his system.

Every behavior setting has a *program.* Barker says:

> Organisms of the same genotype have the same coded programs stored in their nuclei, and behavior settings of the same genotype have the same coded programs stored in their most central zones (zone 6 if the most central region has a single inhabitant, zone 5 if it has multiple inhabitants). . . .
>
> When the program of a setting is incorporated within a person, it is one of his relatively permanent attributes, and he is branded with the code name of the program: Attorney, Postmaster, Grocer, etc. (pp. 80–81).

In businesses, government agencies, and schools, the zone 5 and 6 performers are usually "professionals" who receive salaries or proprietary income for operating the behavior setting. Churches and voluntary associations may have "professionals" in charge of some behavior settings and laymen or "amateurs" in charge of others. A great deal of higher education is concerned with training individuals to serve (in Barker's terminology) as zone 5 or 6 performers in stated genotype behavior settings.

Each grocery store in a town is a *specific* behavior setting; "grocery stores" is a behavior setting *genotype.* Barker used the following cutting point for determining whether two specific behavior settings belong to the same genotype: "Two behavior settings are of the same genotype if, when their zone 5/6 performers are interchanged, they receive and process the same inputs as formerly, in the same way and without delay" (p. 83).

Barker (p. 51) uses a diagram consisting of six equally spaced concentric circles to illustrate the six *zones of penetration* of individuals into a behavior setting. Working from center to periphery, these zones are (6) single leader, (5) joint leaders, (4) active functionary, (3) member or customer, (2) audience or invited guest, and (1) onlooker.

In general, it appears that an individual in zone 6 makes a larger contribution to the output of the behavior setting than an individual in zones 5, 4, 3, 2, or 1, in descending order. In business firms, the line between zones 4 and 3 is the boundary between the business and its customers. Occupants of zone 3 interact to some extent with occupants of zones 4, 5, and 6; occupants of zone 2 evidently play a passive role except for expressing approval or other reactions to the performances of occupants of zone 6, 5, and 4.

Barker (p. 66) also rates behavior settings on five variables, which he calls *behavior mechanisms*: affective behavior, gross motor activity, manipulation, talking, and thinking. The three subscales for each of these variables are: (1) (extent of) participation, (2) tempo, and (3) intensity.

In addition, Barker (p. 52) rates behavior settings in terms of 11 variables that he calls *action patterns*: Aesthetics, business, education, government, nutrition, personal appearance, physical health, professionalism, recreation, religion, and social contact. Subscales for each of these variables are (1) participation, (2) supply relationship (if any) to other settings, (3) evaluation and appreciation, and (4) teaching and learning.

Barker states that "A behavior setting authority system is identified by the *controlling setting*, e.g., Elementary and High School Board Meeting, Baseball Association Committee Meeting. The controlling setting of an authority system is frequently a committee meeting" (p. 90). He classifies the controlling settings into five *authority systems*, (1) business, (2) churches, (3) government, (4) schools, and (5) voluntary associations.

Barker (p. 76) identifies four decisions regarding the operations of a behavior setting; (1) appointment of performers, (2) admittance of members, (3) determination of fees and prices, and (4) establishment of programs and schedules. Each of these decisions may be made (*a*) within the town, (*b*) outside the town but within the school district, (*c*) outside the district but within the county, (*d*) outside the county but within the state, or (*e*) outside the state but within the nation. The loci of these decisions establish the *degree of local autonomy* of the setting.

The demographic characteristics of the occupants of various zones of a behavior setting are also important data. Barker (pp. 47–48) divides residents of the town into 14 *population subgroups*, as follows: infants (under 2 years), preschool (2:0–5:11), younger school (6:0–8:11), older school (9:0–11:11), adolescent (12:0–17:11), adult (18:0–64:11); aged (65:0 and over); male; female; Social Class I; Social Class II; Social Class III; white; Negro. The maximum *degree of penetration* into behavior settings can be rated for individuals or for population subgroups.

Barker (pp. 70–71) recognizes seven categories of *pressure* (outside forces bearing on an individual or a population subgroup) *to approach and enter or to withdraw from and avoid* any specified behavior setting. For example, with respect to a given behavior setting, the presence of children may be (1) required, (2) urged, (3) invited, (4) neutral, (5) tolerated, (6) resisted, or (7) prohibited.

Barker states (p. 75) that the *raison d'être* of a setting with respect to any class of inhabitants is the *welfare attribute*. With respect to children, for example, a specified behavior setting may be classified as follows: (1) not concerned with children, (2) serves child members in this setting, (3) serves children in other settings (e.g., a meeting of the elementary school board), and (4) children serve other members in this setting (e.g., children may provide the program for a PTA meeting).

Barker is definitely concerned with the reproducible measurement of all the aspects of behavior settings just noted. His book *Ecological Psychology* (1968) is a rich source of ideas that may be useful in the development of social accounts, in measures of output applicable to both market and nonmarket systems, and in the specification of objective functions for both market and nonmarket institutions.

We will need still another of Barker's concepts for use in the last section of this chapter. With respect to homeostasis, equilibrium, or stability in the functional level of a behavior setting, Barker states that "One source of the stability of behavior settings is a balance between many independent forces that bear upon them. Some of the forces issue from the larger community, some are intrinsic to the setting itself, and some originate within the individuals who populate the setting" (pp. 161–163). As an example, he lists 12 influences pressing members of a particular school class—some toward an increase and some toward a decrease in its level of activity.

In essence, the functional level of a behavior setting remains quasi-stationary because increases in functional level that would make some members of the setting
better off would make some other members (or supporters) of the setting worse off.
If a member puts more into this setting he must, as a rule, reduce his inputs into some
other settings. The zone 6 performer (e.g., the teacher in a classroom) controls the
basic program of the setting and must generally take the initiative if the functional
level of the setting is to be increased. If membership in the setting for at least some
members is maintained by outside pressure, such as compulsory school attendance
laws, the setting as such can achieve a local optimum at best. The teacher may be
able to restructure the program of the setting so that with no greater demands on
her own time and energy, the marginal utility of the setting to all or most members is
increased (three reading groups instead of two, in Barker's example, might have this
effect).

2.7   A Tentative Integration of Concepts to Measure an Individual's Total Income

Our approach in this section is largely intuitive. However, a number of the concepts
presented in previous sections lend themselves to a tentative synthesis.

Parsons's Media of Social Interchange.   Parsons's media include influence, money,
political power, and value commitments; erotic pleasure; affect (including recognition and response); technological know-how and skill; ideology, conscience, reputation, and faith. Some of these media circulate mainly in specific "authority systems"
(in Barker's sense): money in the economy; political power in the polity, faith in
churches, reputation in scientific and professional communities, technological know-
how and skill in appropriate occupational groups and labor markets, influence in
territorially based communities, and so on.

A number of Parsons's media seem to have "human capital" aspects. This is clearly
true of technological know-how and skill. Higher wages paid to experienced workers
imply that human capital is produced on the job as well as in schools. Influence,
political power, and reputation usually require considerable application over a period
of years—a demonstrated capacity to deliver a specified volume of a desired output
per unit of time. Value commitments may also have to be demonstrated over a period
of years to become media of exchange capable of influencing the behavior of others.
A long record of (almost always) "correct" choices from the standpoint of ideology,
conscience, or faith establishes an empirical relative frequency basis for predicting
such probabilities.

Levinson's Ego Ideal.   Levinson states that a person's ego ideal is his vision of himself
at his future best.

As a step toward measurement, the ego ideal might be represented as a vector of
desired stocks of Parsons's media of exchange at each point in a person's life cycle.
At each point a shortfall in actual stocks relative to desired stocks would call forth
efforts to raise the actual closer to the ideal. This leads to a stock-adjustment equation:

$$e = d(s^* - s); \qquad e, d, s^*, s: n \times 1 \qquad (1)$$

where e ("effort") is a time-and-effort allocation vector, s^* and s are vectors of desired stocks and actual stocks, respectively, and d is a vector of adjustment coefficients per time period. We could rewrite (1) with a time lag as

$$e_t = d(s^*_{t+1} - s_t) \qquad (2)$$

to reflect the dynamic flight-and-pursuit nature of the endeavor, with achievement typically lagging behind aspiration.

A person whose ego ideal is realistic should be able to estimate approximately how much effort will be required to achieve a certain stock (or annual flow) of each medium; he should allocate his effort so that the expected marginal value product of a unit of effort directed at each goal will be the same, measured in terms of his own utility function.

Cantril's ladder-of-life device or Self-Anchoring Striving Scale (1965, p. 22) might be used to help a person express perceived discrepancies between his ego ideal and his actual condition. The discrepancy for each medium would be stated in numbers of ladder steps on a scale ranging from 0 for the worst to 10 for the best possible situation he could visualize for himself with respect to that medium. If one step on the money dimension were taken as unity, the person could express the relative importance of one step with respect to any other medium as a fraction or multiple of one. Furthermore, one step on the money dimension might be stated in terms of dollars (of assets or annual income); if so, the other media also could be given dollar values per step.

Barker's Behavior Settings and Related Concepts.   Several of Barker's concepts link up well with those of Parsons.

1. Barker's five *behavior mechanisms* (affective behavior, gross motor activity, manipulation, talking, and thinking) occupy most if not all the time in public behavior settings; these mechanisms have a long evolutionary history. The established equilibrium for an individual at a particular stage of his life cycle would probably involve certain amounts (duration multiplied by intensity) of use of each of these five behavior mechanisms.

2. Barker's *authority systems* include businesses, churches, governments, schools, and voluntary associations—these control "public" behavior settings. Families could no doubt be added as the authority systems that control behavior settings in private homes.

3. Some of Barker's *action patterns* seem to have very nearly a one-to-one correspondence with specified authority systems, namely, the action patterns called business, religion, government, and education. Professionalism as an action pattern seems to interpenetrate the other four. The remaining six action patterns (nutrition, personal appearance, physical health, aesthetics, recreation, and social contact) seem to be largely independent of authority systems other than families and, in some cases, perhaps, voluntary associations.

4. Barker's degrees of *local autonomy* (town, school district, county, state, nation) might be generalized into successive levels in an administrative decision-making hierarchy, regardless of whether the successive levels were located in a single building or in a hierarchy of central places that controlled system operations over successively larger geographic territories.

We will make use of Barker's basic concept of *behavior settings* shortly in a more formal model.

An Approach to Measurement of a Person's Total Income. If we extend Barker's system of behavior settings to include all places of employment and all residences (plus settings occupied by residents of the community when they leave it temporarily on business or personal trips), we can establish an accounting system that is exhaustive with respect to living time, including sleep and private activities.

Each individual in a behavior setting has a role (student or teacher, grocer or customer, chairman or member, etc.). If two or more persons are involved in a behavior setting, there occur "transactions" [in the terminology of Berne (1964)], involving recognition and response. The utility of a behavior setting to an individual is a function of the setting as such, his own role in the setting, and his perception of his effectiveness in the role as evidenced by the behavior of other participants toward him.

We might postulate, then, that a "rational" personality will allocate his time among behavior-setting-and-role combinations so as to maximize their (expected) total utility. If a role has a quality dimension, more preparation time may be required to perform it well than to perform it at the threshold of adequacy.

If we assume that a consumer can rate any two arrays of commodities as "A preferred to B," "B preferred to A," or "indifferent as between A and B," it may be equally reasonable to assume that a person can make similar orderings of two arrays of behavior setting, role, and quality-of-performance-in-role combinations.

In the case of economic transactions, we multiply observed market prices by quantities of the respective goods and services produced in a nation and compute gross national (economic) product, *GNP*. The ratios of market prices (under certain restrictive assumptions) are equal to the ratios of the marginal utilities of the corresponding commodities to each consumer. If the market prices for some base year are used as fixed weights, we can compute changes in "real" GNP over a period of years.

Would it mean anything to perform the same operation for all Parsons's media of exchange? Perhaps so, if we visualize a person as trying to maximize his total utility from a year of living by using his total capacities in the most effective way. If there are s media of exchange, n potential activities representing essentially all forms of human behavior, and s restrictions limiting the amounts of each medium that a given individual can use ("spend") as inputs into the social system, our model becomes:

$$\max U = f(t_1, t_2, \cdots, t_n) \qquad \text{subject to} \tag{3}$$

$$\sum_{i=1}^{n} t_i p_i = Y = b_1,$$

$$\sum_{i=1}^{n} t_i m_{2i} = M_2 = b_2,$$

$$\sum_{i=1}^{n} t_i m_{3i} = M_3 = b_3,$$

.

.

.

$$\sum_{i=1}^{n} t_i m_{si} = M_s = b_s,$$

$$\sum_{i=1}^{n} t_i = 8760. \tag{4}$$

Then

$$\frac{\partial U}{\partial t_i} - \lambda_1 p_i - \lambda_2 m_{2i} - \lambda_3 m_{3i} - \cdots - \lambda_s m_{si} - \lambda_t = 0, \tag{5}$$

for all $i = 1, 2, 3, \cdots, n,$
and

$$\frac{\partial U / \partial t_i}{\partial U / \partial t_j} = \frac{\lambda_1 p_i + \lambda_2 m_{2i} + \lambda_3 m_{3i} + \cdots + \lambda_s m_{si} + \lambda_t}{\lambda_1 p_j + \lambda_2 m_{2j} + \lambda_3 m_{3j} + \cdots + \lambda_s m_{sj} + \lambda_t}. \tag{6}$$

Each unit of activity i uses up some time; many activities use up some money; some use personal influence; some use professional reputation; and so on. Each activity involves occupying a behavior setting and performing some role in it at a specified quality level. Each medium of exchange corresponds to a goal of activity for some if not all personalities. Some of Parsons's media seem to be *stocks* (e.g., professional reputation) that yield a flow of inputs into the social system and bring in a flow of outputs or rewards from the social system. Intense application may increase professional reputation; diversion of effort to politics or gardening may cause it (or permit it) to decline. In measuring the utility enjoyed by a personality during a given year only the *flows* of rewards associated with possession of stocklike media should be included.

Since some activities bring in only one or two of the s kinds of reward from the social system and use only one or a few kinds of the s resources or "contributions," there would be many zeros in the $n \times s + 1$ "technology" matrix, hence in the expressions for the $\partial U/\partial t_i$, $i = 1, 2, \ldots, n$. If the individual is free to convert time into money income and into flows of each of the other $s - 1$ resources, the initial b_i's can be adjusted until the marginal utilities of time converted into all other limiting resources are equal.

Consider the following matrix of exchange rates among marginal utilities of the s resources (and time):

$$
\begin{array}{c}
\\
\lambda_1 \\ \lambda_2 \\ \lambda_3 \\ \lambda_4 \\ \cdot \\ \cdot \\ \cdot \\ \lambda_s \\ \lambda_t
\end{array}
\begin{array}{cccccccc}
\lambda_1 & \lambda_2 & \lambda_3 & \lambda_4 & \cdots & \lambda_s & \lambda_t \\
\left[\begin{array}{ccccccc}
1 & k_{12} & k_{13} & k_{14} & \cdots & k_{1s} & k_{1t} \\
k_{21} & 1 & k_{23} & k_{24} & \cdots & k_{2s} & k_{2t} \\
k_{31} & k_{32} & 1 & k_{34} & \cdots & k_{3s} & k_{3t} \\
k_{41} & k_{42} & k_{43} & 1 & \cdots & k_{4s} & k_{4t} \\
\cdot & \cdot & \cdot & \cdot & & \cdot & \cdot \\
\cdot & \cdot & \cdot & \cdot & & \cdot & \cdot \\
\cdot & \cdot & \cdot & \cdot & & \cdot & \cdot \\
k_{s1} & k_{s2} & k_{s3} & k_{s4} & & 1 & k_{st} \\
k_{t1} & k_{t2} & k_{t3} & k_{t4} & \cdots & k_{ts} & 1
\end{array}\right]
\end{array}. \tag{7}
$$

The last row k_{tj} indicates the marginal rates at which time can be converted into each of the s media; the corresponding element in the last column, k_{jt}, is the reciprocal of k_{tj} (e.g., $k_{1t} = 1/k_{t1}$).

If so, we have

$$\lambda_t = k_{t1}\lambda_1,$$
$$\lambda_2 = k_{2t}\lambda_t = k_{2t}k_{t1}\lambda_1,$$
$$\lambda_3 = k_{3t}\lambda_t = k_{3t}k_{t1}\lambda_1,$$
$$.$$
$$.$$
$$.$$
$$\lambda_s = k_{st}\lambda_t = k_{st}k_{t1}\lambda_1. \tag{8}$$

In this kind of equilibrium for the individual, we can write

$$\frac{\partial U}{\partial t_i} = \lambda_1[p_i + k_{t1}(1 + k_{2t}m_{2i} + k_{3t}m_{3i} + \cdots + k_{st}m_{si})]. \tag{9}$$

If we multiply $\partial U/\partial t_i$ by t_i/λ_1 and sum over $i = 1, 2, \ldots, n$, the first term, $\sum_{i=1}^{n} t_i p_i = Y$, is a component of GNP (i.e., the total consumption expenditures of the individual). The remaining terms are also expressed in dollars. The sum of all such terms would be the total income received by the individual.

If an individual is making an optimal allocation of his time, the marginal utility of an additional hour per year should be the same in each behavior setting in which he participates. If *cardinal* measures were devised for the s media of exchange and the quantities of each contributed and received per hour in each of $n > s$ behavior settings were measured, it appears that relative marginal utilities such as λ_2/λ_1, λ_3/λ_1, $\ldots$, λ_s/λ_1 might be estimated by statistical means. Each behavior setting would yield an observation equation as follows:

$$\frac{\partial U}{\partial t_i} = \lambda_1 p_i + \lambda_2 m_{2i} + \lambda_3 m_{3i} + \cdots + \lambda_s m_{si} + \lambda_t. \tag{10}$$

However, $\partial U/\partial t_i$ should be the same for all $i = 1, 2, \ldots, n$, and λ_t should be a constant; each observation equation could be rewritten as

$$p_i = \frac{1}{\lambda_1}\left(\frac{\partial U}{\partial t_i} - \lambda_t\right) - \frac{\lambda_2}{\lambda_1}m_{2i} - \frac{\lambda_3}{\lambda_1}m_{3i} - \cdots - \frac{\lambda_s}{\lambda_1}m_{si}. \tag{11}$$

Now, p_i is the money cost per hour of occupying behavior setting i. The variance of p_i among the n behavior settings should be attributable to variations in m_2, m_3, $\ldots$, m_s among the n settings. A least squares estimate of $(-\lambda_2/\lambda_1)$ would indicate that a unit difference in m_2 per hour between two behavior settings would offset a difference of $(-\lambda_2/\lambda_1)$ dollars per hour in the costs of occupying them. If an hour in each of two alternative settings is regarded as an offer with price and nonprice aspects, $(-\lambda_j/\lambda_1)$ translates the jth nonprice difference into a money equivalent; that is, a tradeoff between a price and a nonprice offer variation.

The Place of the Organism in Social System Models.   Parsons states that the outputs of the social system are delivered to personalities—not, except in certain borderline cases, to organisms.

The model in the preceding section, which is formulated in terms of optimizing the flow of rewards to a personality, could perhaps be supplemented by a set of constraints relating to the welfare of the organism. Thus we might specify upper and lower bounds for the amount of use of each behavior mechanism (affective behavior, gross motor activity, manipulation, talking, and thinking) to reflect the needs and limitations of the organism. Lower bounds might be specified for sleep, on behalf of the organism. The *social* rationale for these indulgences is that illness or fatigue of the organism will reduce the ability of the personality to make contributions and to earn (and enjoy) rewards. The prevalence of life, accident, and health insurance symbolizes this dependence of the personality on the survival and good physical condition of the organism. As Cantril points out (1965), "unless the survival needs are satisfied, a person devotes himself almost exclusively to fulfilling them" (p. 315).

There is a tradition of cost-benefit analysis, damage suits and settlements, and percentage disability estimates on which social accounting measurements might build. In general, it appears that injuries to the organism should be evaluated in terms of foregone reward streams, monetary and nonmonetary, as a consequence of the injuries. Where population groups are suffering extensively from malnutrition and illness, the difference between actual total income and potential total income with adequate nutrition and with illness rates characteristic of higher income groups would be an estimate of the potential *social* value of the necessary health and nutrition programs.

Optimizing Within a Behavior Setting.   The concept of optimization in social transactions is at least implicit in Berne. For example, in describing a simple *pastime* (1964), he stated that "the transactions are adaptively programmed so that each party will obtain the maximum gains or advantages during the interval. The better his adaptation, the more he will get out of it" (p. 41). Also, the transactions involved are "complementary"—a word Berne used quite frequently.

Barker's discussion of the various forces acting in and upon a behavior setting to maintain its function at a quasi-stationary level is also illuminating. In his classroom example, it appears that any change in functional level that would make some members better off would make others worse off. However, an innovation (such as dividing the class into a number of groups on the basis of proficiency or interest) might lead to a Pareto-better situation in which no student was worse off and most students were better off than before.

A behavior setting may be regarded as a "cooperative plant" that has no objective function of its own but should be managed so as to maximize the total net benefits distributed to the members, each member profiting in proportion to the amount he puts into the setting. Each member tries to allocate his total resources between this setting and all others in a way that will maximize his expected total utility. If the setting is a classroom, the teacher is responsible for managing the setting for the maximum benefit of the students. The students share in proportion to what they put into the setting (including study outside of the class); the teacher may receive various rewards for good management of the setting in terms of (1) implicit or explicit feedback from students as to how much they are getting out of the course, (2) self-approval for living up to her ego ideal, and (3) higher salary.

Optimization for Sets of Interrelated Behavior Settings.   The cost to a person of participating in one behavior setting is the opportunity cost of not participating in the highest-valued alternative setting.

Suppose that in a given community all children aged 6 to 11 are required to be in school for 30 hours a week. If each child has considerable latitude to choose his activities within the school, he may approximate a local optimum and realize most of the complementarities potentially available (from his standpoint) in the school as a whole. Mutually recognized complementarities might lead to near-optimal study groups without external pressure. Each constraint that was thought to be necessary by teachers or administrators could be evaluated in terms of perceived reductions in the outputs of the settings directly and indirectly affected by it.

As in the theory of general economic equilibrium under perfect competition, it would be possible to *accept* the results of a self-optimizing process without attempting to *measure* them. However, if pressures and restrictions have been imposed on the self-optimizing process (and the continuance of some restrictions is deemed necessary), measurement of the outputs associated with alternative sets of restrictions is needed for policy guidance.

Optimization for a Small Community.   The optimizing model involved in the theory of consumer behavior may be expressed as follows:

$$\max U = f(q_1, q_2, \cdots, q_n), \qquad \text{subject to} \tag{12}$$

$$\sum_{i=1}^{n} p_i q_i = Y, \tag{13}$$

where the q_i are quantities of n consumer goods and services, the p_i are the corresponding market prices, and Y is the consumer's income, assumed to be fixed; the consumer's utility function U depends directly only on the quantities consumed, q_i $(i = 1, 2, \ldots, n)$.

This model implies that the weighted average price elasticity of demand for the q_i is -1 and the weighted average income elasticity is 1; if all prices and money income are multiplied by the same scalar, the q_i will be unchanged.

If there are no externalities of consumption, these elasticity properties apply also to an *aggregate* of consumers, such as the 830 residents of Barker's community, provided each of the 830 incomes is fixed and consumers pay the same price for any given commodity.

Do these elasticity properties apply to our model of a person allocating fixed amounts of s media among n behavior settings? We assume that his input into any behavior setting i is a vector of fixed numbers per hour of occupancy and that the output (reward) he gains from that setting is also a vector of fixed numbers per hour of occupancy.

If the money income constraint is binding for the person, the price and income elasticity properties must hold with respect to his *economic* transactions. By analogy, it seems that the same properties should hold with respect to each of the other media taken separately. If so, the elasticity properties should also hold for each medium separately over an aggregate of consumers whose resource vectors contain fixed amounts of the s media. (These amounts can vary both absolutely and relatively as between different persons.)

Competition among behavior settings for the time of community residents could be conceptualized, recognizing that the total living time of the residents per year is a fixed number; an increase in occupancy time for one genotype setting therefore requires a decrease in occupancy time for one or more other genotype settings.

Suppose a resident is allocating his yearly living time among the n genotype settings available in the community and receiving a vector of rewards per hour in setting i with an equivalent dollar value (to him) of r_i. Then we can write $t = a + Br$ in matrix notation or, in expanded form:

$$
\begin{bmatrix} t_1 \\ t_2 \\ \cdot \\ \cdot \\ \cdot \\ t_n \end{bmatrix} = \begin{bmatrix} a_1 \\ a_2 \\ \cdot \\ \cdot \\ \cdot \\ a_n \end{bmatrix} + \begin{bmatrix} b_{11} & b_{12} & \cdots & b_{1n} \\ b_{21} & b_{22} & \cdots & b_{2n} \\ \cdot & \cdot & & \cdot \\ \cdot & \cdot & & \cdot \\ \cdot & \cdot & & \cdot \\ b_{n1} & b_{n2} & \cdots & b_{nn} \end{bmatrix} \begin{bmatrix} r_1 \\ r_2 \\ \cdot \\ \cdot \\ \cdot \\ r_n \end{bmatrix}, \tag{14}
$$

and $\sum_{i=1}^{n} t_i = 8760$; the total social income of the resident is $\sum_{i=1}^{n} t_i r_i$. Then the following measure might be taken as a surrogate for his *quality of life*:

$$
\frac{\sum_{i=1}^{n} t_i r_i}{\sum_{i=1}^{n} t_i} = \frac{\sum_{i=1}^{n} t_i r_i}{8760} = \bar{r}. \tag{15}
$$

Now, suppose that the matrix B is stated in elasticity form, relating percentage changes in the t_i to percentage changes in the r_i. If every r_i is multiplied by the same scalar, the t_i should not change. Also, if the reward per hour, r_i, for occupying setting i is increased while all r_j's $(j = 1, 2,)$ i $(, \ldots, n)$ remain constant, occupancy time in setting i should increase or, at the least, not decrease. Hence the diagonal elements b_{ii} will be nonnegative and the off-diagonal elements b_{ij} $(j \neq i)$ will, on the average, be nonpositive:

$$
b_{ii} \geq 0; \qquad b_{ii} + \sum_{\substack{j=1 \\ (j \neq i)}}^{n} b_{ij} = 0; \tag{16}
$$

therefore, we have

$$
\sum_{\substack{j=1 \\ (j \neq i)}}^{n} b_{ij} \leq 0.
$$

The genotype behavior settings might be grouped according to "authority systems," using Barker's terminology: business, schools, churches, government, and voluntary associations (also families, since we are including private as well as public behavior settings in our conceptualization). Thus a resident's living time could be allocated exhaustively (for social accounting purposes) among these six authority systems and an average reward per hour calculated for each one; the weighted average of these six quality measures would be the $\bar{r}$ of (15), a surrogate for the overall quality of the person's life during the specified period.

The quality of life of a resident is improving over time if the value of $\bar{r}$ is rising. If we aggregate over all N residents and all n genotype settings and divide by total living time of the residents, we obtain

$$
\frac{\sum_{k=1}^{N} \sum_{i=1}^{n} t_{ki} r_{ki}}{\sum_{k=1}^{N} \sum_{i=1}^{n} t_{ki}} = \bar{r}_N, \tag{18}
$$

$\bar{r}_N$ being the average total income per hour of living time for all area residents. If $\bar{r}_N$ increases over time, the quality of life in the community is improving.

. In addition to the crucial problems of measuring exchange rates between media for a given person and aggregating "rewards" over persons, there would remain some more conventional problems, such as (*a*) comparing rates of change in $\bar{r}_N$ over time as between different communities and (*b*) comparing absolute levels of $\bar{r}_N$ at a given date across communities.

An increase in the value of output of any behavior setting per participant hour will tend (*ceteris paribus*) to increase its share of the community's total living time. Some behavior settings are selective with respect to age or other population subgroups; an improvement in recreational programs for the aged would have its primary impact on behavior settings normally occupied by them.

2.8   Concluding Remarks

The model described is by no means definitive. However, it suggests some of the problems that must be solved in developing social indicators that are equally consistent with leading theories in sociology, psychology, and economics.

In the next chapter, we restate the concept of a person's total income in the language of utility theory and mathematical programming. Hopefully, it will serve as an additional bridge among the three disciplines involved.

III

Derivation and Implications of a Scalar Measure of Total Income[1]

THIS CHAPTER CONTAINS an alternative statement of the model presented in Section 2.7. The terminology and notation are somewhat different, and several statements that were put forward as conjectures in Section 2.7 are rigorously proved here.

We introduce a scalar measure of an individual's social income (SI) which includes returns in terms of social media of exchange other than money, such as professional standing and political power, in addition to money income from property and transfer payments.

We show that such a scalar measure exists if the individual is assumed to optimize the allocation of his time among alternative behavior settings under a number of social constraints. SI is computed with the help of a mathematical programming model: since one of the constraints is financial, the dual variables pertaining to the remaining constraints, and hence SI, can be equally well expressed in dollars.

A number of desirable, and empirically meaningful, properties are derived by mathematical programming techniques. Some implications of our approach for policy models, output measurement, demand analysis, and the study of income distributions are suggested in the concluding sections.

3.1 Sociopsychological and Economic Rationale for the Total Income Concept

The development of national income accounts by Kuznets (1937) and others took a tremendous amount of hard work with crude data. The work was guided by explicit definitions of the scope of economic activity. The input–output models of

[1] This chapter is based on Fox and Van Moeseke (1973). The mathematical sections were written by Paul Van Moeseke, Professor Ordinarius of Mathematical Economics at the University of Louvain.

Leontief (1936, 1951) and the econometric models of Tinbergen (1939) incorporated the national income accounts, and hence embodied the same definitions of the scope of the economy. Essentially the same definitions have been carried forward in subsequent developments of national income accounting, econometric forecasting and stabilization models, and models of economic growth.

The resulting interconnected array of economic accounts and models has been a magnificent achievement. The problems of economic policy within individual countries have been greatly clarified as a result. Use of the same definitions and scope by many different countries has facilitated international comparisons and cooperation. Thus J. A. C. Brown (1969) could design a 20-region model of the world economy emphasizing food and agriculture, with confidence that it could be implemented if the appropriate international agency wished to do so. One of the present authors (Fox 1969b) outlined an extension of the food and agricultural sectors of Brown's model that in principle could generate consistent sets of prices for 20 or more major agricultural commodities and groups in each of 5000 to 10,000 agricultural production areas. Klein (1971) reported substantial progress toward linking econometric models for several countries under a cooperative project looking toward a world model of the short-run or stabilization type.

The current interest in social indicators and social accounts extends to all aspects of a social system. The economist's traditional scope is much narrower, but his methods may be of wider application.

Sections 3.2 through 3.5 are intended as a contribution to the pure theory of social accounts. In Sections 3.6 and 3.7, we point out some implications of our approach for policy models, output measurement, demand analysis, and the study of income distributions.

In our exposition we make use of Roger Barker's (1968) concept of "behavior settings" and Talcott Parsons's (1968) concept of "generalized media of social interchange." The individual is viewed as attempting to optimize the allocation of his time among behavior settings during the current accounting period, subject to constraints on each of the several endowments that limit his contributions to, and rewards from, the social system during the period; these contributions and rewards could presumably be measured in terms of Parsons's media. One of the endowments is money income y from property and transfer payments (i.e., income not dependent on personal effort during the current accounting period). We define the sum of the equivalent dollar values of all rewards during the current accounting period that are derived from the endowments as *social income* (SI).

It is intuitively plausible that an estimate of an individual's social income during a given accounting period could be obtained by the following procedure. (1) Ask him to estimate the proportion of each one of the other media (separately) among his endowments that he would be willing to sacrifice in order to increase his money income during the current period by $1000; from this we can compute a dollar value for the entire amount of each medium available to him for use during the current period. (2) Sum these dollar values over all media, yielding a measure of his social income (*SI*) in dollar equivalents.

The individual's money income for current personal services (wages or salary, etc.) is denoted by p_1x_1, where x_1 is the fraction of his total time devoted to paid employment and p_1 is the wage or salary received per time unit spent in paid employment. His *total income*, then, during the current accounting period is $SI + p_1x_1$.

How does this total income compare with the income attributed to the individual in our traditional national income accounts? The sum of income from property and transfer payments y and income from personal services p_1x_1 would correspond to the *personal income* concept in such accounts, $y + p_1x_1$. The difference between total income and personal income is $(SI + p_1x_1) - (y + p_1x_1)$ or $SI - y$; it is the equivalent dollar value attributed to rewards received in media other than money.

In principle, dollar estimates of social income and total income could be obtained for each individual in a society and summed over individuals to yield societal (e.g., national) totals. In practice, the estimates of nonmoney income $SI - y$ could be based largely on sample survey interviews; some data about time allocation and perceived intensity of use of specified media in specified categories of behavior settings could be obtained in the same way. Objective data of various kinds (school enrollments, numbers of tickets sold for attendance at cultural or athletic events, etc.) could also be used to develop aggregative estimates of time allocation and nonmoney income for national populations and specified subgroups.

A number of independent developments are hastening the time when such an accounting system may become feasible. One of these is the system of demographic accounts developed by Stone (1971) under the auspices of the Organization for Economic Cooperation and Development (OECD), with emphasis on earning and learning activities. Another, in the United States at least, is the current emphasis on "accountability" in higher education and consequent attempts to define, measure, and evaluate the educational, research, and service outputs of universities; some examples of these attempts have been presented by one of us (Fox, ed., 1972). Most important of all is the recent intensification of research on social indicators in several countries and institutional provisions for improved communication among those involved.

A system of social accounts based on behavior settings and generalized media of exchange would require decisions on many questions of definition, classification, and measurement.

As noted in Sections 2.6 and 2.7, Roger Barker (1968) has used his theory of behavior settings to characterize the behaviorally relevant environment of a small town in considerable detail. He has made great progress in defining and classifying behavior settings and measuring their behavioral inputs and outputs. The uniformities seem to be at least as great as those underlying the classification of consumer durable goods or clothing in the national income and product accounts.

We also noted in Sections 2.5 and 2.7 that Talcott Parsons (1968) discusses generalized exchange media in terms of influence, money, power, value commitments, erotic pleasure, affect, recognition, response, technological know-how and skill, ideology, conscience, reputation, and faith. It is not clear that he would regard this list as optimal for measuring all contributions to and rewards from the social system, but he evidently intended it to be quite comprehensive.

A person enjoys participating in behavior settings in which he is "liked," "respected," and "appreciated." Once he has identified himself with a group for which, say, faith is the primary medium in its distinctive behavior settings, his satisfaction per hour of occupancy of these settings may be approximately the same as in settings whose primary medium is reputation, ideology, or conscience. Thus behavior settings sponsored by a wide range of organizations might be lumped together in some measures of social income.

Our exposition in Sections 3.2 through 3.5 will assume the existence of a classification scheme more or less along the lines suggested by Parsons.

3.2 Outline of the Mathematical Derivation and Implications

From a sociological viewpoint, the individual is active in a number of behavior settings belonging to the economy, the polity, the church, the family, the club, and so on. Within each behavior setting, his activity is guided—and restricted—by inputs and outputs (or contributions and rewards) in terms of a number of media of exchange such as money, influence, votes, and professional standing.

We assume in Section 3.3 that the individual optimizes the allocation of his time among alternative behavior settings under a number of constraints pertaining to several media—money included. The resulting programming model theoretically allows the derivation of a scalar measure, called social income (SI) and expressed in dollars, of the individual's rewards in terms of all social media of exchange, and resulting from his activities in all relevant behavior settings. Summation over individuals would then yield a figure, expressed in dollars, for the social income of any specified population aggregate (nation, region, state, age, sex, occupation, or other grouping).

In Section 3.4 empirically meaningful implications of the programming model are derived, in particular: the individual's utility need only be defined up to a monotonic transformation; SI changes proportionately with the general price level in the economy; the individual's choice is invariant under proportional changes (in particular, changes in the unit of measurement) of inputs and outputs of any medium of exchange; his choice further satisfies the elasticity rule and the Le Chatelier principle. In Section 3.5 a quadratic approximation to the individual's utility function is derived.

3.3 The Model

The individual divides one period of time (the current accounting period) over n behavior settings, hereafter interchangeably referred to as *settings* or *activities*, spending the fraction x_j of the unit period on the jth activity. The n tuple $x_j, j = 1, 2, \ldots, n$, is denoted by x (where $x \in R^n+$). Formally, an *individual* is a triple $(u:R^n+ \rightarrow R; A; b)$, where u is his utility function; A and b are real matrices, respectively, $m \times n$ and $m \times 1$; b denotes the endowment (or resources) in terms of the different media of exchange; and the elements a_{ij} of A are input coefficients: a unit of the jth activity absorbs a_{ij} units of b_i. The matrices x, A, b express the individual's *life style*, *environment*, and *endowment*, respectively.[2]

[2] Note that x records the proportions of the individual's time spent in each of the n behavior settings (a complete time budget), hence summarizes his life style. Each column of the matrix A lists the amounts of each of m (economic and social) exchange media absorbed per unit of time spent in a particular setting as an environment for the individual's behavior. The characterization of b as the individual's endowment is straightforward.

MATHEMATICAL PROPERTIES OF THE MODEL   33

He faces the programming model (P),

$$\text{maximize } u(x), \qquad \text{subject to} \tag{1}$$

$$Ax \leq b, \tag{2}$$

$$x \geq 0. \tag{3}$$

The set $X \equiv \{x \geq 0 \,|\, Ax \leq b\}$ is called the *feasible set* of possible activity levels (time allocations to alternative settings).

By way of illustration, we write out the first three rows of (2):

$$-p_1 x_1 + p_2 x_2 + \cdots + p_n x_n \leq y, \tag{4}$$

$$x_1 + x_2 + \cdots + x_n \leq 1, \tag{5}$$

$$-w_1 x_1 - w_2 x_2 - \cdots - w_n x_n \leq -w, \tag{6}$$

and we assume that x_1 denotes time spent at work, x_2, time spent shopping at the grocery store, and so on. Income constraint (4) is the reduced form of $p_2 x_2 + \cdots + p_n x_n \leq y + p_1 x_1$, stating that expenses incurred in activities 2 through n cannot exceed money income (from property and transfer payments y, and current personal services $p_1 x_1$, where p_1 denotes the wage rate). The meaning of time constraint (5) is obvious. Constraint (6) is the reduced form of $w_1 x_1 + w_2 x_2 + \cdots + w_n x_n \geq w$: in the case of, say, a local politician, election requires at least w votes; activity 1 is estimated to yield w_1 votes per unit of time spent at work (law practice or union activity, say), w_2 per unit of time spent at the grocery store, and so on. Put another way, the left side of (6) is a linear approximation to the assumed functional relationship $w = w(x_1, \ldots, x_n)$ between votes obtained and time invested in alternative behavior settings. Such linearization is neither more nor less rebarbative in a social than in an economic context, where linear activity analysis (Koopmans, 1951) in general, and input–output tables (Leontief, 1951) in particular, are standard tools in approximating production functions.

Analogously, in the case of a research worker, w may express an output requirement (e.g., pages or papers published), and the w_j may denote estimated average yields from time spent in such behavior settings as work, professional contacts, and relaxation.

As illustrated by (4) to (6), the a_{ij} may denote inputs or outputs according as $a_{ij} > 0$ or < 0. Furthermore, the b_i denote endowments or requirements according to whether $b_i > 0$ or < 0.

3.4   Mathematical Properties of the Model

We make the standard assumption that u is concave (i.e., has the usual properties of risk aversion and nonincreasing returns). By the saddlepoint theorem (Uzawa, 1958), x^* solves (P)—assuming the Slater regularity condition: $Ax^\circ < b$ for some $x^\circ \geq 0$— if and only if there is a real n tuple $v^* \geq 0$ such that (x^*, v^*) is a *saddlepoint* of the Lagrangian $L(x, v) \equiv u(x) + v(b - Ax)$; that is, if and only if

$$u(x) + v^*(b - Ax) \leq u(x^*) + v^*(b - Ax^*) \leq u(x^*) + v(b - Ax^*)$$
$$\text{for all} \quad x \geq 0, v \geq 0. \tag{7}$$

Clearly, the second inequality holds if and only if

$$v^*(b - Ax^*) = 0. \tag{8}$$

The coordinates x_j, v_i of x, v are called primal and dual variables, respectively.

The standard interpretation of v^* as a price system for endowments b_i (in terms of maximand u) is well known. Consequently, the solution of (P) implies the valuation of total endowment at

$$v^*b \equiv \Sigma v_i^* b_i = v_1^* y + \cdots + v_m^* b_m. \tag{9}$$

We define

$$SI \equiv \frac{v^*b}{v_1^*} = \Sigma \frac{v_i^*}{v_1^*} b_i = \frac{v_1^*}{v_1^*} y$$

$$+ \frac{v_2^*}{v_1^*} b_2 + \cdots + \frac{v_m^*}{v_1^*} b_m, \quad (v_1^* > 0), \tag{10}$$

which evidently has the same dimension as y, namely, dollars.[3] *Total income*, including income from current personal services, is then $p_1 x_1^* + SI$. If u is known, the value of SI is given by (10): we indicate in Section 3.5 how a quadratic approximation to u can be estimated.

We show first that u can be and need be specified only up to a monotonic transformation and that SI is *invariant* on the class of such transformations. Next to (P) consider the problem (P′):

$$\text{maximize } F(x) = F[u(x)], \quad (F \in \mathfrak{F}) \tag{P′}$$

under restrictions (2) and (3). Here $\mathfrak{F}$ designates the class of transformations F that are concave in x and satisfy $F' \equiv dF/du > 0$ on the range of u.

For the first proposition we need the Kuhn-Tucker (1951) *equivalence theorem*: Let u be concave and differentiable (on $R^n +$); then x^* solves (P)—assuming the foregoing regularity condition—if and only if there is a $v^* \geq 0$ such that

$$Ax^* \leq b,$$
$$v^*Ax^* = v^*b,$$
$$u_{x^*} \leq v^*A, \tag{KT}$$
$$u_{x^*}x^* = v^*Ax^*,$$

where u_{x^*} denotes the gradient vector $[\partial u/\partial x] \equiv [\partial u/\partial x_1, \ldots, \partial u/\partial x_n]$ evaluated at x^*, and $u_{x^*}x^*$ is the scalar product $\Sigma(\partial u/\partial x_j)x_j^*$. For u concave and differentiable, conjunction of the four conditions (KT) is equivalent to the single saddlepoint condition (7). The following proposition is obvious.

PROPOSITION 1.   Let u be concave and differentiable and $F \in \mathfrak{F}$. Then x^* solves (P) if and only if it solves (P′).

---

[3] Assuming $v_1^* > 0$ by (2), (8) implies that money constraint (4) is binding. Since v_i^* can be interpreted as the marginal utility $\partial u/\partial b_i$ of the ith endowment (proof in Van Moeseke, 1965), the assumption means that money is a scarce commodity for the individual.

We note further that $F_x = F'u_x$. By the equivalence theorem, applied to (P'), x^* solves (P') if and only if there is a $w^* \geq 0$ such that

$$Ax^* \leq b,$$
$$w^*Ax^* = w^*b,$$
$$F'u_{x^*} \leq w^*A, \qquad \text{(KT')}$$
$$F'u_{x^*}x^* = w^*Ax^*.$$

It is clear that a $v^* \geq 0$ satisfying (KT) exists if and only if there exists a $w^* \equiv F'v^* \geq 0$ satisfying (KT').

COROLLARY 1. SI is invariant on $\mathfrak{F}$.
   Proof.   Substitution of w^* for v^* in (10) yields

$$\frac{w^*b}{w_1{}^*} = \frac{(F'v^*)b}{(F'v_1{}^*)} = \frac{v^*b}{v_1{}^*}. \qquad \text{Q.E.D.} \qquad (11)$$

The unit of measurement for any one medium in (2) is evidently arbitrary: in (4) all p_j and y could be expressed in cents as well as in dollars, time in (5) could be measured in months, years, or other units; clearly, the choice x^* should be invariant under such changes, as shown below. We denote[4] by a^i the ith row of A and by $a^i x \leq b_i$ the ith constraint in (2).

The next proposition requires neither concavity nor differentiability of u. It is valid for any real-valued u whatever.

PROPOSITION 2.   Any solution x^* to (P) is invariant under replacement of (2) by

$$(k_i a^i)x \leq k_i b_i, \qquad k_i > 0, \qquad 1 = 1, 2, \ldots, m. \qquad (12)$$

   Proof.   Proof follows because the feasible set X is unaffected. Indeed, let K be the diagonal $n \times n$ matrix with k_i in the ith position. The new constraints then read

$$KAx \leq Kb. \qquad (13)$$

Clearly, for all $K > 0$, any $x \geq 0$ satisfies (2) if and only if it satisfies (13). Q.E.D.

A solution x^* to (P) is a vector function[5] f, called *choice function*, of the coefficients of A, b. Proposition 2 states that every coordinate f_h is (positively) homogeneous of degree 0 in every $n + 1$-tuple $(a_{i1}, \ldots, a_{in}, b_i)$ of coefficients of row i separately— and, a fortiori, in all the coefficients of A, b jointly:

$$x_h{}^* = f_h(a_{11}, \ldots, a_{1n}, b_1; \ldots; a_{m1}, \ldots, a_{mn}, b_m)$$
$$= f_h(k_1 a_{11}, \ldots, k_1 a_{1n}, k_1 b_1; \ldots; k_m a_{m1}, \ldots, k_m a_{mn}, k_m b_m),$$
$$k_i > 0, i = 1, \ldots, m; \qquad h = 1, \ldots, n. \qquad (14)$$

The proposition imposes empirically meaningful restrictions on small relative changes of the x_h in response to small relative changes (not necessarily proportional) in the coefficients:

[4] Superscripts distinguish vectors (e.g., a^i, x^h); subscripts distinguish coordinates (e.g., b_i, x_j).
[5] It is necessarily single valued if u is strictly quasi-concave. Otherwise, in general, it is a correspondence.

COROLLARY 2 (ELASTICITY RULE[6]).   Let u be concave and differentiable. For any $x_h{}^* > 0$ and any ith constraint, the elasticity of $x_h{}^*$ with respect to b_i equals in absolute magnitude the sum of elasticities with respect to the a_{ij}:

$$\sum_{j=1}^{n} \frac{a_{ij}}{x_h{}^*} \frac{\partial x_h}{\partial a_{ij}} = - \frac{b_i}{x_h{}^*} \frac{\partial x_h}{\partial b_i},$$

$h = 1, \ldots, n; \qquad i = 1, \ldots, m, \qquad$ all differentials taken at x^*.   (15)

Proof.   Homogeneity of degree 0 by Euler's theorem implies, for every h, i,

$$\sum_{j=1}^{n} \frac{\partial x_h}{\partial a_{ij}} a_{ij} + \frac{\partial x_h}{\partial b_i} b_i = 0.$$ (16)

After dividing (16) through by $x_h{}^* > 0$ and rearranging, one obtains (15). Q.E.D.

Observe that (15) provides $m \times n$ verifiable restrictions.

We can further compute how multiplication of the coefficients of the ith constraint by k_i affects the value of $v_i{}^*$, hence of *SI*.

Concavity, but not differentiability, of u is postulated in the remainder of the section.

PROPOSITION 3.   If in (P) the ith constraint is replaced by

$$(k_i a^i)x \le (k_i b_i); \qquad k_i > 0, \quad i = 1, \ldots, m,$$ (17)

then $v_i{}^*/k_i$ can be substituted for $v_i{}^*$.

Proof.   Clearly, for all x,

$$v^*(b - Ax) \equiv \Sigma v_i{}^*(b_i - a^i x) = \Sigma \frac{v_i{}^*}{k_i} (k_i b_i - k_i a^i x).$$ (18)

Hence substitution of $v_i{}^*/k_i$ for $v_i{}^*$ does not affect the first inequality in (7). Since for $x = x^*$, (18) vanishes by (8), the second inequality in (7) is not affected either. Q.E.D.

COROLLARY 3.   Under the conditions of Proposition 3, *SI* is multiplied by k_1.

Proof.   Equation (10) becomes

$$\frac{[\Sigma(v_i{}^*/k_i)(k_i b_i)]}{(v_1{}^*/k_1)} = k_1 \frac{v^*b}{v_1{}^*}. \qquad \text{Q.E.D.}$$ (19)

In particular, if the general price level rises by, say, 5 percent ($k_1 = 1.05$) so, *ceteri. paribus*, does *SI*: consistent measurement of *SI* in dollars evidently requires this result$s$

We finally prove that as one would expect, the marginal value $v_i{}^*$ of the ith endowment increases if its amount is reduced, and vice versa. Similarly, an activity is

---

[6] Implies, as a special case, the elasticity rule (Samuelson, 1947, Chapter 5) for consumer equilibrium under a single equality constraint.

stepped up if its cost (in terms of endowment inputs) decreases, and vice versa. These are instances of the *Le Chatelier principle*.[7]

In the next two propositions we consider, next to (P), the problem $(\overline{P})$, where $\overline{b}$ has been substituted for b, so that, for $(\overline{P})$, (2) becomes

$$Ax \leq \overline{b}. \tag{2'}$$

Let (x^*, v^*) be a saddlepoint of (P) and $(\overline{x}, \overline{v})$ a saddlepoint of $(\overline{P})$ so that
$$u(x) + \overline{v}(\overline{b} - Ax) \leq u(\overline{x}) + \overline{v}(\overline{b} - A\overline{x}) \leq u(\overline{x}) + v(\overline{b} - A\overline{x})$$
$$\text{for all} \quad x \geq 0, \quad v \geq 0. \tag{7'}$$

Again, the second inequality holds if and only if

$$\overline{v}(\overline{b} - A\overline{x}) = 0. \tag{8'}$$

We denote $\Delta b \equiv \overline{b} - b$, $\Delta x \equiv \overline{x} - x^*$, $\Delta v \equiv \overline{v} - v^*$.

PROPOSITION 4 (LE CHATELIER PRINCIPLE I).

$$\Delta v \Delta b \leq 0. \tag{20}$$

Proof. (A) By the *first* saddlepoint inequalities in (7) and (7') respectively, one has
$$u(\overline{x}) + v^*(b - A\overline{x}) \leq u(x^*) + v^*(b - Ax^*), \tag{21}$$
$$u(x^*) + \overline{v}(\overline{b} - Ax^*) \leq u(\overline{x}) + \overline{v}(\overline{b} - A\overline{x}). \tag{21'}$$
Adding (21), (21'), and canceling yields $\overline{v}A(\overline{x} - x^*) \leq v^*A(\overline{x} - x^*)$, or
$$\Delta v A \Delta x \leq 0. \tag{22}$$

(B) Equalities (8) and (8'), equivalent to the *second* saddlepoint inequalities in (7) and (7') respectively, yield
$$v^*Ax^* = v^*b, \tag{23}$$
$$\overline{v}A\overline{x} = \overline{v}\overline{b}. \tag{23'}$$
Since $x^*, \overline{x}$ satisfy (2) and (2'), respectively, and $v^*, \overline{v} \geq 0$, one has further
$$\overline{v}Ax^* \leq \overline{v}b, \tag{24}$$
$$v^*A\overline{x} \leq v^*\overline{b}. \tag{24'}$$
Subtraction of (23) from (24), and of (23') from (24'), yields respectively
$$\Delta v\, Ax^* \leq \Delta v b, \tag{25}$$
$$-\Delta v\, A\overline{x} \leq -\Delta v \overline{b}. \tag{26}$$
Addition of these two inequalities yields $\Delta v\, \Delta b \leq \Delta v A\, \Delta x$ so that, by (22), one obtains (20). Q.E.D.

If but one of the b_i changes, say, b_g (i.e., $\Delta b_i = 0$, all $i \neq g$), then $\Delta v\, \Delta b \equiv \Sigma \Delta v_i \Delta b_i = \Delta v_g \Delta b_g \leq 0$, so that b_i and v_i^* change in opposite directions.

---

[7] If one alters one of the parameters (pressure, temperature, concentration of any one compound, etc.) of a system in a physical or chemical equilibrium, the remaining parameters will adjust to counteract the disturbance.

Putting $r^* \equiv v^*A$, one has $r^*x^* = v^*Ax^* = \Sigma r_j^*x_j^* = \Sigma_j(\Sigma_i v_i^* a_{ij})x_j^*$. Also, by (8), $r^*x^* = v^*b$. Hence r_j^* can be interpreted as the *cost* $\Sigma_i v_i^* a_{ij}$ of resources used up per unit of activity level j. Total cost r^*x^* equals total resource value v^*b. One would expect activity level j to be reduced if its cost r_j^* increases, as shown in Corollary 4. We denote $\Delta r \equiv \bar{r} - r^*, \bar{r} \equiv \bar{v}A$.

COROLLARY 4 (LE CHATELIER PRINCIPLE II).

$$\Delta r \, \Delta x \leq 0. \tag{27}$$

Proof. $\Delta r \, \Delta x = (\bar{r} - r^*) \, \Delta x = (\bar{v} - v^*)A \, \Delta x = \Delta v A \, \Delta x$, so that, by (22), one obtains (27). Q.E.D.

Given the optimal x^*, there is, by the saddlepoint condition, an associated v^*, hence an r^* that can be interpreted as a cost, as just explained. But *given* the value v^* of resources used, $r_j^*x_j$ can be viewed as the value created by, or the return from, activity j, so that r^*x should be maximized on X.

PROPOSITION 5. x^* maximizes r^*x on X.

Proof. All $x \in X$ satisfy $r^*x \equiv v^*Ax \leq v^*b = v^*Ax^* \equiv r^*x^*$, where the inequality follows from (2) and the equality from (8). Q.E.D.

This dual interpretation of r^* reflects, of course, the dual character of a saddlepoint.

3.5   Measurement

One can compute u by quadratic approximation,

$$u(x) = a + qx + \tfrac{1}{2} xQx. \tag{28}$$

Without loss of generality, Q is assumed symmetric; thus apart from the constant a, one must compute $n' \equiv n + n(n + 1)/2 = n(n + 3)/2$ coefficients (the elements q_j of q and q_{ij} of Q). If the individual specifies n' points $x^h \in R^n+$ among which he is indifferent [i.e., $u(x^h) = k$, all h, where k is a constant], one obtains n' equations linear in and normally solvable for the q_j and q_{ij}:

$$\sum_j x_j^h q_j + \tfrac{1}{2} \sum_j x_j^2 q_{jj} + \sum_{i<j} x_i^h x_j^h q_{ij} = k - a \equiv k' \qquad (h = 1, \ldots, n'). \tag{29}$$

Clearly, the x^h belong to the same indifference locus, whether the utility function be u or any other member of $\mathfrak{F}$. Consequently,[8] we can choose an arbitrary $k' > 0$.

The quadratic approximation to u affords a verification, both theoretical and empirical, of (27). By Corollary 4, one has, in the limit $dr \, dx \leq 0$; hence $dr \, dx = dr(\partial x/\partial r) \, dr \equiv \sum_{i,j} (\partial x_i/\partial r_j) \, dr_i \, dr_j \leq 0$, where $\partial x/\partial r$ denotes a Jacobian evaluated at $x = x^*$ and the summand denotes the corresponding quadratic form. Hence $\partial x/\partial r$ is negative semidefinite. By the third (KT) condition

$$r^* \equiv v^*A \geq u_{x^*} = q + Qx^*. \tag{30}$$

---

[8] $k' \leq 0$ is inapposite (e.g., in the case of u homogeneous).

By the fourth (KT) condition, $x^* > 0$ implies equality in (30). Since for the purpose of measurement, one will limit the domain of u to the behavior settings the individual actually engages in (so that $x^* > 0$), one has $r^* = q + Qx^*$; thus assuming Q non-singular, $x^* = Q^{-1}(r^* - q)$ and $\partial x/\partial r = Q^{-1}$, which means that Q^{-1}, hence Q, must be negative semidefinite (indeed, definite, because nonsingular).

This is confirmed by the observation that the quadratic u is concave if and only if Q is negative semidefinite. Furthermore, one can check empirically whether the solution to (29) satisfies that condition.

3.6   Implications for the Study of Income Distributions

Our demonstrations in Sections 3.3 through 3.5 are evidently consistent with standard assumptions and proofs in economic theory and mathematical programming. Since an individual's utility function need be specified only up to a monotonic transformation, we can obtain all our empirically meaningful results without assigning a numerical value to the individual's "utility" or total subjective experience of well-being. Moreover, we do not need to compare the "utilities" experienced by different individuals.

We do not suggest that interpersonal comparisons of well-being are impossible simply because interpersonal comparisons of utility are unnecessary either for our derivations or for those of consumer theory. Distributions of money income are of considerable political interest, and distributions of nonmoney income and total income (if measured with the same degree of accuracy) would be of equal or greater concern.

Tinbergen (1956) held that comparison of the satisfaction of different individuals is implicit in the policy aim of social justice:

> Social justice, whatever its meaning, is an aim of economic and social policy which, in the minds of many citizens of many countries, ranks very high. An attempt at defining social justice, in such a way as to appeal to most people's feelings and to be amenable to scientific analysis, might be of great importance. Social justice has, essentially, to do with comparing the satisfaction of different individuals (p. 22).
>
> Such comparisons are declared impossible by many economists. Nevertheless, they seem to be the basis for many decisions taken by family heads as well as organizers, judges, etc. Furthermore, individuals who have undergone a "transformation" such as training or a medical treatment seem to be able to make comparisons. Finally it would sometimes seem possible to determine, with the help of medical and similar standards, the compensations needed to neutralize certain "handicaps" and by so doing to find a method of making different individuals "equally happy" (pp. xiv–xv).
>
> In ways like this it may be possible to make fruitful contributions to this problem, which is not the first in the history of sciences to have been regarded—by renowned scientists—to be insoluble in principle (p. 24).

Our model at least offers a novel and systematic way of considering such comparisons. Suppose we had estimates of p_1x_1, y, and $(SI - y)$ for each of 20,000 individuals in a representative sample of a country's population. How large is $(SI - y)$

relative to $p_1x_1 + y$? Are the nonmoney and money components significantly correlated? If so, how closely and with what sign? Is the coefficient of variation of nonmoney income larger or smaller than that of money income? How do various measures of inequality of total income, $p_1x_1 + SI$, compare with those for money income only, $p_1x_1 + y$?

The distributions and intercorrelations of specific nonmoney media would also be of interest. Power, influence, and recognition may all be rather highly correlated (positively) with money income. Technological know-how and skill presumably result from specific learning experiences and are a form of "human capital," positively correlated with money income.

The exclusion of p_1x_1 from our definition of social income is not a crucial feature of the approach. For example, technological know-how and skill s at the beginning of the current accounting period could be included in the endowment vector, and p_1x_1 could be ascribed to using this endowment on the job. In addition to (4), we would then include (4a):

$$-p_1x_1 + p_2x_2 + \cdots + p_nx_n \leq y \qquad (4)$$

$$p_1x_1 \qquad\qquad\qquad \leq s \qquad (4a)$$

In equilibrium, the dollar value attributed to s would be $p_1x_1{}^*$, and the sum of (4) and (4a) would be $p_2x_2 + \cdots + p_nx_n = y + p_1x_1{}^*$; the right-hand term is, of course, the money component of total income. One medium—skill—is transformed into (sold for) another medium—money—within the expanded model.

Health was not mentioned by Parsons as a medium of exchange. His broader conceptual scheme distinguishes between the *organism* and the *personality*, and it is primarily the personality that is involved in social interchange. In some passages, however, Parsons speaks of the organism as a component of the personality, and this is evidently the appropriate view for our purposes. At the beginning of the current accounting period health h might perhaps be included in the endowment vector, and its value (as a flow during the period) might enter into total income.

Care must be taken to avoid double counting. For example, part of p_1x_1 may be attributable not to skill but to physical health. The first term of (4a) might then be written $\lambda(p_1x_1)$, where $0 \leq \lambda \leq 1$; the first term of the new row in h might be written as $(1 - \lambda)(p_1x_1)$. All of skill s and part of health h would be transformed into money income for personal services within the revised model. Part of health might also be transformed into affect or other nonmoney media; here, again, the constraint structure must reflect these transformations without double counting any component of nonmoney income, $SI - y$.

It may be objected that our approach involves an unrealistic degree of self-knowledge on the part of the individual. We have already suggested that an individual be asked to compare the loss of some *proportion* of his ith endowment with a gain of $1000 in money income. We need not ask him to specify a unit of measure for any of the nonmoney endowments. His endowment vector becomes $(y, 1, 1, \ldots, 1)$, each a_{ij} becomes $\alpha_{ij} = a_{ij}/b_i$, and each constraint $\sum a_{ij}x_j \leq b_i$ becomes $\sum \alpha_{ij}x_j \leq 1$.

As a matter of fact, the numbers of resources, their definitions, and their degrees of aggregation could differ substantially from one individual to another and still yield appropriate measures of social income for each; these dollar measures could be summed over individuals. The list of resources for an individual should include all those that he perceives as affecting his well-being during the accounting period. Over the longer run, it would be desirable to set up uniform classification systems for media of social interchange, states of health, and behavior settings, thus permitting the publication of national and regional aggregates of social and total income on a uniform basis across areas and over time.

Barker (1968) has outlined a detailed classification scheme for behavior settings; this could be refined and extended. The classification of media of social interchange may require several years of experimentation and discussion by scholars prior to its use in any publicly sponsored system of social accounts. A suitable classification of states of health and degrees of physical handicap may already exist, although some modifications might be needed for social accounting purposes.

It may turn out that estimates obtained by interviewing individuals show systematic biases relative to those based on objective data of various sorts. This is not a new problem, of course. It would be interesting to compare the results of such interviews with analyses based on independent studies of variables such as professional recognition, influence, political power, prestige rankings of small groups or organizations (e.g., university departments), and rankings of occupations on the basis of prestige.

3.7 Implications for Policy Models, Output Measurement, and Demand Analysis

A fully developed system of social accounts should enable us to address problems of growth, stability, and equity in terms of total income ($SI + p_1x_1$) and each of its major components, p_1x_1, y, and ($SI - y$). Models of national economies would then be perceived as components of models of the social system as a whole. Tinbergen's (1952) "theory of economic policy" might be extended to include in quantitative models noneconomic as well as economic targets and instruments of national policy. At the least, attempts to estimate, in nonmoney as well as money terms, the costs to individuals associated with different combinations of inflation and unemployment might lead to revisions in the relative weights assigned to these targets in the objective functions of policy models. The same might be said of target and instrument variables generally. Similarly, the general Efficiency Criterion (Van Moeseke, 1968) may be redefined relatively to a decision space including noneconomic dimensions.

The allocation of an individual's resources among behavior settings also has considerable interest. Recall that utility u in our mathematical model depends only on x, the "life style" vector of proportions of the individual's time spent in the various behavior settings. In equilibrium, he pays "total prices" of r_j^*/v_1^* and r_k^*/v_1^* per unit of time spent in the jth and kth settings, respectively; these prices must stand in the same ratios as their marginal utilities:

$$\frac{r_j^*/v_1^*}{r_k^*/v_1^*} = \frac{\partial u}{\partial x_j^*} \bigg/ \frac{\partial u}{\partial x_k^*}.$$

(31)

Indeed, by the fourth (KT) condition x_j^*, $x_k^* > 0$ implies equalities for the corresponding indices j, k in the third condition:

$$u_{x_j}^* = \sum_i a_{ij}v_i^*; \qquad u_{x_k}^* = \sum_i a_{ik}v_i^*.$$

(32)

Since $r^* = v^*A$, one has further, by the implicit-function rule:

$$-\frac{\partial x_k}{\partial x_j} = \frac{u_{x_j}^*}{u_{x_k}^*} = \frac{\sum_i a_{ij} v_i^*}{\sum_i a_{ik} v_i^*} = \frac{r_j^*}{r_k^*}. \tag{33}$$

Note, further, that $r_j^* x_j^* / v_1^*$ can be regarded as an output or reward produced in setting j and valued at resource cost. In extended notation, $r_j^* = \sum_i v_i^* a_{ij}$, and in dividing both sides of the equation by the marginal utility of money v_1^*, the cost of each resource is converted into dollars.

Our model requires that $r^* x^* / v_1^* = (v^* b)/v_1^*$. If we expand the endowment vector to include skill and health, thus including income from personal services $p_1 x_1^*$ in $(v^* b)/v_1^*$, the equality states that the individual's total income $(SI + p_1 x_1^*)$ equals his total expenditures $r^* x^* / v_1^*$. The relation

$$(r_1^* x_1^* + r_2^* x_2^* + \cdots + r_n^* x_n^*)/v_1^* = SI + p_1 x_1^* \tag{34}$$

is formally analogous to the money income constraint in the theory of consumer choice. The dollar unit of measure applies to all individuals, and the equality holds when total income is aggregated over individuals.

Hence the demand for life styles (i.e., for occupancy of, and participation in, behavior settings) should be amenable to quantitative representation. The elasticity rules derived in Section 3.4 can be regarded as generalizations of corresponding rules in demand theory, and Frisch (1959) has shown that those rules have important consequences for models of national economies. In principle, time series observations on (1) the proportions of time allocated to specified categories of behavior settings, (2) the total costs per hour of occupying them, and (3) total income per capita, should permit us to estimate statistical demand functions for participation in each kind of behavior setting. In practice, an initial rough approximation to such functions might be based on a priori information. If n categories of behavior settings were used to classify total hours of living time per person per year, Frisch's approach would yield an $n \times (n + 1)$ matrix of elasticity coefficients with respect to the n measures of total price per hour and to total income per capita. Although some pairs of behavior settings might be complementary, competitive relationships would predominate. The $n + 1$ coefficients in each row would sum to zero. The n coefficients with respect to total income would have a weighted average of 1 and the $n \times n$ coefficients with respect to total prices per hour would have a weighted average of -1; the weight applied to all coefficients in the ith row would be the proportion of total income that was expended on the ith category of behavior settings. An equal percentage increase in all total prices and in total income per capita would leave the allocation of time among behavior settings unchanged.

The present model applies to a single accounting period. It could be extended to deal with generalized human capital transactions and the evaluation of policy interventions that affect the trajectory of the endowment vector over a period of years. The distinctly new and difficult problems would arise in implementing the suggested social accounts and verifying their usefulness initially for a single period. For example, (34) implies that dollar values could be assigned to the current behavioral outputs of universities, government agencies, and scientific communities, as well as to those of business firms!

To say that such things are possible is not to say that they are easy or that they will soon be achieved. The gap between aspiration and accomplishment may be closed from either direction.

IV

Some Other Attempts to Combine Economic
and Noneconomic Variables
in Theoretical Models

Aᴄᴄᴏʀᴅɪɴɢ ᴛᴏ ʟᴇɢᴇɴᴅ, John o' Groats built an octagonal dining hall so that eight guests could enter simultaneously without quarreling over precedence. The current state of the social sciences calls for similar etiquette.

Scholars in many fields have had to make partial syntheses of concepts from two or more parent disciplines. In many instances, they have found it easier to do the job from scratch than to search all the potentially relevant literatures. Independent formulations of similar models may be taken as evidences of convergent thinking, which is prerequisite to the implementation of practical systems of social indicators.

This chapter juxtaposes a number of (mostly recent) formulations by others which are broadly consistent with the models of Chapters 2 and 3.

4.1 Organization Theory and Industrial Relations

The scientific study of human behavior in formal organizations has expanded rapidly since World War II. Key figures in this development have acknowledged major intellectual debts to Chester I. Barnard, a practicing executive and amateur scholar. According to Kenneth R. Andrews (1968), Barnard's book, *The Functions of the Executive* (1938) was

> a direct outcome of Barnard's failure to find an adequate explanation of his own executive experience in classic organization or economic theory. His own extensive, unsystematic, and multidisciplinary reading offered him few clues until his encounter with Pareto and with L. J. Henderson, a biochemist of interdisciplinary bent who studied and wrote about Pareto. Barnard was thus stimulated by what sociology could explain that classical

economic and organization theory could not. His acquaintance with Henderson, Donham, Mayo and the other members of the coalition of social scientists and clinicians who were rediscovering human motivation in the Hawthorne Works was indispensable to the development of his central thesis . . . (p. x).

Barnard (pp. 142–149) describes two classes of *incentive* that can be used to induce an individual (employee) to contribute his efforts to a formal organization: (1) those that can be specifically offered to the individual and (2) general incentives.

The specific inducements may be (*a*) material (money, things), (*b*) personal but nonmaterialistic (distinction, prestige, power), (*c*) desirable physical conditions of work, and (*d*) "ideal benefactions" (the capacity of the organization to satisfy such personal ideals as pride of workmanship, sense of adequacy, altruistic service, patriotism, or aesthetic or religious feeling). The general incentives include (*e*) associational attractiveness, (*f*) customary working conditions, (*g*) the feeling of enlarged participation, and (*h*) "the condition of communion" (opportunity for companionship and for mutual support in personal attitudes).

Barnard states that if an organization cannot afford incentives adequate to the personal contributions it requires, it will perish "unless it can by persuasion change the minds of enough men that the incentives it can offer will be adequate" (p. 144).

At the time his book was published, Barnard had worked 29 years in private industry, including 11 years as president of New Jersey Bell Telephone (Roethlisberger, 1968). It is particularly significant, therefore, that his models of the individual and the organization include such a wide range of noneconomic variables.

The complexity of motivation is recognized in most subsequent works on human behavior in organizations. Influential examples include Simon (1947), March and Simon (1958), and March (1965). The literature is now vast. As a spot example, Oliver Williamson (1963, 1964) cites Barnard (1938), Simon (1947), and R. A. Gordon (1961) for a largely overlapping list of managerial motives: salary, security, power, prestige, and professional excellence.

The literature on industrial relations has reflected a similar complexity. We mentioned in Section 2.5 Zytowski's (1970) review of 72 references on "work values" of employees. Recently Doeringer and Piore (1971) have given a sophisticated treatment of the *internal labor market*,

an administrative unit, such as a manufacturing plant, within which the pricing and allocation of labor is governed by a set of administrative rules and procedures. The internal labor market . . . is to be distinguished from the *external labor market* of conventional economic theory where pricing, allocating, and training decisions are controlled directly by economic variables. These two markets are interconnected, however, and movement between them occurs at certain job classifications which constitute *ports of entry and exit* to and from the internal labor market. The remainder of the jobs within the internal market are filled by the promotion and transfer of workers who have already gained entry. Consequently, these jobs are shielded from the *direct* influences of competitive forces in the external market.

. . . The phenomenon of internal labor markets is thus closely akin to the problems which other authors have identified as "industrial feudalism," "the balkanization of labor markets," and "property rights" in a job (pp. 1–2).

4.2   Regional Science (Isard et al.)

Walter Isard, in association with Peter Isard and Tze Hsiung Tung, has made a most ambitious attempt to include "noneconomic commodities" in a model of "general social, political, and economic equilibrium for a system of regions." The noneconomic commodities were described in Walter Isard and T. H. Tung (1964) and the general equilibrium model in which they were incorporated appeared in two articles by Walter Isard and Peter Isard (1965a, 1965b). All three articles were subsequently included in a major book by Walter Isard and four associates, *General Theory: Social, Political, Economic, and Regional* (1969).

The economic component of the model is based on a classic article by Arrow and Debreu (1954), "Existence of an Equilibrium for a Competitive Economy." Isard and Ostroff (1958) extended this approach to a system of regions in their paper, "Existence of a Competitive Interregional Equilibrium."

Isard et al. (1969) express dissatisfaction with the ability of the current general equilibrium theory of economics and regional science to identify and cast light on interrelations of the many social, political, and economic forces of actuality. Economic theory emphasizes efficiency and profit maximization. However, basic decisions on plant locations, allocation of investment funds among regions, design of urban transportation systems, designation of urban places as growth centers for a system of regions, and many other matters also involve

(1) the interplay of political forces wherein individuals and groups seek to maximize at least to some extent their power and network of influence;

(2) the strivings of cultural and social institutions to optimize the probability of their continued existence and/or growth;

(3) the operation of cultural and social values and norms which highly restrict action spaces and make infeasible input–output vectors which otherwise might maximize increases in per capita income, or employment opportunities, etc. (p. 598).

Isard et al. (1969, pp. 494–497) state that their conception of a social system draws heavily on the works of Talcott Parsons. Thus they refer to (1) the adaptive or economy subsystem, (2) the goal-attainment or polity subsystem, (3) the integrative subsystem, and (4) the pattern-maintenance subsystem.

The authors deal at length with "noneconomic commodities" (Isard et al., 1969, pp. 563–596), indicating (p. 564, fn. 2) that Harold Lasswell's writings have been most influential in their tentative definitions of these commodities. They emphasize that their own list is by no means complete. It includes solidarity, power, respect, rectitude, affection, sociality, participation, well-being, skill, enlightenment, achievement, and some others.

Isard et al. recognize the difficulty of defining and measuring these noneconomic commodities for inclusion in a formal model. They require four different price concepts; (1) money price (a price that is or can easily be stated in terms of currency),

(2) nontangible price (a price that is implicit and cannot easily be stated in terms of currency), (3) market price (a money price or a nontangible price), and (4) effective price (a market price associated with a unit of a commodity *plus* the value of society's net approval or disapproval of the commodity). There is an income concept (money, nontangible, market, effective) corresponding to each price concept.

Isard and his colleagues discuss in detail the existence and probable nature of supply and demand schedules for each of the noneconomic commodities (pp. 571–586). They also comment on possible ways of choosing an objectively definable unit of measurement for each. Given appropriate units of quantity measurement, demand schedules, and supply schedules, it would be possible to determine equilibrium prices for each noneconomic commodity simultaneously with those for economic commodities.

They stress that these efforts, first reported in Isard and Tung (1964), represent only a beginning and that their value "will stem from the extensive and sharp criticism that should be provoked, and the drastic revisions of the conceptual framework that will be required" (p. 594).

4.3   Becker's Theory of the Allocation of Time

Gary Becker (1965) presented a theory of the allocation of time that is compatible with the models in Section 2.7 and Chapter 3. He indicates (1965, p. 494) that he, J. Mincer, J. Owen, E. Dean, and other participants in the Labor Workshop at Columbia University had for some years been occupied "with introducing the cost of time systematically into decisions about non-work activities."

Becker pointed out that economic development has led to a secular decline in the work week and that in most countries, as of 1965, it occupied less than one-third of the total time (168 hours) available:

> Consequently the allocation and efficiency of non-working time may now be more important to economic welfare than that of working time; yet the attention paid by economists to the latter dwarfs any paid to the former. . . .
>
> Most economists have now fully grasped the importance of foregone earnings in the educational process and, more generally, in all investments in human capital, and criticize educationalists and others for neglecting them. In the light of this it is perhaps surprising that economists have not been equally sophisticated about other non-working uses of time. For example, the cost of a service like the theater or a good like meat is generally simply said to equal their market prices, yet everyone would agree that the theater and even dining take time, just as schooling does, time that often could have been used productively. If so, the full costs of these activities would equal the sum of market prices and the foregone value of time used up. In other words, indirect costs should be treated on the same footing when discussing all non-work uses of time, as they are now in discussions of schooling (pp. 493–494).

In Becker's formal model (pp. 495–497), households are both producing units and utility maximizers. Market goods x_i and time inputs T_i are used to produce more basic commodities Z_i (e.g., seeing a play), that directly enter a household's utility function.

The household then chooses the best combination of Z_i by maximizing a utility function

$$U = U(Z_1, \ldots, Z_m); \tag{1}$$

each Z_i is the output of a production function,

$$Z_i = f_i(x_i, T_i), \qquad i = 1, 2, \ldots, m, \tag{2}$$

and maximization is subject to a budget constraint

$$g(Z_1, \ldots, Z_m) = Z, \tag{3}$$

"where g is an expenditure function of Z_i and Z is the bound on resources" (p. 496).

Becker notes that separate resource constraints could be specified for (a) market goods and (b) time. However, time can be converted into goods by using less time at consumption and more at work; on certain assumptions, therefore, the two constraints could be converted into one:

$$\sum (p_i b_i + t_i \bar{w})Z_i = V + T\bar{w}, \tag{4}$$

with (p. 497)

$$\pi_i \equiv p_i b_i + t_i \bar{w}, \qquad \text{and} \qquad S \equiv V + T\bar{w}. \tag{5}$$

Here, b_i is the quantity of market goods and t_i the amount of time used per unit of Z_i, $\bar{w}$ is earnings per unit of time spent at work, T is total time available, and V is other income. Then, π_i is the "full price" of a unit of Z_i: "the full price of consumption is the sum of direct and indirect prices in the same way that the full cost of investing in human capital is the sum of direct and indirect costs." Correspondingly, S, "full income," is the money income achieved if all the available time were spent at work (p. 497).

If a household chooses to forego part of its potential money income S, the amount of earnings foregone or "lost" L is a function of the consumption set chosen:

$$L(Z_1, \ldots, Z_m) \equiv S - I(Z_1, \ldots, Z_m), \tag{6}$$

where I is total money income. Equation (6) can also be written

$$\sum p_i b_i Z_i + L(Z_1, \ldots, Z_m) \equiv S. \tag{7}$$

When utility is maximized subject to (7), the equilibrium conditions are

$$\frac{\partial U}{\partial Z_i} = U_i = T(p_i b_i + L_i), \qquad i = 1, \ldots, m, \tag{8}$$

"where $p_i b_i$ is the direct and L_i the indirect component of the total marginal price $p_i b_i + L_i$." (pp. 498–499).

Becker suggests a number of applications of his approach to (a) the determination of hours of work, (b) the productivity of time, (c) income elasticities of demand, (d) transportation, and (e) the division of labor within families. He concludes his article as follows:

> Rough estimates suggest that foregone earnings are quantitatively important and therefore that full income is substantially above money income. Since

foregone earnings are primarily determined by the use of time, considerably more attention should be paid to its efficiency and allocation. In particular, agencies that collect information on the expenditure of money income might simultaneously collect information on the "expenditure" of time. The resulting time budgets, which have not been seriously investigated in most countries, including the United States and Great Britain, should be integrated with the money budgets in order to give a more accurate picture of the size and allocation of full income (p. 517).

4.4   The Harried Leisure Class (Linder)

Staffan Linder (1970) has written a highly readable book on the theme of "an increasing scarcity of time" associated with rising levels of money income. On page 9 he states that "even though work on this book had reached a relatively late stage before Becker's paper became available, it has naturally been extremely valuable to be able to utilize Becker's line of thinking."

Linder notes that the optimal allocation of time is quite analogous to the optimal allocation of money income. One's time resources "must be so distributed as to give an equal yield in all sectors of use. Otherwise, it would pay to transfer time from an activity with a low yield to one with a high yield and to continue to do this until equilibrium had been reached" (p. 3).

Linder's formal model (pp. 147–148) involves an individual's utility function and two constraints:

$$\text{maximize} \quad U = f(Q, T_c) \qquad \text{subject to} \tag{9}$$

$$Q = pT_w \tag{10}$$

and

$$T = T_w + T_c, \tag{11}$$

where Q is the number of units of consumption goods and T_c the number of hours devoted to consumption purposes; p is a productivity index measuring the number of units of consumption goods earned per hour of work (T_w), and T is the total number of hours available during the accounting period (e.g., a year). He forms the Lagrangian function,

$$L = f(Q, T_c) - \lambda[Q - p(T - T_c)] \tag{12}$$

and sets the partial derivatives equal to zero:

$$\frac{\partial L}{\partial Q} = \frac{\partial U}{\partial Q} - \lambda = 0, \tag{13}$$

$$\frac{\partial L}{\partial T_c} = \frac{\partial U}{\partial T_c} - \lambda p = 0, \tag{14}$$

$$Q - p(T - T_c) = 0. \tag{15}$$

Since utility U is assumed to be an increasing function of Q and T_c, $\partial U/\partial Q$ and $\partial U/\partial T_c$ are positive; hence λ, the marginal utility of consumption goods, and λp, the marginal utility of time devoted to consumption, are both positive. The productivity index p is the opportunity cost of time devoted to consumption; $pT \equiv p(T_w + T_c)$ would correspond to Becker's concept of full income.

For purposes of discussion, Linder classifies time into five categories (pp. 13–15):

1. Working time (i.e., time devoted to specialized production).
2. Time for personal work, including (a) the maintenance of consumption goods and (b) the maintenance of one's body (sleep, personal hygiene, etc.).
3. Consumption time (i.e., time involving the use of consumption goods).
4. Culture time (i.e., "time devoted to the cultivation of mind and spirit").
5. Idleness, or slack time.

Linder's main theme is a criticism of the continued intense pursuit of economic growth in the now-affluent countries: ". . . a constant hunt to secure the basic necessities of life is presently regarded as a degrading existence. Perhaps being constantly chased by a scarcity of time will some day be recognized as an equally undignified way of life" (p. 145). Thus Linder views a theory of the allocation of time as a useful framework for social criticism, including reflections on the relation of economic growth to the "quality of life."

4.5   Nonmarket Components of National Income (Sirageldin)

Ismail Sirageldin (1969) uses household survey data from Morgan, Sirageldin, and Baerwaldt's classic *Productive Americans* (1966) to estimate the value of nonmarket output: "namely the value of those nonmarket activities done by American families in 1964 which were not included in the conventional national accounts" (p. 2). He concluded that the average value of a family's nonmarket output was almost $4000, equivalent to about 50 percent of its disposable income.

Sirageldin's calculations, in terms of means for the families surveyed, are as follows (p. 55):

1.	Family disposable income	$ 8,115
2.	Plus:	
	(a) Value of housework and home production	3,523
	(b) Volunteer work	204
	(c) Education of heads of families	141
	(d) Value of the family's car(s) services	44
	(e) Free help received by the family	18
3.	Equals: family full income	$12,045

Sirageldin also presents an estimate of *potential income*, which includes two additional items:

4.	Plus:	
	(a) Value of time lost because of sickness or unemployment	$ 500

> (b) Value of desired more or fewer hours of   92
>   work by heads of families
>
> 5. Equals: potential income $12,638

The significance of Sirageldin's work stems partly from its sponsorship by the Survey Research Center of the University of Michigan, with its distinguished tradition of data collection and analysis based on interviews with probability samples of households. We make considerable use of Survey Research Center data in Chapter 5.

Sirageldin follows Becker (1965) closely in his approach to the value of time. He regards the family unit as

> a technical unit in which commodities are produced, sold, or purchased. Its manager (or board of directors!) decides on the allocation and utilization of total input resources (including time in all its uses) into a large number of activities or production relations, in order to maximize the expected utility of a stream of consumption of some basic commodities (activities) (p. 13).

The family maximizes utility subject to a time constraint

$$T = LE_s' + JE_r' + HE_k' \tag{16}$$

and to a budget constraint

$$\sum P_i X_i + \sum Q_i Y_i = I = V + JW' + HN', \tag{17}$$

where P_i = market prices of goods and services bought by the family,

$\quad Q_i$ = imputed prices of nonmarket goods and services used in consumption activities,

$\quad V$ = nonearned income,

$\quad I$ = total income,

$\quad W = (W_1, W_2, \ldots, W_r)$ = hourly earnings in the various occupations (at which family members work for money),

$\quad J = (J_1, J_2, \ldots, J_r)$ = hours spent in the various occupations,

$\quad N = (N_1, N_2, \ldots, N_k)$ = imputed dollars per hour in the various nonmarket productive activities,

$\quad H = (H_1, H_2, \ldots, H_k)$ = hours spent in the various nonmarket productive activities,

$\quad L = (L_1, L_2, \ldots, L_s)$ = hours spent in the various consumption activities, including leisure activities,

and E_s, E_r, E_k are unit vectors $(1, 1, \ldots, 1)$ of $s, r,$ and k elements, respectively (p. 14).

Using Lagrangian multipliers, Sirageldin obtains the now-familiar expressions for marginal utilities of (a) money expenditures and (b) "leisure," or time (pp. 15–17).

4.6 Prospects for Convergence

Becker (1965), Sirageldin (1969), and Linder (1970) all present compatible models involving the simultaneous allocation of money income and time. These are two of the constraints used in my own model (Section 2.7) and its extension by Fox and Van Moeseke (Chapter 3).

Isard and his associates (1969) follow Talcott Parsons in their characterization of the four subsystems of the social system as a whole. Their concept of "noneconomic commodities" evidently draws on both Lasswell and Parsons; it is quite similar to our interpretation of Parsons's *generalized media of social interchange* in Section 2.7 and Chapter 3. The lists of employee inducements and managerial objectives used by Barnard (1938) and attributed by Williamson (1963, 1964) also to Simon and to R. A. Gordon correspond closely with several of Parsons's media.

Barnard mentions *general incentives*, which are properties of an organization as such and cannot be cut up and parceled out to individual employees; some of Isard's *noneconomic commodities* (e.g., solidarity) also have this "public goods" quality for all organization members (employees). Doeringer and Piore's (1971) concept of an *internal labor market* connected only at certain job classifications with the external labor market should help in linking total organizational outputs to total incomes of individual employees. Zytowski's (1970) list of "work values" seems to be long enough to accommodate any demands placed on it by the authors mentioned.

Only the Fox (Section 2.7) and Fox-Van Moeseke (Chapter 3) models make use of Roger Barker's (1967, 1968) concept of behavior settings. My own interest in this concept dates from a symposium (October 1966) at which Barker presented a preliminary draft of his 1967 paper. His data on occupancy of behavior settings in the town of "Midwest" during 1963–1964 at once suggested to me the ideas of a complete time budget and the optimal allocation of a person's time among behavior settings. My first public use of these ideas was at a conference in December 1967 and in the resulting paper (Fox, 1969a). I developed them further and incorporated Parsons's concept of generalized media of social exchange in another article (Fox, 1969b), written in 1968.

Sirageldin applied his model to Survey Research Center data on the use of time by a sample of households in 1965, establishing a strong link between the theory of time allocation and the empirical-analytical tradition of household surveys.

Examining the various, largely independent developments cited in this chapter, we see a considerable degree of convergence and no evidence of basic incompatibility.

V

Time Budgets, Behavior Settings, and Total Income

SEVERAL OF THE THEORETICAL MODELS outlined in Chapter 4, as well as those presented in Section 2.7 and Chapter 3, call for an exhaustive allocation of an individual's time as a basis for estimating his total income in a given accounting period. The time allocation results from the individual's attempt to maximize a utility function subject to constraints on time and other resources.

In this chapter we discuss the tradition of empirical research on time budgets, which has taken a new and promising turn in the past few years. After pointing out potential linkages between time budget surveys and other approaches, we present an illustrative synthesis of time budget data with the models of Section 2.7 and Chapter 3.

5.1 Time Budgets (Converse)

According to Philip E. Converse (1968), a time budget is

> a log or diary of the sequence and duration of activities engaged in by an individual over a specified period, most typically the 24-hour day. Time budget research involves the collection of numerous such protocols from members of a population to analyze main trends and subgroup differences in the allocation of time.
>
> ... the phrase "time budget" has arisen because time, like money, is a resource that is continually being allocated by the individual, although with varying degrees of consciousness and short-term discretion. Like money, time is thought of as being spent, saved, invested, or wasted. It is presumed that analysis of the structure of time allocation gives behavioral evidence of a peculiarly "hard" kind concerning individual preferences and values, especially in the more optional forms of time use (pp. 42–43).

However, it turns out that time budgets by themselves "provide extensive but not intensive information; the data are broad but shallow. . . ." (p. 46).

Despite improvements in survey design in the mid-1960s, Converse states that

> a wide gulf still exists between the manifest activity as it is recorded and the latent functions of the activity for the individual which give it ultimate meaning or significance. The act of repairing an appliance in one's home may reflect a desire to convert free time into money saved to piece out one's income, or an inability to secure sufficiently rapid service from outside, or a hobby of tinkering, or some combination of the three. More theoretically satisfying ways of grouping detailed activities into broader classes are often avoided because of just such difficulties. Where ingenious activity group- ings are made, there lurks the inevitable suspicion that were the truth known, the same activities might fall in quite different classes for various subjects and that the substantive results may be artifacts of such "forcings" of the data.
>
> It is for reasons of this sort that time budgets seem to have been found less useful for investigations of life style than might be expected on the surface. Activity designations tend to be more incisive about the forms of activities than about their content. The fact of watching television or having a con- versation with a neighbor is recorded, but the types of programs watched or the subjects of informal discourse are rarely catalogued. And variations in what is called "life style" seem thoroughly muted in the process . . . (pp. 46–47).

5.2   The Survey Research Center Survey of Time Use in the United States, 1966

The most advanced time-budget survey that has come to my attention was carried out by the Survey Research Center of the University of Michigan in 1966. The tables in this section are based on data from John P. Robinson and Philip E. Converse, *Sixty-six Basic Tables of Time Budget Data for the United States*, Survey Research Center, Institute for Social Research, the University of Michigan, Ann Arbor, Michigan, May 30, 1966.[1]

According to Robinson and Converse,

> There were four major goals of the United States time use project: first, the collection and comparison of basic behavioral data across eleven widely different nations; second, the tabulation of these basic data as general de- scriptive information on life in the United States; third, the use of these data as benchmarks in the measurement and assessment of social change; and finally, investigation into the major activities and objects which bring gratification and satisfaction to individuals in different parts of society (p. 1).

The survey results were based on a probability sample of the urban population of the United States in 1966. The time budgets refer to adults under 65 years of age

[1] These data, with some modifications and corrections, have been published in Szalai (ed., 1973); the authors (Robinson and Converse) give a more extended treatment of the United States time budget data there and place them in their proper institutional context.

(except for a very few persons aged 66 or over in households having an eligible respondent under 65).

Tables 5.1 through 5.4 are illustrative of the data obtained. Table 5.1 shows the allocation of total time (24 hours per day) among 27 primary activities. The lower portion of the table aggregates these activities into seven major categories: work-related, housework, personal care (including sleep), family tasks, education and organizations, mass media, and leisure.

Table 5.2 uses the same format to display the amounts of time during which certain secondary activities were going on simultaneously with primary ones. The major secondary activities were conversation and mass media (radio, television, and reading); eating, resting, and social life were reported as secondary activities involving relatively small amounts of time. It is not possible from the published data to determine the primary activities with which the various secondary activities were associated.

Table 5.3 allocates approximately 24 hours a day according to the categories of people with whom time was spent (alone, with members of nuclear family, with colleagues, etc.). In Table 5.4 the 24 hours in a day are apportioned according to the categories of places in which they were spent (at home, at place of work, in streets, parks, and other public places, etc.).

The data in Table 5.1 are broken down by sex, marital status, and employment status. The May 30, 1966, report also contains breakdowns by age, education, and occupation; by numbers and ages of children in the household; by day of the week; by place of residence (central business district, suburbs, etc.); and by distance from home to work. The data in Tables 5.2 through 5.4 are broken down in similar fashion. Still other data, including income level, are presumably available on magnetic tapes. Thus different combinations of these variables could be used in multiple regression formats to "explain" differences in time use among the 1244 actual, or 2536 weighted, respondents. Alternatively, the data could be analyzed by the stepwise regression procedure developed by James Morgan and others at the Survey Research Center (Sonquist and Morgan, 1964; Morgan, Sonquist, and Andrews, 1967).

5.3   Time Budget Data in Behavior Setting Format: One Individual

Let us suppose that the second column of figures in Table 5.1 relates to a specific individual. Suppose, further, that this individual has also supplied us with the information called for by the model presented in Chapter 3 (i.e., about behavior setting occupancy, equivalent dollar values of various exchange media used in total and in each behavior setting genotype, earnings from current personal services, and income from property and transfer payments); we also assume that his total income is equivalent to $48 per average 24-hour day. Then if x_i is the number of hours spent in the ith primary activity and r_i is the total price per hour spent in the ith activity, we have

$$\sum_{i=1}^{27} x_i r_i = \$48, \tag{1}$$

$$\sum_{i=1}^{27} x_i = 24 \text{ hours}, \tag{2}$$

and

$$\bar{r}_i = \frac{\sum\limits_{i=1}^{27} x_i r_i}{\sum\limits_{i=1}^{27} x_i} = \$2.00 \text{ per hour.} \tag{3}$$

At this point we might ask the individual to take his perceived utility of the marginal hour per week of one primary activity, say, eating, as a base ($r'_{eating} = 1$), and assign the marginal hour per week of each of the other 26 activities an r_i' value relative to eating. If $\sum_{i=1}^{27} x_i r_i' \neq 48$, we could multiply every r_i' by whatever scalar k is required to make the total $\sum_{i=1}^{27} x_i(k r_i')$ equal \$48 and the weighted average $k\bar{r}_i'$ equal \$2.00 per hour.

However, part of the \$48 should evidently be attributed to the 5.1 hours per day of *secondary activities* listed in the second column of Table 5.2. The most extensive secondary activity is conversation, at 3.3 hours per day. To estimate the relative marginal utility of "secondary" conversation, the individual would probably have to associate appropriate fractions of the 3.3 hours with specific primary activities. Thus the 6.2 hours of regular work might include 4.0 hours without conversation and 2.2 hours with conversation as a secondary activity; the utility of the marginal hour per week with conversation is presumably higher than that of the marginal hour without, or at least different from it.

Tables 5.1 and 5.2 tell us very little about the individual's interactions, although some categories (e.g., conversation) imply contact with others. Column 2 of Table 5.3 indicates that he spends 4.1 hours a day with colleagues, 2.1 hours with friends and relatives, 14.4 hours all alone, and so on. However, we do not know whether the entire 4.1 hours spent with colleagues is associated with the primary activity of regular work or whether substantial portions are spent watching television or engaged in social life with colleagues.

Column 2 of Table 5.4 identifies the functional categories of the places in which the individual spends his time. Since these data are not linked to Table 5.3, we do not know how much time he spent with colleagues at home, at work, and in restaurants and bars, respectively. Without linkages among the four tables, the data are, as Converse suggested, "broad but shallow."

The situation would be improved if the data in the four tables were integrated into a behavior setting format. In Table 5.5, we have taken the data from column 1 in each of the first four tables (men, married, employed) and forced them into a set of 46 behavior settings. The 46 figures on time spent in primary activities (row 1) add to 24.0 hours a day, as do the 46 figures on categories (*a*) persons and (*b*) places. Thus behavior setting 1 consists of (*a*) being engaged in regular work, (*b*) all alone, (*c*) at one's place of work. Setting 2 consists of (a) being engaged in regular work, (*b*) with colleagues, (*c*) at one's place of work. The respondent spends 2.7 hours a day in setting 1 and 2.6 hours in setting 2.

The 46 settings can readily be grouped into a few clusters:

(*a*) Work-related (paid employment), settings 1 through 9,
(*b*) Home- and household-related, settings 10 through 27,
(*c*) Education, setting 28,

Table 5.1. United States Time Use Survey, 1966: Time Spent by Respondents in Primary Activities, by Respondents' Sex, Employment Status, and Marital Status (hours per 24-hour day)

Primary Activities	Men Employed		Men Unemployed		Women Employed		Women Unemployed	
	Married (1)	Single (2)	Married (3)	Single (4)	Married (5)	Single (6)	Married (7)	Single (8)
N =	449	72	16	6	190	152	342	17
Weighted N =	945	127	41	17	398	243	724	41
1 Regular work	6.1	6.2	0.2	1.6	4.7	4.6	0.1	0.7
2 Second job	0.2	0.1				0.1		
3 Nonwork breaks	0.6	0.6			0.4	0.5		0.1
4 Trips to and from work	0.7	0.6		0.1	0.5	0.5		
5 Preparing food	0.1	0.2	0.5	0.3	1.0	0.5	1.6	1.1
6 Cleaning house	0.2	0.1	0.8	0.1	1.2	1.0	2.0	1.6
7 Laundry, mending		0.1			0.6	0.3	1.0	0.7
8 Other house upkeep	0.3	0.1	0.1	0.2	0.3	0.1	0.4	0.3
9 Gardening, pets			0.1		0.1		0.1	0.1
10 Sleep	7.6	7.5	8.5	8.4	7.7	7.5	7.7	8.3
11 Personal care	0.9	1.2	0.8	1.0	1.2	1.5	1.2	1.3
12 Eating	1.2	1.0	1.6	1.7	1.0	1.0	1.3	1.1
13 Resting	0.3	0.2	0.4	0.2	0.3	0.5	0.4	0.2
14 Child care	0.1			0.4	0.4	0.2	1.1	0.9
15 Shopping	0.4	0.3	0.6	0.4	0.5	0.6	0.7	0.6
16 Nonwork trips	0.8	0.8	1.5	1.4	0.7	0.8	0.9	0.9

17 Education	0.1	0.5	1.5	1.9		0.3	0.1	0.8
18 Organizations	0.2	0.2	0.5		0.1	0.3	0.4	0.5
19 Radio	0.1	0.1				0.1		
20 Television	1.7	1.4	2.6	1.9	1.0	1.2	1.6	2.5
21 Reading	0.7	0.6	0.7	1.0	0.5	0.3	0.6	0.4
22 Social life	1.0	1.2	1.7	1.7	1.0	1.2	1.5	1.1
23 Conversation	0.2	0.2	0.4	0.2	0.3	0.3	0.5	0.3
24 Walking			0.2					
25 Sports	0.2	0.1			0.1	0.1	0.1	0.1
26 Various leisure	0.2	0.2	0.8	0.2	0.3	0.3	0.5	0.3
27 Spectacles	0.1	0.3		1.5	0.1	0.3	0.1	0.1
28 Work-related	7.6	7.5	0.3	1.7	5.6	5.7	0.1	0.8
29 Housework	0.6	0.5	1.6	0.6	3.0	1.9	5.1	3.8
30 Personal care	10.0	9.9	11.3	11.2	10.1	10.4	10.6	10.9
31 Family tasks	1.3	1.2	2.1	2.1	1.6	1.6	2.7	2.3
32 Education and organizations	0.4	0.7	2.0	1.9	0.2	0.5	0.5	1.3
33 Mass media	2.5	2.2	3.4	2.9	1.6	1.6	2.2	2.9
34 Leisure	1.7	2.0	3.2	3.6	1.8	2.2	2.8	2.0
35 Grand total	24.0	24.0	24.0	24.0	24.0	24.0	24.0	24.0
36 Free time	4.8	5.1	9.0	8.6	3.9	4.8	5.9	6.4

Source. John P. Robinson and Philip E. Converse, *Sixty-six Basic Tables of Time Budget Data for the United States.* Ann Arbor: Survey Research Center, University of Michigan, May 30, 1966. 11 pages plus 66 tables (xeroxed). Adapted from Table 1.

Table 5.2. United States Time Use Survey, 1966: Time Spent by Respondents in Secondary Activities, by Respondents' Sex, Employment Status, and Marital Status (hours per 24-hour day)

Secondary Activities	Men Employed		Men Unemployed		Women Employed		Women Unemployed	
	Married (1)	Single (2)	Married (3)	Single (4)	Married (5)	Single (6)	Married (7)	Single (8)
N =	449	72	16	6	190	151	342	17
Weighted N =	945	127	41	17	398	242	724	41
1 Regular work								
2 Second job								
3 Nonwork breaks								
4 Trips to and from work								
5 Preparing food								
6 Cleaning house							0.1	
7 Laundry, mending							0.1	
8 Other house upkeep								
9 Gardening, pets								
10 Sleep								
11 Personal care								0.2
12 Eating	0.1				0.1	0.1	0.1	0.1
13 Resting	0.1	0.1		0.2	0.1	0.1	0.1	
14 Child care		0.1	0.1	0.2	0.1	0.1	0.4	0.3
15 Shopping								
16 Nonwork trips								0.1

	Activity								
17	Education								
18	Organizations		0.1	0.3					
19	Radio	0.8	0.9	0.7	0.8	0.9	1.2	0.9	1.0
20	Television	0.4	0.2	1.0	0.4	0.6	0.5	1.0	0.6
21	Reading	0.4	0.2	0.3	0.1	0.2	0.3	0.2	0.2
22	Social life	0.2	0.1	0.4		0.2	0.1	0.3	0.1
23	Conversation	3.1	3.3	1.3	3.7	2.7	2.4	1.8	1.6
24	Walking								
25	Sports								
26	Various leisure	0.1	0.1		0.1	0.1	0.2	0.3	0.4
27	Spectacles			0.1					
28	Work-related					0.1	0.1		
29	Housework					0.2	0.2	0.2	
30	Personal care	0.3	0.1		0.2	0.1	0.1	0.3	0.3
31	Family tasks	0.1	0.1	0.1	0.2			0.4	0.5
32	Education and organizations		0.1	0.3					
33	Mass media	1.5	1.3	2.0	1.2	1.7	2.0	2.1	1.9
34	Leisure	3.4	3.5	1.9	3.7	3.0	2.8	2.5	2.1
35	Grand Total	5.3	5.1	4.4	5.3	5.2	5.3	5.5	4.8
36	Free time	5.0	4.9	4.2	5.1	4.8	5.0	4.7	4.0

Source. John P. Robinson and Philip E. Converse, *Sixty-six Basic Tables of Time Budget Data for the United States.* Ann Arbor: Survey Research Center, University of Michigan, May 30, 1966. 11 pages plus 66 tables (xeroxed). Adapted from Table 17.

Table 5.3. United States Time Use Survey, 1966: Time spent by Respondents Alone and with Specified Categories of Persons, by Respondents' Sex, Employment Status, and Marital Status (hours per 24-hour day)

	Categories of Persons	Men Employed	
		Married (1)	Single (2)
	N =	450	72
	Weighted N =	947	127
1	All alone	13.7	14.4
2	Alone in a crowd		
3	Family--no children	1.9	
4	Family--spouse and children	1.4	
5	Family--no spouse	0.6	0.4
6	Other household adults	0.1	1.0
7	Other friends and relatives	1.3	2.1
8	Colleagues	3.4	4.1
9	Organization members	0.2	0.2
10	Neighbors and children	0.3	0.8
11	Officials		
12	Others	1.0	0.9
13	Control columns	1.4	1.6
14	Alone	13.7	14.4
15	Nuclear family	3.9	0.4

Table 5.3. (*Continued*)

Men Unemployed		Women Employed		Women Unemployed	
Married (3)	Single (4)	Married (5)	Single (6)	Married (7)	Single (8)
16	6	190	156	341	17
41	17	398	242	722	41
15.7	12.2	14.0	14.5	14.4	14.8
3.0	0.3	2.0	0.1	2.0	
1.3	0.3	0.8		1.6	
0.8	0.3	1.2	1.2	3.1	2.9
0.8	2.5	0.4	1.7	0.3	3.6
1.7	6.7	1.4	2.4	1.8	1.3
0.5	0.6	2.5	2.7	0.1	1.0
0.2		0.1	0.2	0.2	0.3
	0.1	0.8	0.7	0.6	0.6
0.1					0.1
0.5	1.1	1.0	1.3	0.6	0.9
0.7	2.6	1.3	1.5	0.6	0.5
15.7	12.2	14.0	14.5	14.4	14.8
5.1	0.9	4.1	1.3	6.6	2.9

Source. John P. Robinson and Philip E. Converse, *Sixty-six Basic Tables of Time Budget Data for the United States.* Ann Arbor: Survey Research Center, University of Michigan, May 30, 1966. 11 pages plus 66 tables (xeroxed). Adapted from Table 33.

Table 5.4. United States Time Use Survey, 1966: Time Spent by Respondents in Specified Categories of Places, by Respondents' Sex, Employment Status, and Marital Status (hours per 24-hour day)

Categories of Places	Men Employed	
	Married (1)	Single (2)
N =	449	72
Weighted N =	945	127
1 At home	13.7	12.9
2 Just outside home	0.2	
3 Place of work	6.5	6.8
4 Another's home	0.5	0.9
5 Streets, parks, etc.	1.6	1.5
6 Business places	0.8	0.8
7 Indoor leisure	0.2	0.3
8 Outdoor leisure	0.1	0.1
9 Restaurants, bars	0.4	0.5
10 Others	0.2	0.1
11 Home	13.8	12.9
12 Grand total	24.0	24.0

Table 5.4. *(Continued)*

Men Unemployed		Women Employed		Women Unemployed	
Married (3)	Single (4)	Married (5)	Single (6)	Married (7)	Single (8)
16	6	190	151	342	17
41	17	398	242	724	41
17.5	15.1	15.8	15.4	20.5	19.4
0.5		0.1		0.1	0.1
0.2	1.6	5.0	4.8	0.1	1.1
1.1	1.3	0.7	0.6	0.8	0.5
1.7	1.5	1.2	1.4	1.0	1.0
2.5	2.4	0.8	1.1	1.1	1.6
	0.5	0.2	0.3	0.2	0.1
	0.9				0.1
0.5	0.7	0.2	0.3	0.1	
		0.1	0.1	0.1	
17.9	15.1	15.9	15.5	20.6	19.5
24.0	24.0	24.0	24.0	24.0	24.0

Source. John P. Robinson and Philip E. Converse, *Sixty-six Basic Tables of Time Budget Data for the United States*. Ann Arbor: Survey Research Center, University of Michigan, May 30, 1966. 11 pages plus 66 tables (xeroxed). Adapted from Table 45.

Table 5.5. Illustrative Rearrangement of Time Budget Data into Behavior Setting Format, Using Figures in Column 1, "Men, Married, Employed," in Tables 5.1 through 5.4

Primary activity number[a]	1	1	1	1	2	3	4	4	4
Behavior setting number	1	2	3	4	5	6	7	8	9
Number of hours (x_i)	2.7	2.6	0.4	0.4	0.2	0.6	0.3	0.2	0.2
Value per hour (r_i)									
Setting structure (per hr.)									
Primary activity	1	1	1	1	1	1	1	1	1
Secondary activity									
Eating									
Resting·									
Radio								1	
TV									
Reading									1
Social life									
Conversation						1			
Place occurring									
At home									
Place of work	1	1	1		1	1			
Another's home									
Streets, parks, etc.							1	1	1
Business places				1					
Indoor leisure[b]									
Restaurants, bars									
Other places									
Persons involved									
All alone	1						1	1	1
Nuclear family									
Friends, relatives									
Colleagues		1				1			
Organization members									
Neighbors and children									
Others			1	1	1				

Table 5.5. (*Continued*)

5	6	7	8	8	9	10	11	11	12	12	12	12	13	14
10	11	12	13	14	15	16	17	18	19	20	21	22	23	24
0.1	0.2	--	0.2	0.1	--	7.6	0.7	0.2	0.6	0.2	0.2	0.2	0.3	0.1
1	1	--	1	1	--	1	1	1	1	1	1	1	1	1
	1							1						
										1				
											1			
									1			1		1
1	1		1	1		1	1	1	1	1	1		1	1
												1		
						1	1	1					1	
1	1			1					1	1	1			1
												1		
			1											

65

Table 5.5.   Illustrative Rearrangement of Time Budget Data into Behavior Setting Format (*Continued*)

Primary activity number[a]	15	16	16	17	18	19	20	20	20
Behavior setting number	25	26	27	28	29	30	31	32	33
Number of hours (x_i)	0.4	0.6	0.2	0.1	0.2	0.1	0.7	0.9	0.1
Value per hour (r_i)									
Setting structure (per hr.)									
Primary activity	1	1	1	1	1	1	1	1	1
Secondary activity									
Eating									1
Resting						1			
Radio			1						
TV									
Reading									
Social life									
Conversation								1	
Place occurring									
At home				1		1	1	1	1
Place of work									
Another's home									
Streets, parks, etc.		1	1						
Business places	1								
Indoor leisure[b]									
Restaurants, bars									
Other places						1			
Persons involved									
All alone	1	1	1	1	1				
Nuclear family							1	1	1
Friends, relatives									
Colleagues									
Organization members						1			
Neighbors and children									
Others									

Source. Arbitrary rearrangement (by Karl A. Fox) of time use data for "men, married, employed" in column 1 of Tables 1, 17, 33, and 45 from John P. Robinson and Philip E. Converse, *Sixty-six Basic Tables of Time Budget Data for the United States.* Ann Arbor; Survey Research Center, University of Michigan, May 30, 1966. 11 pages plus 66 tables (xeroxed).

Table 5.5. (*Continued*)

21	21	22	22	22	22	23	24	25	25	26	26	27	Total hours per day
34	35	36	37	38	39	40	41	42	43	44	45	46	
0.2	0.5	0.5	0.2	0.2	0.1	0.2	--	0.1	0.1	0.1	0.1	0.1	24.0
1	1	1	1	1	1	1	--	1	1	1	1	1	24.0
													0.1
													0.1
													0.8
			1										0.4
													0.4
						1							0.2
		1	1		1								3.3
1	1		1	1		1							13.7
													6.5
		1											0.5
										1			1.6
													0.8
							1	1				1	0.3
			1								1		0.4
													0.2
1													13.8
	1							1			1	1	4.0
		1	1	1	1	1			1				1.3
													3.4
													0.2
													0.3
													1.0

[a] There are 27 primary activities, listed in the same order as in the stub of Table 5.1. Thus Primary Activity 1 is Regular Work, Primary Activity 2 is Second Job, and so on.
[b] Includes 0.1 hour of outdoor leisure (behavior setting number 46).

 (*d*) Organizations, setting 29,
 (*e*) Mass media, settings 30 through 35, and
 (*f*) Leisure, settings 36 through 46.

We could also disaggregate the home- and household-related cluster into:

 (*b*1) Housework, settings 10 through 15,
 (*b*2) Personal care, settings 16 through 23, and
 (*b*3) Family tasks, settings 24 through 27,
as is done in lines 29, 30, and 31 of Table 5.1.

5.4 Time Budget Data in Behavior Setting Format: Implications for Samples and Populations

Table 66 in Robinson and Converse (1966) indicates that data were collected on 41 variables that could be used in cross-classifying or explaining variations in time use among the 2536 weighted respondents. Six variables (day of diary, work day or not, day normal, weather, etc.) are of use primarily in judging the representativeness of the sample. At least eight variables relate to attributes of the respondent as an individual, and five more involve the respondent's work shift, hours worked per week and per day, distance to work, and mode of transport to work. Eight variables are concerned with demographic aspects of households: five with the dwelling, garden (if any), kind of neighborhood, distance to the city (central business district?), and plumbing; and seven deal with presence and number of telephones, radio and television sets, books, clocks and watches, bicycles, scooters, and automobiles. It is not clear whether the income variable relates to the household or the respondent, or whether religion is that of the respondent or of the head of the household (when these are different individuals).

How do these variables help us to interpret the behavior setting data in Table 5.5? In the first place, the respondent depicted is *male, married,* and *employed.* His *occupation, industry, education, annual earnings,* and *age* would all help to characterize the work-related behavior settings he occupies, the roles he plays in them, and the probable quality levels of his performance in them. Thus settings 1 through 6 link the respondent into the national structure of occupations, the demand for occupational skills stemming from levels of activity in different industries, and the derived demand for experience, training, and education to support such skills. The 1713 respondents who were employed should constitute (apart from special restrictions on age and urban residence in this survey) a representative sample of the employed labor force of the nation; settings 1 through 6 for all respondents would represent the intersections of 1713 "life styles" with the production sectors of the economy as represented in the national income accounts.

The respondent's age, sex, employment status, and marital status, plus the attributes of the household of which he is a member, the size and type of dwelling and its equipment, and the numbers of books, radio and TV sets, autos, scooters, and bicycles owned should all contribute to an interpretation of settings 10 through 27. The type of dwelling, presence or absence of garden, the type of neighborhood (ecology?), and distance from the central business district should also help to char-

TOTAL INCOME FOR AN INDIVIDUAL   69

acterize the convenience and amenity of the area in which household members make their shorter excursions—to stores, schools, parks, and so on.

The weighted number of households, including one-person households, is 2536, the same as the weighted number of respondents. Hence settings 10 through 27 for all respondents represent the intersections of 2536 "life styles" with the household sector. Settings 10 through 15 are sometimes classified as household *production* activities and settings 16 through 27 as consumption activities.

Setting 28, education, could of course be disaggregated by subject matter and level. In this survey, all respondents were adults and very few were taking formal courses or training programs. A respondent's age, sex, previous education, occupation, marital status, and annual earnings would all be relevant to the interpretation of setting 28.

Setting 29, organizations, is hard to interpret without further disaggregation into religious, political, cultural, community service, and social or recreational types.

Settings 30 through 35, mass media, are hard to interpret without further detail on the books, articles, and programs read, watched, or heard. The content attended to no doubt varies somewhat by level of education, employment status, age, sex, and other characteristics.[2]

Settings 36 through 46, leisure, must also vary in content with level of education, income, age, sex, employment status, and other variables.

Some of the variables are relevant to the broader aspects of city planning and the quality of urban life; these include distance from home to work, mode of transportation to work, and distance from home to central business district.

5.5   Behavior Settings, Resources, and Total Income for an Individual: A Numerical Illustration

In Table 5.5, the row for "value per hour (r_i)" has been left blank. The Fox-Van Moeseke model (Chapter 3) would require us to specify an endowment vector b of the amounts of m resources available for expenditure by the individual during the current accounting period. In choosing the "life style" vector $(x_i, i = 1, 2, \ldots, 46)$ that maximized his utility function, he would generate a set of m shadow prices v_j, one for each resource; since v_1 is the shadow price (marginal utility) of money, we can convert each of the other $m - 1$ shadow prices into a money equivalent by dividing it by v_1, yielding $v_j/v_1, j = 1, 2, \ldots, m$. The individual's total income is

$$\sum_{j=1}^{m} \frac{v_j}{v_1} b_j = SI + p_1 x_1. \tag{4}$$

We can normalize the left-hand side of (4) by dividing each resource quantity b_j by itself and multiplying the corresponding price $(v_j/v_1$ by b_j:

$$\sum_{j=1}^{m} \frac{v_j}{v_1} b_j(1) = SI + p_1 x_1. \tag{5}$$

[2] Bower (1973) gives the results of a detailed national survey of television viewing patterns and respondent attitudes made in 1970 and compares them with similar data obtained in 1960.

Table 5.6.   Illustrative Allocations of an Individual's Resources Among Behavior Setting Aggregates (figures hypothetical unless otherwise noted)

Resources Available						Behavior
Name of Resource	Total Amount of Resource (0)	Work-related (1)	Pre-paring Food (2)	Laundry and Mending (3)	Other House-work (4)	Shopping (5)
1 Time[b]	1.00	.20	.03	.02	.07	.02
2 Money[c]	1.00	.14	.04	.03	.04	.01
3 Skill: work-related	1.00	1.00				
4 Skill: other	1.00	.05	.15	.05	.10	.10
5 Value commitments	1.00	.40	.03	.02	.07	.06
6 Health	1.00	.30	.03	.02	.09	.02
7 Sexuality	1.00					
8 Affect	1.00	.25			.15	.02
9 Power: in formal organizations	1.00	.90				
10 Power: political	1.00	.10				
11 Prestige	1.00	.50				.05

The term $(v_j/v_1)b_j$ is the equivalent money value of the entire quantity of the jth resource available for expenditure in the current period; the resource quantity vector is simply a unit vector of m elements, $(1, 1, \ldots, 1)$.

With m resources and n behavior settings, we must also elicit from the individual a set of coefficients α_{ji}, where α_{ji} is the proportion of the jth resource expended per hour in the ith behavior setting; many of the α_{ji}'s may be zeros. Then the total resource cost (price) per hour spent in the ith behavior setting is

$$r_i = \sum_{j=1}^{m} \alpha_{ji} b_j \frac{v_j}{v_1}. \tag{6}$$

The total value of resources expended in the ith setting is

$$r_i x_i = x_i \sum_{j=1}^{m} \alpha_{ji} b_j \frac{v_j}{v_1}, \tag{7}$$

and the total value of resources expended in all settings is

$$\sum_{i=1}^{n} r_i x_i = \sum_{i=1}^{n} x_i \left[\sum_{j=1}^{m} \alpha_{ji} b_j \frac{v_j}{v_1} \right] = SI + p_1 x_1. \tag{8}$$

Table 5.6.   (*Continued*)

Setting Aggregates[a]							
Nonwork Trips	Sleeping and Resting	Personal Care	Eating	Mass Media	Leisure	Education	Organi- zations
(6)	(7)	(8)	(9)	(10)	(11)	(12)	(13)
.03	.33	.05	.05	.09	.09	.01	.01
.06	.14	.09	.24	.05	.10	.03	.03
.05		.10	.05	.15	.15		.05
.03		.05	.05	.09	.09	.01	.10
.03		.10	.10	.09	.20	.01	.01
					1.00		
.03		.08	.10	.09	.25		.03
							.10
			.10	.05	.05		.70
			.10	.05	.20		.10

[a] The figures in each row are proportions of the total amount of the resource specified in the stub and sum to 1.00.
[b] Time allocation based on "total sample," column 15, Table 1, from John P. Robinson and Philip E. Converse, *Sixty-six Basic Tables of Time Budget Data for the United States.* Ann Arbor: Survey Research Center, University of Michigan, May 30, 1966. 11 pages plus 66 tables (xeroxed).
[c] Based on rough allocations of 1972 estimates of personal consumption expenditures in the United States national income accounts.

We will try to gain some insight into the operationality of this model through another illustrative use of time budget data, in this case averages for all 2536 respondents. In Table 5.6 we have grouped the 27 primary activity figures from Table 1, column 15, of Robinson and Converse (1966) into 13 categories, which we will regard as behavior setting aggregates. We have listed 11 resources b_j and the figures in the 11 $\times$ 13 array are the α_{ji}; $\sum_{i=1}^{13} \alpha_{ji} = 1.00$ along each row $j, j = 1, 2, \ldots, 11$.

The time allocations α_{1i} come directly from column 15 of Robinson and Converse's Table 1, as we have just mentioned. The money allocations α_{2i} are based on some crude judgmental prorations of 1972 data on personal consumption expenditures from the United States national income accounts. Setting 7, sleeping and resting, is assumed to require no resources except time and money; hence resources 3 through 11 are allocated over the active hours only. Some are allocated entirely to one or two settings (work-related skill and sexuality); some, like power in formal organizations, political power, and prestige, are allocated only to settings in which the individual is interacting with others (this is true of affect, except for one activity). Other skills are a diverse lot, some useful in one setting (driving a car) and some in another (cooking a meal); health and value commitments are assumed to be more salient in some settings than others but also to contribute to the individual's performance throughout his waking hours.

We have not ventured to assign weights to the various resources in Table 5.6, but this problem must be clarified. At any given time, resources 3, 4, 5, 6, 7, and 8 are built into the individual. His work-related skills can be tested and demonstrated; so can his other skills. His value commitments can be appraised through attitude tests and by skilled interviewers. His physical health, affect (emotional health), and sexuality can also be appraised through medical examinations and clinical interviews. Many millions of such tests and appraisals are made every year, and a good deal is known about their validity and reliability. Resources 9, 10, and 11 (power in formal organizations, political power, and prestige) consist of the individual's capacity to evoke specified kinds of response from others; his self-perceptions could be determined by tests and interviews, and (in principle) appropriate others could be asked to rate him on the same points. The same batteries of tests could be administered to large numbers of individuals, and a test score s_{jk} could be associated with the jth resource of the kth individual. (We will leave open the question of the forms of the functions that would transform the test scores s_{jk} into measures of the quantities of resources b_{jk} needed to construct Table 5.6 for the kth individual.)

It will also be helpful to compare our list of resources with Erik Erikson's (1968) list of favorable outcomes associated with successive stages of the individual's life cycle. In chronological sequence, these outcomes are basic trust or hope, will power, purpose, competence, fidelity, love, care, and wisdom. Presumably, many individuals in many different cultures (past and present) have developed these qualities in this chronological order. Several of them involve *value commitments*: will power, purpose, fidelity, care, and wisdom. Basic trust or hope is evidently associated with *affect* (emotional health), and love with *affect* and *sexuality*. Competence is associated with *work-related skills* and *other skills*.

So far we have named all eight of Erikson's favorable outcomes but only five of our eleven resources. A sixth resource, time, is universal and a seventh, physical health, can be appraised in simple societies as well as complex ones. The eighth resource, money (personal income), represents claims on consumer goods and services produced by others in a complex society. Power in formal organizations, political power, and prestige undergo much more differentiation in large modern societies than in traditional small ones. Work-related skills have been tremendously differentiated in modern societies; the individual converts these skills into money, and the money into consumer goods. (If we include his income from personal services p_1x_1 in his total income $SI + p_1x_1$, we must not include the value of his work-related skills, also p_1x_1, as an additional item; this would be double counting.)

We might consider grouping the individual's resources (except time) as follows:

1. Health, affect, sexuality;
2. Value commitments;

3. Work-related skills, other skills; and

4. Money, prestige, power in formal organizations, political power.

Group 1 would correspond roughly to the id (Murray, 1968, following Freud) or Child (Berne, 1964) and group 2 to the superego or Parent. Groups 3 and 4 involve ego- or Adult-directed activities. At the beginning of a particular accounting period, the amounts of the various group 3 and 4 resources exist and can be appraised independently of one another. Over a succession of periods, the group 3 skills can be greatly modified and also redirected to produce different amounts and proportions of the group 4 resources.

In Table 5.7, we have assigned equivalent dollar values to the total amounts of each resource available to a hypothetical individual in a given year. We assume him to be unmarried, to sell his work-related skills for $8000, and to spend the $8000 in the various behavior setting aggregates. We further assume that in response to an appropriate set of questions about tradeoffs between marginal quantities of his resources at or near the point of optimal allocation, we obtain the following evaluations of his other resources *relative to* his money income: skill, work-related, 1.000; skill, other, 0.250; value commitments, 0.500; health, 0.250; sexuality, 0.125; affect, 0.125; power in formal organizations, 0.125; power, political, 0.062; prestige, 0.062. We assume these ratios to hold with sufficient accuracy for variations of plus or minus 10 percent (say) in the quantities of any or all of his resources; they do not, for example, imply that the individual would give up *all* his health for a year to obtain an increase of 25 percent in his money income. The above-specified ratios of shadow prices or marginal utilities lead to values of $2000 each for "skill: other," and for health; $4000 for value commitments; $1000 each for sexuality, affect, and power in formal organizations; and $500 each for "power: political," and prestige. These amounts are recorded in the extreme left-hand column of Table 5.7.

The figures in the second row of Table 5.7 are obtained by multiplying money income ($8000) by the appropriate proportions in row 2 of Table 5.6; the other rows of Table 5.7 are generated in like fashion.

Since all elements are stated in dollars, the elements in any ith column can be added to give the total dollar value of all resources spent in the ith behavior setting aggregate (e.g., $4870 for setting 1, work-related settings; $3235 for setting 11, leisure activities, etc., as shown in the row labeled "total per year"). If we divide these figures by the proportions of time spent in each setting (from row 1 of Table 5.6), we obtain measures of the cost of the individual's spending *all* his time in the ith setting ($i = 1, 2, \ldots, 13$); when these measures are divided by 8760 (the total number of hours in a year), we obtain the figures in the row labeled "Average per Hour (r_i)." The r_i average is $2.28 in this illustration. The two extreme values are $0.39 per hour for sleeping and resting and $14.73 per hour for organizations; the latter figure results from dividing all the individual's contributions to organizations (money, political power and value commitments) by the small amount of time allocated to "organizations" in Table 1, column 15, of the University of Michigan survey. The other r_i values range from $1.84 per hour for other housework (setting 4) to $5.98 per hour for eating (setting 9).

The figures in Table 5.8 are obtained by dividing total income ($20,000) into the corresponding elements of Table 5.7. The extreme left-hand column indicates the proportions of the individual's total income that are attributed to his various re-

Table 5.7. Illustrative Conversion of Table 5.6 Figures into Equivalent Dollar Amounts per Year, Based on Assumed Equivalent Dollar Values for Total Amounts of Each Resource.

Resources Available						Behavior
Name of Resource	Total Amount Dollar Equivalent	Work-Related (1)	Preparing Food (2)	Laundry and Mending (3)	Other Housework (4)	Shopping (5)
1 Time [b]						
2 Money [c]	8000	1120	320	240	320	80
3 Skill: work-related [d]						
4 Skill: other	2000	100	300	100	200	200
5 Value commitments	4000	1600	120	80	280	240
6 Health	2000	600	60	40	180	40
7 Sexuality	1000					
8 Affect	1000	250			150	20
9 Power: in formal organizations	1000	900				
10 Power: political	500	50				
11 Prestige	500	250				25
Total per year	20000	4870	800	460	1130	605
Average per hour (r_i)	2.28	2.32	3.04	2.63	1.84	3.45
Groups of resources						
1 Resources 6, 7, 8	4000	850	60	40	330	60
2 Resource 5	4000	1600	120	80	280	240
Subtotal groups 1 and 2	8000	2450	180	120	610	300
3 Resources 3, 4	10000 [e]	8100 [e]	300	100	200	200
4 Resources 2, 9, 10, 11	10000	2320	320	240	320	105
Subtotal groups 3 and 4	12000 [f]	2420 [f]	620	340	520	305

sources; the top row shows what proportions of his total income are spent in (allocated to) the various behavior setting aggregates. According to the Fox-Van Moeseke terminology of Chapter 3, the left-hand column is a profile of his *endowment b* at the beginning of the accounting period, and the top row is a profile of his *life style x*, weighted by the total resource cost per hour *r* spent in each setting. (Note that since *x* and *r* are measures of duration and intensity, respectively, the figures in the top row have the dimension "duration × intensity.")

Table 5.7. (*Continued*)

Setting Aggregates[a]

Nonwork Trips (6)	Sleeping and Resting (7)	Personal Care (8)	Eating (9)	Mass Media (10)	Leisure (11)	Education (12)	Organizations (13)
480	1120	720	1920	400	800	240	240
100		200	100	300	300		100
120		200	200	360	360	40	400
60		200	200	180	400	20	20
					1000		
30		80	100	90	250		30
							100
			50	25	25		350
			50	25	100		50
790	1120	1400	2620	1380	3235	300	1290
2.98	0.39	3.20	5.98	1.73	4.10	3.42	14.73
90		280	300	270	1650	20	50
120		200	200	360	360	40	400
210		480	500	630	2010	60	450
100		200	100	300	300		100
480	1120	720	2020	450	925	240	740
580	1120	920	2120	750	1225	240	840

[a] The figures in each column are equivalent dollar amounts of the specified resources used in a given behavior setting aggregate.
[b] No value is assigned to "time" in this exercise.
[c] Earnings from personal services obtained by selling "skill:work-related" for $8000.
[d] Value of "skills:work-related" ($8000) is deleted to avoid double counting (with "money").
[e] Includes $8000 of "skills: work-related."
[f] Excludes $8000 of "skills: work-related" to avoid double counting with $8000 of "money."

Table 5.8. Illustrative Conversion of Table 5.7 Figures into Proportions of an Individual's Total Income[a]

| Resources Available | | | | | | Behavior |
Name of Resource	Total Amount of Resource	Work-Related (1)	Pre-paring Food (2)	Laundry and Mending (3)	Other House-work (4)	Shopping (5)
Total, all resources	1.000	.244	.040	.023	.056	.030
1 Time[b]						
2 Money[c]	.400	.056	.016	.012	.016	.004
3 Skill: work-related[d]						
4 Skill: other	.100	.005	.015	.005	.010	.010
5 Value commitments	.200	.080	.006	.004	.014	.012
6 Health	.100	.030	.003	.002	.009	.002
7 Sexuality	.050					
8 Affect	.050	.012			.008	.001
9 Power: in formal organizations	.050	.045				
10 Power: political	.025	.003				
11 Prestige	.025	.012				.001
Groups of resources						
1 Resources 6, 7, 8	.200	.042	.003	.002	.017	.003
2 Resource 5	.200	.080	.006	.004	.014	.012
Subtotal groups 1 and 2	.400	.122	.009	.006	.031	.015
3 Resources 3, 4	.500[e]	.405[e]	.015	.005	.010	.010
4 Resources 2, 9, 10, 11	.500	.116	.016	.012	.016	.005
Subtotal groups 3 and 4	.600[f]	.121[f]	.031	.017	.026	.015

Table 5.8. (*Continued*)

Setting Aggregates

Nonwork Trips (6)	Sleeping and Resting (7)	Personal Care (8)	Eating (9)	Mass Media (10)	Leisure (11)	Education (12)	Organi- zations (13)
.040	.056	.070	.131	.069	.162	.015	.064
.024	.056	.036	.096	.020	.040	.012	.012
.005		.010	.005	.015	.015		.005
.006		.010	.010	.018	.018	.002	.020
.003		.010	.010	.009	.020	.001	.001
					.050		
.002		.004	.005	.004	.012		.002
							.005
			.003	.001	.001		.017
			.003	.001	.005		.003
.005		.014	.015	.013	.082	.001	.003
.006		.010	.010	.018	.018	.002	.020
.011		.024	.025	.031	.100	.003	.023
.005		.010	.005	.015	.015		.005
.024	.056	.036	.102	.022	.046	.012	.037
.029	.056	.046	.107	.037	.061	.012	.042

[a] Proportions of total income spent, by resource and setting.

[b] No value is assigned to "time" in this exercise.

[c] Earnings from personal services obtained by selling "skill: work-related" worth 0.400.

[d] Value of "skill: work-related" (.400 of total income) is deleted to avoid double counting (with "money").

[e] Includes .400 of "skill: work-related."

[f] Excludes .400 of "skill: work-related" to avoid double counting with 0.400 of "money."

VI

Individuals and Families

SOME IMPORTANT ECONOMIC and social indicators are available for households or nuclear families but not for their individual members. In this chapter we explore some implications of extending the approach outlined in Tables 5.5 through 5.8 to families of two or more individuals.

6.1 Differences in Time Use by Adults Associated with Employment Status, Marital Status, and Sex, United States, 1966

The greatest differences in time use by adults are associated with differences in employment status. The first three columns of Table 6.1 show "unemployed men" spending 6.9 hours a day less than "employed men" in work-related activities and 1.6 hours more on housework and family tasks, 1.3 more on personal care, 1.6 more on education and organizations, and 2.4 more on mass media and leisure. In the lower section of the table, column 3 expresses these figures as proportions of a 24-hour day, the reduction of .29 in work-related time being offset by increases of .08, .05, .06, and .10 in housework and family tasks, personal care, education and organizations, and mass media and leisure, respectively.

Joblessness represented an involuntary status for most men listed in the survey as "unemployed." In contrast, most of the women listed as "unemployed" were housewives voluntarily performing this role. They spent 5.6 hours a day less than "employed women" in work-related activities (paid employment), but 3.6 hours more on housework and family tasks, 0.4 more on personal care, 0.3 more on education and organizations, and 1.4 more on mass media and leisure.

The time spent on housework and family activities by "unemployed women" (7.8 hours) is about the same as that spent on work-related activities by "employed men" (7.6 hours). Columns 7 and 8 show that the sum of hours spent on work-related activities and on housework and family tasks was 9.1 for "all men" and 8.8 for "all

Table 6.1. United States Time Use Survey, 1966: Time Spent by Respondents in Primary Activities, by Respondents' Sex and Employment Status

Primary Activities	Men			Women			All Men	All Women	Difference (8)-(7)	All Respondents
	Employed	Unemployed	Difference (2)-(1)	Employed	Unemployed	Difference (5)-(4)				
	(1)	(2)	(3)	(4)	(5)	(6)	(7)	(8)	(9)	(10)
A. Hours per 24-hour day										
Work-related	7.6	0.7	-6.9	5.7	0.1	-5.6	7.2	2.7	-4.5	4.7
Housework and family tasks	1.8	3.4	1.6	4.2	7.8	3.6	1.9	6.1	4.2	4.3
Personal care	10.0	11.3	1.3	10.2	10.6	0.4	10.1	10.4	0.3	10.3
Education and organizations	0.4	2.0	1.6	0.3	0.6	0.3	0.5	0.4	-0.1	0.5
Mass media and leisure	4.2	6.6	2.4	3.6	5.0	1.4	4.3	4.3	0.0	4.3
Total	24.0	24.0	--	24.0	24.1	0.1	24.0	23.9	-0.1	24.1
B. Proportions of total time										
Work-related	.32	.03	-.29	.24	--	-.24	.30	.11	-.19	.20
Housework and family tasks	.07	.15	.08	.17	.32	.15	.08	.26	.18	.18
Personal care	.42	.47	.05	.43	.44	.01	.42	.43	.01	.42
Education and organizations	.02	.08	.06	.01	.03	.02	.02	.02	--	.02
Mass media and leisure	.17	.27	.10	.15	.21	.06	.18	.18	--	.18
Total	1.00	1.00	--	1.00	1.00	--	1.00	1.00	--	1.00

Source. John P. Robinson and Philip E. Converse, *Sixty-six Basic Tables of Time Budget Data for the United States.* Ann Arbor: Survey Research Center, University of Michigan, May 30, 1966. 11 pages plus 66 tables (xeroxed). Adapted from Table 1.

Table 6.2. United States Time Use Survey, 1966: Time Spent by Employed Respondents in Primary Activities, by Respondents' Sex and Marital Status

Primary Activities	Men			Women			Men Plus Women		
	Married (1)	Single (2)	Difference (1)-(2) (3)	Married (4)	Single (5)	Difference (4)-(5) (6)	Married (1)+(4) (7)	Single (2)+(5) (8)	Difference (7)-(8) (9)
A. Hours per 24-hour day									
Work-related	7.6	7.5	0.1	5.6	5.7	-0.1	13.2	13.2	--
Housework and family tasks	1.9	1.7	0.2	4.6	3.5	1.1	6.5	5.2	1.3
Personal care	10.0	9.9	0.1	10.1	10.4	-0.3	20.1	20.3	-0.2
Education and organizations	0.4	0.7	-0.3	0.2	0.5	-0.3	0.6	1.2	-0.6
Mass media and leisure	4.2	4.2	0.0	3.4	3.8	-0.4	7.6	8.0	-0.4
Total	24.1	24.0	0.1	23.9	23.9	--	48.0	47.9	0.1
B. Proportions of total time									
Work-related	.32	.32	--	.24	.24	--	.56	.56	--
Housework and family tasks	.08	.07	.01	.19	.15	.04	.27	.22	.05
Personal care	.41	.41	--	.42	.43	-.01	.83	.84	-.01
Education and organizations	.02	.03	-.01	.01	.02	-.01	.03	.05	-.02
Mass media and leisure	.17	.17	--	.14	.16	-.02	.31	.33	-.02
Total	1.00	1.00	--	1.00	1.00	--	2.00	2.00	--

Source. John P. Robinson and Philip E. Converse, Sixty-six Basic Tables of Time Budget Data for the United States. Ann Arbor: Survey Research Center, University of Michigan, May 30, 1966. 11 pages plus 66 tables (xeroxed). Adapted from Table 1.

80

women," suggesting that the two categories are treated simply as different kinds of work and that adults of both sexes are expected to "work" about the same total number of hours. The two sexes spent very similar amounts of time on mass media and leisure, on education and organizations, and on personal care.

Table 6.2 indicates that marital status seems to make little difference in the allocation of time by employed men among the major categories of primary activities listed. Among employed women, wives evidently spend 1.1 hours a day more on housework and family tasks than do single women, and 0.3, 0.3, and 0.4 hours less, respectively, on personal care, education and organizations, and mass media and leisure. When "couples" are created by adding the figures in columns 1 and 4 for "marrieds" and, alternatively, the figures in columns 2 and 5 for "singles," the marrieds spend 1.3 hours a day more (out of 48) on housework and family tasks and 0.2, 0.6, and 0.4 hours less, respectively, on personal care, education and organizations, and mass media and leisure. These differences probably imply that the marrieds, on the average, spend more time caring for other household members (children, in particular) than do the singles.

Table 6.3A shows time spent in primary and secondary activities by married respondents, namely, employed men, employed women, and unemployed women. For the same three types of respondent, Table 6.3B gives the amounts of time spent with specified categories of people and in specified place categories. Unemployed women reported more time spent with family tasks and television as secondary activities and less time with conversation as a secondary activity than did the other groups. Unemployed women spent 20.6 hours a day at home, compared with 15.9 hours for employed women, and 6.7 hours a day with members of their families, as against 4.0 hours for employed women.

6.2 Extending the Fox-Van Moeseke Model to a Married Couple and to a Four-Person Family

Tables 6.4 through 6.6 are illustrative rearrangements of time budget data from Tables 5.1 through 5.4 into a behavior setting format, using somewhat larger aggregates of primary activities, people, and places than in the original tables. The degree of aggregation can be seen by comparing Table 6.4 with Table 5.5. The hours spent on primary activities are taken directly from the 1966 United States time use survey; however, the assignment to particular behavior setting aggregates of hours spent in secondary activities, with people, and in places, was made arbitrarily by the author. The arbitrary element should not be exaggerated; it is based on reasonable assumptions, such as "married people do all or most of their sleeping at home and conduct their work-related activities (and interactions with colleagues) mainly at their places of work."

It could be argued that we are converting the 1966 data to purposes for which they were not designed. However, I believe it is important to keep these "real-world" magnitudes before us as we consider the feasibility and desirability of the more speculative aspects of the Fox-Van Moeseke approach.

The values per hour (r_i) in Tables 6.4 through 6.6 have been derived from the figures on average values of resources used per hour in Table 5.7 by a process of weighting, rounding, and conversion to relatives (the average r_i over the 24-hour day is set at 1.0). The proportions of resources in the lower sections of Tables 6.4 through

Table 6.3A. United States Time Use Survey, 1966: Time Spent in Primary and Secondary Activities by Married Respondents—Employed Men, Employed Women, and Unemployed Women (hours per 24-hour day)

Activities	Primary Activities			Secondary Activities		
	Men	Women		Men	Women	
	Employed (1)	Employed (2)	Unemployed (3)	Employed (4)	Employed (5)	Unemployed (6)
Work-related	7.6	5.6	0.1	—	—	—
Housework	0.6	3.0	5.1	—	0.1	0.2
Family tasks	1.3	1.6	2.7	0.1	0.1	0.4
Sleep	7.6	7.7	7.7	—	—	—
Personal care, eating, resting	2.4	2.4	2.9	0.3	0.2	0.3
Education and organizations	0.4	0.2	0.5	—	—	—
Mass media						
Radio	0.1	—	—	0.8	0.9	0.9
Television	1.7	1.0	1.6	0.4	0.6	1.0
Reading	0.7	0.5	0.6	0.4	0.2	0.2
Leisure						
Social life	1.0	1.0	1.5	0.2	0.2	0.3
Conversation	0.2	0.3	0.5	3.1	2.7	1.8
Sports	0.2	0.1	0.1	—	—	—
Various leisure	0.2	0.3	0.5	0.1	0.1	0.3
Spectacles	0.1	0.1	0.1	—	—	—
Total, all activities	24.1	23.8	23.9	5.4	5.1	5.4

Source. John P. Robinson and Philip E. Converse, *Sixty-six Basic Tables of Time Budget Data for the United States.* Ann Arbor: Survey Research Center, University of Michigan, May 30, 1966. 11 pages plus 66 tables (xeroxed). Adapted from Tables 1 and 17.

Table 6.3B.   United States Time Use Survey, 1966: Time Spent with Specified Categories of Persons and at Specified Categories of Places by Married Respondents—Employed Men, Employed Women, and Unemployed Women (hours per 24-hour day)

Categories of Persons with Whom, and Places at Which, Respondents' Time Is Spent	Men	Women	
	Employed (1)	Employed (2)	Unemployed (3)
Persons with whom			
All alone	13.7	14.0	14.4
Family--no children	1.9	2.0	2.0
Family--spouse and children	1.4	0.8	1.6
Family--no spouse	0.6	1.2	3.1
Other household adults	0.1	0.4	0.3
Other friends and relatives	1.3	1.4	1.8
Colleagues	3.4	2.5	0.1
Organization members	0.2	0.1	0.2
Neighbors and children	0.3	0.8	0.6
Others	1.0	1.0	0.6
Total	23.9	24.2	24.7
Places at which			
At home and just outside	13.9	15.9	20.6
Place of work	6.5	5.0	0.1
Another's home	0.5	0.7	0.8
Streets, parks, etc.	1.6	1.2	1.0
Business places	0.8	0.8	1.1
Indoor leisure	0.2	0.2	0.2
Outdoor leisure	0.1	--	--
Restaurants, bars	0.4	0.2	0.1
Others	0.2	0.1	0.1
Total	24.2	24.1	24.0

Source.   John P. Robinson and Philip E. Converse, *Sixty-six Basic Tables of Time Budget Data for the United States.* Ann Arbor: Survey Research Center, University of Michigan, May 30, 1966. 11 pages plus 66 tables (xeroxed). Adapted from Tables 33 and 45.

6.6 are based on the resource groupings shown in Table 5.7 (group 1, group 2, and the subtotal of groups 3 and 4 with double counting eliminated) and reflect the relative weights assigned to the individual resources in Tables 5.7 and 5.8. Here, again, it seems desirable to use numbers rather than abstract symbols, for an operational system of social accounts must generate numbers.

Table 6.7 shows the main features involved in extending the Fox-Van Moeseke approach to a married couple (with no children living at home). The man's allocation of time and other resources is based on Table 6.4 and the woman's on Table 6.5; both spouses are employed. Their behavior settings are combined into five major aggregates, as follows:

1. Settings occupied simultaneously (shared) by man and wife,

Table 6.4. Man, Married, Employed: Illustrative Rearrangement of Time Budget Data from Table 5.5 into Larger Aggregates of Behavior Settings and Categories of Activities, Places, and Persons

Item	Behavior Setting Aggregates									Total Hours Spent All Settings
	1 Work-Related	2 Household Production	3 Family Tasks	4 Sleeping and Resting	5 Personal Care	6 Eating	7 Mass Media	8 Leisure	9 Education, Organizations	
	(1)	(2)	(3)	(4)	(5)	(6)	(7)	(8)	(9)	(10)
Primary activity (hours)	7.6	0.6	1.3	7.8	0.9	1.2	2.5	1.7	0.4	24.0
Value per hour (r_i)	1.0	1.0	1.5	0.2	1.5	3.0	0.7	2.0	2.0	5.3
Secondary activities (hours)						1.1	2.5	1.7		24.0
Place occurring										
Place of work	6.5									6.5
At home or just outside		0.6	0.5	7.8	0.9	1.0	2.5	0.6		13.9
Another's home								0.5		0.5
Other places	1.1		0.8			0.2		0.6	0.4	3.1
										24.0
Persons involved										
Colleagues	3.4									3.4
All alone	3.9	0.6		7.8	0.9		1.2			13.8
Nuclear family			0.5			1.0	1.2	0.6		3.9
Other household adults							0.1			0.1
Other friends, relatives						0.2		1.1		1.3
Neighbors and children			0.3							0.3
Organization members									0.2	0.2
Others	0.3		0.5						0.2	1.0
Proportion of total resource used										
Time	.32	.03	.05	.32	.04	.05	.10	.07	.02	1.00
Group 1	.30	.05	.05	--	.05	.15	.05	.35	--	1.00
Group 2	.50	.05	.10	--	.05	.05	.10	.10	.05	1.00
Groups 3 and 4	.30	.02	.08	.11	.07	.20	.07	.10	.05	1.00

Source. Table 5.5.

84

Table 6.5. Woman, Married, Employed: Illustrative Rearrangement of Time Budget Data from Tables 5.1 through 5.4 into Behavior Setting Aggregates Format

Item	1 Work-Related	2 Household Production	3 Family Tasks	4 Sleeping and Resting	5 Personal Care	6 Eating	7 Mass Media	8 Leisure	9 Education, Organizations	10 Total Hours Spent All Settings
	(1)	(2)	(3)	(4)	(5)	(6)	(7)	(8)	(9)	(10)
Primary activity (hours)	5.6	3.0	1.6	8.0	1.2	1.0	1.6	1.8	0.2	24.0
Value per hour (r_i)	1.0	1.0	1.5	0.2	1.5	3.0	0.7	2.0	2.0	
Secondary activities (hours)		0.8				1.0	1.6	1.8		5.2
Place occurring										24.0
Place of work	5.0									5.0
At home or just outside		3.0	0.8	8.0	1.2	0.8	1.6	0.5		15.9
Another's home								0.7		0.7
Other places	0.6		0.8			0.2		0.6	0.2	2.4
Persons involved										24.0
Colleagues	2.5									2.5
All alone	2.8	2.0		8.0	1.2					14.0
Nuclear family		0.6	0.8			0.8	1.2	0.6		4.0
Other household adults							0.4			0.4
Other friends, relatives			0.2					1.2		1.4
Neighbors and children		0.4	0.2			0.2				0.8
Organization members									0.1	0.1
Others	0.3		0.4						0.1	0.8
Proportion of total resource used										
Time	.23	.12	.07	.33	.05	.04	.07	.08	.01	1.00
Group 1	.20	.05	.10	--	.10	.10	.05	.40	--	1.00
Group 2	.30	.20	.20	--	.10	.05	.05	.10	--	1.00
Groups 3 and 4	.24	.13	.08	.11	.07	.17	.05	.12	.03	1.00

Source. Tables 5.1 through 5.4.

85

Table 6.6. Woman, Married, Unemployed: Illustrative Rearrangement of Time Budget Data from Tables 5.1 Through 5.4 into Behavior Setting Aggregates Format

Item	1	2	3	4	5	6	7	8	9	10
				Behavior Setting Aggregates						Total Hours Spent All Settings
	Work-Related	Household Production	Family Tasks	Sleeping and Resting	Personal Care	Eating	Mass Media	Leisure	Education, Organizations	
	(1)	(2)	(3)	(4)	(5)	(6)	(7)	(8)	(9)	(10)
Primary activity (hours)	0.1	5.1	2.7	8.1	1.2	1.3	2.2	2.8	0.5	24.0
Value per hour (r_i)	1.0	1.0	1.5	0.2	1.5	3.0	0.7	2.0	2.0	
Secondary activities (hours)						1.1	1.6	2.8		5.5
Place occurring										24.0
Place of work	0.1									0.1
At home or just outside		5.1	1.5	8.1	1.2	1.1	2.2	1.4		20.6
Another's home								0.8		0.8
Other places			1.2			0.2		0.6	0.5	2.5
Persons involved										24.0
Colleagues	0.1									0.1
All alone		3.8	1.3	8.1	1.2					14.4
Nuclear family		1.3	0.5			1.1	1.9	1.2		6.0
Other household adults							0.3			0.3
Other friends, relatives						0.2		1.6		1.8
Neighbors and children			0.6							0.6
Organization members									0.2	0.2
Others			0.3						0.3	0.6
Proportion of total resource used										
Time	--	.22	.11	.34	.05	.05	.09	.12	.02	1.00
Group 1	--	.10	.10	--	.10	.15	.05	.50	--	1.00
Group 2	--	.35	.30	--	.05	.05	.05	.15	.05	1.00
Groups 3 and 4	--	.22	.13	.11	.07	.18	.07	.17	.05	1.00

Source   Tables 5.1 through 5.4.

Table 6.7. Illustrative Extension of Fox-Van Moeseke Model to a Married Couple: Man and Wife Both Employed

Item	Behavior Setting Aggregates					Total Resources Available	Shadow Prices of Resources
	Shared by Man and Wife	Man Not Shared		Wife Not Shared			
		Work-Related	Other	Work-Related	Other		
	(1)	(2)	(3)	(4)	(5)	(6)	(7)
Value of resources used per unit of time							
Man (r_i)	r_1	r_2	r_3	--	--		
Wife (s_i)	s_1	--	--	s_4	s_5		
Proportions of total time							
Man (x_{1i})	.63	.32	.05	--	--	1.00	ρ_t
Wife (x_{2i})	.63	--	--	.23	.14	1.00	σ_t
Behavior setting structure per unit of time							
Man's resources							
Time	1.00	1.00	1.00	--	--	1.00	ρ_t
Group 1	1.03	.94	1.00	--	--	1.00	ρ_1
Group 2	.71	1.56	1.00	--	--	1.00	ρ_2
Groups 3 and 4	1.00	.94	1.40	--	--	1.00	ρ_3
Wife's resources							
Time	1.00	--	--	1.00	1.00	1.00	σ_t
Group 1	1.03	--	--	.87	1.07	1.00	σ_1
Group 2	.71	--	--	1.30	1.79	1.00	σ_2
Groups 3 and 4	1.00	--	--	1.04	.93	1.00	σ_3

2. Work-related settings occupied by the husband separately,
3. Other settings occupied by the husband separately,
4. Work-related settings occupied separately by the wife, and
5. Other settings occupied separately by the wife.

The total values per unit of time of resources used by the husband in settings 1, 2, and 3 are denoted by r_1, r_2, and r_3, respectively; the corresponding values of resources used by the wife in settings 1, 4, and 5 are denoted by s_1, s_4, and s_5, respectively. The shadow prices of the husband's resources (time, group 1, group 2, and groups 3 and 4) are denoted by ρ_t, ρ_1, ρ_2, and ρ_3 and the wife's by σ_t, σ_1, σ_2, and σ_3. The utilities experienced by husband and wife cannot be summed directly; however, when the husband converts his shadow prices into dollar equivalents (as in the left-hand column of Table 5.7) and the wife does likewise, these dollar equivalents can be summed to yield a total income figure for the couple.

Table 6.8 extends the model to a family of four persons, all living at home. Behavior settings are aggregated into 15 categories which, in turn, fall into four major groups:

1. Settings occupied jointly by all four persons,
2. Settings occupied jointly by three persons (four combinations are possible),
3. Settings occupied jointly by two persons (six possible combinations), and
4. Settings occupied by one person (a different aggregate for each of four persons).

Shadow prices for each person's resources (time, group 1, group 2, and groups 3 and 4) are denoted by a separate Greek letter. Conversion of utilities into dollar equivalents must be done separately for each person; the dollar equivalents can then be summed to yield a total income figure for the family of four.

The novel element in Table 6.7 is the behavior setting (aggregate) shared by husband and wife. By definition, they both spend the same proportion of their time in the shared settings; they need not spend the same proportions of their other resources in those settings.

Formally, the problem(s) may be stated as follows:

Husband's problem:

$$\text{maximize} \quad u_1(x_{11}, x_{12}, x_{13}) \qquad \text{subject to}$$
$$x_{11} + x_{12} + x_{13} = 1.00,$$
$$a_{11}x_{11} + a_{12}x_{12} + a_{13}x_{13} \leq 1.00,$$
$$a_{21}x_{11} + a_{22}x_{12} + a_{23}x_{13} \leq 1.00,$$
$$a_{31}x_{11} + a_{32}x_{12} + a_{33}x_{13} \leq 1.00,$$
$$x_{1i} \geq 0, \quad i = 1, 2, 3,$$

and

$$x_{11} = x_{21}.$$

Wife's problem:

$$\text{maximize} \quad u_2(x_{21}, x_{24}, x_{25}) \qquad \text{subject to}$$
$$x_{21} + x_{24} + x_{25} = 1.00,$$

$$b_{11}x_{21} + b_{14}x_{24} + b_{15}x_{25} \leq 1.00,$$
$$b_{21}x_{21} + b_{24}x_{24} + b_{25}x_{25} \leq 1.00,$$
$$b_{31}x_{21} + b_{34}x_{24} + b_{35}x_{25} \leq 1.00,$$
$$x_{2i} \geq 0, i = 1, 4, 5,$$

and

$$x_{21} = x_{11}.$$

The solution of the husband's problem would yield a shadow price for time (ρ_t), one for each of his three groups of resources (ρ_1, ρ_2, ρ_3), and one (call it ρ_{12}) for the sharing restriction $x_{11} = x_{21}$. Similarly, the solution of the wife's problem would yield a shadow price for time (σ_t), one for each of her three groups of resources ($\sigma_1, \sigma_2, \sigma_3$), and one (call it σ_{21}) for the sharing restriction $x_{21} = x_{11}$.[1]

It is not clear that these optimization problems for husband and wife have a unique joint solution. A reasonable approach might run as follows:

1. Solve the husband's problem assuming that he can choose x_{11} without regard to the sharing restriction, and calculate his total income Y_1^* in dollar equivalents.

2. Solve the wife's problem assuming that she can choose x_{21} without regard to the sharing restriction, and calculate her total income Y_2^* in dollar equivalents.

3. Recalculate the husband's income $Y_1^* - d_1$, setting x_{11} equal to the wife's optimal value of x_{21}: the sum of the two incomes is $Y_1^* - d_1 + Y_2^*$.

4. Recalculate the wife's income $Y_2^* - d_2$, setting x_{21} equal to the husband's optimal value of x_{11}: the sum of the two incomes is $Y_1^* + Y_2^* - d_2$.

5. Search for values of $x_{11} = x_{21}$ intermediate between the separate optimal values of x_{11} and x_{21} that yield a higher sum ($Y_1' + Y_2'$) of the two incomes than the larger of either ($Y_1^* - d_1 + Y_2^*$) or ($Y_1^* + Y_2^* - d_2$).

6. Select a final value of $x_{11} = x_{21}$ that exactly or approximately maximizes the sum of the two incomes, say ($Y_1' + Y_2'$)*.

In the four-person family of Table 6.8, the number of sharing restrictions would increase to 11, as follows:

$$x_{11} = x_{21} = x_{31} = x_{41}, \tag{1}$$

$$x_{12} = x_{22} = x_{32}, \tag{2}$$

$$x_{13} = x_{23} = x_{43}, \tag{3}$$

$$x_{14} = x_{34} = x_{44}, \tag{4}$$

$$x_{25} = x_{35} = x_{45}, \tag{5}$$

$$x_{16} = x_{26}, \tag{6}$$

$$x_{17} = x_{37}, \tag{7}$$

$$x_{18} = x_{48}, \tag{8}$$

$$x_{29} = x_{39}, \tag{9}$$

[1] We disregard here the technical point that the number of nonzero shadow prices in a linear programming problem cannot exceed the number of activities included at positive levels in the optimal solution. We could easily disaggregate the behavior settings into four or more each for husband and wife separately, plus the shared-setting aggregate.

Table 6.8. Illustrative Extension of Fox-Van Moeseke Model to a Family of Four Persons: A, B, C, and D

Behavior Setting Aggregate:		1	2	3	4	5	6	7
Persons Sharing in Setting:		ABCD	ABC	ABD	ACD	BCD	AB	AC
		(1)	(2)	(3)	(4)	(5)	(6)	(7)
Proportion of total time spent in setting by:								
Person A		x_{11}	x_{12}	x_{13}	x_{14}		x_{16}	x_{17}
Person B		x_{21}	x_{22}	x_{23}		x_{25}	x_{26}	
Person C		x_{31}	x_{32}		x_{34}	x_{35}		x_{37}
Person D		x_{41}		x_{43}	x_{44}	x_{45}		
Resources used per unit of time by:								
Person A		r_1	r_2	r_3	r_4		r_6	r_7
Person B		s_1	s_2	s_3		s_5	s_6	
Person C		u_1	u_2		u_4	u_5		u_7
Person D		v_1		v_3	v_4	v_5		
Behavior setting structure per unit of time, by person and resource:								
Person A:	Time	1.00	1.00	1.00	1.00	0	1.00	1.00
	Group 1	$a_{1.1}$	$a_{1.2}$	$a_{1.3}$	$a_{1.4}$	0	$a_{1.6}$	$a_{1.7}$
	Group 2	$a_{2.1}$	$a_{2.2}$	$a_{2.3}$	$a_{2.4}$	0	$a_{2.6}$	$a_{2.7}$
	Groups 3 and 4	$a_{3.1}$	$a_{3.2}$	$a_{3.3}$	$a_{3.4}$	0	$a_{3.6}$	$a_{3.7}$
Person B:	Time	1.00	1.00	1.00	0	1.00	1.00	0
	Group 1	$b_{1.1}$	$b_{1.2}$	$b_{1.3}$	0	$b_{1.5}$	$b_{1.6}$	0
	Group 2	$b_{2.1}$	$b_{2.2}$	$b_{2.3}$	0	$b_{2.5}$	$b_{2.6}$	0
	Groups 3 and 4	$b_{3.1}$	$b_{3.2}$	$b_{3.3}$	0	$b_{3.5}$	$b_{3.6}$	0
Person C:	Time	1.00	1.00	0	1.00	1.00	0	1.00
	Group 1	$c_{1.1}$	$c_{1.2}$	0	$c_{1.4}$	$c_{1.5}$	0	$c_{1.7}$
	Group 2	$c_{2.1}$	$c_{2.2}$	0	$c_{2.4}$	$c_{2.5}$	0	$c_{2.7}$
	Groups 3 and 4	$c_{3.1}$	$c_{3.2}$	0	$c_{3.4}$	$c_{3.5}$	0	$c_{3.7}$
Person D:	Time	1.00	0	1.00	1.00	1.00	0	0
	Group 1	$d_{1.1}$	0	$d_{1.3}$	$d_{1.4}$	$d_{1.5}$	0	0
	Group 2	$d_{2.1}$	0	$d_{2.3}$	$d_{2.4}$	$d_{2.5}$	0	0
	Groups 3 and 4	$d_{3.1}$	0	$d_{3.3}$	$d_{3.4}$	$d_{3.5}$	0	0

Table 6.8.   (*Continued*)

8	9	10	11	12	13	14	15	Total Resources Available	Shadow Prices of Resources
AD	BC	BD	CD	A	B	C	D		
(8)	(9)	(10)	(11)	(12)	(13)	(14)	(15)	(16)	(17)
x_{18}				$x_{1,12}$				1.00	ρ_t
	x_{29}	$x_{2,10}$			$x_{2,13}$			1.00	σ_t
	x_{39}		$x_{3,11}$			$x_{3,14}$		1.00	μ_t
x_{48}		$x_{4,10}$	$x_{4,11}$				$x_{4,15}$	1.00	ν_t
r_8				r_{12}					
	s_9	s_{10}			s_{13}				
	u_9		u_{11}			u_{14}			
v_8		v_{10}	v_{11}				v_{15}		
1.00	0	0	0	1.00	0	0	0	1.00	ρ_t
$a_{1.8}$	0	0	0	$a_{1.12}$	0	0	0	1.00	ρ_1
$a_{2.8}$	0	0	0	$a_{2.12}$	0	0	0	1.00	ρ_2
$a_{3.8}$	0	0	0	$a_{3.12}$	0	0	0	1.00	ρ_3
0	1.00	1.00	0	0	1.00	0	0	1.00	σ_t
0	$b_{1.9}$	$b_{1.10}$	0	0	$b_{1.13}$	0	0	1.00	σ_1
0	$b_{2.9}$	$b_{2.10}$	0	0	$b_{2.13}$	0	0	1.00	σ_2
0	$b_{3.9}$	$b_{3.10}$	0	0	$b_{3.13}$	0	0	1.00	σ_3
0	1.00	0	1.00	0	0	1.00	0	1.00	μ_t
0	$c_{1.9}$	0	$c_{1.11}$	0	0	$c_{1.14}$	0	1.00	μ_1
0	$c_{2.9}$	0	$c_{2.11}$	0	0	$c_{2.14}$	0	1.00	μ_2
0	$c_{3.9}$	0	$c_{3.11}$	0	0	$c_{3.14}$	0	1.00	μ_3
1.00	0	1.00	1.00	0	0	0	1.00	1.00	ν_t
$d_{1.8}$	0	$d_{1.10}$	$d_{1.11}$	0	0	0	$d_{1.15}$	1.00	ν_1
$d_{2.8}$	0	$d_{2.10}$	$d_{2.11}$	0	0	0	$d_{2.15}$	1.00	ν_2
$d_{3.8}$	0	$d_{3.10}$	$d_{3.11}$	0	0	0	$d_{3.15}$	1.00	ν_3

$$x_{2,10} \qquad = x_{4,10}, \qquad\qquad (10)$$

$$x_{3,11} = x_{4,11}. \qquad\qquad (11)$$

In addition to shadow prices for his time and each of his three groups of resources as indicated in the right-hand column of Table 6.8, each person would have shadow prices for seven sharing restrictions (some shadow prices, of course, might be zero).

Approximately optimal solutions for the family might be found by an extension of the procedure suggested for the two-person case, starting from the equivalent dollar values of the total incomes of each of the four persons if he allocated his time without regard to the sharing constraints. If the separately optimal solutions yielded incomes of Y_1^*, Y_2^*, Y_3^*, and Y_4^*, a "satisficing" approach might be tried under which any solution yielding incomes $Y_i \geq \alpha Y_i^*$ for all i ($i = 1, 2, 3, 4$) and for $\alpha = .95$, say, and satisfying all the sharing constraints would be regarded as acceptable.

To go further than this would be to divert attention from the conceptual problems that are our fundamental concern. Computational techniques are not likely to become limiting factors in any realistic system of social accounts and indicators.

6.3   Some Problems in Implementing a Life Cycle Model of an Individual's Resources and Total Income

In Section 2.2 we cited with approval Erik Erikson's (1968) characterization of an individual's life cycle in terms of eight stages. In Table 6.9, with an eye to customary tabulations of demographic and other data, we have expanded Erikson's seventh and eighth life stages into six periods (each covering 5 or 10 years) and have equated each of his first six stages with a definite age range.

Table 6.9 lists all but one of the 10 resources (other than time) named in Tables 5.6 through 5.8; these 10 are arranged in groups 1, 3, and 4 as in the tables mentioned. We have expanded the remaining resource, value commitments (group 2), to incorporate with equal weights seven of the qualities the individual acquires, according to Erikson, if he successfully negotiates the crises associated with seven of his life stages. The eighth quality, competence, we subsume under group 3 as work-related and other skills.

The figures in Table 6.9 represent the values of each resource used annually during the specified periods, measured in terms of relative marginal utilities experienced by the individual. We have assigned a value of 100 units per year to health in each period except the last two, and 100 units to affect, which we identify with emotional and mental health. We assign increasing values to sexuality up to the age range 18.0–34.9 and declining values thereafter.

In most cases, we introduce a value of 20 for each of the qualities listed by Erikson at the end of the period during which he says it is usually acquired; we continue to value the quality at 20 units per year in all subsequent periods. If value commitments are construed as "character," we represent character as being built, quality by quality, in successive life stages.

We show the value of work-related skills increasing with age (and presumably associated experience and education) up to the 45.0–54.9 age range and then declining. For simplicity, we have assigned precisely the same values to money income, assuming it to be obtained exclusively from current employment. We have assigned roughly similar time patterns to other skills and to the values of prestige, power in formal organizations, and political power.

Table 6.9 illustrates concretely the kinds of measurement and definitional problems that would be involved in attempts to quantify the concept of total income and its components over the life span of an individual. The requirements include:

1. A list of resources that exhausts total income,

2. For each resource, a method of measurement that will yield a consistent series of numbers at successive ages (or stages) in an individual's life cycle—a resource trajectory, and

3. At each age (or stage), a method for determining a set of weights for combining the numerical measures of individual resources into numerical measures of total income and various subaggregates (such as groups 1, 2, 3, and 4 in Table 6.9).

Since one of the resource trajectories for any individual would record annual money income in dollars, it follows that

4. The weights mentioned in step 3 can be used to convert the measures of each resource and of total income into dollars.

5. Since the money incomes of different individuals are all measured in dollars and can be aggregated, averaged, arrayed in frequency distributions, and the like, the same operations can be applied to the dollar measures of total income and its various subaggregates for different individuals.

Tables 6.10 and 6.11 are taken from a study by Melichar (1968). Using nearly 200,000 observations from the 1966 National Register of Scientific and Technical Personnel, Melichar was able to explain 54 percent of the variance in the (logarithms of) salaries of scientists by means of such variables as years of experience, type of employer, highest academic degree, primary work activity, age, sex, and profession (i.e., scientific discipline). The relation of salary to years of experience and type of employer is shown in Table 6.10 and Figure 6.1; the relation of salary to the remaining variables appears in Table 6.11.

Figure 6.1 is based on cross-sectional data for a single year. However, it shows about the same general relationship of real salary to years of experience that we would expect in individual careers extending through time. The relationships of salaries to years of experience are quite similar in contour for the various employer groups. The *levels* of all salary curves in Figure 6.1 assume a particular set of values of the variables in Table 6.11—namely, highest academic degree, primary work activity, age, sex, and field of science.

Figure 6.2 combines the net effects of age and experience, assuming that the relevant experience for all members of a particular cohort of scientists begins at age 25. The points on the curve labeled "Ph.D. (50; T)" are estimated directly from Melichar's regression equation; "T" refers to teaching as the primary activity and "50" designates the fiftieth percentile in an assumed normal distribution of the (logarithms of) salaries of individual scientists around the regression line. The curves labeled "Ph.D. (90; T)," "Ph.D. (75; T)," and "Ph.D. (50; T)" represent the 90th, 75th, and 50th percentile points in such a distribution. (The standard error of esti-

Table 6.9. Hypothetical Pattern of Total Income and Its Components for an Individual, by Life Stages

Life Stage No.:	1	2	3	4	5
Age (years):	0–0.9	1.0–2.9	3.0–4.9	5.0–13.9	14.0–17.9
Resources	(1)	(2)	(3)	(4)	(5)
Group 1 (health)	220	240	260	280	300
Health	100	100	100	100	100
Affect	100	100	100	100	100
Sexuality	20	40	60	80	100
Group 2 (value commitments)	0	20	40	60	70
Trust or hope	–	20	20	20	20
Will power	–	–	20	20	20
Purpose	–	–	–	20	20
Fidelity	–	–	–	–	10
Love	–	–	–	–	–
Care	–	–	–	–	–
Wisdom	–	–	–	–	–
Group 3 (skills)	0	0	0	30	60
Work–related	0	0	0	20	40
Other	0	0	0	10	20
Group 4 (social rewards)	0	0	0	30	60
Money income	0	0	0	20	40
Prestige	0	0	0	10	15
Power in organizations	0	0	0	0	5
Political power	0	0	0	0	0
Group 3 + Group 4 (double counting eliminated)	0	0	0	40	80
Total, all groups (double counting eliminated)	220	260	300	380	450

mate associated with Melichar's regression equation is taken as the standard deviation of the salary distribution cited.)

The last age group reflected in Figure 6.2 is 55 to 64. The National Register was primarily concerned with scientists engaged in full-time professional work; therefore, only 1.4 percent of the respondents were 65 or older. The money income trajectory in Table 6.9 is roughly similar to the salary curves in Figure 6.2 through age 64 but declines sharply thereafter.

Tremendous quantities of wage, salary, and other income data are available in

Table 6.9.   (*Continued*)

6	7	7	7	8	8	8
18.0–24.9 (6)	25.0–34.9 (7)	35.0–44.9 (8)	45.0–54.9 (9)	55.0–64.9 (10)	65.0–74.9 (11)	75.0 and over (12)
320	320	300	280	260	220	180
100	100	100	100	100	80	60
100	100	100	100	100	100	100
120	120	100	80	60	40	20
80	100	120	140	140	140	140
20	20	20	20	20	20	20
20	20	20	20	20	20	20
20	20	20	20	20	20	20
20	20	20	20	20	20	20
–	20	20	20	20	20	20
–	–	20	20	20	20	20
–	–	–	20	20	20	20
120	150	180	195	180	115	60
80	100	130	150	140	80	40
40	50	50	45	40	35	20
120	150	195	225	220	140	70
80	100	130	150	140	80	40
20	25	30	35	35	30	20
10	15	20	25	25	15	0
10	10	15	15	20	15	10
160	200	245	270	260	175	90
560	620	665	690	660	535	410

the United States and, I presume, in most other developed economies. Blau and Duncan (1967) have also made extensive studies of the American occupational structure, the interrelations between education, income, and occupation, and the measurement of occupational status or prestige. An operational set of measures of total income and its components should be consistent, and integrated, with such data and studies.

Table 6.12 contains some illustrative calculations related to "the value of a life plan." Time preference implies that a person will prefer $100 available now to a

Table 6.10. Net Relationship Between Professional Salaries and Employer-Experience Characteristics: All Professions—1966 National Register (shown as percentage difference from national geometric mean)

Type of Employer	Experience (years)						
	1 or Less	2 to 4	5 to 9	10 to 14	15 to 19	20 to 29	30 and Over
Educational institutions							
Academic year base	-36.6	-31.9	-25.7	-17.6	-11.5	-4.3	0
Calendar year base	-28.8	-23.4	-16.5	-7.3	-.5	7.6	12.4
Government							
Federal	-26.0	-15.8	-5.7	.9	7.2	16.0	24.7
Other	-36.5	-27.8	-19.1	-13.5	-8.0	-.5	7.0
Other employer							
Nonprofit organization	-20.9	-16.7	-9.0	-1.2	6.5	15.6	24.8
Industry or business	-10.8	-6.0	2.7	11.5	20.2	30.5	40.8
Self-employed	.7	6.1	15.9	25.9	35.7	47.4	59.0

Source. E. Melichar, "Factors Affecting 1966 Basic Salaries in the National Register Professions." Supplement to *American Economic Review*, **58** (December 1968), 62.

guarantee of $100 a year hence. If he puts $100 in a savings account now at a compound interest rate of 5 percent, he will have $105 a year hence, $110.25 2 years hence, and about $200 in 14 years. Conversely, the sum of $200 guaranteed payable 14 years hence (given a discount rate of 5 percent) would have a present value of $100.

When interest is compounded over a period of years comparable to a human life span, the results are quite astonishing. If the interest rate is 5 percent, $100 now will grow to $265 in 20 years, $1147 in 50 years, and $4956 in 80 years. Conversely, the present values of $100 to be paid (alternatively) in 20, 50, or 80 years would be $37.69, $8.72, and $2.02, respectively.

Columns 4, 5, and 6 show the present values at age 0 of real incomes of $1.00 at specified numbers of years in the future. If the discount rate is zero, an income stream of $1.00 a year for 80 years will have a present value of $80. The same income stream would have a present value of $30.20 if the discount rate were 3 percent, $19.60 if the rate were 5 percent, and $14.22 if the rate were 7 percent. If the discount rate is zero, only 18/80 or 22 percent of the present value is derived from the first 18 years of the income stream; this percentage rises to 46, 60, and 71 for discount rates of 3, 5, and 7 percent. The present value at age 0 of the last 35 years of the income stream would account for 44, 19, 9, and 4 percent of the total present value with discount rates of 0, 3, 5, and 7 percent, respectively. Thus high discount rates are roughly equivalent to short planning horizons.

In columns 7, 8, 9, and 10 of Table 6.12, these four different discount rates have been applied to the total income figures in the bottom row of Table 6.9. The hypothetical income stream is not constant, but varies over the individual's life cycle. However, the proportionate reductions in the present value of this income stream with successively higher values of the discount rate are much like those previously

Table 6.11. Net Relationships Between Professional Salaries and Specified Characteristics: All Professions—1966 National Register

Characteristic	Percentage Difference from National Geometric Mean, 1966	Percentage of Respondents in Class
Highest academic degree		
Professional medical	38.9	2.5
Ph.D.	15.5	41.5
Master's	− 8.5	25.1
Bachelor's	−13.6	28.8
Other or not reported	−18.3	2.1
Primary work activity		
Management	14.9	23.0
Research and development	− 1.5	35.4
Production and inspection	− 5.5	7.9
Teaching	− 9.4	19.9
Other or not reported	− 2.3	13.8
Age		
Under 30	−12.8	13.8
30–34	− 4.2	17.6
35–39	1.9	19.2
40–44	4.7	17.0
45–54	5.9	22.0
55–64	2.7	8.8
65 and over	− 2.8	1.4
Not reported	− 1.5	0.2
Sex		
Male	1.1	93.4
Female	−15.0	6.6
Field of science		
Mathematics	13.3	9.6
Economics	11.6	5.7
Statistics	8.5	1.3
Physics	7.9	11.0
Anthropology	1.0	0.4
Meteorology	− 0.4	1.7
Sociology	− 0.6	1.5
Psychology	− 1.4	8.2
Earth sciences	− 2.7	7.9
Chemistry	− 4.7	27.2
Biological sciences	− 4.9	12.4
Linguistics	− 6.7	0.5
Agricultural sciences	−15.5	4.8
Other	3.7	7.7

Source. E. Melichar, "Factors Affecting 1966 Basic Salaries in the National Register Professions." Supplement to *American Economic Review*, **58** (December 1968), 66.

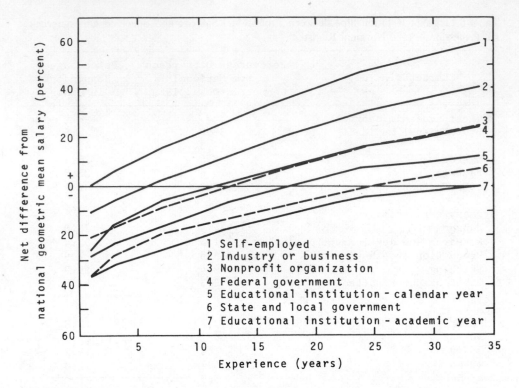

Figure 6.1.   Net relationship between professional salaries and years of experience by employer groups: all professions—1966 National Register. *Source.* E. Melichar, "Factors Affecting 1966 Basic Salaries in the National Register Professions." Supplement to *American Economic Review,* **58** (December 1968), 63.

described for the constant income stream. The percentages of total present value at age 0 contributed by the last 35 years of income are 47, 24, 13, and 7, with discount rates at 0, 3, 5, and 7 percent, respectively.

The choice of discount rates in comparing alternative life plans for an individual or evaluating the costs and benefits of medical and educational services provided to people of different ages can evidently be of great quantitative importance.

6.4   Life Cycle Models and the Holmes-Rahe (1967) Social Readjustment Rating Scale: The Impacts of Life Events on the Value of an Individual's Life Plan

Richard L. Meier (1972) reproduced Table 6.13 from a 1967 article by Thomas H. Holmes and Richard H. Rahe (1967) and made some additional comments based on papers by Masuda and Holmes (1967a, 1967b). Meier states:

> In subsequent studies a ratio scale for stressful events indicates that the making and breaking of close human relationships (bonds within small groups) are by far the strongest historic predictors of the onset of disease, while those of life style (including diet) and physical milieu are much less important, though still significant. Table [6.13] shows the relative weights

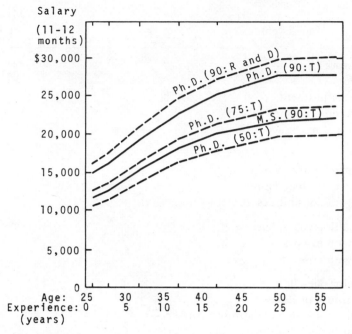

Figure 6.2.   Estimated 1968–1969 national salary structure for economists employed by educational institutions on an 11 to 12-month basis. *Source.* K. A. Fox, "Objective Functions and Optimization Models," in K. A. Fox, ed., *Economic Analysis for Educational Planning: Resource Allocation in Nonmarket Systems.* Baltimore: Johns Hopkins University Press, 1972, p. 319.

of these pathology-inducing events. Very surprisingly, the constitution of the relationship to characteristics of the person becoming ill, whether varied by his age, sex, social class, race, education, or the number of generations of acculturation in America, did not affect the weights to any significant degree. A comparable study in Japan revealed remarkable cross-cultural agreement. For the Japanese it was found that detention in jail and trial for minor violations of the law more often preceded illness, as did the threat of major personal injury, but in America marital conflicts and religious conversions are relatively more important (p. 299).

Rearrangement of the items in Table 6.13 into such categories as changes in relations with (1) spouse, (2) other family members, and (3) close friends, changes in job relations and lines of work, and other events affecting the respondent, suggests some interesting gradients of intensity of feeling. Consider the following clusters:

Life Event	Mean Value of Rating
Death of spouse	100
Death of close family member	63
Death of close friend	37
Divorce	73
Marital separation	65

Life Event	Mean Value of Rating
Fired at work	47
Retirement	45
Business readjustment	39
Change to different line of work	36
Foreclosure of mortgage or loan	30
Marriage	50
Gain of new family member	39
Son or daughter leaving home	29
Change in responsibilities at work	29
Sex difficulties with spouse	39
Trouble with in-laws	29
Trouble with boss	23
Jail term for oneself	63
Personal injury or illness	53
Change in health of close family member	44
Change in financial state	38
Change in number of arguments with spouse	35
Wife begins or stops work	26
Begin or end school (oneself)	26
Change in work hours or conditions	20
Change in living conditions	25
Revision of personal habits	24
Change in residence	20
Change in schools	20
Change in recreation	19
Change in church activities	19
Change in social activities	18
Change in sleeping habits	16
Change in eating habits	15
Vacation	13
Christmas	12
Minor violations of the law	11

Unsurprisingly, the intensity of stress felt by a respondent in connection with objectively comparable events is highest when they involve his spouse or himself and next highest if they happen to close family members or if they impinge on his career or job. If a weight of 1.0 is assigned to a given event happening to the respondent or his spouse, it appears that a weight of 0.6 or 0.7 could be assigned to comparable events involving close family members or career and job. The ratings are mean values for a number of respondents, and individual variations evidently exist, although Meier states that they are not significantly related to "age, sex, social class, race, education or the number of generations of acculturation in America."

Table 6.12. Present Values at Age 0 of Total Income Flows (Table 6.9) at Various Discount Rates and at Specified Life Stages, for an Individual

Life Stage Number	Period Number	Age Range (years) (1)	Age at Midpoint (years) (2)	Duration (years) (3)	Present Value at Age 0 of a Unit of Income at Midpoint Age			Present Value at Age 0 of Table 6.9 Total Income in Each Period			
					i=0.03 (4)	i=0.05 (5)	i=0.07 (6)	i=0 (7)	i=0.03 (8)	i=0.05 (9)	i=0.07 (10)
1	1	0.0- 0.9	1	1	0.971	0.952	0.935	220	214	209	206
2	2	1.0- 2.9	2	2	0.943	0.907	0.873	520	490	472	454
3	3	3.0- 4.9	4	2	0.888	0.823	0.763	600	533	494	458
4	4	5.0-13.9	10	9	0.744	0.614	0.508	3,420	2,544	2,100	1,737
5	5	14.0-17.9	16	4	0.623	0.458	0.339	1,800	1,121	824	610
6	6	18.0-24.9	22	7	0.522	0.342	0.226	3,920	2,046	1,341	886
7	7	25.0-34.9	30	10	0.412	0.231	0.131	6,200	2,554	1,432	812
7	8	35.0-44.9	40	10	0.307	0.142	0.067	6,650	2,042	944	446
7	9	45.0-54.9	50	10	0.228	0.087	0.034	6,900	1,573	600	235
8	10	55.0-64.9	60	10	0.170	0.054	0.017	6,600	1,122	356	112
8	11	65.0-74.9	70	10	0.126	0.033	0.009	5,350	674	177	48
8	12	75.0-79.9	78	5	0.100	0.022	0.005	2,050	205	45	10
Total, ages 0-79.9				80	30.201	19.596	14.222	44,230	15,118	8,994	6,014
Subtotals											
Ages 0.0-17.9				18	13.754	11.690	10.059	6,560	4,902	4,099	3,465
Ages 18.0-44.9				27	10.765	6.084	3.547	16,770	6,642	3,717	2,144
Ages 45.0-79.9				35	5.682	1.822	0.616	20,900	3,574	1,178	405

Table 6.13. Social Readjustment Rating Scale

Rank	Life Event	Mean Value
1	Death of spouse	100
2	Divorce	73
3	Marital separation	65
4	Jail term	63
5	Death of close family member	63
6	Personal injury or illness	53
7	Marriage	50
8	Fired at work	47
9	Marital reconciliation	45
10	Retirement	45
11	Change in health of family member	44
12	Pregnancy	40
13	Sex difficulties	39
14	Gain of new family member	39
15	Business readjustment	39
16	Change in financial state	38
17	Death of close friend	37
18	Change to different line of work	36
19	Change in number of arguments with spouse	35
20	Mortgage over $10,000	31
21	Foreclosure of mortgage or loan	30
22	Change in responsibilities at work	29
23	Son or daughter leaving home	29
24	Trouble with in-laws	29
25	Outstanding personal achievement	28
26	Wife begin or stop work	26
27	Begin or end school	26
28	Change in living conditions	25
29	Revision of personal habits	24
30	Trouble with boss	23
31	Change in work hours or conditions	20
32	Change in residence	20
33	Change in schools	20
34	Change in recreation	19
35	Change in church activities	19
36	Change in social activities	18
37	Mortgage or loan less than $10,000	17
38	Change in sleeping habits	16
39	Change in number of family get-togethers	15
40	Change in eating habits	15
41	Vacation	13
42	Christmas	12
43	Minor violations of the law	11

Source. Thomas H. Holmes and Richard H. Rahe, "The Social Readjustment Rating Scale," *Journal of Psychosomatic Research* **11** (1967), Table 3, p. 216.

Some of the changes in life style (in the last cluster of items) can be interpreted as a change in the pattern of occupancy of genotype and/or specific behavior settings. The stress associated with such a change should bear some relation to the proportion of his total resources the individual has been using in the settings abandoned or cut off.

Some of the life events have financial implications. For example, a voluntary change in responsibilities at work, or to a different line of work, may be motivated by a guaranteed increase in salary. If the change is made at (say) age 40 and the person expects to gain $4000 a year (relative to his old job) for 25 years, a financial magnitude of $100,000 is associated with the change. However, we must discount the income stream if we wish to arrive at a present value that might reasonably motivate the person now, at the time he makes his decision. At discount rates of 3, 5, and 7 percent, the present value of the $100,000 shrinks to $47,761, $29,530, and $18,425, respectively.

If the same discount rate applies to all components of the person's expected total income stream, the *ratio* of the present values of the benefits and costs associated with the change will be the same regardless of the discount rate chosen, *if* the cost and benefit streams have the same time shape. If the time shapes are different, a high discount rate will assign larger proportions of the total present values to the first few years of the income streams than will a moderate or low one, and the ratio of benefits to costs will depend on the rate chosen.

Suppose that the well-being of a person at age 34 is characterized by the resource flows in column 7 of Table 6.9 and the present values at age 34 of the resource flows in columns 8 through 12. A life event occurring when the person is 34 could be viewed as changing certain of these resource flows in specified time periods. The readjustments after Christmas or a vacation would presumably be completed within a few weeks; they could be regarded as normal seasonal variations in the flows of total income and its components—variations around the annual averages shown in Table 6.9. The readjustment after the death of a spouse or close family member would extend over a number of years; a jail term might, in effect, place a permanent ceiling on a person's money income, prestige, and power in formal organizations. A serious accident or illness at age 34 might permanently reduce the individual's earning power and his capacity to engage in valued activities.

To the extent that some of the life events listed by Holmes and Rahe (1967) have direct financial consequences or have a tradition of financial indemnity under workmen's compensation or other laws, it appears that reasonable dollar-equivalent values might be assigned to the remaining events with respect to any given individual. The numerical ratings assigned by Holmes and Rahe (Table 6.13) may not be cardinally related to changes in the present values of an individual's expected income streams, but an attempt to integrate the concepts underlying Tables 6.9, 6.12, and 6.13 might have important consequences for social accounts and indicators.

VII

National Goals Accounting and Policy Models

So FAR, WE HAVE EMPHASIZED concepts relating to individuals and (at most) families. We have pointed out that measures of the total incomes (in dollar equivalents) of different individuals can be added up to form totals for a nation or any other aggregate of individuals.

But most of the interest in social indicators has been directed toward aggregative measures for the nation as a whole and for metropolitan areas and other territorial units. For example, Senator Mondale in 1967 proposed an annual social report of the President, a Council of Social Advisers, and a Joint Committee (of Congress) on the Social Report—all presumably to focus on national trends and policy concerns. Economic indicators, accounts, and policy models have also emphasized national concerns.

Biderman (1966) examined *Goals for Americans*, the report of the President's Commission on National Goals (1960), and enumerated 81 specific goals. He then searched *Statistical Abstract of the United States 1962* and *Historical Statistics of the United States from Colonial Times to 1957* to see "for how many of the commission's goals any relevant indicators could be found" (p. 87). He did not require that the indicators be measures of attainment of a specific goal, only that they be at least remotely related to phenomena that were pertinent to each goal statement.

Biderman decided that the two volumes contained data pertinent to only 48 of the 81 specific goals. Some major goal areas had better statistical support than others, as suggested by the following tabulation (aggregated from the 11 goal areas in Biderman's Table 2.1, p. 88):

Major Goal Areas	Number of Specific Goals	Number of Goals to Which Some Indicator Is Relevant
Health and welfare, economic growth, education, agriculture, equality	32	30

Major Goal Areas	Number of Specific Goals	Number of Goals to Which Some Indicator Is Relevant
Democratic economy, the individual, democratic process	26	13
Living conditions, technological change, arts and sciences	23	5
	—	—
Total, all 11 major areas	81	48

Since 1960, the National Planning Association (NPA) has conducted a number of studies relating to national goals. Some of this work has been reported by Lecht (1966) and Terleckyj (1970, 1971).

As of 1973, the NPA Goals Accounting Study, under the direction of Nestor E. Terleckyj, was well advanced. The following section is based on his "Estimating Possibilities for Improvement in the Quality of Life in the United States, 1972–1981," in the NPA's monthly publication *Looking Ahead* (January 1973, pp. 1–12). A book-length report, similarly titled (Terleckyj, 1973b), was in second draft stage in mid-1973.

7.1   Nestor Terleckyj's Framework for National Goals Accounting (1973)

Terleckyj (1973a) states that

> A wide-ranging search is currently underway to develop better means by which social and institutional performance can be judged (p. 1).

> NPA's present work is related to this search. It represents an *attempt to devise an analytical framework for systematically assessing possibilities for social change.* More specifically, it focuses on the *possibilities for effecting change in social conditions that represent particular aspects of the quality of life, conditions that are measured by a set of quantitative indicators* (p. 2).

> The analytical system for estimating possibilities for social change is based on the following six elements:

> 1. *selection and definition of areas of concern (such as health and public safety) and identification of indicators (such as average life expectancy and the rate of violent crime) to measure those social conditions that are the main objects of the given concerns. . . .*

> 2. *projection of trend levels of the conditions measured by the indicators and of resource uses associated with various categories of objectives. . . .*

> 3. *a distinction between fixed and discretionary activities in society, on the part of individuals, private institutions and governments. . . .*

> 4. *identification of discretionary activities, their cost and their effect on the conditions selected for measurement by the indicators. . . .*

> 5. *projections of the resources available for discretionary activities* broken down by two subperiods (first four vs. later six years) and into public and private components. . . .

> 6. *calculation of the maximum feasible output of combinations of discretionary ac-*

tivities which can be undertaken within the estimated resource supply. These are derived by making "least-cost" calculations for different combinations of output, and serve as benchmark estimates of the maximum potential for achieving social improvements that are both technically and economically feasible. . . .

Elements (1) to (4) are combined within a set of productive relationships linking resource cost to improvements in the different conditions measured by the indicators.

All estimates used in this study are highly tentative, primarily because the knowledge that would permit more concrete estimates simply does not exist. To the extent possible in a research study of this scope, the best available information has been utilized. In successive revisions, new knowledge, data and analysis will be incorporated; but, in view of the limitations of basic knowledge, this progress will no doubt be gradual. Yet, without repeated attempts to make such preliminary estimates, it would be difficult, if not impossible, to gain an understanding of those areas in which data and analysis are most needed and of the directions in which they can be applied most productively (p. 3).

The national goal output indicators and activities in Terleckyj's model are of great substantive interest, and we list them in full.

Goal Output Indicators.   In the heading of his Table 1 (p. 4), Terleckyj lists 22 goal output indicators, as follows:

Health and safety:
 1. Average life expectancy at birth—years.
 2. Number of persons with major disabilities—millions.
 3. Number of violent crimes per 100,000 persons per year.

Education, skills, and earnings:
 4. Index of performance in education based on standard tests.
 5. Number of persons completing college—thousands.
 6. Number of persons not in the mainstream of labor force—millions.
 7. Median earnings of individuals, 1971 dollars—thousands.

Adequacy and continuity of income:
 8. Number of persons below poverty standard—millions.
 9. Number of persons in near-poverty conditions—millions.
10. Number of persons with living standard loss of over 30 percent—millions.

Economic equality:
11. Age adjusted family income ratio—20th percentile to 90th.
12. Mean family income, Negroes as a percentage of whites.
13. Hourly earnings of women as percent of earnings of men (adjusted).

Human habitat:
14. Percentage of persons living in adequate houses.
15. Percentage of persons living in satisfactory neighborhoods.
16. Number of persons exposed to bothersome pollution—millions.
17. Percentage of persons regularly taking part in recreation.
18. Number of areas maintained for preservation of life and natural forms.

Science and art: [1]

19. Number of scientists active in basic science—thousands.
20. Number of active artists—thousands.

Leisure and GNP: [2]

21. Time free from work and chores—hours per person per year.
22. GNP—billions of 1971 dollars.

Terleckyj presents the numerical value of each goal output indicator in 1971 and a 1981 "base value," which assumes that current trends continue. Thus the 1971 figure for average life expectancy at birth is 71.0 and the 1981 base value is 72.4. Various activities may be undertaken to improve the actual values of the goal output indicators in 1981. For example, Terleckyj estimates that a program to change health-related habits and patterns could increase average life expectancy as of 1981 by a maximum of 4.8 years over the 1981 base of 72.4; he estimates the total cost of the program over the 1972–1981 period as $66 billion (in 1971 dollars). This program would also affect certain other goal output indicators, reducing the number of persons with major disabilities and the number of violent crimes per person per year. Furthermore, life expectancy would be affected by other activities—health services related to specific conditions, special health services for vulnerable population groups, and improved recreation facilities in neighborhoods.

Activities.   Terleckyj lists 31 activities for improving the levels of the 22 goal output indicators. Certain activities affect only one goal output while others have impacts on two or more:

> In most cases, the effects of multiple activities on the given indicator are not additive. When undertaken at the same time, these activities may either interfere with each other or achieve the *maximum possible effect on the given indicator at levels lower than their full capacity.* Therefore, the possible combined effect of more than one activity directed toward the same social area is, as a rule, less than the sum of the individual effects of each activity taken separately. To a considerable extent, then, identification of multiple activities reflects the existence of alternative approaches. The maximum effect of all activities relevant to a particular indicator, if pursued together, is shown on the bottom line in Table 1. For the life expectancy indicator, this effect is 8.5 years compared to the sum of individual effects of 10.1 years (p. 5).

The 31 activities are listed in Terleckyj's Chart A (pp. 7–8). The author does not group them, since many of the activities would affect goal output indicators in two or more major categories; this is shown by the many nonzero elements in Table 7.2 that lie far below or above the major diagonal. For expository purposes, I have grouped them under nine headings that should be regarded as descriptive rather than operational classifications, although they correspond as much as possible to blocks of nonzero coefficients around the major diagonal.

[1] Terleckyj included *free time* (item 21) in this group under the heading "arts, science, and free time."
[2] Terleckyj placed GNP in a category by itself. I have combined leisure and GNP because they are both basic, highly flexible resources.

Health-related:
1. Changing health-related habits and patterns.
2. Health services related to specific conditions.
3. Special health services for vulnerable population groups.

Law enforcement, and opportunities for the young:
4. Improvement of law enforcement systems.
5. Full employment and opportunities for the young.

Education: elementary and secondary, and day care:
6. Selective expansion of conventional school inputs.
7. Remedial tutoring and augmentation of educational inputs.
8. Improved educational technology and new educational approaches.
9. General day care for children.

Higher education, updating of job skills, and training for workers outside the mainstream of labor force:
10. Universal free higher education.
11. Structural improvements in higher education.
12. Maintenance, updating, and improvement of job skills.
13. Specialized training for workers outside the mainstream of labor force.

Private and public retirement pensions and programs to abolish poverty:
14. Private savings, insurance, and pension plans.
15. Provision of old age pensions up to 42 percent of current earnings.
16. Extension of welfare programs to abolish poverty and near-poverty.

Depressed communities, housing, neighborhood, city and regional design, and transportation systems:
17. Aid to depressed communities.
18. Construction and maintenance of houses.
19. Design and testing of new neighborhood, city, and regional environments.
20. Innovations in cars, roads, and other transportation system components.

Pollution control, environment, parks, scenery, design:
21. Pollution control.
22. Basic environmental improvements.
23. Provision of recreation facilities in neighborhoods.
24. Creation of major parks and facilities.
25. Preservation of wilderness and scenery.
26. The encouragement of beauty and good design.

Arts and science:
27. Increased support for pure science.
28. Increased support for the arts.

Longer vacations, early retirement, and time-saving innovations:
29. Provision of three weeks' additional vacation.
30. Retirement at age 60.
31. Extended use of time-saving innovations.

The figures in Table 7.1 are reproduced directly from Terleckyj's article (1973a). Column 1 shows the 1971 values of the 22 goal output indicators, and column 2 gives their projected values in 1981 if recent trends continue. Column 3 displays the maximum additional effects on 1981 values of the indicators if the 31 discretionary activities listed previously were carried out during 1972–1981 at specified levels. The total cost of these 31 activities over the 1972–1981 decade is estimated by Terleckyj at $3563 billion 1971 dollars.

It should be stressed that the total cost and simultaneous occurrence of all 31 activities is not economically feasible even when it is technically feasible; therefore, the tradeoffs between the various goal outputs are an essential part of Terleckyj's analysis. Resource constraints impose a fairly strict ceiling on what is actually feasible within the domain of the technically feasible.

7.2 Some Relations Between Terleckyj's Concepts and Those in the Fox-Van Moeseke Model

Some of Terleckyj's goal output indicators can be related to the group 1, 2, 3, and 4 resources ascribed to individuals in our earlier chapters. Thus health and safety goals relate mainly to group 1 resources, and education, skill and earnings goals to groups 3 and 4. Adequacy and continuity of income goals and goals of economic equality involve directly the distribution of money income (group 4) and indirectly an increase in prestige and power (group 4) and self-respect (group 2).

Human habitat goals relate in part to improved health (group 1) and in part to improvements in the physical and aesthetic qualities of behavior settings that may operate through self-respect and human dignity (group 2) and prestige or status (group 4). Preservation of wildlife and natural forms appeals to group 2 (value commitments). Science and art goals in this context seem to be largely matters of value commitment (group 2), although basic science may also advance all the other goals mentioned. The leisure and GNP goals involve increases in money income (group 4) and in discretionary time (i.e., time not committed to work, housework, and family tasks). Discretionary time should contribute to health (group 1), value commitments (group 2), "other skills," not work-related (group 3), and prestige and political power (group 4).

Most or all of Terleckyj's activities can be described in terms of changes in the pattern of occupancy of behavior settings and/or changes in the quality levels at which behavior settings are operated.

7.3 An Adaptation of Terleckyj's System to Illustrate the Structure of a Policy Model

In this section we use data from Terleckyj's basic goals-and-activities matrix (Table 1, p. 4, Terleckyj, 1973a) to illustrate the structure of a policy model and to describe the coordination problem associated with it. We are not concerned here with Terleckyj's numerical estimates but only with the structure of his matrix, which reflects careful study of the real structure of this country's economy and society. It therefore provides a realistic example with considerable intrinsic interest instead of a purely hypothetical one to which we might otherwise resort.

Suppose that the 22 indicator values for 1971 measure the "position" of the United States social system—that is, they are the coordinates of a point (call it point 1) in 22-dimensional space. A change in the value of the ith indicator means that the

Table 7.1. NPA National Goals Accounting Study: Goal Output Indicators, 1971 Actual, 1981 (Trend), and Maximum Additional Effects of Discretionary Activities on 1981 Position

Goal Output Indicators and Units of Measure	Base 1971 (1)	Base 1981 (2)	Maximum Additional Effect of Identified Activities 1981 (3)
1 Average life expectancy at birth (years)	71.0	72.4	8.5
2 Number of persons with major disabilities (millions)	33.4	34.8	-15.7
3 Number of violent crimes (per 100,000 persons per year)	591	981	-687
4 Index of performance in education (based on standard tests)	100	105	29
5 Number of persons completing college (thousands per year)	816	1200	1550
6 Number of persons not in the mainstream of labor force (millions)	9.0	6.7	-6.7
7 Median earnings of individuals (1971 dollars, thousands)	5.2	6.9	1.3
8 Number of persons below poverty standard (millions)	25	19	-19
9 Number of persons in near-poverty conditions (millions)	15	9	-9

10 Number of persons with living standard loss of more than 30 percent (millions)	17	19	-15
11 Age adjusted family income ratio (20th percentile to 90th)	34	39	6
12 Mean family income; Negroes as a percent of whites	65	72	13
13 Hourly earnings of women as percent of earnings of men (adjusted)	60	60	12
14 Percent of persons living in adequate houses	87	92	8
15 Percent of persons living in satisfactory neighborhoods	75	85	15
16 Number of persons exposed to bothersome pollution (millions)	135	110	-87
17 Percent of persons regularly taking part in recreation	14	28	38
18 Number of areas maintained for preservation of life and natural forms	400	450	450
19 Number of scientists active in basic science (thousands)	72	130	85
20 Number of active artists (thousands)	88	149	321
21 Time free from work and chores (hours per person per year)	2303	2399	729
22 GNP (billions of 1971 dollars)	1050	1662	178

Source. Nestor E. Terleckyj, "Estimating Possibilities for Improvement in the Quality of Life in the United States, 1972–1981," *Looking Ahead,* **20**, No. 10 (January 1973), 1–12. (National Planning Association, 1606 New Hampshire Ave., N.W., Washington, D. C.)

point changes its position in a direction parallel to the ith axis but does not move parallel to any of the other 21 axes. The 1981 base values specify a second point (point 2) in 22-space, and the maximum additional effects in column 3 of Table 7.1, if added to the 1981 base values, specify a third (point 3). The social system will move from point 1 in 1971 to point 2 in 1981 if recent trends continue; it can be moved from point 1 in 1971 to point 3 in 1981 by operating 31 discretionary activities at specified levels of program costs.

If for the sake of illustration each activity is regarded as a policy input or instrument, the 31 cost figures associated with each of the three points in the goal output or target space will specify a point in a 31-dimensional instrument space; call them point $1(i)$, point $2(i)$, and point $3(i)$ respectively.[3] Points $1(i)$ and $2(i)$ are at the origin of the coordinate system and are represented by vectors of 31 zeros. Point $3(i)$ is represented by a vector of 31 cost estimates totaling $3563 billion. The movement of the instrument vector from point $2(i)$ to point $3(i)$ has the net effect of moving the goal output (target) vector from point 2 to point 3.

Table 7.2 is based on Terleckyj's estimates of the contribution of each of the 31 activities to each of the 22 output indicators. The coefficients in each row add up to 1.00; they allocate the maximum additional effect in column 3 of Table 7.1 among the activities that contributed to it, on the assumption that these effects are linear and additive. (This assumption is made only to simplify our exposition.)

In the units of Table 7.2, point 2 becomes a vector of 22 zeros and point 3 a vector of 22 ones; point $2(i)$ is a vector of 31 zeros and point $3(i)$ is an allocation vector of 31 proportions of total costs adding up to 1.000. If the allocation vector is held constant, a 1 percent increase in total activity costs implies a 1 percent increase in each of the 31 activity levels. This in turn leads to an increase of 1 percent in each of the 22 goal outputs.

Is it worthwhile to move the social system from $(0, 0, \ldots, 0)$ to $(1, 1, \ldots, 1)$ at a cost of $3563 billion? That depends on the equivalent dollar value, v_i, $i = 1, 2, \ldots, 22$, attributed to a change of one unit in each of the 22 goal indicators. The total value of the outputs of activity 1 operated at a cost level of $(.019)(3563) = $68 billion would be $(.47 v_1 + .43 v_2 + .18 v_3 + .09 v_{10} + .30 v_{17} + .08 v_{21})$; total output values or benefits could be similarly calculated for each of the other 30 activities. Since the dollar costs of each activity are given by Terleckyj and can be constructed (except for rounding errors) from the allocation vector in Table 7.2 and Terleckyj's total cost figure of $3563 billion, a benefit–cost ratio could then be calculated for each activity and also for the movement of the entire system from point 2 to point 3 in the 22-space of benefits and from point $2(i)$ to point $3(i)$ in the 31-space of costs.

It is difficult, of course, to determine appropriate dollar values for some of the v_i, since the different goals are not obviously comparable. Table 7.3 assumes that the problem of comparability can be solved satisfactorily within each of seven clusters of goals. The symbol A_{68} stands for a matrix of two rows and two columns in which the Table 7.2 coefficients in each row have been multiplied by the appropriate v_i.

---

[3] Actually, Terleckyj's activities represent technological possibilities and not program or policy elements. In practice, to identify specific policy elements or units within Terleckyj's model of activities, additional matrix information would be required to disaggregate the organizational components, the output indicators, and the time periods.

If the two activities represented in the two columns are combined in fixed proportions as in the allocation vector of Table 7.2, a 1 percent increase in the cost level of activity group 8 will produce a 1 percent increase in the output attributed to A_{68}. The six zeros in the "science and art" *column* indicate that no other goal cluster will be affected by the increase in activity group 8. However, the symbol A_{64} in the "science and art" *row* indicates that the output of goal cluster 6 is also affected by activity group 4, "higher education and skills." If the level of activity group 4 is chosen primarily because of its effects on goal clusters 7, 2, 3, and 4, the A_{64} contribution to goal cluster 6 is essentially a by-product; the level of activity group 8 could then be set to make up the gap between some output target for goal cluster 6 and the contribution to it through A_{64} by activity group 4.

Activity groups 7 and 5 each affect two goal clusters, whereas groups 1, 9, 6, 2, 4, and 3 each affect four or five goal clusters. Conversely, goal clusters 6 and 1 are affected by two and three activity groups, respectively; cluster 5 is affected by four, clusters 7 and 2 by five, and clusters 3 and 4 by six! Thus if specific targets are to be met for each of the seven goal clusters, the levels of the nine activity groups must be carefully coordinated.

It appears intuitively that activity groups 8, 7, and 5, which affect only one or two goal clusters each, would be particularly useful and flexible policy instruments, requiring only moderate degrees of interagency coordination. More generally, the pattern of zeros in the first three rows and first three columns of the Table 7.3 matrix (28 zeros out of 39) implies that the number of major interactions among these three goal clusters and activity groups, and between them and the remaining clusters and groups, is limited. For example, activity groups 3 and 5 have no effects on any of the first three goal clusters, and activity groups 9, 6, 2, and 4 each affect only one of the three. Similarly, activity groups 8 and 7 have no effects on any of the four remaining goal clusters, and activity group 1 affects only two of the four.

In contrast, the remaining block of 24 elements formed by activity groups 9, 6, 2, 4, 3, and 5 and goal clusters 7, 2, 3, and 4 contains only four zeros. Evidently, plans relating these six activity groups to the four goal clusters mentioned should be carefully coordinated.

To simplify the exposition, we drop the terms "cluster" and "group" and assume that the matrix expresses the relations between seven individual goals, y_i, $i = 1, 2, \ldots, 7$, and nine individual instruments, $z_j, j = 1, 2, \ldots, 9$, as follows:

$$
\begin{bmatrix} y_6 \\ y_5 \\ y_1 \\ \text{--} \\ y_7 \\ y_2 \\ y_3 \\ y_4 \end{bmatrix} = \begin{matrix} \begin{bmatrix} z_8 & z_7 & z_1 & z_9 & z_6 & z_2 & z_4 & z_3 & z_5 \end{bmatrix} \\ \begin{bmatrix} a_{68} & 0 & 0 & 0 & 0 & 0 & a_{64} & 0 & 0 \\ 0 & a_{57} & a_{51} & a_{59} & a_{56} & 0 & 0 & 0 & 0 \\ 0 & a_{17} & a_{11} & 0 & 0 & a_{12} & 0 & 0 & 0 \\ \hline 0 & 0 & a_{71} & a_{79} & a_{76} & 0 & a_{74} & a_{73} & 0 \\ 0 & 0 & 0 & a_{29} & a_{26} & a_{22} & a_{24} & a_{23} & 0 \\ 0 & 0 & a_{31} & 0 & a_{36} & a_{32} & a_{34} & a_{33} & a_{35} \\ 0 & 0 & 0 & a_{49} & a_{46} & a_{42} & a_{44} & a_{43} & a_{45} \end{bmatrix} \end{matrix} \tag{1}
$$

The z_j's are placed above the appropriate columns.

Table 7.2. Illustrative Calculations Based on NPA National Goals Accounting Study: Linearized and Normalized Version of Terleckyj's Matrix, Relating Maximum Additional Effects on Goal Output Indicators, 1981, to Total Costs of Discretionary Activities During 1972–1981

Goal Output Indicator Number	Change in Level of Indicator (normalized)	1	2	3	4	5	6
		Proportions of Total Change					
1	1.00	.47	.17	.25			
2	1.00	.43	.39	.12			
3	1.00	.18	.11		.36	.35	
4	1.00					.10	.15
5	1.00						
6	1.00					.10	
7	1.00						
8	1.00					.05	
9	1.00					.04	
10	1.00	.09	.05				
11	1.00						
12	1.00					.11	
13	1.00						
14	1.00						
15	1.00						
16	1.00						
17	1.00	.30					
18	1.00						
19	1.00						
20	1.00						
21	1.00	.08	.07				
22	1.00						
Proportion of total cost of activities	1.000	.019	.017	.024	.014	.015	.030

Table 7.2. (*Continued*)

7	8	9	10	11	12	13	14	15

in Each Indicator Produced by Specified Activities

7	8	9	10	11	12	13	14	15
.35	.40							
.02	.02		.50	.21	.25			
		.12			.20	.39		
.08	.08		.15	.08	.15			
		.10			.05	.08	.05	.10
		.13	.04		.09	.04	.07	.07
							.45	.27
		.33	.11		.22	.11		
.05			.05		.21	.16	.05	.05
		.33			.50			
			.21	.21	.10			
			.10	.03	.05			
		.16						
.07	.07	.17	.11	.04	.13	.07		
.020	.048	.033	.082	.018	.095	.024	.056	.018

Table 7.2. Illustrative Calculations Based on NPA National Goals Accounting Study (*Continued*)

Goal Output Indicator Number	Change in Level of Indicator (normalized)	16	17	18	19	20	21
		Proportions of Total Change					
1	1.00						
2	1.00						
3	1.00						
4	1.00						
5	1.00						
6	1.00		.19				
7	1.00		.15				
8	1.00	.49	.05	.03			
9	1.00	.39	.09	.04			
10	1.00	.14					
11	1.00		.22				
12	1.00	.16	.11	.05			
13	1.00						
14	1.00		.29	.57	.14		
15	1.00		.16	.12	.31		.16
16	1.00		.03	.03	.14	.07	.42
17	1.00		.06		.08		
18	1.00						
19	1.00						
20	1.00						
21	1.00					.10	
22	1.00		.14				
Proportion of total cost of activities	1.000	.020	.045	.028	.053	.041	.050

Source. Calculations (by Karl A. Fox) based on Table 1, p. 4, in Nestor E. Terleckyj, "Estimating Possibilities for Improvement in the Quality of Life in the United States, 1972–1981."

Table 7.2. (*Continued*)

in Each Indicator Produced by Specified Activities

22	23	24	25	26	27	28	29	30	31
	.11								
	.06								
									.31
									.17
	.16			.09					
.25				.06					
.12	.24	.06						.06	.08
.22		.11	.67						
				.48					
						.82			
							.08	.07	.44
									.20
.087	.033	.021	.007	.014	.010	.007	.028	.019	.024

Looking Ahead, **20**, No. 10 (January 1973), 1–12. (National Planning Association, 1606 New Hampshire Ave., N.W., Washington, D. C.)

Table 7.3.   Aggregation and Rearrangement of Terleckyj's National Goals Accounting Matrix to Emphasize "Policy Structure": The Effects of Particular Groups of Activities (Instruments) on Particular Clusters of Goal Output Indicators (Targets)

Goal Cluster Number	National Goal Cluster	Maximum Additional Effect on Goals, 1981	8 Science and Art	7 Environ- ment	1 Health Programs
6	Science and art	1.00	A_{68}	0	0
5	Human habitat	1.00	0	A_{57}	A_{51}
1	Health and safety	1.00	0	A_{17}	A_{11}
7	Leisure and GNP	1.00	0	0	A_{71}
2	Education, skills, and earnings	1.00	0	0	0
3	Adequacy and continuity of income	1.00	0	0	A_{31}
4	Economic equality	1.00	0	0	0
	Proportion of total cost of activities	1.000	.017	.212	.060

We pose the coordination problem by specifying a target value y_i^* for each of the seven goals and considering how a set of values of the instruments might be selected to meet the seven targets exactly. A plausible procedure might be comprised of the following steps.

Step 1.   Consider the four targets y_7^*, y_2^*, y_3^*, and y_4^* and the six instruments z_9, z_6, z_2, z_4, z_3, and z_5. Under the terms of our problem, the four targets could be achieved exactly with any set of four of these six instruments. There are 15 possible combinations of six things taken four at a time; however, each of the 15 solutions obtained in this way would leave two of the six instruments at the zero level. However, since appropriately weighted combinations of any two or more of these 15 solution sets of four z_j's would also achieve the four targets exactly, there exists an infinite number of sets of values of the six instruments exactly meeting the targets.

As a by-product, whatever set is selected will make some contributions (positive or negative) to the other three goals y_6, y_5, and y_1, by way of the coefficients a_{64}, a_{59}, and a_{56}. The amounts of these goal outputs that must be obtained by purposeful action are, therefore,

$$y_6' = y_6^* - a_{64}z_4, \tag{2}$$

Table 7.3. *(Continued)*

Activity Group Number					
9	6	2	4	3	5
Leisure-Increasing Programs	Housing and Transportation	Youth Opportunities	Higher Education and Skills	Elementary and Secondary Education	Income Maintenance
0	0	0	A_{64}	0	0
A_{59}	A_{56}	0	0	0	0
0	0	A_{12}	0	0	0
A_{79}	A_{76}	0	A_{74}	A_{73}	0
A_{29}	A_{26}	A_{22}	A_{24}	A_{23}	0
0	A_{36}	A_{32}	A_{34}	A_{33}	A_{35}
A_{49}	A_{46}	A_{42}	A_{44}	A_{43}	A_{45}
.071	.167	.029	.219	.131	.094

Source. Special aggregation and rearrangement (by Karl A. Fox) of figures in Table 7.2. Table 7.2 is based on Nestor E. Terleckyj, "Estimating Possibilities for Improvement in the Quality of Life in the United States, 1972–1981," *Looking Ahead*, **20**, No. 10 (January 1973), 1–12. (National Planning Association, 1606 New Hampshire Ave., N.W., Washington, D. C.)

$$y_5' = y_5{}^* - a_{59}z_9 - a_{56}z_6, \tag{3}$$

$$y_1' = y_1{}^* - a_{12}z_2. \tag{4}$$

Step 2. We can now use the three remaining instruments z_8, z_7, and z_1 to produce y_6', y_5', and y_1' exactly, thus satisfying the targets $y_6{}^*$, $y_5{}^*$, and $y_1{}^*$. Two of the instruments, z_8 and z_7, do not affect the other four goals; however, z_1 contributes the amount $a_{71}z_1$ to y_7 and the amount $a_{31}z_1$ to y_3.

Step 3. At the end of step 2, five targets were being met exactly, but y_7 and y_3 were off the marks by $a_{71}z_1$ and $a_{31}z_1$, respectively. However, any attempt to reach $y_7{}^*$ and $y_3{}^*$ exactly by changing the levels of two instruments would displace some other goals from their target values. We can isolate $y_6{}^*$ from the interconnected system by holding z_8 and z_4 at the values they reached at the ends of steps 2 and 1, respectively. If we also hold z_7 at the level reached at the end of step 2, we can make a final adjustment in which changes in z_1, z_9, z_6, z_2, z_3, and z_5 are used to hold y_5, y_1, y_2, and y_4 at their target values while restoring y_7 and y_3 to their target values $v_7{}^*$ and $y_3{}^*$:

$$
\begin{bmatrix} \Delta y_5 \\ \Delta y_1 \\ \hline \Delta y_7 \\ \Delta y_2 \\ \Delta y_3 \\ \Delta y_4 \end{bmatrix}
=
\begin{bmatrix} 0 \\ 0 \\ \hline a_{71}z_1 \\ 0 \\ a_{31}z_1 \\ 0 \end{bmatrix}
=
\begin{bmatrix}
a_{51} & a_{59} & a_{56} & 0 & 0 & 0 \\
a_{11} & 0 & 0 & a_{12} & 0 & 0 \\
\hline
a_{71} & a_{79} & a_{76} & 0 & a_{73} & 0 \\
0 & a_{29} & a_{26} & a_{22} & a_{23} & 0 \\
a_{31} & 0 & a_{36} & a_{32} & a_{33} & a_{35} \\
0 & a_{49} & a_{46} & a_{42} & a_{43} & a_{45}
\end{bmatrix}
\begin{bmatrix} \Delta z_1 & \Delta z_9 & \Delta z_6 & \Delta z_2 & \Delta z_3 & \Delta z_5 \end{bmatrix}
\tag{5}
$$

In matrix notation we can write

$$\Delta y = A\ \Delta z; \tag{6}$$

hence

$$\Delta z = A^{-1}\ \Delta y, \tag{7}$$

yielding a set of six Δz_j values that will move the system into exact conformity with the targets $y_5{}^*$, $y_1{}^*$, $y_7{}^*$, $y_2{}^*$, $y_3{}^*$, and $y_4{}^*$.

We have more to say about the theory of policy coordination in the next section. By implication, Terleckyj is concerned with means of describing alternative positions of a social system and estimating the capacities of various sets of discretionary programs (using both public and private resources) to steer the social system to such positions. The goals chosen by a society may result from political processes at various levels, and the levels at which programs are funded (also as a result of political processes) may steer the social system at an angle to the direction implied by the stated goals.

Terleckyj's model provides a useful framework for thinking about all kinds of social indicators relevant to national policies. In Section 7.4 we set forth an approach that has been applied fruitfully to economic policy. Formally, it can be extended to the full range of goal output indicators and activities presented by Terleckyj. The usefulness of the extension will depend on further progress in measuring social system outputs and interrelationships among economic and noneconomic variables.

7.4   Jan Tinbergen's Theory of Economic Policy

Jan Tinbergen (1952, 1954, 1956) made a major breakthrough in the analysis of economic policies. Further extensions and applications have been made by Theil (1958, 1964), van Eijk and Sandee (1959), Fox, Sengupta, and Thorbecke (1966), and others. Tinbergen was primarily concerned with the development of consistent economic policies at the national level. However, his model can readily be adapted to smaller areas and political jurisdictions.

I developed Figure 7.1 in 1961 to provide a visual description of Tinbergen's framework (Fox, 1961) and have used it since in many other publications. For con-

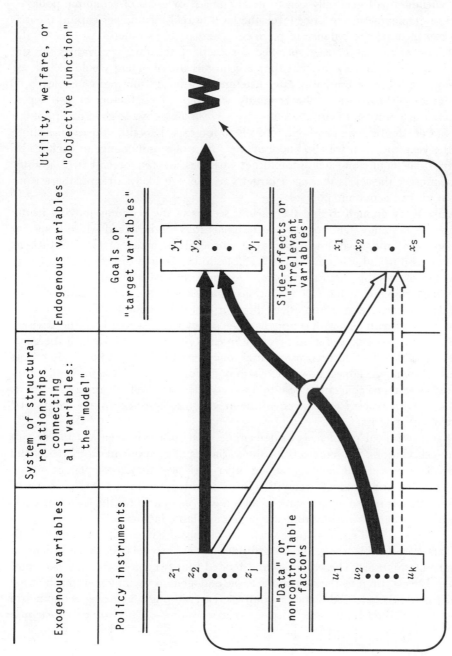

Figure 7.1. The theory of economic policy. Classification of variables is based on Jan Tinbergen. The "data" or noncontrollable factors are those not subject to control by the policy maker or level of government that sets the goals and uses the policy instruments in question.

creteness, let us assume that we are looking at the United States economy from the viewpoint (say) of a chairman of the Council of Economic Advisers.

Our first requirement is accurate knowledge of the workings of the economy. Certain variables will generally constitute the *targets* or goals of economic policy—the level of employment, the price level, the level of real income per capita, the distribution of income, the balance of payments, and perhaps others. Assume for the moment that values have been specified for each of the target variables for the coming year—let us simply say that they are targets the president would like to see the economy achieve (presumably after listening to advice from many people).

The actual performance of the economy will depend on factors of two types. First, there are a number of variables that are *not controllable* by the government of the United States; the best we can hope to do is to forecast the values they will assume during the year ahead. If we also know the net effect of a unit change in each of the noncontrollable factors on each of the target variables, we can forecast (with greater or less accuracy) the levels that each target variable will likely attain if there is no change in present economic policies.

If we are lucky enough to find the various sectors of the economy moving in the right directions at the right speeds, all the goals may be achieved without special effort. However, the government has at its disposal an array of *policy instruments* that can be used to influence the target variables in the desired direction if it appears that the noncontrollable factors (or "*data*," as Tinbergen calls them) will not do the job. These instruments include all the actions legally permitted to the federal government and its agencies that would affect the course of the economy.

To use these instruments with confidence, the policy maker (or at least the adviser) should know the net effect of a unit change in each instrument on each of the goals or target variables. In addition, use of the policy instruments will have side effects on other economic variables; however, we may decide that these are not sufficiently important to warrant concern. These minor variables, which Tinbergen refers to as "irrelevant" with respect to a given problem, are also affected by the "data" or noncontrollable factors.

The basic technical problem is to determine with sufficient accuracy the system of structural relations that connects all the variables and constitutes a model of the economy. This model will include, among other variables, major components of the national income and product accounts. Given an adequate model, the problem of economic policy is to use instruments in such a way as to achieve the specified goals in spite of disturbances arising from the noncontrollable factors.

Let us examine Tinbergen's approach more closely. First, all the variables in his scheme are measurable economic magnitudes. They are related by a system of simultaneous equations. The variables are divided into two categories, *exogenous* and *endogenous*. Effects run *from* the exogenous *to* the endogenous variables within the time unit for which the model is designed (usually a year, although the newer econometric models of the United States are based on quarterly data). The equation system is designed to answer the following questions.

1. Given a set of known or projected values of the exogenous variables for the coming year, what values of the endogenous variables are likely to emerge?
2. Given desired values of the target variables and forecasts of the noncontrollable

factors, what "settings" of the policy instruments are required to achieve the target values?

The second major element in Tinbergen's approach is introduced not by the economist but by the policy maker. In principle, the model of the economy is objective, reproducible, and nonpolitical—"value free." In Tinbergen's scheme, the policy maker is responsible for classifying the endogenous variables into those having significant effects on welfare (target variables) and those having negligible effects (irrelevant variables). He may judge also that a unit increase in target y_1 contributes three times as much to welfare as a unit increase in y_2 but only half as much as a unit increase in y_3. He classifies the exogenous variables into noncontrollable factors and potential instruments. For the most part, changes in both categories affect welfare through their influence on the target variables. However, the policy maker may decide that the use of certain instruments involves direct welfare losses that must be offset against the welfare gains resulting from the instruments' effects on the target variables.

Different policy makers would assign different value weights to the same target. Given the same facts about the structure of the economy and its current position, one might be willing to accept a 3 percent rise in prices to achieve a 1 percent increase in employment, while another would accept only a 1 percent price rise for the same employment gain. The two policy makers have different marginal rates of substitution between these goals—different value systems or "welfare functions," symbolized by the large W in Figure 7.1.

A More Technical Exposition.   Tinbergen (1939) was the first to construct an econometric model of a national economy. Later, his series of books on the theory of economic policy supplied a bold new interpretation of the relationship of econometric models to the practical formulation of economic policies. For these contributions, Tinbergen (jointly with Ragnar Frisch) received the first Nobel prize in economics in 1969.[4]

The three basic ingredients of Tinbergen's quantitative economic policy model are as follows: a welfare function W of the policy maker which is a function of I target variables y_i and J instrument variables z_j; a quantitative model M, which sets up statistical or empirical relationships essentially between the I target variables and the J instrument variables; and a set of boundary conditions or constraints on the target, the irrelevant, and the instrument variables. The policy model may be a fixed target or a flexible target model; in the former W contains fixed target values, but in the latter such target values are chosen as will optimize the welfare function W.

The model M specifies the set of quantitative relations among the variables. Such relations in their original form, as distinct from the "reduced form," are called structural relations, and their coefficients are called structural coefficients. These structural relations may be divided into three groups: behavioral, technical, and definitional. The most important equations are the behavioral ones, which contain essentially quantitative theories and hypotheses about empirical economic behavior,

---

[4] Most of the following section is excerpted from Fox, Sengupta, and Thorbecke (1966; also, revised second edition, 1973).

for example, demand or supply relations or the reactions of economic groups to risk and uncertainty.

The variables of the model M may be classified into four different types, the target variables y_i, which are to be purposefully (though indirectly) influenced by the policy maker; the instrument variables z_j, which are the means available to him; the data u_k, which are not subject to his control; and the irrelevant variables x_s, which are side effects in which the policy maker is not interested.

If for ad hoc reasons we regard some economic variables x_s as irrelevant for a given policy decision, we can usually eliminate them from a complete model by algebraic means, leaving a set of equations containing only policy instruments and targets (plus the effects of strictly noncontrollable variables). Figure 7.1 may help to clarify the classification of variables in the Tinbergen type of policy model. The random components of the policy model are not explicit in the diagram. Furthermore, the light arrow running from the instrument vector to the welfare function W probably understates the importance of this connection, because in most cases a cost imputation on the basis of either shadow prices or direct monetary expenditure can be made for the instrument variables used by a policy maker. In any case, the welfare function W can incorporate as elements instrument variables in addition to the target variables as such.

Assuming linearity and eliminating the vector x of irrelevant variables, an economic policy model may be very simply specified in terms of three systems of equations:

optimize $W = a'y + b'z$ (preference function) $\qquad\qquad$ (8)

under the conditions:

$$Ay = Bz + Cu \text{ (the model } M\text{)}, \qquad\qquad (9)$$

and

$$\left.\begin{array}{l} y_{\min} \leq y \leq y_{\max} \\ z_{\min} \leq z \leq z_{\max} \end{array}\right\} \text{ (boundary conditions)}, \qquad\qquad (10)$$

where A, B, and C are matrices of coefficients of appropriate orders and y, z, and u are appropriate column vectors of targets, instruments, and data.

Since for the policy problem our unknown is the vector z of instruments, we solve for z from (9):

$$Bz = Ay - Cu. \qquad\qquad (11)$$

If the matrix B has constant elements and is square and nonsingular, the inverse of B exists, hence the vector of instruments z can be uniquely solved from (11) by premultiplying both sides by B^{-1}; that is,

$$z = (B^{-1}A)y - (B^{-1}C)u = Gy + Hu. \qquad\qquad (12)$$

The nature of the dependence of z on y is associated with different types of structures of the matrices B and A:

1. If B and A are strictly diagonal matrices, then to each target there corresponds one and only one instrument, and vice versa. There is no simultaneity in the relationship between the instruments and the targets. The practical implication would

be that the policy maker could pursue each target with a single highly specific instrument. Or, he could afford to assign responsibility for each target and its unique instrument to a different cabinet officer or agency head without providing any mechanism for coordination or even communication among these officials!

2. If the matrices B and A are strictly triangular and of similar dimensionality, the policy model given by (11) is called recursive (or correspondingly consecutive). In this case we have a "pure causal chain" model, to use a concept developed by Wold (1956) in his theory of estimation. The two-way simultaneity of relations between the vectors z and y (i.e., z affecting y and y affecting z) can be reduced to a unilateral dependence.

We must emphasize that z and y are vectors:

$$z = \begin{bmatrix} z_1 \\ z_2 \\ \cdot \\ \cdot \\ \cdot \\ z_J \end{bmatrix}, \qquad y = \begin{bmatrix} y_1 \\ y_2 \\ \cdot \\ \cdot \\ \cdot \\ y_I \end{bmatrix}.$$

Even if most of the z_j's were unilaterally dependent on certain of the y_i's, the vectors z and y would be interdependent (or show two-way simultaneity) if any one (or more) of the y_i's depended on one or more of the z_j's.

If the matrices A and B are strictly triangular, the first element z_1 of the vector z will depend only on the single element y_1 of vector y and other data (u). The second element z_2 will depend on z_1, y_1, y_2 and other data, but since z_1 has already been solved in terms of y_1, we have z_2 depending only on y_1, y_2, and not on any y_i higher than $i = 2$. Apart from the advantages of this pattern for statistical estimation, the strictly recursive model allows a very simple policy interpretation. Specifically, if each equation were assigned to a different policy maker, the system of equations would specify a hierarchy such that a policy maker in a given position would not need to look at the instruments selected by those who are below his position in the hierarchy of equations to determine his own optimal policy.

3. If many of the elements of the matrices B and A are zero (which sometimes occurs in practice in input–output models and in investment planning), such matrices may be quasi-diagonal or block-diagonal rather than strictly diagonal. This means that each matrix contains square submatrices that, after appropriate arrangement of rows and columns, form blocks on the principal diagonal, the off-diagonal elements being zero.

In this case of a block-diagonal policy model, the overall model could be split (or decomposed) into two or more independent parts, depending on the number of blocks in the block-diagonal form. A centralized plan (model) could thus be decentralized into "relatively independent" subplans (submodels) which would permit efficient decentralized decision making.

4. Again, if the matrices B and A are quasi-triangular or block-triangular (i.e., triangular in blocks of submatrices), the set of instruments corresponding to any given block can be solved for without any knowledge of other instruments belonging to blocks lower in the hierarchy. In this case the overall central plan (or model) could be split into separate unilaterally dependent plans (or models).

So far we have assumed implicitly, if not explicitly, that we are discussing a fixed-target policy model; we may presume that some welfare function W lies behind the selection of target values, but W itself is not specified. In fact, however, a Tinbergen type of policy model may be fixed, flexible, random, or mixed. In the flexible case we select the instruments to optimize the welfare function W subject to the conditions of the model. In the random case we optimize the expected value (or some appropriate deterministic equivalent, such as the variance or the probability that W takes a particular value or falls within a particular confidence interval) of the preference function. The randomness in the model may enter either through errors of statistical estimation of the model M from past observational data or because the targets set have random components (or intervals within which random variation will be tolerated). A model is mixed when some targets are fixed, some are flexible, and still others are random. Various other combinations are possible; for example, some targets may be allowed to take only integral values, and some may be continuous except at some "jump points."

The concept of "efficiency" used in the theory of economic policy is also important. This concept is applicable to a flexible target policy model and also to the random and mixed cases. Suppose for simplicity we write the welfare function W as a scalar function of the target variables, the instruments and random terms (v); that is,

$$W = W(y_1, y_2, \ldots, y_I; \quad z_1, z_2, \ldots, z_J, v) \tag{13}$$

after appropriate substitutions through the model. Then, assuming differentiability and other regularity conditions, we can state that the optimum set of instruments would be given by solving the following set of J partial differential equations which are the necessary conditions for an extremum (optimum):

$$\frac{dW}{dz_j} = \sum_{i=1}^{I} \frac{\partial W}{\partial y_i} \frac{\partial y_i}{\partial z_j} + \frac{\partial \dot{W}}{\partial z_j} = 0, \qquad j = 1, 2, \ldots, J, \tag{14}$$

provided the random term v is identically zero and the second-order condition for a maximum or minimum is fulfilled. The term $(\partial y_i / \partial z_j)$ expresses the effectiveness of the instrument z_j in inducing a change in the value of the target y_i when all other instruments are kept constant. Hence the term $\sum_{i=1}^{I} (\partial W / \partial y_i)(\partial y_i / \partial z_j)$ expresses the sum of all marginal (partial) effects upon W of a unit change in z_j acting indirectly through the target variables y_i. The direct effect of the instrument z_j on W is specified by the term $\partial W / \partial z_j$.

These efficiency indicators, which are partial measures of impact of the use of instruments, may be used to construct numerical tables to indicate the rates of substitution between different instruments. It should be noted that these indicators are not in terms of elasticities, hence comparisons of the effectiveness of different instruments are not free from the units in which these instruments are measured.

The specification of objective functions in the theory of economic policy involves essentially the same problem that confronts us in specifying objective functions for universities and other nonmarket institutions—that is, the absence of generally recognized prices for all or many of the outputs. Van Eijk and Sandee (1959), analyzing the context of economic policy in the Netherlands as of 1956, decided that against a 100 million guilder balance of payments surplus could be set 400 million guilders of government expenditure, or 500 million guilders of investment, or a 2 percent increase in real wages, or a 1.33 percent decrease in consumer prices, or an 0.5 percent increase in employment, or a 200 million guilder surplus of government receipts over government expenditures. These were marginal rates of substitution or "barter terms of trade" among the six variables listed; from these a linear objective function could be written as:

$$W = 1.0(E - M) + 0.25x_G + 0.20i + 5.0w_R - 7.5p_c + 0.20a$$
$$+ 0.50S_G + \text{constant}, \quad (15)$$

subject to specified upper and lower limits within which the targets, and implicitly the instruments, could be varied. (In this equation, the balance of payments surplus $E - M$, government expenditures x_G, investment i, and the surplus of government receipts over expenditures S_G are expressed in *billions* of guilders; real wages w_R and consumer prices p_c are expressed as *decimal fractions* of 1; and employment a is expressed in units of 1 *percent*. Hence the coefficients of w_R, p_c, and a are smaller by factors of 10, 10, and 1000 than they would be if the units of the statement immediately preceding the equation had been retained.)

Theil (1964) specified quadratic objective functions representing (1) the trade unionist position, (2) the employer position, and (3) a neutral position and worked out the implications of each for optimal time paths of the same set of target and instrument variables in the Netherlands over a 3-year horizon, using the same 40-equation model of the Dutch economy to link target and instrument variables in all cases. On one level, the barter terms of trade could be discussed as matters of taste or intuition, with different policy makers bringing to bear their own judgments and experiences as tempered by recent political platforms and by the public and private statements of persons wielding political or intellectual influence. On another level, they suggest the need for further clarification as to who is hurt (or helped), how, and how much by a unit change in each national aggregative variable.

Ordinal Versus Cardinal Objective Functions in the Theory of Economic Policy.   Theil (1958) drew a very specific analogy between the theory of economic policy and the theory of consumption. He pointed out that ordinal utility was sufficient in principle to lead the policy maker to select the optimal set of values of the instrument variables (according to his own preference ordering, of course). Theil's model is essentially

$$\max W = f(x, y) \qquad x:m.1, \qquad\qquad (16)$$
$$y:n.1,$$

subject to

$$Qy = Rx + s, \qquad Q:n.n, \qquad\qquad (17)$$
$$R:n.m,$$
$$s:n.1,$$

where x is a vector of m instruments, y is a vector of n targets, Q is a matrix with scalar numbers on the diagonal and zeros elsewhere, R is a matrix of coefficients specifying the effects of the instruments on values of the (normalized) targets $q_i y_i$, and s is a vector of constants (each s_i is a linear combination of the data variables, whose values are regarded as predetermined constants during the optimization period, and any constant term in the equation expressing y_i as a function of the instruments and data). The y_i may be expressed in different units, such as per capita disposable income (in dollars), total employment (millions of workers), the consumer price index, and so on; the diagonal elements in Q, $q_i (i = 1, 2, \ldots, n)$ may be thought of as analogous to prices per unit of y_i, in that each unit of y_i uses up q_i units of the restriction imposed (or resource provided) by the ith equation.

The income constraint of consumption theory is here replaced by the set of n reduced-form equations derived from the econometric model (i.e., those equations which express the target variables as functions of the instruments and data after the vector of irrelevant variables has been eliminated from the original structural system). To impose the present constraint set, we write

$$\max W - \lambda'(Qy - Rx - s), \tag{18}$$

where λ is a column vector of n Lagrangian multipliers. Maximization leads to

$$\frac{\partial W}{\partial x} + R'\lambda = 0 \tag{19}$$

and

$$\frac{\partial W}{\partial y} - Q'\lambda = 0, \tag{20}$$

where $\partial W/\partial x$ and $\partial W/\partial y$ are column vectors of the marginal welfare contributions or "utilities" of the instruments and the target variables, respectively.

For clarity, we may write typical individual rows of the vectors of first derivatives as

$$\frac{\partial W}{\partial x_j} + (\lambda_1 r_{1j} + \lambda_2 r_{2j} + \cdots + \lambda_n r_{nj}) = 0, \qquad j = 1, 2, \ldots, m \tag{21}$$

and

$$\frac{\partial W}{\partial y_i} - \lambda_i q_i = 0, \qquad i = 1, 2, \ldots, n. \tag{22}$$

If W has been given a cardinal specification, each $\partial W/\partial x_j$ will be a cardinal number and each λ_i will be the shadow price of the ith equation, in units of W, at the optimal solution. If W has been given an ordinal specification, the ratio of the marginal utilities of any two instruments x_j and x_k can be expressed as

$$\frac{\partial W/\partial x_j}{\partial W/\partial x_k} = \frac{(\lambda_1 r_{1j} + \lambda_2 r_{2j} + \cdots + \lambda_n r_{nj})}{(\lambda_1 r_{1k} + \lambda_2 r_{2k} + \cdots + \lambda_n r_{nk})}. \tag{23}$$

This ratio will not be affected if we multiply both numerator and denominator by the same scalar k (say) where k is any real number whatsoever.

An Illustrative Example.   As a simple example let us consider a linear macroeconomic model[5] with two fixed targets: a given value of balance of payments ($B = B^*$) and a given volume of employment ($N = N^*$) and two instruments: government expendi-

---

[5] This has been adapted from Theil (1956).

ture for consumption (G_c) and for investment (G_i). The model is

$$\text{domestic output:} \quad Y = C + I + X + G_c + G_i \text{ (definition),}$$
$$\text{imports:} \quad M = a_1C + a_2I + a_3X + a_4G_c + a_5G_i$$
$$\text{(behavior equation),}$$
$$\text{consumption:} \quad C = bY \text{ (behavior equation),}$$
$$\text{employment:} \quad N = eY \text{ (technical relation),}$$
$$\text{balance of payments:} \quad B = p_xX - p_mM \text{ (definition).}$$

The boundary conditions on each of the variables are that they must belong to the real nonnegative interval $(0, \infty)$, which is closed at the left end but open at the right end. Here we have

$$\text{5 endogenous variables:} \quad Y, M, C, B, N,$$
$$\text{4 exogenous variables:} \quad I, X, G_c, G_i,$$
$$\text{2 target variables:} \quad B = B^*, N = N^*,$$
$$\text{2 instrument variables:} \quad G_i, G_c,$$
$$\text{2 data variables:} \quad I, X,$$
$$\text{3 irrelevant variables:} \quad Y, M, C.$$

After rearrangement of terms and appropriate substitution, we get

$$N = N^* = b_1(I + X) + b_1G_c + b_1G_i,$$
$$B = B^* = p_xX - g_2I - g_3X - g_4G_c - g_5G_i, \tag{24}$$

where the constant coefficients are $b_1 = e/(1 - b)$ and $g_i = p_ma_i + p_ma_1b/(1 - b)$ for $i = 2, 3, 4, 5$.

Since the data variables I, X are not controlled by the policy maker, they must be either forecast from past data (projected) or replaced by judgment estimates. We denote these values by I_0 and X_0. Substituting these known values in system (24), we can check the system for mathematical consistency in the sense of the existence of solutions. Since the number of targets equals the number of instruments, in this case we can solve for "unique" values of the instruments G_i, G_c, if their coefficient matrix is nonsingular; that is,

$$\begin{bmatrix} G_i \\ G_c \end{bmatrix} = \begin{bmatrix} b_1 & b_1 \\ -g_4 & -g_5 \end{bmatrix}^{-1} \begin{bmatrix} N^* - b_1(I_0 + X_0) \\ B^* - (p_x - g_3)X_0 - g_2I_0 \end{bmatrix}. \tag{25}$$

Suppose we reduce our two instruments to only one (i.e., $G = G_i + G_c$) by defining $a_4 = a_5$, hence $g_4 = g_5$. We cannot now achieve the two arbitrarily fixed targets in general, because the system (24) now defines two equations in one unknown (G). However, if we reduce the two equations to one by defining $W = w_1N + w_2B$, where $W = W^*$ is the value of the fixed target, we again have consistency in the policy sense, and under the usual regularity conditions the policy model can be solved. We note that the nonnegative weights w_1, w_2 specify the barter terms of trade between the two objectives N and B, which together specify the preference function of the policy maker.

It should be clearly noted that the two targets are competitive. To increase N (employment) we must increase Y (total domestic output) by increasing government expenditures for consumption (G_c) or investment (G_i) or both. But if Y increases, private consumption (C) will also increase, which in turn will increase imports M; and an increase in M will reduce the balance of payments B.

VIII

Social Indicators and Models for Cities and Regions

THERE IS CONSIDERABLE INTEREST in social indicators for cities, metropolitan areas, states, and regions. Such indicators should be compatible, broadly speaking, both with national aggregates such as those in Terleckyj's model and with measures of individual resources and total income.

Tinbergen's policy model (Figure 7.1) can evidently be applied to the problems of a state or to those of a smaller political jurisdiction. In any given year, legislation and policies of the federal government would be "data" or noncontrollable factors for the state. The array of policy instruments available to the governor would differ from the array available to the president. Also, in assigning weights to the various policy targets subject to his influence, the governor's responsibilities would run to the people of the state, rather than to citizens of the entire nation. In general, side effects on residents of other states would be disregarded, and events in other states would be noncontrollable factors. Targets and instruments would be related through a model of the economy of the state.

We can also apply Figure 7.1 to the policy problems confronting a mayor, a city council, or a county board of supervisors. Actions of the state government must now be taken as "data"; the model needed relates to the economy of a town or county; and actions of governments, consumers, or businessmen in other towns and counties within the state also affect the ease or difficulty with which local officials can achieve their goals.

In principle, policy models for any territorial jurisdiction can be extended to include noneconomic variables. In this chapter we consider (1) the problem of specifying the objective function for policy models of metropolitan areas, (2) some implications of differences among American cities as indicated by a factor analysis, (3) the choice of appropriate regions for policy models, (4) the regionalization or decentralization of national models, and (5) the use of simulation models of economic systems at city, county, and multicounty area levels.

130

8.1   Jones and Flax on the Quality of Life in Metropolitan Areas (1970)

Jones and Flax (1970) presented indicators for 14 "quality of life" areas in a number of large metropolises in the United States. These quality areas and indicators are listed in Table 8.1.

We will not concern ourselves with the specific indicators used; Jones and Flax were severely limited in their selections by lack of data that were (*a*) appropriate measures of quality in particular facets of life and (*b*) available on a comparable basis for 18 metropolitan areas. We are, however, interested in their conceptual framework.

Suppose we are asked to devise a numerical criterion to measure changes in the "quality of life" in a particular metropolitan area annually from (say) 1971 to 1981. After consulting with elected officials and opinion leaders in the area, we select a set of indicators y_i and a set of weights λ_i for combining the indicators into an index of the quality of life:

$$W = \sum_i \lambda_i y_i. \tag{1}$$

The y_i would be aggregative measures for the metropolitan area as a whole, and the λ_i could be viewed as expressing the preferences of a composite policy maker who thinks in terms of such aggregates.

Now, suppose we are given funds to conduct an annual sample survey of (say) 2000 households to elicit from area residents themselves some direct measures of changes in the quality of their lives. The object would be to obtain a "quality of life" measure for each resident or household

$$w_h = \sum_j v_j b_j; \tag{2}$$

by averaging w_h over households we would obtain a measure

$$W_h = \frac{\sum_{k=1}^{N} w_{h.k}}{N} \tag{3}$$

of the average quality of life for the population of the area.

If money income per capita (adjusted for price changes over time) is included in W as y_1 and we set λ_1 equal to 1.00, we can convert each of the other components of W, namely, $\lambda_i y_i$, $i \neq 1$, into equivalent dollar values. For example, if $\lambda_1 y_1 / W = 0.4$ and $\lambda_2 y_2 / W = 0.1$, then $\lambda_2 y_2 / \lambda_1 y_1 = 0.25$. If $y_1 = \$4000$ and $\lambda_1 = 1$, then $\lambda_2 y_2 = 0.25 \ (\$4000) = \$1000$. Similarly, since $W = \lambda_1 y_1 / 0.4$ and $\lambda_1 y_1 = \$4000$, it follows that $W = \$10,000$.

Furthermore, if money income per capita (adjusted for price changes over time) is included in w_h for each resident as b_1, we can set $v_1 = 1$ and express each of the other components of w_h, namely, $v_j b_j$, $j \neq 1$, in equivalent dollar terms; the same applies to w_h itself. Since $W_h = \sum_{k=1}^{N} w_{h.k} / N$ is simply the arithmetic mean of the w_h's for all residents in the sample and would now be expressed in dollar terms, W_h could be compared directly with W. The two measures might differ substantially both as to level and as to movements over time.

Table 8.1. Quality Areas and Selected Indicators

Quality Areas	Indicators Used
Income	Per capita money income adjusted for cost-of-living differences
Unemployment	Percent of labor force unemployed
Poverty	Percent of households with less than $3000 income
Housing	Cost of housing a moderate-income family of four
Education	Selective Service mental test rejection rate
Health	Infant (i.e., under 1 year) deaths per 1000 live births
Mental health	Suicides per 100,000 population
Air pollution	A composite index of pollutants
Public order	Reported robberies per 100,000 population
Traffic safety	Deaths from automobile accidents per 100,000 population
Racial equality	Ratio between nonwhite and white unemployment rates
Community concern	Per capita contributions to United Fund appeal
Citizen participation	Percent of voting-age population that voted in recent presidential elections
Social disintegration	Known narcotics addicts per 10,000 population

Source. Martin V. Jones and Michael J. Flax, *The Quality of Life in Metropolitan Washington, D. C.: Some Statistical Benchmarks*. Washington, D. C.: Urban Institute, March 1970, p. 6.

Several of the Jones-Flax quality areas can be interpreted as attributes of individuals. Income, education, health, and mental health correspond to some of the resources enumerated in Chapter 5. Unemployment disrupts the resident's life style (pattern of behavior setting occupancy), subjects him to some degree of stress, and may reduce his prestige and self-respect. Poverty is usually defined (for indicator purposes) in terms of money income. Housing involves the physical and aesthetic qualities of behavior settings, with some implications for health, mental health, prestige, and self-respect.

Hence at least seven of the indicators intended for use at the metropolitan area level could be aggregated directly from attributes of individuals, households, and their dwelling units. So could an eighth, racial equality, if based on such measures as ratios of average incomes and/or unemployment rates for nonwhite and white residents. Traffic congestion might be reflected in individuals' estimates of their own time losses through traffic delays. Some effects of air pollution could be represented by reporting of eye irritation, breathing difficulties, and respiratory diseases attributed by the individuals to this cause. Traffic accidents happen to individuals and robberies are perpetrated on them. Individuals also vote and make contributions to their United Funds, and some individuals are narcotic addicts or have been directly affected by them.

We conclude that so far as possible, measures of the "quality of life" in a metropolitan area should be based on attributes of, and effects on, individuals and households. This would lead to an indicator of the W_h type. The proportion of W_h contributed by any "quality of life" area would be an average of the proportions of $w_{h.k}$, $k = 1, 2, \ldots, N$, attributed to that life area. The proportions should be broadly consistent with the proportions of total income attributed by individuals to their various groups of resources (health, value commitments, skills, money income, prestige, and power in our Chapter 5 formulations).

If officials and opinion leaders in a metropolis believed that additional indicators should be included which could only be defined and measured at an aggregative level, we might suggest a composite indicator,

$$W_c = c_1 A + (1 - c_1) W_h, \tag{4}$$

which is a weighted average of W_h and an index A, made up of directly perceived aggregates for the area as a whole.

Initially, A might include some zero-or-one variables reflecting the presence or absence of an art museum, a symphony orchestra, a professional baseball team, and the like. However, further analysis might lead to the estimation of the values of the services of these institutions as contributions to the total incomes of individuals. These effects might then be incorporated into W_h and the corresponding items withdrawn from A; the weight assigned to A, namely, c_1, would be reduced and that assigned to W_h (i.e., $1 - c_1$) would be increased.

8.2 Berry's Factor Analysis of Differences Among United States Cities in 1960

Comparisons of the "quality of life" in different metropolitan areas and in different states, counties, and cities have been attempted by various authors. An early and rather sophisticated example was Margaret Jarman Hagood's "farm operator family level of living indexes" for every county in the United States, based on data from successive U.S. censuses of agriculture from about 1929 to 1949. Hagood applied factor analysis to data on 15 or more variables (all or most of those available in a given census that seemed relevant to a level-of-living concept) and selected four or five variables that accounted for a large proportion of the total variance in the original set. Her index was a weighted combination of such variables as (1) average cash receipts per farm from the sale of farm products, (2) percentage of farm operator families owning automobiles, (3) percentage owning radios, and (4) percentage of farm operator dwellings with running water. With increased prosperity after 1939, the percentages of farm operator families equipped with automobiles, radios, and running water began to approach 100 in more and more counties; thus more and more of the variance in the index was accounted for by the cash receipts variable (a proxy for family income).

Brian J. L. Berry (1972) set out "to define and describe principal dimensions of American urban structure in 1960." He started with 97 primary variables for each of the 1762 urban places with 1960 populations of 10,000 or more. All 97 variables were based on census or other publicly available data; Berry converted some of these into logarithmic or square root forms. Principal axis factor analysis was then applied, yielding 14 factors that together accounted for 77 percent of the original variance of the 97 variables. Each city was given a numerical score on each factor in terms of its deviation (in standard deviation units) from the mean score for all cities on that factor, yielding a "community profile" in terms of 14 numbers.

Berry identified the three most significant sources of variation among cities as (1) *functional size of urban centers in the urban hierarchy*, (2) *socioeconomic status*, and (3) *stage in family cycle*.

Other factors identified in the analysis focused on (4) proportion of population nonwhite, (5) proportion of population foreign-born or of foreign stock, (6) extent of female participation in the labor force, and (7) extent of participation of males in the labor force beyond age 65. Additionally, factors relating to (8) population growth, 1950–1960, and (9) employment expansion, 1950–1960 appeared to be independent of previous dimensions. Finally, the economic specializations of places appeared to be uncorrelated with their sociodemographic characteristics. Economic specializations recognized as important in differentiating towns on a national basis were (10) manufacturing, (11) mining, (12) colleges, (13) military installations, and (14) "services—central places."

Berry was not concerned with social indicators in this study but simply with means of classifying cities. Several of his factors are based on only two or three of the 97 primary variables (e.g., the score on "mining" is based on the percentage of the labor force engaged in mining and on total mining employment). At the other extreme, his size factor is based on 21 of the primary variables, and all but one are measures of absolute size of population, labor force, and of employment in various economic sectors. The intercorrelations among these 21 variables must be extremely high. The "loadings" of these variables on the size factor were as follows:

Class Interval	Number of Loadings
.900 to .974	9
.800 to .899	5

Class Interval	Number of Loadings
.700 to .799	3
.600 to .699	2
.500 to .599	1
.400 to .499	1

The information contained in the 21 variables was evidently highly redundant.

We are mainly interested here in Berry's factor for "socioeconomic status of community residents." This factor is based on 12 primary variables, as follows: median family income, percentage of incomes exceeding $10,000, percentage of incomes below $3000, percentage of adults with high school education (or more), median school years completed by persons over 25, value per occupied housing unit, median rent, percentage housing units sound, percentage housing units owner-occupied, median rooms per housing unit, percentage white collar, and unemployment rate. Three of the variables involve money income, two education, one occupation, and one unemployment; the remaining five are related to housing.

As I understand Berry's procedure, his socioeconomic status factor is uncorrelated with the other 13 factors. If so, it should in principle give a measure of "pure" status for each city, with the other 13 factors held constant. This would contrast with the original set of 97 primary variables, in which the 12 constituent variables of the status factor may have been intercorrelated with constituent variables of other factors, such as proportion of nonwhite population or stage in family cycle.

Suppose we choose a set of measures of attributes of individuals (and households) and compute from them an index W_h for each of Berry's 1762 cities. Suppose we find, on comparing the W_h values for different cities, that they and their components are strongly affected by the age distributions of their respective populations. We would then want to consider whether the W_h values should be "standardized" or adjusted for the effects of age distribution. Comparisons of death rates are meaningless without such standardization; so are many statistics on the incidence of particular diseases. Years of education completed are also associated with age distribution; so are crime rates.

If the unadjusted value of W_h is regarded as the objective function of a policy maker, the effectiveness of various activities in increasing its value may also depend on age distribution. Other variables, such as proportion of population nonwhite, may in one sense "explain" differences in W_h; at the same time, reduction of these differences may be an object of policy. We will not pursue the standardization problem further here.

Many of the cities in Berry's analysis are political subdivisions embedded in metropolitan areas. Berry raises and answers the following question:

> Why mix intermetropolitan and intrametropolitan differences by using legal cities as units of observation? . . . Might not the structural dimensions be confounded by this mixture? Parallel analyses at the intermetropolitan and intrametropolitan levels do not suggest this. The principal dimensions of intermetropolitan and intrametropolitan differentiation appear to be the same: size, socioeconomic status, stage in life cycle, recent growth behavior, and the like (p. 47).

Berry further comments that "An increasing number of economic activities are now market-oriented. ... the more important elements of socioeconomic differentiation are increasingly *intra*-metropolitan in a nation that is fully metropolitanized" (pp. 44–47).

8.3   Appropriate Regions for Social Indicators and Social Policy Models

The social indicators movement faces questions concerning area delineation similar to those encountered by the regional (economic) accounting movement a decade ago.

At the Conference on Regional Accounts in 1962, Jesse Burkhead (1964) began an excellent substantive paper as follows:

> Those who have worked in recent years at the development of regional concepts and at the measurement of regional economic activity are by this time aware that their efforts have no clear-cut policy orientation. Regional accounting is not directed toward a set of regional policies nor toward an organizational structure, public or private, with responsibility for regional well-being. The measurement of levels of private economic activity within a region does not in any sense imply, for example, that there is or should be a regional trade policy or a regional development policy, a point which was well made by Werner Hochwald in his 1957 paper. And, as Clark Bloom pointed out in his review of Isard's *Methods of Regional Analysis*, there is no compelling problem that dominates the field of regional analysis to give it focus in the same way that economic stabilization has dominated macroeconomics, and the monopoly problem has dominated microeconomics (p. 51)

Immediately after the conference I wrote and circulated some comments (Fox, 1962b) in which the paragraph just quoted served as a point of departure, and I proceeded to outline (1) a new approach to delineating policy-oriented regions and (2) Jan Tinbergen's theory of economic policy. The following paragraphs are excerpted from my 1962 comments; I believe they still comprise a useful introduction to the delineation of regions with special significance for social indicators and socioeconomic policies.

Burkhead's statements are indeed applicable to much recent and current work in regional accounting. But it is possible to delineate a set of regions that will provide a compelling problem and a policy orientation for regional accounts. Given an appropriate region, a rigorous logical framework is available for stating and analyzing the corresponding set of policy problems.

Appropriate Regions for Economic Policy.   In principle, a complete set of regional accounts could be maintained for any area large enough for a person to stand on while conducting some economic activity. The same format could be applied to the United States as a whole. Accounts for the United States would be useful; those for the arbitrary area would be "an answer without a question."

The neutrality of accounting concepts may divert our attention from important problems that are not invariant with respect to type or size of region. The papers delivered at the 1962 Conference on Regional Accounts by Harris (1964) and Niskanen (1964) derive some of their sharpness from the fact that they are dealing with metropolitan areas. A metropolitan area is an ecological entity. Certain policy problems involve the metropolitan area as a whole and cannot be solved within arbitrary geographic subdivisions of it.

Outside the metropolitan areas, we seem to lose this ecological perspective. We permit ourselves to be trapped by political boundaries and by particular features of the current data system. I refer particularly to the county, the standard metropolitan statistical area (SMSA), and the state economic area (SEA).

The SMSA delineations may approximate ecological entities for metropolitan areas with several million residents. Our estimates of population and income in the New York metropolitan area are not greatly distorted by the exclusion of small-town and farm people in the neighboring counties.

The problem becomes more acute when we come to an SMSA such as Des Moines. The SMSA includes about 274,000 people—the population of Polk County. But an additional 250,000 or more people are linked with Des Moines by commuting, shopping, and recreational trip patterns.

As we descend the scale of city sizes, we find complete ecological units with central cities of 25,000 to 49,000 and total populations of 200,000 or more simply falling through the meshes of the SMSA–SEA classification system. Fort Dodge, Iowa, a city of 29,000, is the central business district and administrative center of an area covering $5\frac{1}{2}$ or 6 counties with a total population of 130,000. Similar areas of from 6 to 11 counties (3000 to 6000 square miles) can be delineated around Mason City and Ottumwa, cities of 30,000 to 35,000 people.

It seems to me that Iowa, with its 2.8 million people, can be divided into about a dozen *functional economic areas*.[1] Some of these extend into adjoining states. These states also can be subdivided into functional economic areas.

A system of ecologically meaningful regions covering the entire area of the United States would have obvious advantages. If such a system (let us call it an FEA system) were substituted for the present SMSA–SEA system, it might simply amount to a perfecting amendment for the four or five largest SMSAs. But it would be much more revealing than the SMSA delineation for areas with central cities of 50,000 to 1 million people, and it would fill in the rest of the map with regions of similar economic significance.

I submit, therefore, that a "policy-oriented" system of regional accounts and models could be set up on the basis of functional economic areas. Each FEA would be a relatively self-contained labor market in the short run. Its residents could purchase within its boundaries a complete or nearly complete line of consumer goods and could enjoy a full range of local government services. Relatively few people living in one FEA would work or shop (to any major extent) in another.

Apart from megalopolis, it appears that we may reasonably hope to define a network of FEA boundaries with the following characteristics:

1. The flow of daily home-to-job trips across any stretch of boundary would be about the same in each direction.

2. The number of boundary crossings of the home-to-work type would be noticeably increased if arbitrary boundaries were drawn more than a mile or two from the

---

[1] My first statement of the functional economic area (FEA) concept was written in March 1961 and presented at the opening session of the Community Development Seminar at Iowa State University, April 18, 1961 (Fox, 1961).

true ones. Also, the percentage of total labor force commuting across area boundaries would be only slightly smaller for an aggregate of (say) four FEAs than for a single FEA.

I have not studied a map of the entire United States from this standpoint, but I feel quite confident that the nation could be divided (for purposes of regional social accounts and a major cluster of policy problems) into some 400 or 500 functional economic areas. The total number of FEAs would be about the same as the number of SMSAs plus the number of SEAs in the present census classification system. And as noted previously, all but the largest SMSAs are deficient for regional accounting and policy purposes.

Home-to-work commuting patterns would be the most important single factor in delineating an FEA. A very high percentage of income produced by persons residing in the FEA would be gained at places of employment within its boundaries. A large part of the total income produced by area residents would also be consumed by them in the forms of private goods and local government services, or it would take the form of construction activity on public and private capital improvements. The remainder of income produced would take the forms of goods and services "exported" to other FEAs.

The policy problems appropriate to a functional economic area should be substantially the same as those of a city of 100,000 to 500,000 people that had political boundaries roughly coextensive with its economic ones. To me, it seems useful to regard an FEA as a city spatially extended to accommodate a low-density pattern of land use and residential location over the bulk of its area.[2] A further implication is that agriculture, despite its space-filling and eye-catching qualities, is simply another export industry and source of employment from the standpoint of an FEA classification and accounting scheme.

A set of accounts, an economic model, and a central policy-making body would seem to be just as desirable for a functional economic area as for a metropolitan area. This does not necessarily imply that there should be *only* one policy-making body in an FEA—for example, there could be a mayor or similar official in each of several small towns—but there should be *some* policy-making body that could deal with problems of area-wide significance.

The significance of Tinbergen's theory of economic policy in relation to the application of regional accounts to functional economic areas is simply this: it shows how detailed information about the structure of the area's economy can be explicitly incorporated into the design of development and other policies for the area. At the same time, it enables us to separate questions of fact about economic relationships from questions of value about community goals and the acceptability of alternative means for achieving them.

From 1961 to 1967 I made a number of extensions of the FEA concept. Figures 8.1 and 8.2 were developed in 1964. Figure 8.1 encloses the seven Iowa SMSAs as of 1960 in squares representing 50-mile (or approximately 60-minute) commuting distances from their central business districts over Iowa's predominantly rectangular road grid. Figure 8.2 shows 50-mile commuting perimeters around a dozen FEA

[2] In an informal discussion, Wilbur Thompson reformulated my hypothesis as stating that "the United States is made up not of states but of city-states."

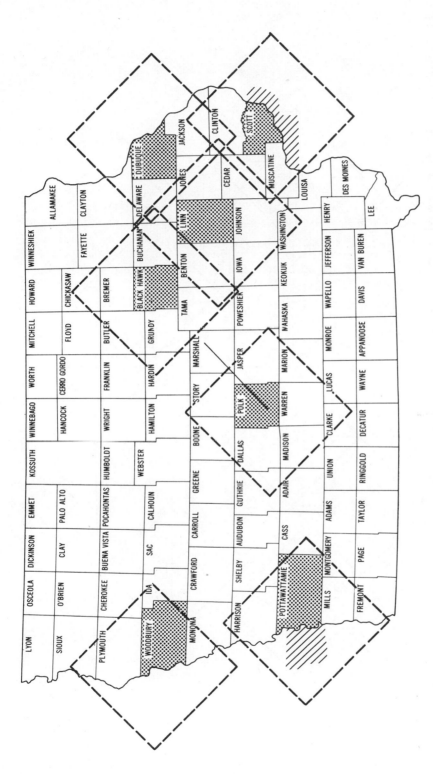

Figure 8.1. Fifty-mile commuting distances from the central business districts of Iowa SMSA central cities (50,000 people or more) in 1960. Each shaded county or pair of shaded contiguous counties is an SMSA.

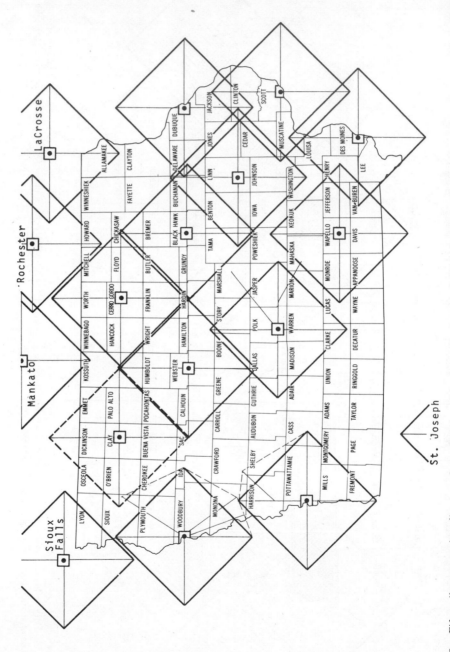

Figure 8.2. Fifty-mile commuting distances from the central business districts of all FEA (including SMSA) central cities in or near Iowa. Central cities selected on the basis of range of economic activities performed and relationship to surrounding area.

central cities in Iowa, including the seven SMSAs of Figure 8.1 and five cities of less than 50,000 population.[3] The 12 areas included 80 percent of the state's area and 90 percent of its population. The theoretical delineations were approximately confirmed by pilot studies (Fox and Kumar, 1965, 1966) of commuting data from the 1960 census.

During 1965–1967, Berry, under the auspices of the Social Science Research Council Committee on Areas for Social and Economic Statistics, analyzed 1960 commuting data for the entire United States. His results were reported in Berry et al. (1968), and his recommendations, adopted by the SSRC Committee, were also summarized by Fox (1967).

The smaller regions in Figure 8.3 are the 358 Functional Economic Areas delineated by Berry et al. (1968). The larger regions are tentative delineations by myself, done in 1970 and published in Fox (1973a), of 24 National Metropolitan Regions.

Starting from Berry's FEA delineations, Robert E. Graham (Regional Economics Division, Office of Business Economics, 1969) of the U.S. Department of Commerce delineated economic areas to facilitate its program of regional measurement and analysis, and projections of economic activity. The result, as of January 1969, is shown in Figure 8.4.

The procedure used by Graham was described as follows in Olsen and Westley (1973a):

> First, economic centers were identified. Standard metropolitan statistical areas were chosen where possible. Each SMSA has a large city at its center which serves both as a wholesale and retail trade center and as a labor market center. However, not all SMSA's were made centers of economic areas because some are integral parts of larger metropolitan complexes. The New York City area, for instance, encompasses not only the New York City SMSA but also Jersey City, Newark, Patterson-Clifton-Passaic, Stamford, Norwalk and Bridgeport SMSA's. The Seattle economic area includes the Seattle-Everett and Tacoma SMSA's. In rural parts of the country, where there were no SMSA's, cities of from 25,000 to 50,000 population were utilized as economic centers provided that two other criteria were met. These other criteria were: (1) that the city form a wholesale trade center for the area, and (2) that the area as a whole have a population minimum of about 200,000 people. (There are some exceptions to the size criteria in sparsely populated areas.) After identifying economic centers, intervening counties were allocated to the centers. This assignment was made on the basis of comparative time and distance of travel to the economic centers, the journey to work pattern around the economic centers, the interconnection between counties because of journey to work, the road network, the linkage of counties by such other economic ties as could be found, and certain geographic features.
>
> In places where the commuting patterns of adjacent economic centers overlap, counties were included in the economic area containing the center with which there was the greatest commuting connection. In the case of

[3] The area bounded by dashed lines in Figure 8.2 meets commuting-field criteria for an FEA, but its central city does not meet the criteria of population size and retail trade volume that should probably be included in the definition of an FEA. In Chapter 12 I refer several times to the *regional capitals* of Iowa's *eleven* FEAs.

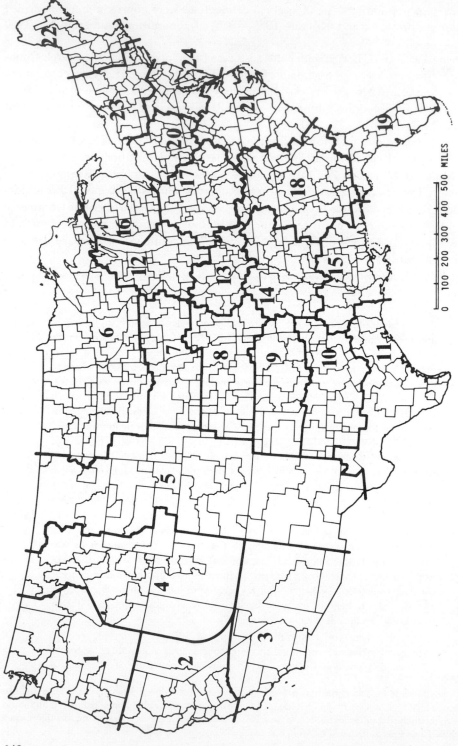

Figure 8.3. National metropolitan regions of the United States.

cities where the commuting pattern overlapped to a great degree, no attempt was made to separate the two cities; instead, both were included in the same economic area.

In the more rural parts of the country, the journey to work information was insufficient to establish boundaries of the economic areas. In these areas, distance of travel to the economic centers was the major determinant (pp. 6–9).

The result was 171 economic areas for the continental United States and one each for Alaska and Hawaii—a total of 173. Olsen and Westley (1973a) commented on these delineations as follows:

> OBE Economic Areas seem destined for a lifetime at least as useful and durable as that already experienced by SMSA's. First, OBE areas have been delineated for the entire United States whereas FEA's as defined by others have usually covered only a portion of the nation. Second, OBE areas incorporate many of the criteria often suggested for FEA delineation. Third, OBE areas have been used by the Regional Economics Division of OBE and the Economic Research Service of the U.S. Department of Agriculture in a joint venture in regional measurement, analysis, and projection of economic activity for the U.S. Water Resources Council. In the process OBE's county personal income, employment and population estimates have been cumulated to OBE areas and published with the likelihood that regional scientists will use these data and demand more on the same spatial grid for some time to come. Fourth, the OBE is currently attempting to implement a "National-Regional Impact Evaluation System" which will essentially be a simulation model of the macro economy of OBE areas. Finally, the Bureau of the Census has decided to publish the Public Use Samples of Basic Records from the 1970 Census by "County Groups" which are very closely related to OBE areas (U.S. Bureau of the Census, 1972). The nation has been divided into areas and subareas called "county groups" where "the 'areas' delineated correspond to economic areas designated by the Bureau of Economic Analysis (formerly the Office of Business Economics), Regional Economics Division [or occasionally combinations of related economic areas where necessary to meet (minimum of 250,000) population criteria]. All of these characteristics and applications of OBE areas would seem to ensure their use or the use of similarly defined areas for analytical purposes for years to come (pp. 9–10).

Olsen and Westley (1973a) developed a program for assigning county data from several major data systems to the appropriate OBE areas; this will be of continuing usefulness.[4] They also (1973b) published cumulations to OBE areas of all or most items in the *County and City Data Book* (U.S. Bureau of the Census, 1968, and earlier years) for the years 1967, 1962, 1956, and 1952.

In Figure 8.3, Berry delineated his FEAs as clusters of contiguous whole counties approximating a commuting field. In superimposing my national metropolitan regions (NMRs) I delineated them as clusters of contiguous whole FEAs. Hence, data

[4] These include, among others, Social Security Administration county data (Office of Research and Statistics, 1969) on employers, workers, and self-employed persons.

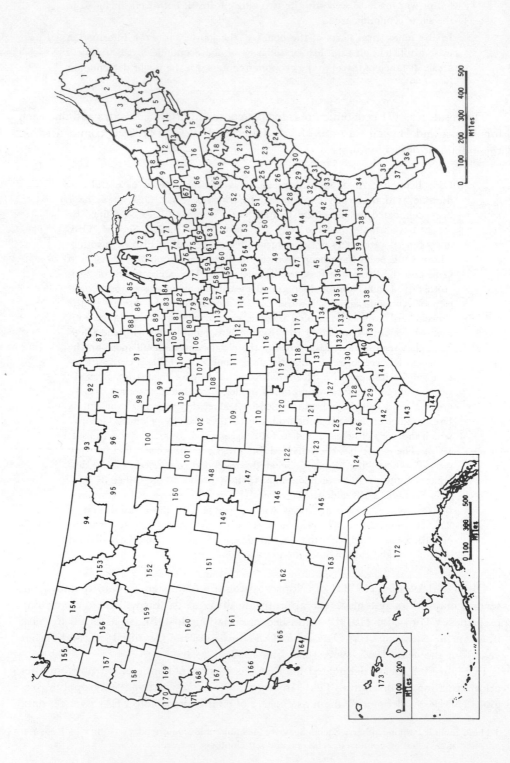

Figure 8.4. OBE economic areas.

1 Bangor, Maine	36 Miami, Fla.	69 Lima, Ohio	103 Sioux City, Iowa-Nebr.	140 Beaumont-Port Arthur-Orange, Tex.
2 Portland, Maine	37 Tampa-St. Petersburg, Fla.	70 Toledo, Ohio	104 Fort Dodge, Iowa	141 Houston, Tex.
3 Burlington, Vt.	38 Tallahassee, Fla.	71 Detroit, Mich.	105 Waterloo, Iowa	142 San Antonio, Tex.
4 Boston, Mass.	39 Pensacola, Fla.	72 Saginaw, Mich.	106 Des Moines, Iowa	143 Corpus Christi, Tex.
5 Hartford, Conn.	40 Montgomery, Ala.	73 Grand Rapids, Mich.	107 Omaha, Nebr.-Iowa	144 Brownsville-Harlingen-San Benito, Tex.
6 Albany-Schenectady-Troy, N.Y.	41 Albany, Ga.	74 Lansing, Mich.	108 Lincoln, Nebr.	145 El Paso, Tex.
7 Syracuse, N.Y.	42 Macon, Ga.	75 Fort Wayne, Ind.	109 Salina, Kans.	146 Albuquerque, N.M.
8 Rochester, N.Y.	43 Columbus, Ga.-Ala.	76 South Bend, Ind.	110 Wichita, Kans.	147 Pueblo, Col.
9 Buffalo, N.Y.	44 Atlanta, Ga.	77 Chicago, Ill.	111 Kansas City, Mo.-Kans.	148 Denver, Col.
10 Erie, Pa.	45 Birmingham, Ala.	78 Peoria, Ill.	112 Columbia, Mo.	149 Grand Junction, Col.
11 Williamsport, Pa.	46 Memphis, Tenn.-Ark.	79 Davenport-Rock Island-Moline, Iowa-Ill.	113 Quincy, Ill.	150 Cheyenne, Wyo.
12 Binghamton, N.Y.-Pa.	47 Huntsville, Ala.	80 Cedar Rapids, Iowa	114 St. Louis, Mo.-Ill.	151 Salt Lake City, Utah
13 Wilkes-Barre-Hazleton, Pa.	48 Chattanooga, Tenn.-Ga.	81 Dubuque, Iowa	115 Paducah, Ky.	152 Idaho Falls, Idaho
14 New York, N.Y.	49 Nashville, Tenn.	82 Rockford, Ill.	116 Springfield, Mo.	153 Butte, Mont.
15 Philadelphia, Pa.-N.J.	50 Knoxville, Tenn.	83 Madison, Wis.	117 Little Rock-North Little Rock, Ark.	154 Spokane, Wash.
16 Harrisburg, Pa.	51 Bristol, Va.-Tenn.	84 Milwaukee, Wis.	118 Fort Smith, Ark.-Okla.	155 Seattle-Everett, Wash.
17 Baltimore, Md.	52 Huntington-Ashland, W. Va.-Ky.-Ohio	85 Green Bay, Wis.	119 Tulsa, Okla.	156 Yakima, Wash.
18 Washington, D.C.-Md.-Va.	53 Lexington, Ky.	86 Wausau, Wis.	120 Oklahoma City, Okla.	157 Portland, Ore.-Wash.
19 Staunton, Va.	54 Louisville, Ky.-Ind.	87 Duluth-Superior, Minn.-Wis.	121 Wichita Falls, Tex.	158 Eugene, Ore.
20 Roanoke, Va.	55 Evansville, Ind.-Ky.	88 Eau Claire, Wis.	122 Amarillo, Tex.	159 Boise City, Idaho
21 Richmond, Va.	56 Terre Haute, Ind.	89 La Crosse, Wis.	123 Lubbock, Tex.	160 Reno, Nev.
22 Norfolk-Portsmouth, Va.	57 Springfield, Ill.	90 Rochester, Minn.	124 Odessa, Tex.	161 Las Vegas, Nev.
23 Raleigh, N.C.	58 Champaign-Urbana, Ill.	91 Minneapolis-St. Paul, Minn.	125 Abilene, Tex.	162 Phoenix, Ariz.
24 Wilmington, N.C.	59 Lafayette-West Lafayette, Ind.	92 Grand Forks, N.D.	126 San Angelo, Tex.	163 Tucson, Ariz.
25 Greensboro-Winston Salem-High Point, N.C.	60 Indianapolis, Ind.	93 Minot, N.D.	127 Dallas, Tex.	164 San Diego, Calif.
26 Charlotte, N.C.	61 Muncie, Ind.	94 Great Falls, Mont.	128 Waco, Tex.	165 Los Angeles-Long Beach, Calif.
27 Asheville, N.C.	62 Cincinnati, Ohio-Ky.-Ind.	95 Billings, Mont.	129 Austin, Tex.	166 Fresno, Calif.
28 Greenville, S.C.	63 Dayton, Ohio	96 Bismarck, N.D.	130 Tyler, Tex.	167 Stockton, Calif.
29 Columbia, S.C.	64 Columbus, Ohio	97 Fargo-Moorhead, N.D.-Minn.	131 Texarkana, Tex.-Ark.	168 Sacramento, Calif.
30 Florence, S.C.	65 Clarksburg, W. Va.	98 Aberdeen, S.D.	132 Shreveport, La.	169 Redding, Calif.
31 Charleston, S.C.	66 Pittsburgh, Pa.	99 Sioux Falls, S.D.	133 Monroe, La.	170 Eureka, Calif.
32 Augusta, Ga.	67 Youngstown-Warren, Ohio	100 Rapid City, S.D.	134 Greenville, Miss.	171 San Francisco-Oakland, Calif.
33 Savannah, Ga.	68 Cleveland, Ohio	101 Scottsbluff, Nebr.	135 Jackson, Miss.	172 Anchorage, Alaska
34 Jacksonville, Fla.		102 Grand Island, Nebr.	136 Meridian, Miss.	173 Honolulu, Hawaii
35 Orlando, Fla.			137 Mobile, Ala.	
			138 New Orleans, La.	
			139 Lake Charles, La.	

145

published on a county basis could be aggregated to national totals in three successive steps—FEAs, NMRs, and the United States.

The OBE areas embody most of the desirable features of FEAs and (like FEAs) are clusters of contiguous whole counties. The NMRs can be delineated as clusters of contiguous OBE areas and, in turn, aggregated to United States totals.

The NMRs are centered on large cities (e.g., New York, Chicago, Los Angeles, and Atlanta), which serve as economic and cultural centers for sizable regions. Their usefulness for purposes of general economic and social policy has not been sufficiently studied; they were recommended by Fox (1973a) as promising regions for transportation planning and coordination. Their central cities are analogous to the *metropoles* (eight or nine large cities) that figure prominently in French regional planning as counterbalances to the extreme concentration of population, power, and cultural activities in Paris.

8.4 Decentralization or Regionalization of National Models

The 358 FEAs delineated by Berry et al. (1968) and displayed as the finer network in Figure 8.3 included 96 percent of the 1960 population of the United States. As of 1973, probably 97 to 98 percent of all labor market activity and nearly 100 percent of retail trade and service activities requiring direct contact with the public (as customers, pupils, students, patients, clients, voters, taxpayers, churchgoers, etc.) occur within functional economic areas (FEAs) or urban-centered commuting fields. Broadly speaking, an FEA may be regarded as a "macro household" that is essentially self-contained with respect to resident-oriented activities that account for about 60 percent of total employment. The remaining employment (on the order of 40 percent) in each FEA is part of an interarea trading system. The "export-oriented" activities include agriculture, most manufacturing, most mining and forestry, tourist attractions, state universities, state capitals, and many other private and public establishments that, although located in one FEA, are designed to serve residents of several or many FEAs.

Thus, we might view the United States economy in terms of an intersectoral flow matrix of the following structure:

$$
\begin{array}{c}
\text{Destinations} \\
\begin{array}{c c}
 & \begin{array}{cccc} R_1 & R_2 & E_1 & E_2 \end{array} \\
\text{Sources} \begin{array}{c} R_1 \\ R_2 \\ \\ E_1 \\ E_2 \end{array} &
\left[\begin{array}{cc|cc}
X & 0 & 0 & 0 \\
0 & X & 0 & 0 \\
\hline
X & X & X & X \\
X & X & X & X
\end{array}\right]
\end{array}
\end{array}
$$

where R_i and E_i are respectively the residentiary and the export sectors of the ith FEA. In ideal form, no residentiary establishment in the ith region would provide goods or services to any firm or consumer in R_j ($i \neq i$) or to any firm in any E_i or E_j. Deliveries from any export sector to any residentiary sector might be regarded as deliveries to final demand (in the "macro-household" sense) while deliveries from E_i to E_j would be regarded as interindustry sales.

The special definition of final demand just mentioned would lead to the following input-output type of matrix:

Export sector originating sales and deliveries — Sales to export sectors — Deliveries to "final demand" — Total gross sales of export sector

$$
\begin{array}{cc}
\begin{matrix} E_1 \\ E_2 \\ \vdots \\ \vdots \\ \vdots \\ E_n \end{matrix}
\begin{bmatrix}
e_{11} & e_{12} & \cdots & e_{1n} \\
e_{21} & e_{22} & \cdots & e_{2n} \\
\vdots & \vdots & & \vdots \\
\\
\\
e_{n1} & e_{n2} & \cdots & e_{nn}
\end{bmatrix}
+
\begin{bmatrix}
r_{11} & r_{12} & \cdots & r_{1n} \\
r_{21} & r_{22} & \cdots & r_{2n} \\
\vdots & \vdots & & \vdots \\
\\
\\
r_{n1} & r_{n2} & \cdots & r_{nn}
\end{bmatrix}
=
\begin{bmatrix}
X_{1e} \\ X_{2e} \\ \vdots \\ \vdots \\ \vdots \\ X_{ne}
\end{bmatrix}
\end{array}
$$

$$+$$

Primary inputs of export sector
$$
\begin{bmatrix}
w_{1e} & w_{2e} & \cdots & w_{ne} \\
k_{1e} & k_{2e} & \cdots & k_{ne}
\end{bmatrix}
$$

$$=$$

Total gross outlays of export sector
$$
\begin{bmatrix}
X_{1e} & X_{2e} & \cdots & X_{ne}
\end{bmatrix}
\tag{5}
$$

or

$$
E + R = X = E' + w' + k', \tag{6}
$$

where the w_{ie} are total payments to labor (broadly defined) and the k_{ie} are total payments for other factors of production (net rent, interest, depreciation, etc.).

The matrix E could be expanded to include any number m of export-oriented production activities in each of the n regions. Most extractive and manufacturing industries would be included in the E matrix (along with strictly inter-FEA transportation); most personal, professional, and public services and retailing, a great deal of wholesaling, and intra-FEA transportation would be included in the residentiary sector. [Matrix R simply records deliveries from the export sectors to the residentiary sectors valued essentially at manufacturers' f.o.b. prices plus freight. To show the employment-generating activities within the residentiary sector, we would need a different and more detailed model, as presented in Fox, Sengupta, and Thorbecke (1973, pp. 396–415).]

If disposable consumer income in the jth FEA is increased (e.g., because of a reduction in tax rates on personal incomes) at least some of the n r_{ij}'s will increase. We assume here that the price vector p_{ij} $(i = 1, 2, \ldots, n)$ does not change, so that the r_{ij}'s are essentially indexes of quantities demanded. The increased demands will ramify through the interregional trading system, so that employment and income payments in the n export sectors (or nm region-and-industry sectors) will increase to varying degrees. An increase in purchases from E_j by the federal government or by other countries (not explicitly provided for in the model) would also increase employment and income in the jth FEA, with effects on the r_{ij}'s and the general economy as before.

In Section 7.4 we outlined the theory of quantitative economic policy in terms of aggregative variables at the national level and considered a linear macroeconomic model with five equations. The target variables were employment (N) and the balance of payments (B); the instruments were government expenditures for current operations (G_c) and government expenditures (G_i) on new buildings, roads and other types of gross capital formation.

We could extend this model to indicate the relations between national and local (FEA-level) policy makers with respect to a particular FEA, say FEA$_1$, as follows:

FEA$_1$ output: $$Y_1 = C_1 + I_{1p} + X_{1p} + G_{1c} + G_{1i}$$
$$+ (\lambda_{11} + \lambda_{21} + \lambda_{31})G_f,$$

FEA$_1$ imports: $$M_1 = a_{11}C_1 + a_{21}I_{1p} + a_{31}X_{1p} + a_{41}G_{1c} + a_{51}G_{1i}$$
$$+ (a_{21}\lambda_{11} + a_{31}\lambda_{21} + a_{51}\lambda_{31})G_f,$$

FEA$_1$ consumption: $$C_1 = b_1(1 - t_1)Y_1,$$

FEA$_1$ employment: $$N_1 = e_1Y_1,$$

FEA$_1$ balance of
payments: $$B_1 = p_{x1}X_1 - p_{m1}M_1,$$
$$I_{1f} = \lambda_{11}G_f,$$
$$X_{1f} = \lambda_{21}G_f,$$
$$G_{1i(f)} = \lambda_{31}G_f,$$

Federal instruments: $\lambda_{11}, \lambda_{21}, \lambda_{31}, t_1, G_f$ (note that $\lambda_{11} + \lambda_{21} + \lambda_{31} = 1$),
Targets: $N_1{}^*, C_1{}^*.$

In these equations, Y is income, C consumption, I_p private investment, X_p private exports, G_c expenditures by local government for current operations, G_i expenditures of local government for investment purposes, and G_f expenditures by the federal government. The subscript 1 stands for region or FEA$_1$. The remaining variables are M imports, N employment, B balance of payments, p_x prices of exports, p_m prices of imports, I_f federal investment projects in the local FEA *or* investments induced by federal expenditures, X_f exports purchased by the federal government, and $G_{i(f)}$ local government investment activities *induced* by federal subsidies or other expenditures.

The endogenous variables of greatest concern to residents of the FEA are presumably N_1, C_1, and perhaps Y_1. The instruments available to the federal government in this model are the personal income tax (t_1), federal expenditures to encourage local private investment $(\lambda_{11}G_f)$, federal expenditures for "exports" from the FEA$(\lambda_{21}G_f)$, and federal expenditures to encourage local government investment $(\lambda_{31}G_f)$. The λ's are allocation coefficients that can presumably be set at different levels for different FEAs; so can the total federal expenditure in the area, G_f.

So far, the FEA$_1$ model ignores the interarea trading system. We can illustrate the effects of interarea trade by means of an even simpler macroeconomic model. We assume to begin with a closed system, consisting of two areas (FEAs). The models for each area separately are (see Fox, 1969d):

Area 1:

$$Y_1 = C_1 + I_1 + G_1 + E_1 - M_1$$

$$C_1 = c_1 Y_1$$
$$I_1 = i_1 Y_1$$
$$M_1 = m_1 Y_1$$

Area 2:

$$Y_2 = C_2 + I_2 + G_2 + E_2 - M_2$$
$$C_2 = c_2 Y_2$$
$$I_2 = i_2 Y_2$$
$$M_2 = m_2 Y_2.$$

In area 1, we may (initially and naively) assume that E_1 (exports) is exogenous; G_1 (government expenditure) is our main policy instrument. Four variables, Y_1 (gross area product), C_1 (consumption), I_1 (domestic private investment), and M_1 (imports), are regarded as endogenous.

In our two-area model, of course, $E_1 = M_2$ and $E_2 = M_1$, so the export variables become *endogenous* to the closed system, which can be displayed as follows:

$$\begin{bmatrix} 1 & -1 & -1 & & & & 1 & & -1 & & -1 & \\ -c_1 & 1 & 0 & & 0 & & & & & & & \\ -i_1 & 0 & 1 & & & & & & & & & \\ & & & 1 & -1 & -1 & 1 & & -1 & & & -1 \\ & 0 & & -c_2 & 1 & 0 & & & & & & \\ & & & -i_2 & 0 & 1 & & & & & & \\ -m_1 & & & & & & 1 & & & & & \\ & & & -m_2 & & & & 1 & & & & \\ & & & & & & & & -1 & 1 & & 0 \\ & & & -1 & & & & & & & 1 \end{bmatrix} \begin{bmatrix} Y_1 \\ C_1 \\ I_1 \\ Y_2 \\ C_2 \\ I_2 \\ M_1 \\ M_2 \\ E_1 \\ E_2 \\ G_1 \\ G_2 \end{bmatrix} = \begin{bmatrix} 0 \\ 0 \\ 0 \\ 0 \\ 0 \\ 0 \\ 0 \\ 0 \\ 0 \\ 0 \end{bmatrix} \qquad (7)$$

In this system there are now ten endogenous variables and only two exogenous or autonomous ones, G_1 and G_2. Because of feedbacks through area 2, the multiplier effect upon Y_1 of an increase in G_1 is larger than if imports (M_1) were a genuine and complete leakage from the economy of area 1. For example, let $c_1 = c_2 = 0.5$, $i_1 = i_2 = 0.2$, and $m_1 = m_2 = 0.3$.

If M_1 were simply a leakage, the multiplier in area 1 would be

$$\frac{\partial Y_1}{\partial G_1} = \frac{1}{1 - 0.5 - 0.2 + 0.3} = \frac{1}{1 - 0.4} = \frac{1}{0.6} = 1.67. \qquad (8)$$

However, in the two-area system the corresponding multiplier becomes

$$\frac{\partial Y_1}{\partial G_1} = \frac{(1 - 0.5 - 0.2 + 0.3)}{(1 - 0.5 - 0.2 + 0.3)^2 - (0.3)^2} = \frac{0.6}{0.36 - 0.09} = 2.22. \qquad (9)$$

If the policy maker in each area understands the structure of the complete system, he will presumably take account of the fact that his multiplier is 2.22 rather than 1.67 in deciding by how much government expenditures should be modified.

A four-area model (again treated as a closed system) opens up the possibility of multilateral trade. If we express the G_i (government expenditures in area i) as functions of the Y_i, $i = 1, 2, 3, 4$, we obtain

$$G_1 = \quad k_1 Y_1 - m_{12} Y_2 - m_{13} Y_3 - m_{14} Y_4 \tag{10}$$

$$G_2 = -m_{21} Y_1 + k_2 Y_2 - m_{23} Y_3 - m_{24} Y_4 \tag{11}$$

$$G_3 = -m_{31} Y_1 - m_{32} Y_2 + k_3 Y_3 - m_{34} Y_4 \tag{12}$$

$$G_4 = -m_{41} Y_1 - m_{42} Y_2 - m_{43} Y_3 + k_4 Y_4 \tag{13}$$

where

$$k_i = 1 - c_i - i_i + \sum_{\substack{j=1 \\ (i \neq j)}}^{4} m_{ji}; \quad i = 1, 2, 3, 4. \tag{14}$$

Or,

$$\begin{bmatrix} G_1^* \\ G_2^* \\ G_3^* \\ G_4^* \end{bmatrix} = \begin{bmatrix} k_1 & -m_{12} & -m_{13} & -m_{14} \\ -m_{21} & k_2 & -m_{23} & -m_{24} \\ -m_{31} & -m_{32} & k_3 & -m_{34} \\ -m_{41} & -m_{42} & -m_{43} & k_4 \end{bmatrix} \begin{bmatrix} Y_1^* \\ Y_2^* \\ Y_3^* \\ Y_4^* \end{bmatrix} \tag{15}$$

or

$$G^* = (k - M)Y^*, \tag{16}$$

where the Y_i^* are desired values of gross area product and the G_i^* are the values of government expenditures needed to attain the Y_i^*. The model could be expanded to include any number of areas n.

The model just outlined would also apply if the Y_i^* $(i = 1, 2, \ldots, n)$ were selected by a national policy maker and if the G_i^* $(i = 1, 2, \ldots, n)$ were also computed and implemented by him. As written, the model is just-identified, with n targets and n instruments.

In practice, the matrix $(k–M)$ might be rather stable for a year or two at a time, because most firms would try to maintain continuing relations with their existing customers wherever they are located. If the Y_i^* were the explicit target variables of national policy, national GNP $(= \sum_{i=1}^{n} Y_i^*)$ and total federal expenditures $(= \sum_{i=1}^{n} G_i^*)$ would be calculated by simple addition. Employment N_i^* would be a more likely target of national policy than gross area product Y_i^*, but if $Y_i^* = w_i N_i^*$ (where w_i is average gross area product per worker in area i), we can simply rewrite the model as

$$G^* = (k - M)N^* w'. \tag{17}$$

Since the functional economic area is a commuting field and a relatively self-contained labor market in the short run, there is much to be said for maximizing employment FEA by FEA as a short-run policy goal (see Fox, 1969e).

In a large metropolitan area regarded as a compound FEA, the employment targets should probably be stated for each R-level trade area within the metropolis.[5]

---

[5] The rationale for delineating R-level trade areas within a metropolis is presented in Fox (1967d, 1969e, 1969f) and in Leven, Legler, and Shapiro (1970); it is also described very briefly in Section 12.1 of this book.

Interarea commuting would be fairly extensive. If the employment target N_i^* applies to members of the labor force *residing* in area i and the G_i^* are calculated to increase the number of workers employed in *establishments* in area i, there is a potential difference between employment impacts by place of residence and those by place of work. If the initial interarea commuting pattern is known and can be assumed stable, we have

$$N^* = CN, \tag{18}$$

where a typical row is

$$N_1^* = c_{11}N_1 + c_{12}N_2 + \cdots + c_{1m}N_m, \tag{19}$$

and there are m R-level trade areas in the metropolis and environs. To find the set of N_i's that will achieve the desired set of N_i^*, we multiply the first equation by C^{-1}, obtaining

$$N = C^{-1}N^*. \tag{20}$$

8.5 *The Fullerton-Prescott Simulation Model of Economic Systems at City, County, and Multicounty Area Levels*

The capacity to deal with quantitative economic models of systems of cities and small regions has grown rapidly in recent years. The most sophisticated model I have seen for nonmetropolitan areas was developed by Herbert H. Fullerton and James R. Prescott (1973). A research program conducted by Wilbur R. Maki from 1960 to 1968 provided some of the data, relationships, and experience upon which these authors built.

Figure 8.5, reproduced from the Fullerton-Prescott study, illustrates the structure of their model at a high level of aggregation. Central to the model is the interindustry relations sector, including a 15×15 input–output matrix aggregated from a more detailed (approximately 100×100) matrix. Connected with the interindustry sector are labor, capital, income, and demographic sectors, and also a water resources sector; the sectors interact recursively over time. In this schematic flow chart of a six-component model, recursive dependence is depicted by the time-dated directional arrows. For example, the authors explain that "model output from the demographic sector in year (t) provides an input to the labor sector in the same year; output from the latter sector is input to the demographic sector in year $(t + 1)$. Broken lines indicate constraining relationships among sectors pertaining to capacity constraints due to capital stock and industrial water supply availability."

The basic geographic units of the model include Iowa's 99 counties, with 21 of them further divided between a city of 10,000 or more people and the rest of the county—120 units in all. These could be aggregated to approximate FEAs, other economic areas, watersheds, or any other logical or arbitrary regions.

Fullerton and Prescott describe the general structure of their model as follows:

> The [model] may be classified as a dynamic simulation model of the deterministic type . . . and has the following principal characteristics:
>
> 1. The model is decomposable into major component sectors or blocks. Each block may be simulated in isolation from other blocks provided that

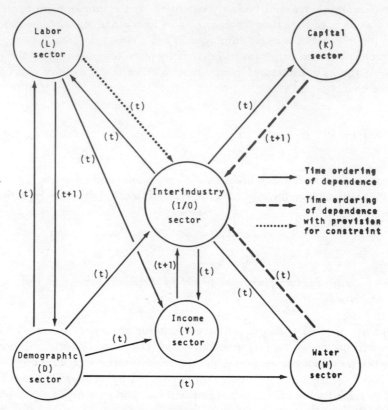

Figure 8.5.   Recursive dependence among major sectors in the reference region economy. *Source.* Herbert H. Fullerton and James R. Prescott, *An Economic Simulation Model for Regional Development Planning.* Ann Arbor: Ann Arbor Science Publishers, Inc., forthcoming 1975. (Figure II.5 in 1973 manuscript version).

values for the exogenous and lagged endogenous variables could be provided; many of these variables are outputs from other component sectors.

2. The model is recursive in that time lagged and sequential dependence occurs among variables within and among component sectors. Model outputs become model inputs in the recursive sequence from block to block and from one time period to the next.

3. The model is balanced spatially. Aggregate model outputs were obtained by summation where they were generated at the standard level. Conversely, spatially disaggregated model outputs generated at the reference area level were forced to be consistent with their main counterparts (Section II.5).

Although computational problems in handling social system models of cities and regions are far from trivial, the limiting factors at present are deciding what variables to measure, how to measure them, and how to estimate (or establish a priori) causal or structural relationships among them.

IX

Accounts and Indicators for the Higher Education Sector

W̲E̲ ̲H̲A̲V̲E̲ ̲S̲A̲I̲D̲ ̲V̲E̲R̲Y̲ ̲L̲I̲T̲T̲L̲E̲ about formal organizations in relation to social accounts and indicators. It seems best to fill this gap with a discussion of universities, departments, and the higher education sector.[1] In the process we should obtain some insights into the problems of evaluating the outputs of nonmarket institutions.

9.1 Resource Allocation Problems of a University President

The university is an important kind of nonmarket institution. Cyert (1973), in his review of Fox (ed., 1972), commented on the problem of determining appropriate prices or weights for university outputs as follows:

> The major problem in planning is, of course, the lack of market prices and Professor Fox argues (in Chapter 10) for substituting weights as estimated by the relevant administrator to units of various outputs as a substitute for a pricing system. Conventional techniques can then be used to determine an optimum allocation of resources, given the weighting scheme. I have some sympathy for this approach, but I think that it is not sufficiently sophisticated. I believe that the whole problem of determining these weights is the central consideration the solution of which is lacking not only in most universities, but also in many profit-making organizations. The decisions

[1] Some examples of quantitative approaches to problems of resource allocation in universities and departments are presented in McCamley (1967); Fox, McCamley, and Plessner (1967); Plessner, Fox, and Sanyal (1968); Fox and Sengupta (1968); Koenig, Keeney, and Zemach (1968); Sengupta and Fox (1970); Wagner and Weathersby (1971); Sengupta (1972); Feinberg (1972); Kumar (1972a, 1972b); and Sanyal (1972).

involving the internal allocation of resources in a firm pose exactly the same problems as decisions determining the allocation for a university; one problem is the inability to determine the benefits from allocating certain resources to particular kinds of activities—advertising being one example. More generally, I am arguing that a major problem in making planning more quantitative is the determination of the goals of the organization. In universities, in particular, we lack knowledge on how to determine a set of goals and priorities. Without such a set of goals and priorities, the process of resource allocation is one that is political. The resources allocated to a particular output depend on the kinds of influence that can be asserted by various deans and department heads on the various administrative officers making the allocation decisions. Thus an allocation of resources is made that is not related directly to either the value of output in the market or the goals of the institution. Even the procedure recommended by Fox might still fall into this category because the weights might be determined politically. . . .

. . . one of the major factors that is untouched in the book is the need for more elaborate information systems than currently exist within most universities. We need to have better cost data and better means of searching the environment for trends and changes in the values of various potential outputs of the university in both education and research (p. 592–593).

We will try to shed some additional light on these problems. To begin, assume that a university president understands the internal "technology" of the university very well and can compute rather accurately what would happen to various measurable outputs (numbers of B.S., M.S., and Ph.D. graduates in specific fields, numbers of research publications in specific fields, etc.) if a million dollars a year were withdrawn from one cluster of activities and added to another cluster. For simplicity, assume that all outputs are aggregated into two and that all limiting resources are converted into two, say (1) funds for current operations (mostly salaries for professors and supporting staff) and (2) physical plant (classrooms, office space, laboratories, library facilities, etc.). Given these two constraints, he chooses to operate the two activities Q_1 and Q_2 at the levels q_1 and q_2.

We infer a utility function and an optimizing model

$$\max W = f(Q_1, Q_2), \tag{1}$$

subject to the nonlinear production functions

$$Q_1 = f_1(F, B), \tag{2}$$

$$Q_2 = f_2(F, B). \tag{3}$$

the production transformation curve

$$g(Q_1, Q_2) = 0, \tag{4}$$

and the constraints

$$F \leq F_0, \tag{5}$$

$$B \leq B_0. \tag{6}$$

We assume that the president's utility function (like the consumer's) is simply ordinal but has the property of diminishing marginal rates of substitution of Q_i for Q_j $(i, j = 1, 2, i \neq j)$; also, that the production possibilities frontier has the property of diminishing marginal rates of transformation of Q_i into Q_j.

If the point (q_1, q_2) is optimal under the specified restrictions, it is a point of tangency between the president's utility function and the transformation function. Assume that the (continuous) transformation function is specified numerically over a reasonable range of values of Q_1 and Q_2; then the slope $-r$ of the tangent at (q_1, q_2) is

$$-r = \frac{\partial Q_1}{\partial Q_2} = \frac{\{\partial g(Q_1, Q_2)\}/\partial Q_2}{\{\partial g(Q_1, Q_2)\}/\partial Q_1}. \tag{7}$$

If a vice-president agrees with the specification of the transformation function but believes that the (constrained) optimal point at which to operate would be (q_1', q_2') at which the absolute value of the slope of the tangent is $|r'| > |r|$, we infer that he sets a higher value on Q_2 relative to Q_1 than does the president. If both utility functions are ordinal and no marketlike prices are available for Q_1 and Q_2, there is no objective way to choose between the two views. Quantification of the ratios determined from the transformation function as (say) $r = 1.5$ and $r' = 2.0$ might provoke a clarifying exchange of "reasons why." If Q_1 and Q_2 are disaggregated into more sharply defined components, such as Ph.D. degrees in biological sciences versus Ph.D. degrees in social sciences, each party can specify his "barter terms of trade" at this more detailed level. Different assumptions about *facts* can be checked against factual data, and the areas of disagreement over as yet unmeasurable values can be more clearly delimited. The result might lead to some changes in both objective functions and the selection of a point (q_1'', q_2'') as optimal.

If the detailed components of Q_1 can be assigned marketlike prices, such as the net increases in expected career earnings associated with taking B.S. degrees rather than starting work with high school diplomas, we can compute a "market" price P_1 and infer an implicit price, $P_2 = rP_1$, for Q_2. The next challenge would be to analyze the suboutputs of Q_2 in more detail as inputs into various subsystems of the society; determine the media of exchange (in Parsons's sense) in which these inputs should be priced; and probe more deeply into the measurement of exchange rates between media which would be more or less appropriate for a society rather than simply for a particular individual.

The analogy of GNP calculations based on market prices seems to be the logical starting point. Many problems of measurement and aggregation are involved in computing gross national product. Yet the development of national income and product accounts in the 1930s and 1940s was prerequisite to the development and implementation of rational macroeconomic policies and the theory of quantitative economic policy in general. We should regard the "prices" of university outputs not as unmeasurable but simply as not yet measured.

We should note also that the concept of external economies among firms in a shopping center is directly transferable to clusters of departments within a university. Suppose that Q_1 and Q_2 are aggregates of two kinds of outputs, say Ph.D. degrees (Q_{1i}) and B.S. degrees (Q_{2i}) in m departments $(i = 1, 2, \ldots, m)$. If each department operates independently, we have a set of m production possibilities frontiers, one for each department. Suppose now that by pooling one or more of the limiting resources among all the departments, we are able to advance the production possibilities frontiers for all m departments simultaneously. The economies which were external to the departments individually are now internal to the cluster as a whole.

If we assume that the ith department policy maker (chairman or faculty consensus) has an ordinal preference function such that an increase in either or both outputs Q_{1i} and/or Q_{2i} will be regarded as an improvement, the external economies can be allocated among departments in many different patterns all of which will leave some departments better off than before and none worse off than before. All these solutions are Pareto-better than the situation prevailing before certain resources were pooled.

The president might allocate the benefits according to his own ordinal preference function. However, he may perceive features of "technology" that are not perceived by department chairmen generally but may be recognized by those most directly involved. For example, the president may have good reason to believe that department i is operating in a range of increasing returns to scale and should therefore be given considerably more resources. A Schumpeterian innovation in one department may stimulate a wave of emulation in others. As in the market economy, new "profit" opportunities are continually appearing within (and between) universities—"profit" as perceived by particular decision makers at various levels in the universities. So long as all or most weights (prices) are unspecified, comparisons between the expected "profits" from alternative innovations remain highly subjective.

It seems clear that careful measurement of the quantities of outputs (and inputs) of universities should be attempted, so that at least the quantity component of "gross university output" will be defined. Even if the prices were left relatively arbitrary, any specified set of (price) weights could be used to compute quantity index numbers for a given university over a period of years and to make rough but numerically reproducible comparisons between the quantities of output of different universities. The same (price) weights could be used in specifying *cardinal* objective functions for optimizing models of different universities; discussions of the implications of the results would lead to further clarification as to the rationales for (1) relative prices and (2) absolute prices ascribed to the various outputs.

On the operational level, perhaps, these endeavors are justified by the prospect of "increasing the efficiency of the university." On the scientific level, they would contribute to our understanding of the manner in which the market and nonmarket subsystems of the society are linked and how their functioning might be improved both "within and between"—initially and primarily by providing fuller and more accurate information about the system as a whole to decision makers active in the various subsystems.

9.2   *Resource Allocation Problems of a Department Chairman*

A typical department in a large public university operates in two principal environments: (1) the undergraduate programs, data systems, and administrative constraints of its own university, and (2) the graduate training, research, and publication system of its national scientific or scholarly community. Let us explore these from the viewpoint of the chairman of such a department, Department 1.

Within the broad admissions policies of the university and the average level of resources per student available to it for undergraduate programs, each department is obligated to supply courses of reasonable quality to all qualified undergraduates who may request enrollment. An increase in its undergraduate enrollments relative to other departments in the university constitutes a reasonable claim for the allocation of additional resources to Department 1.

Let us assume that an index of the attractiveness of each course in Department 1 that is available to undergraduates can be computed and all such indexes aggregated into a measure v of the overall attractiveness of Department 1's "undergraduate program offer." The measure v may contain at least three components: (1) expectations of the students concerning the contribution Department 1's courses will make to increasing their earning power and improving their employment prospects, (2) appraisals by students concerning the relevance of Department 1's subject matter to their concerns as citizens and members of society, and (3) appraisals by students of the quality of teaching performance in Department 1.

Suppose there are 70 departments in a university, each offering some undergraduate work, and the sum of all enrollments in undergraduate courses in the university in a given year is a fixed number n_u, resulting from the size of the student body. The prospective enrollments in the individual departments can be expressed by the following matrix equation:

$$n = a + Bv, \tag{8}$$

where n, a, and v are column vectors of 70 elements (departments) each and B is a square matrix of 70 rows and 70 columns. This set of 70 linear equations is assumed to determine the undergraduate enrollment in each department subject to the constraint that the sum of enrollments in all departments equal n_u, the total undergraduate enrollment in the university.

An increase in v_1 (the attractiveness of Department 1's undergraduate program offer as perceived by students) will increase n_1, the number of student quarters of enrollment in Department 1's courses, if the other v_i remain constant ($i = 2, 3, \ldots, 70$). Since total university enrollment for the given year is fixed, an increase in n_1 must be offset by decreases in some or all of the enrollments in other departments, n_2 through n_{70}. Thus the first column of the matrix B will contain an element b_{11} which is greater than zero, while most of the remaining elements in that column will be zero or negative.

If all v_i other than v_1 remain constant while v_1 increases, the net effect of v_1 on the enrollment pattern is given by

$$\frac{\partial n}{\partial v_i} = b_{11} + b_{21} + b_{31} + \cdots + b_{70,1}. \tag{9}$$

The corresponding net effect of a change in the perceived attractiveness of the undergraduate program offer of any other department i is

$$\frac{\partial n}{\partial v_i} = b_{1i} + b_{2i} + \cdots + b_{ii} + \cdots + b_{70,i}; \tag{10}$$

hence increases in any or all v_i ($i = 2, 3, \ldots, 70$) relative to v_1 will affect (i.e., in most cases, decrease) n_1.

We can visualize the matrix equation $n = a + Bv$ as a student preference function, with the restriction on total enrollments taking the place of the budget constraint in consumption theory. The v_i play the role of prices or perceived rewards that induce enrollment responses by students.

We assume that the national environment of the department is a scientific community that includes 50 departments with graduate programs ranging from distinguished to barely adequate. The demand function for enrollment in the department's undergraduate courses has a substantial downward slope. In contrast, the demand function for the department's contribution to the national output of graduate training and published research must slope downward rather gently (because the department accounts for a small percentage of the national output of its discipline).

Now, suppose that the national demand function for graduate training and research rises sharply while the department's total resources remain fixed. Department 1 will tend to seek a new equilibrium at which a smaller proportion of its regular budget resources is used in the undergraduate and a larger proportion in the graduate program. Conversely, a sharp drop in the national demand function for graduate training and research would tend to result in the allocation of a larger proportion of its fixed resources to the undergraduate program and a smaller proportion to graduate training and research. This situation is replicated in each of the 50 departments in our hypothetical scientific community.

Assume now that an agency of the federal government recognizes that (1) the benefits of graduate training and research are diffused over the nation and not fixed in particular states, and (2) state legislatures will not appropriate sufficient funds to support the volumes of graduate training and research that appear to be desirable from a national viewpoint. Assume further that the director (policymaker) of this federal agency has two major policy instruments: (1) an allocation of funds for research grants and contracts to be awarded to university professors, and (2) an allocation of funds to provide fellowships for graduate students. The research grants and contracts may be used (1) to pay salaries of professors during the summer months, (2) to provide stipends for research assistants and associates who are graduate or postdoctoral students in the department, and (3) to pay some proportion of the academic year salaries of professors.

If federal funds for research are increased, some professors in Department 1 will transfer additional time to such funds, releasing salary savings that (under the circumstances) can and should be used for additional part-time instructors and teaching assistants. The total number of graduate students in the department may be expanded somewhat (on research assistantships even if the number of federal fellowships is held constant); also, the kinds of research performed by university professors are usually complementary with the preparation of dissertations by graduate students.

The number of persons engaged in nationally oriented research and graduate training may also be expanded by adding temporary faculty members whose salaries are paid from research grants and contracts. Also, some persons who have recently completed Ph.D.s may find it advantageous to accept a temporary teaching position in the same department to replace regular professorial teaching resources that are temporarily transferred to federally financed research.

The quality of the research output and the teaching programs of a department will depend partly on the quality of the graduate students it attracts. Suppose that a specified number of graduate students, all meeting the admission standards of at least the less prestigious departments in the community, seeks admission to various of the 50 departments. Formally, the situation may be modeled in a manner much like that presented for undergraduate enrollment choices among departments in a single university. We assume that the total number of graduate students who will be admitted to the 50 departments in the coming year is a fixed number m_T. Each department has an "offer" for prospective graduate students, and we denote its attractiveness by u. This measure of the attractiveness of the department to prospective graduate students is closely associated with the rated quality of its graduate faculty, which in turn is strongly correlated with the reputed effectiveness of its graduate program. Graduate students in the most highly rated departments will usually be made aware of the most promising ideas and methods in their discipline, will engage in dissertation research reasonably close to the frontiers of their specialties, and will have considerably better than average employment opportunities; and judgments of faculty and graduate program reflect these conditions.

The allocation of beginning graduate students among the departments in the discipline may be represented by the matrix equation

$$m = c + Du, \tag{11}$$

where m, c, and u are column vectors of 50 elements each and D is a square matrix with 50 rows and 50 columns. If u_1 is perceived as increasing while the other u_i remain constant, the number of students seeking to enroll in Department 1 will increase, and (since we assume $\sum_{i=1}^{50} m_i = m_T$ to be fixed) the numbers seeking to enroll in other departments will on balance decline.

The same model can be extended to the allocation of prospective graduate students among disciplines. Assume that the u_i for the 50 departments in discipline 1 can be combined into an aggregative measure, U_1, of the perceived attractiveness of obtaining a Ph.D. in discipline 1. Suppose that similar measures U_2, U_3, ... , U_k, are calculated for other disciplines requiring Ph.D.s or comparably long graduate training. Then a perceived increase in U_1 relative to the other U_i will tend to increase the number of potential graduate students seeking admission to discipline 1. If total admissions to the 50 departments in discipline 1 were held constant, the average quality of the graduate students admitted to them would rise.

One component of a vector of U_i's ranging over disciplines would be the vector of expected salaries for persons with given characteristics who take their Ph.D.s in the various fields. A multiple regression analysis of the salaries of scientists on the National Register of Scientific and Technical Personnel in 1966 was published by Emanuel Melichar (1968). Melichar's principal results are reproduced in Tables 6.10 and 6.11 and Figure 6.1.

The net relations between salaries and years of experience in Table 6.11 are presumed to be the same for all sciences. The salary differentials in the bottom portion of Table 6.11 imply that graduate students with the same ability and motivation may receive considerably different salaries, depending on the discipline in which they earned their Ph.D.s[2] We do not know the stability of the 1966 salary structure over time.

---

[2] There is, of course, a wide variation in salaries of individuals within each discipline; the standard error of the residuals from Melichar's equation was approximately $\log_{10} = 0.114$. About two-thirds of the individual salaries in any given science lay within a range of 30 percent above and 23 percent below the corresponding regression estimates. A superior scientist in a low-salaried field still earned more than an average scientist in a high-salaried field in 1966.

We return to our assumed federal policy maker who has the power to expand or contract the volume of research grants and contracts (and graduate fellowships) available to the 50 departments of our hypothetical scientific community. A given number of dollars allocated to university professors in the form of research grants and contracts will support fewer graduate students than the same number of dollars awarded as graduate fellowships. Thus these two policy instruments should enable the policy maker to achieve (approximately) target values of two separate variables: (1) the number of graduate students trained, and (2) the volume of published research. These two target variables would normally tend to move in the same direction, but the instruments (research grants versus fellowships) could be manipulated to insure that they changed by different percentages. Under certain circumstances, the volume of published research could be caused to expand moderately at the same time that the number of graduate students completing Ph.D.s was moderately reduced, or vice versa.

Our policy maker should presumably use his two instruments with a view to approximating some "optimal" time paths of the two target variables. The optimal time path for numbers of graduate students enrolled or numbers completing the Ph.D. degree could hardly be chosen without some notion of the associated time path of salaries for Ph.D.s in discipline 1 relative to salaries in other fields involving similar training and life styles.

Complementarities Between Graduate and Undergraduate Programs: Combining Subject Matter Quality with Teaching Proficiency.   The values u and v of a department's offers to graduate and undergraduate students, respectively, might each be viewed schematically as containing four components, as follows:

$$u = w_1(\lambda_1 t + \lambda_2 p) + w_2(\gamma_1 s + \gamma_2 r) \tag{12}$$

and

$$v = w_3(\lambda_3 t + \lambda_4 p) + w_4(\gamma_3 s + \gamma_4 r), \tag{13}$$

where t is an index of the quality of teaching techniques used, p is an index of the quality of subject matter learned, s is an index of the expected average salary of professional workers in the discipline, and r is an index of the expected riskiness of employment prospects in the discipline; the w's, λ's, and γ's are weights such that $w_1 + w_2 = 1$, $\lambda_1 + \lambda_2 = 1$, $\gamma_1 + \gamma_2 = 1$, $w_3 + w_4 = 1$, $\lambda_3 + \lambda_4 = 1$, and $\gamma_3 + \gamma_4 = 1$.

The variables s and r are properties of the national market for professional workers trained in the discipline and cannot be significantly altered by the actions of a single department; they are matters of major importance to potential graduate students and substantial importance to undergraduates considering a B.A. or B.S. major in the field. The variables t and p are properties of the department's own program and can be influenced by choice of personnel, in-service training and learning opportunities, incentives, facilities and equipment, choice of course content, textbooks and reading lists, curriculum design, and other local actions. The quality of subject matter learned (including theory and methodology), crucial at the graduate level, is somewhat less important at the upper and lower division levels, respectively; the quality of teaching techniques used is least important at the graduate level and progressively more so at the upper and lower division levels. Our hypothesis might be depicted as follows:

	Relative Importance of	
Level of Instruction	Teaching Techniques, t	Quality of Subject Matter, p
Graduate division	0.2	0.8
Upper division	0.4	0.6
Lower division	0.6	0.4

The figures are illustrative only.

The gradients in a national scientific community are dominated by productivity in the creation of new knowledge, which implies proximity to the frontier of the subject matter field (and a high rating on the variable p in our equations). In contrast, the faculty of a strictly undergraduate department is in some danger of becoming detached from the national scientific community and teaching obsolescent subject matter (implying a low rating on the variable p). The undergraduate faculty may, however, take considerable pride in its teaching skills (leading to a high rating on t); a strictly graduate faculty may be impervious to advice on teaching techniques (leading to a low rating on t).

For numerical illustration of the potential leverage of t and p in increasing program quality, we separate v into upper division (v_{ud}) and lower division (v_{ld}) components and supply values for all coefficients, as follows:

$$u = 0.5(0.2t + 0.8p) + 0.5(0.5s + 0.5r), \tag{14}$$

$$v_{ud} = 0.7(0.4t + 0.6p) + 0.3(0.5s + 0.5r), \tag{15}$$

$$v_{ld} = 0.9(0.6t + 0.4p) + 0.1(0.5s + 0.5r). \tag{16}$$

The following partial derivatives are of interest:

Index of Program Quality or Value	Partial Derivative with Respect to	
	t	p
u	0.10	0.40
v_{ud}	0.28	0.42
v_{ld}	0.54	0.36

Let us relate this discussion to Table 9.1, a display of Department 1's instructional program in activity analysis format, and particularly to the top row of figures labeled "assumed relative value per unit of activity with average quality." This implies that $v_{ld} = 1$ for activities 1, 2, and 3; $v_{ud} = 1$ for activities 4, 5, and 6; and $u = 1$ for activities 9, 10, 11, 12, 13, and 14. Suppose these are the values realized in year 1. We would like to consider realistic ways of increasing these values. The values of s

Table 9.1. Department 1: Consistency Model of Instructional Program for Year 1

	X_1	X_2	X_3	X_4	X_5	X_6	X_7	X_8	X_9	X_{10}
Assumed Relative Value per Unit of Activity, with Average Quality (3 credit hours of lower division teaching = 1.00):	280	100	34	136	68	68	1.25	1.25	140	105
Number of Units of Activity:	8	9	93	25	35	0	0	130	8	5
Activity Number:	X_1	X_2	X_3	X_4	X_5	X_6	X_7	X_8	X_9	X_{10}
A. Outputs										
1. Lower division teaching	-280	-100	-34							
2. Upper division teaching				-68	-34	-34				
3. Undergraduate advising							-1	-1		
4. Graduate division teaching									-40	-30
5. Dissertation research, etc.										
6. Transfers										
7. Faculty research time (residual)										
B. Inputs of Budgeted Resources (man-years)[b]										
1. Professors	0.125	0.083		0.083	0.083		0.005		0.083	0.083
2. Instructors			0.083			0.083		0.005		
3. Teaching assistants	0.500	0.083			0.083				0.083	
C. Inputs of Student Time (man-years)[c]										
1. Lower division students	17.500	6.250	2.125							
2. Upper division students				4.250	2.125	2.125				
3. Graduate students (courses)									3.333	2.500
4. Graduate students (dissertations, etc.)										

and r (salary and employment prospects in our discipline), which are beyond our control, are not of much concern to the lower-division students anyway.

Our assumed values of the w's and λ's imply that the partial derivative or "efficiency" of p in raising quality is about the same (from 0.36 to 0.42) at all three levels of instruction, whereas the "efficiency" of t appears to be twice as high at the lower division as at the upper division level (0.54 as against 0.28) and to be quite low at the graduate level. Our search for ways to improve quality now becomes an examination of ways to increase t and p.

A systematic attempt at program improvement in a department with both undergraduate and graduate responsibilities might be guided by an objective function with six components as follows:

$$W_{\text{total}} = W_l + W_u + W_{adv} + W_g + W_{gsq} + W_{r(s+gc)}, \qquad (17)$$

where the subscripts l, u, adv, g, gsq, and $r(s + gc)$ refer, respectively, to lower-division teaching, upper-division teaching, advising undergraduate majors, graduate teaching, dissertation research and related graduate study, and research involving regular university budget resources (s) and/or grants and contracts (gc) typically

Table 9.1. (*Continued*)

X_{11}	X_{12}	X_{13}	X_{14}	X_{15}	X_{16}	X_{17}	X_{18}		B_0 Restrictions: Outputs Demanded and Budgeted Resources Available	B_1 Places Provided; Budget Resources and Student Time Used	B_1-B_0 Places Provided Minus Enrollments; Resources Used Minus Resources Available
70	52.5	35	10.5	0	0	0	0				
10	4	14	300	2.009	0.860	0.341	3.623				
								=	−6300	−6302[a]	−2[a]
								=	−2880	−2890	−10[a]
								=	−130	−130	0
−20	−15	−10						=	−870	−870	0
			−1					=	−300	−300	0
				−1	−1	−1		=	−3.210	−3.210	0
						−1	−1	≤	0	−3.964	−3.964
0.083	0.083	0.083	0.008	1.000	1.000		1.000	=	19.400	19.400	0
				2.325				≥	3.730	8.400	4.670
					2.906			≥	5.000	7.500	2.500
								=	393.750[d]	393.750[d]	0
								=	180.000[d]	180.000[d]	0
1.667	1.250	0.833						=	72.500	72.500	0
			0.083					=	25.000	25.000	0

[a] Student places available under this instructional pattern slightly exceed actual student enrollments.
[b] Assumes academic man years of 9 months and work weeks of 44 hours.
[c] Assumes academic student years of 9 months; 16 courses a year is full-time load for undergraduates and 12 courses a year is full-time load for graduates. Courses are assumed to be on the quarter system and to carry three credit hours each.
[d] Excludes assumed 2.061 student years of time associated with academic advising.

from federal sources. The W's are scalar valued objective functions; let us assume for the moment that they are expressed in dollars. (This would mean that each figure in the top row of Table 9.1 should be multiplied by $400; e.g., the value of output of one unit of activity 1, a lecture-plus-recitation-section pattern involving 280 lower-division students, would be rated at $112,000 with average quality, i.e., with v_{ld} equal to 1.00.)

From Table 9.1, the sum of the first five components of W_{total} for Department 1 in year 1 can be computed at $7,302,000. On certain assumptions the sixth component, $W_{r(s+gc)}$ amounted to $700,000; thus the resulting value of Department 1's total gross output in year 1 would be about $8 million. A first approximation to the production possibilities frontier for the department as of (say) year 5 might be stated as a series of conjectures by the chairman and faculty members most knowledgeable concerning each of the six program segments. For example, the computed value of output of the lower division program in year 1 is $2,520,000. Maximum feasible gains in the value of output of this program by year 5, and the prospective sources of such gains, might be conjectured as follows: (1) better teaching materials, 10 percent; (2) better instructors and teaching assistants in terms of basic ability and motivation, 10 percent; (3) better training and supervision of instructors and teaching assistants in their teaching functions, 10 percent; and (4) better preparation and performance in lecture groups of 280 and 100 students, respectively, by present faculty members, 10 percent.

Plans for implementation could start from such a point. The importance of the various sources of potential improvements would differ substantially from one program segment to another.

Some Elements of an Equilibrium System.   The foregoing considerations lead us to a tentative integration of the graduate and undergraduate components of a set of universities with major programs at both levels.

If there are k disciplines and J universities we can write

$$v = (w_1\lambda_1 t + w_1\lambda_2 p) + (w_2\gamma_1 s + w_2\gamma_2 r) \tag{18}$$

and

$$u = (w_3\lambda_3 t + w_3\lambda_4 p) + (w_4\gamma_3 s + w_4\gamma_4 r), \tag{19}$$

where all variables are column vectors with $k \times J$ elements. Furthermore, assuming that linear relations exist over relevant ranges of the variables, we can write

$$n = a + Bv \tag{20}$$

and

$$m = c + Du, \tag{21}$$

where n, m, a, c, v, and u are column vectors with $k \times J$ elements and B and D are square matrices with $k \times J$ rows and $k \times J$ columns. Substituting, we obtain

$$n = a + B[(w_1\lambda_1 t + w_1\lambda_2 p) + (w_2\gamma_1 s + w_2\gamma_2 r)] \tag{22}$$

and

$$m = c + D[(w_3\lambda_3 t + w_3\lambda_4 p) + (w_4\gamma_3 s + w_4\gamma_4 r)], \tag{23}$$

where B consists of J diagonal blocks of k rows and k columns, each block representing the enrollment preference matrix of undergraduates in a particular university, and D consists of k diagonal blocks of J rows and J columns, each block representing the enrollment preference matrix of graduate students in a particular discipline. The variables s and r each take k distinct national average values, one for each discipline; their time paths should be predicted, analyzed, and if necessary modified in line with federal responsibility for national manpower data, analysis, and broad policy. The variables t and p are subject to influence in each of k departments in each of j universities; this is the level at which activity analysis models can be used and attempts can be made to achieve optimal relationships between graduate and undergraduate programs.

Whereas the chairman of each department might reasonably try to maximize v_{ij} for his own undergraduate program, the university president (once he has designated a total dollar amount e_j for undergraduate instruction in the university) should evidently try to maximize $\bar{v}_j = \sum_{i=1}^{k} (n_{ij}/n_j)v_{ij}$, where $n_j = \sum_{i=1}^{k} n_{ij}$ is total undergraduate enrollment in the university and each v_{ij} is a function of the amount of budget resources e_{ij} allocated for the undergraduate program of department ij. Formally, the e_{ij} should be allocated such that

$$\frac{\partial \bar{v}_j}{\partial e_{1j}} = \frac{\partial \bar{v}_j}{\partial e_{2j}} = \frac{\partial \bar{v}_j}{\partial e_{3j}} = \cdots = \frac{\partial \bar{v}_j}{\partial e_{kj}}, \tag{24}$$

and $\sum_{i=1}^{k} e_{ij} = e_j$.

Similarly, the chairman of each department might reasonably seek to maximize u_{ij} for his own graduate program. Once a total dollar amount f_i has been designated for federally financed research grants, contracts, and graduate fellowships, however, our hypothetical federal policy maker, with a constructive interest in the national scientific community of discipline i, might aspire to maximize $\bar{u}_i = \sum_{j=1}^{J} (m_{ij}/m_i)u_{ij}$, where $m_i = \sum_{j=1}^{J} m_{ij}$ is total graduate enrollment in the discipline and each u_{ij} is a function of the amount of federal resources f_{ij} made available (through whatever mechanisms) for the graduate training and research program of department ij. Evidently, the f_{ij} should be allocated such that

$$\frac{\partial \bar{u}_i}{\partial f_{i1}} = \frac{\partial \bar{u}_i}{\partial f_{i2}} = \frac{\partial \bar{u}_i}{\partial f_{i3}} = \cdots = \frac{\partial \bar{u}_i}{\partial f_{iJ}}, \tag{25}$$

and $\sum_{j=1}^{J} f_{ij} = f_i$.

Federal policy makers must (should) also be concerned about the allocation of total federal resources for research and graduate training among disciplines, $f = \sum_{i=1}^{k} f_i$. The equilibrium conditions at this level would evidently be

$$\frac{\partial \bar{u}}{\partial f_1} = \frac{\partial \bar{u}}{\partial f_2} = \frac{\partial \bar{u}}{\partial f_3} = \cdots = \frac{\partial \bar{u}}{\partial f_k}, \tag{26}$$

where $\bar{u} = \sum_{i=1}^{k} (m_i/m)\bar{u}_i$. To the extent that complementarities existed and were realized between program quality at undergraduate and graduate levels in each department, there would be multiple links between the undergraduate program equilibrium system of each university and the graduate program equilibrium system within and between national scientific (and scholarly) communities.

9.3 Correlates of Quality in Graduate Education

Lawton Hartman (1969) presented some extremely useful data and analyses on correlates of quality in graduate education in the United States. The data in the upper portion of Table 9.2 are taken directly from Hartman's report. Hartman used numerical ratings of the perceived qualities of the graduate faculties of 29 departments in each of 106 universities as of 1964, reported by Allan Cartter (1966), to arrive at quality ratings for the graduate faculties of entire universities. He grouped the top 70 or so universities into four quality classes, A, B, C, and D. For universities within each class, he determined the median value of each of the variables in rows 1 through

Table 9.2. Correlates of Quality in Graduate Education in the United States: Attributes and Performance Measures as of 1963–1964 to 1967–1968

Quality Attribute or Performance Measure	Perceived Quality Class of University's Graduate Faculty, 1963–1964[a]			
	A	B	C	D
1. Ratio of doctorates to baccalaureates[b]	0.202	0.110	0.070	0.055
2. Index of library resources[c]	Over 2.00	1.00–1.49	0.75–0.99	0.50–0.74
3. Average compensation of full professors (9 months)[c]	$18,838	$17,616	$16,600	$15,200
4. Professors as percent of all faculty members[d]	42	38	32	30
5. Number of full professors[d]	375	308	210	160
6. Federal obligations for academic research and development (1000)[b]	$22,878	$10,898	$6,479	$3,447
7. Postdoctoral students in science and engineering (number)[e]	174	84	47	22
8. Selection of institutions by recipients of graduate fellowships (number)[f]	362	62	26	10

9.	Graduate students enrolled[g]	3,100	2,130	1,172	757
10.	Number of doctoral awards per year[b]	316	205	102	56
11.	Doctoral awards per graduate student[h]	0.102	0.096	0.087	0.074

Amounts and Numbers per Full Professor

12.	Federal obligations for academic research and development[i]	$61,000	$35,400	$30,900	$21,500
13.	Postdoctoral students in science and engineering[j]	0.464	0.273	0.224	0.138
14.	Graduate students enrolled[k]	8.27	6.92	5.58	4.73
15.	Number of doctoral awards per year[l]	0.843	0.666	0.486	0.350

Source. Lawton M. Hartman, *Graduate Education: Parameters for Public Policy.* Washington, D. C.: National Science Board, National Science Foundation, 1969. 168 pp. See especially Chapter II, "Correlates of Quality," pp. 49–121. Lines 1–11 compiled into this table by K. A. Fox; lines 12–15 computed by K. A. Fox.

[a] Classification made by the National Science Board for the purpose of distributing 106 universities over seven class intervals. Only the top four classes, containing about 70 universities, are included in this table.
[b] As of 1963–1964.
[c] As of 1967–1968 (salary plus employee benefits, adjusted to a 9-month basis).
[d] As of 1967–1968.
[e] Fall 1966.
[f] Total, 1963–1967.
[g] Line 10 divided by line 11.
[h] Doctoral awards in 1965–1966 divided by graduate students enrolled (science and engineering).
[i] Line 6 divided by line 5.
[j] Line 7 divided by line 5.
[k] Line 9 divided by line 5.
[l] Line 10 divided by line 5.

11 in the table. The "amounts and numbers per full professor," rows 12 to 15, were computed by Fox (1974).

The significant feature of Table 9.2 is that the "independent" variable used to classify the universities was noneconomic and not obviously susceptible to cardinal measurement, namely, prestige. The individual respondent was asked to assign the graduate faculties of each of a specified list of departments in his discipline to one of the following categories: distinguished, strong, good, adequate, marginal, not sufficient to provide acceptable doctoral training, and insufficient information. The number of respondents per discipline ranged from less than 100 to more than 200, according to the "size" of the discipline in terms of numbers of Ph.D.s granted annually and numbers of departments granting the Ph.D.

Although the adjective ratings given by the individual respondents were ordinal and the classification of universities in Table 9.2 derived from them must also be regarded as ordinal, they prove to be highly and consistently correlated with a large number of cardinally measured variables. It seems evident that the variables in rows 1 to 11 could be combined into an index number, $Q_j = \sum_{i=1}^{11} \lambda_i x_{ij}$, where the λ_i are weights adding up to 1.00 and x_{ij} is the ratio of the value of the ith variable for the jth quality class to the value of the ith variable for class A, which would correlate very highly with the quality variable and might be used as a cardinal surrogate for it. For example, if the 11 variables (in ratio form) are given equal weights $\lambda_i = 1/11$ for all i, the values of the index number are 1.00, .66, .47 and .36 for classes A, B, C, and D, respectively. If "quality of graduate faculty" is perceived as a measure of average prestige per full professor, we can construct an equally weighted index of the four variables in rows 12 to 15 (as ratios to their values for class A universities); this yields index number values of 1.00, .70, .55 and .41, respectively, for classes A, B, C, and D.

The ranking of a graduate faculty in Cartter's survey seems to depend almost entirely on its full professors. Francis Boddy, using confidential information on average salaries by rank in 45 of the 71 economics departments rated in that survey, found a coefficient of simple determination (r^2) of .57 between the score for faculty quality and the average salary of all full professors in a department; when the average of the top one-third of full professor salaries in each department ("superior full professors") was related to the quality score, the coefficient was even higher, .63. The coefficients of determination (r^2) between faculty quality and the average salaries for successively lower ranks ("superior associate professors," associate professors, and assistant professors) were .22, .13, and .03, respectively. When the graduate faculty quality index was used as the dependent variable and salary levels for each of six ranks (the five listed above plus "superior assistant professors") as the independent variables, the coefficient of multiple determination (R^2) was .72. It is not clear whether these coefficients were adjusted for degrees of freedom. If not, this adjustment would bring R^2 for the equation based on six ranks down to .68, compared with .62 for the $\bar{r}^2$ based on salaries of "superior full professors" alone.

Figure 9.1 shows the relationship between the graduate faculty quality scores of 71 economics departments and an index of publications *per department* in article equivalents per year. Since the number of full professors per university (hence, on the average, per department) is correlated with perceived quality, it seems likely that the index of publications *per full professor* would show a more nearly linear relationship to the faculty quality rating. Figure 9.2 indicates that the *visibility* of a department,

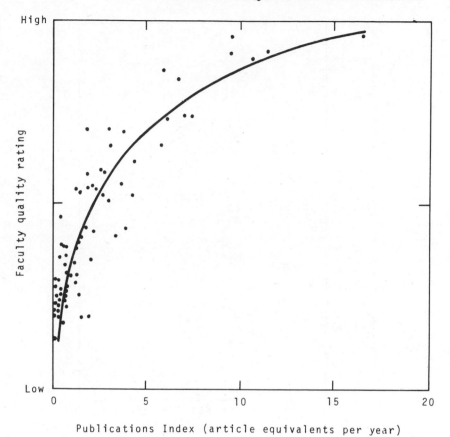

Figure 9.1.   Relationship of rated quality of graduate faculty to index of publications, 71 economics departments. *Source.* Allan M. Cartter, *An Assessement of Quality in Graduate Education* (Washington, D. C.: American Council on Education, 1966), p. 80.

as measured by the percentage of respondents who gave it substantive ratings, was also closely related to the perceived quality of its graduate faculty.

A similar survey of graduate programs as of 1969 made by Roose and Andersen (1970) refrained from publishing index number points for each program but gave ranks from 1 (top) to *n* for the *n* departments in each discipline that received scores of 3.0 to 5.0 as computed by Cartter's method. Roose and Andersen surveyed a total of 2626 graduate programs in 36 disciplines. The survey included 130 universities, and the number of graduate programs ranged from 125 for chemistry to 17 for Russian.

The graduate faculties of 802 programs received numerical ratings between 3.0 and 5.0, corresponding to the "strong" and "distinguished" categories as defined by Cartter (1966). The number of programs in this range as of 1969 varied from 38 for chemistry to 7 for Russian. The raters in each discipline were selected members of that discipline; the number of usable replies ranged from 263 for chemistry to 64 for Russian. For each department in the 3.0-to-5.0 category, Roose and Andersen give the percentage of respondents who indicated that they had insufficient information to rate it. We will call this the invisibility percentage, I, and its complement, $V = 100 - I$, the visibility percentage, or simply "visibility."

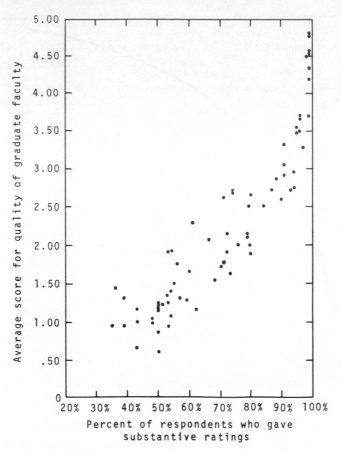

Figure 9.2.   Rated quality of economics faculty, by percentage of respondents providing ratings. *Source.* Allan M. Cartter, *An Assessment of Quality in Graduate Education* (Washington, D. C.: American Council on Education, 1966), p. 85.

The results of a multiple regression analysis of visibility V for the 802 departments are as follows:

$$V = 100.47 - 1.02R - 0.30N - 15.2D_1 - 13.3D_2 - 9.9D_3 - 8.6D_4 \quad (27)$$
$$(0.04) \quad (0.05) \quad\ (0.6) \quad\ \ (0.9) \quad\ \ (1.9) \quad\ \ (1.9)$$

Standard error of V = 7.7 percent of respondents.
Coefficient of multiple determination = .72.

In this equation, N is the number of graduate faculties rated in a discipline, and $R = 1, 2, \ldots, N$ is the perceived rank of the given faculty within its discipline. For faculties in the biological sciences, $D_1 = 1$; for faculties in engineering, $D_2 = 1$; D_3 and D_4 each apply to a single discipline.

The visibility of a graduate faculty in the physical sciences, social sciences, or humanities is estimated by setting D_1, D_2, D_3, and D_4 at zero:

$$V = 100.47 - 1.02R - 0.30N, \quad (28)$$
$$(0.04) \quad (0.05)$$

or in round numbers,

$$V = 100 - 1.0R - 0.3N. \tag{29}$$

Note that the change of R from 1 to 2 signifies a decline in rank (as we usually speak of it) from first place (top) to second place. If $N = 10$, $V = 97 - 1.0R$; hence $V = 96$ for the top-ranking department, 95 for the second, and 87 for the tenth. If $N = 38$, as in the case of chemistry, $V = 88$ for the top-ranking department, 87 for the second, 79 for the tenth, and 51 for the thirty-eighth.

The coefficient of N implies that visibility diminishes as the size of the scientific or scholarly community increases. The seventh-ranking department in Russian would have an estimated visibility of $V = 90$, but the seventh-ranking department in chemistry would have an estimated visibility of 81.

Visibility V is closely associated with R, a measure of "quality" or prestige. The standard error of the regression coefficient is very small (0.04); thus the coefficient is quite accurately determined.

Equation (27) tells us that to increase the national visibility of a graduate program, we must improve its rank R. Table 9.1 has indicated that rank is favorably associated with the average compensation of full professors C and with the number of full professors P. Also, it is easier to achieve a given numerical rank in a small discipline (e.g., Russian, $N = 7$) than in a large one (e.g., chemistry, $N = 38$).

Analyses using makeshift data are often helpful in demonstrating how much we could learn if we had access to better information. In this spirit, I tabulated C and P as of 1970–1971 for 58 universities from the June 1971 issue of the *AAUP Bulletin*; P was the total number of full professors in the university, and C was the average compensation of all full professors in the university. These 58 universities included 766 of the 802 graduate faculties which were given numerical rankings ($R = 1, 2, \ldots, N$) in the Roose and Andersen report. Thus (30) and (31) relate to essentially the same set of faculties as (27) to (29).

University-wide averages and totals being exceedingly blunt instruments for operating on individual disciplines, we should not expect high coefficients of determination of R by C and P. Equation (30) is nevertheless quite suggestive:

$$R = 41.1 + 0.41N - 1.43C - 0.87P - 4.61D_6 \tag{30}$$
$$(0.04) \quad (0.12) \quad (0.12) \quad (0.65)$$
$$+ f(D_2, D_3, D_4, D_5)$$

Standard error of $R = 6.1$ ranks.
Coefficient of multiple determination $= .39$.

The units of R and N are integers; C is measured in thousands of dollars; P is measured in hundreds of full professors; $D_6 = 1$ for universities located on the West Coast and zero otherwise. The variables D_2, D_3, D_4, and D_5 were of negligible importance.

For expository purposes, we will round (30) further, to

$$R = 41.1 + 0.4N - 1.4C - 0.9P - 4.6D. \tag{31}$$

The mean values of these variables for the 766 observations are approximately $\overline{R} = 12$, $N = 23$, $\overline{C} = 24$, $\overline{P} = 4.7$, and $\overline{D} = 0.16$.

As possible policy instruments, C and P operate at the university level. Suppose that the average rank of a university's graduate faculties in 36 disciplines is $R = 13$ and that the graduate dean would like to improve this position by 3 ranks, to $R = 10$. From (31) it appears that an increase of $1000 in the average compensation of full professors will improve rank by 1.4 positions, and an increase of 100 in the total number of full professors will improve rank by 0.9 positions. If so, the desired improvement of 3 ranks might be accomplished by means of an increase of $2143 in the average compensation of full professors, an increase of 333 in the number of full professors, or a combination of increases in C and P such as $2143λ and 333 $(1 - λ)$ full professors, where $λ$ can take any value from 0 to 1.

Suppose the university presently has 400 full professors and their average compensation is $24,000. To gain 3 ranks by using the compensation instrument would evidently cost $2143 (400) = $857,200 a year; to gain 3 ranks by adding full professors would evidently cost 333 ($24,000) = $8 million a year. Apparently, the average compensation approach buys at least 9 times as much rank per million dollars as the strategy of adding full professors. However, if the 333 full professorships were obtained by liquidating an equal number of positions at lower ranks, the net cost might be more like $4 million.

Equation (31) is a reflection of three or four aspects of a much more complex reality; it does not give us an operational grip on reality. The compensation instrument C will work as specified only if we succeed in losing some professors who are worth less than $24,000 and gaining some who are worth more than $26,000 *in the national market*. To attract or retain the latter group, we may have to increase our spending for laboratories and libraries and make many other adjustments.

Similarly, if expanding the total number of professors P at its existing average level of compensation really would move a university from thirteenth place to tenth, most of this effect might result from adding 33 professors at $30,000 or more and very little of it from adding 300 professors at $25,000 or less.

The standard error of 6.1 ranks associated with (30) applies to individual disciplines. The standard error of the mean rank for 36 disciplines in a university should be on the order of 1.0 rank. If we were to regress the mean rank of all graduate programs in each university on the other variables in (30), the coefficient of multiple determination would probably exceed .80 and might approach .90 (recall that 1.00 means perfect correlation and zero standard error). If we had information on C and P for the graduate faculties in each discipline in each university, we should be able to reduce the standard error of R for individual disciplines considerably below 6.1. This might provide a starting point for more realistic appraisals of departmental performance using data internal to one's own university.

We now present two alternative formulations of (30). In the first, we use as the dependent variable $R' = 5.00 - 2(R/N)$. If $N = 20$ for a particular discipline, R' will range from 4.90 when $R = 1$ to 3.00 when $R = 20$, giving a *rough* approximation to the unpublished numerical scores underlying R. The resulting equation is

$$R' = 0.89 + 0.114C + 0.070P + 0.366D_6$$
$$(0.010) \quad (0.010) \quad (0.055)$$
$$+ f(D_2, D_3, D_4, D_5) \tag{32}$$

Standard error of $R' = 0.51$ points.
Coefficient of multiple determination $= .24$.

In the second formulation, we convert R', C, and P into logarithms to the base 10 and obtain

$$\log R' = -0.518 + 0.655 \log C + 0.079 \log P + 0.040 D_6$$
$$\qquad\quad (0.059) \qquad\quad (0.011) \qquad\quad (0.006)$$
$$+ f(D_2, D_3, D_4, D_5) \qquad\qquad\qquad (33)$$

Standard error of $\log R' = 0.058$.
Coefficient of multiple determination $= .23$.

The coefficients of $\log C$ and $\log P$ in this equation hold considerable interest. Note that CP is the total amount of compensation S paid by a university to its full professors. Since $S = CP$, a 1 percent increase in either C (with P held constant) or P (with C held constant) will cause a 1 percent increase in the salary budget S. In logarithmic form, we have $\log S = \log C + \log P$, $\partial \log S / \partial \log C = 1.000$ and $\partial \log S / \partial \log P = 1.000$; hence an increase of one unit in $\log P$ will cost the university the same amount of money as an increase of one unit in $\log C$.

A unit increase in $\log C$ is $0.655/0.079 = 8.3$ times as powerful as a unit increase in $\log P$ in its effects on $\log R'$. This is consistent with the idea that R' is primarily a measure of prestige *per full professor*. At the same time, the coefficient of $\log P$ is highly significant, indicating that the prestige of the graduate faculty of a department does increase with the number of its full professors, average compensation per full professor being held constant. Together, the coefficients imply that the following combinations of P and C would yield the same level of prestige R':

University Number	P	C
1	200	$29,550
2	400	$27,175
3	800	$25,000

We assume implicitly that the average number of full professors per department increases in direct proportion to the number for the university as a whole.

Most of the departments underlying (33) must be from the universities making up classes A and B in Table 9.2. Our equally weighted indexes of the variables in Table 9.2 were as follows:

Rows	Class A	Class B	Logarithmic Difference
1–11	1.00	0.66	0.180
12–15	1.00	0.70	0.155

We do not know what values of R' would be associated with the median universities in classes A and B in that table. Some hypothetical pairs of values would be:

Pair Number	Class A	Class B	Logarithmic Difference
1	4.00	3.00	0.125
2	4.00	2.80	0.155
3	4.00	2.64	0.180

The average change in R' per unit change in rank (as constructed for our analysis of 1969 data) is 0.087. On this basis, the differences between the hypothetical values of R' for classes A and B would be equivalent to differences of 11, 14, and 17 ranks, respectively. Hartman's description of Table 9.2, with about 70 universities grouped into four classes, would suggest a difference of 17 or so in the ranks of the median universities in classes A and B.

The index based on rows 12 to 15 includes research funds, postdoctoral students, graduate students, and numbers of Ph.D.s granted *per full professor*. Pair 2 in our tabulation would imply that R' (prestige) increases in direct proportion to the row 12 to 15 index. Equation (33) implies that R' increases by 0.655 percent for each 1 percent increase in average compensation C per full professor.

It is hard to avoid the conclusion that R' behaves very much like a cardinal measure of output per full professor.

X

Occupations and Earnings

WORK IS A MAJOR COMPONENT of the time budget for adults and education or training to acquire work related skills is a major preoccupation of young adults and teenagers.

In this chapter we juxtapose a number of concepts and frameworks relating to occupations and earnings. We do not attempt to integrate them into a unified system, although this seems to be quite possible, and probably desirable, on both conceptual and empirical levels. We begin with a schematic account of the determination of incomes in particular occupations in a simplified (theoretical) economy. We then proceed to an exposition of Becker's (1964) theory of human capital, some aspects of the Blau and Duncan (1967) study of the American occupational structure, and some elements of Stone's (1971) approach to demographic accounting and model building, with emphasis on earning and learning activities.

10.1 Occupations, Earnings, Training, and Retraining in a Theoretical Economy

The following is a simplified account of the place of the labor force and labor skills in a theoretical economic system. The model implies that each specialized occupational skill is rewarded, in dollars, at its marginal contribution to GNP. It also implies that training costs are a necessary evil, borne entirely by the individual and justified only if their present value is more than offset by the present value of the resulting increase in earnings. Noneconomic motives are ignored in this section, which also serves as an introduction to our discussion of human capital from the perspective of an individual in Section 10.2.

Suppose the economy of the United States is described in an input–output format (Leontief, 1951) as follows:

$$X = (I - A)^{-1}F, \tag{1}$$

where X is a vector of gross outputs from each of n industries or sectors of the economy, F is a vector of deliveries to final demand from the n industries, and A is an $n \times n$ matrix of technical coefficients (assumed constant) whose typical element is $a_{ij} = X_{ij}/X_j$, the dollar value of output from industry i which is used as an input by industry j per dollar of output of industry j; I is an $n \times n$ matrix with ones in the diagonal and zeros elsewhere. The sum of deliveries to final demand is the gross national (economic) product:

$$GNP = \sum_{i=1}^{n} F_i; \tag{2}$$

X and F are measured in dollars.

Equation (1) permits us to do the following: for any given set of deliveries to final demand $(F_1, F_2, \ldots, F_n)$, we can calculate the levels of gross output $(X_1, X_2, \ldots, X_n)$ required from each of the n industries, *if* the technical coefficients remain constant.

Assume now that each industry uses workers from each of m occupations in fixed numbers per unit of gross output:

$$N_1 = b_{11}X_1 + b_{12}X_2 + \cdots + b_{1n}X_n$$
$$\vdots \qquad \qquad \vdots \; ; \tag{3}$$
$$N_m = b_{m1}X_1 + b_{m2}X_2 + \cdots + b_{mn}X_n$$

the matrix generalization is

$$N = BX. \tag{4}$$

Since $X = (I - A)^{-1}F$, we can express N as a function of F, namely,

$$N = B(I - A)^{-1}F. \tag{5}$$

Equation (5) implies that for any given set of deliveries to final demand, we can calculate the numbers of workers in each occupation who will be employed, *if* both the b_{ij} and the a_{ij} remain constant.

If the number of workers skilled in occupation i is denoted by $L_i = N_i + U_i$, where $U_i \geq 0$ is the number unemployed, and if the L_i are regarded as fixed numbers (no transferability of workers from one occupation to another) over the relevant time period, we can pose the following problem:

$$\text{maximize } GNP \left(= \sum_{i=1}^{n} F_i \right) \quad \text{subject to} \tag{6}$$

$$F_i \geq F_{i(1970)}, \quad i = 1, 2, \ldots, n, \tag{7}$$

and

$$B(I - A)^{-1}F \leq L = (N + U). \tag{8}$$

Some (perhaps all) of the L_i will prove to be limiting resources and will have positive shadow prices or marginal value products s_i. For example, suppose that $s_1 = \partial GNP/\partial L_1 = \partial \sum_{i=1}^{n} F_i/\partial L_1 = \$20,000$; in the terms of our problem this would mean that an additional worker with the skills of occupation 1 would permit us to raise GNP by \$20,000. At the same time, suppose $s_2 = \partial \sum_{i=1}^{n} F_i/\partial L_2 = \$10,000$, implying that an additional worker with occupation 2 skills would permit us to raise GNP by \$10,000. The total incomes allocated to members of the two occupations would be \$20,000 L_1 and \$10,000 L_2.

Now, suppose we work out a set of $m(m-1)$ possible training programs for transforming the skills of persons currently in occupation i into those required for occupation j ($i = 1, 2, \ldots, m; j \neq i = 1, 2, \ldots, m$). The matrix of training costs T with elements t_{ij} would imply that some workers in occupation i should retrain for occupation j whenever s_j exceeded s_i by more than the training cost t_{ij}. If the wage structure is in equilibrium, no wage differential $s_j - s_i$ will exceed t_{ij}, nor will $s_i - s_j$ exceed t_{ji}. If for any reason the wage structure is out of equilibrium, we propose to bring it back into line at the minimum total cost of training $T = \sum_{i=1}^{m} \sum_{j \neq 1}^{m} t_{ij} L_{ij}$, where L_{ij} is the number of workers in occupation i to be trained for occupation j.

Assume that each shadow price s_i declines linearly with increases in the corresponding L_i, and that the total labor force $L^* = \sum_{i=1}^{m} L_i$ is a fixed number. Then we have

$$
\begin{aligned}
s_1 &= k_1 + d_1 L_1, \\
s_2 &= k_2 + d_2 L_2, \\
& \cdot \\
& \cdot \\
& \cdot \\
s_m &= k_m + d_m L_m;
\end{aligned}
\tag{9}
$$

also, in equilibrium we write

$$
s_j - s_i \leq t_{ij}
\tag{10}
$$

and

$$
s_j - s_i \geq -t_{ji},
\tag{11}
$$

for all $i = 1, 2, \ldots, m$ and $j \neq i = 1, 2, \ldots, m$.

The least cost training effort to correct any disequilibrium set of the s_i will include at most $m-1$ specific programs. In general, occupations with s_i values below the weighted average $\bar{s} = (\sum_{i=1}^{m} s_i L_i)/L^*$, are likely sources of trainees, and occupations with s_i values above $\bar{s}$ are likely destinations. This problem has the same formal structure as the spatial price equilibrium model (Fox, 1953, 1963; Fox and Taeuber, 1955; Takayama and Judge, 1971), and it can be solved readily for moderate values of m.

In a real planning situation extending over a number of years, workers will be leaving each occupation by retirement or death; also, an approximately predetermined number of young people will reach school-leaving age each year. Suppose that all school leavers have completed the same general education and must now be channeled into specialized curricula that will prepare them for occupations $i = 1$ or 2 or 3 $\cdots$ or m at an instructional cost $h_1, h_2, \ldots, h_m$ specific to each occupation.

If no established workers were retrained, the values of s_i and L_i in a given year would be determined by the size of the total labor force, by (9), and by the restrictions $(s_i - s_j) = (h_i - h_j)$ for all i and j.

If retraining programs were also available, the equilibrium wage structure would be dependent partly on the retraining costs t_{ji} and partly on differences in curriculum costs $h_i - h_j$. At any given time, recruits into occupation i would come either from curriculum i or from retraining, but not from both.

10.2 Human Capital

The concept of "human capital" has been very widely applied by economists since its introduction by T. W. Schultz (1960, 1962), Gary Becker (1964), and others, Everyday speech contains many references to time as something that can be spent. saved, or invested, including Benjamin Franklin's succinct proverb, "Time is money." Familiar, too, are references to education as a good investment. In the older economic literature, Becker (1964) cites a number of passages in Adam Smith (1776) and Alfred Marshall (1890) in which skills and knowledge embodied in people are recognized as a form of capital. However, Becker (1964) in particular developed the concept in a rigorous way and applied it to empirical data.

Our presentation in Section 10.1 implies a narrow interpretation of human capital, and some economists with only a casual interest in the concept may think of it in these terms. Becker (1964) saw it in a broader context:

> "Real" earnings are the sum of monetary earnings and the monetary equivalent of psychic earnings. Since many persons appear to believe that the term "investment in human capital" must be restricted to monetary costs and returns, let me emphasize that essentially the whole analysis applies independently of the division of real earnings into monetary and psychic components. Thus the analysis applies to health, which has a large psychic component, as well as to on-the-job training, which has a large monetary component. When psychic components dominate, the language associated with consumer durable goods might be considered more appropriate than that associated with investment goods; to simplify the presentation, investment language is used throughout (p. 38).

Becker's central point is illustrated by Figure 10.1, based on Chart 1 of his book (1964). Line UU assumes that untrained persons receive the same earnings regardless of age. Then trained persons would receive lower earnings during the training period because training is paid for at that time, and higher earnings at later ages because the return is collected then.

Line $T'T'$ represents a hypothetical case in which training causes a one-time jump in earnings immediately after completion; earnings then remain constant regardless of age, but at a level above UU. But TT is the more typical case.

A good deal of training is done on the job, and Becker discusses the question of who should pay for it—the employer or the trainee—in terms of three hypothetical situations.

1. Assume a "rational" employing firm operating in a perfectly competitive market for its product and for labor. If the firm provided "general training" that would raise the marginal productivity of the trainees by the same amount in any other firm as in itself, it would charge trainees the entire cost of the training; the trainees would be willing to pay this cost, since they would carry the benefits with them if and when they moved to another firm.

Earnings

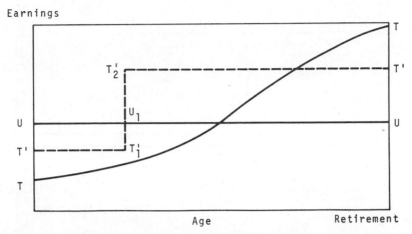

Figure 10.1. Relation of earnings to age. *Source.* Based on Gary S. Becker, *Human Capital: A Theoretical and Empirical Analysis, with Special Reference to Education* (New York: Columbia University Press, 1964), Chart 1, p. 15.

2. On the other hand, suppose a firm has patented a unique technology that requires special training for its workers. Because the training would have no value to the workers in any other firm, the trainees would be foolish to pay for it; the firm would therefore pay the entire cost of this "specific training."

3. Between these extremes would be many intermediate cases in which a firm might have (1) a monopoly within its own labor market area of a particular technology, and/or (2) a differentiated product that permits it to charge somewhat higher prices than its competitors. In such cases the costs of on-the-job training would ("rationally") be paid partly by the firm and partly by the trainees, and the benefits of the training presumably would be shared between worker and employer in rough proportion to the training costs paid by each.

In the next few pages we assume that all training costs are paid by the trainee.

Becker says that the earning curves of untrained workers are relatively flat (i.e., do not increase much with age); let UU in Figure 10.1 represent the pure case.

If there were no discounting of future income relative to present income, and if training costs of $20,000 were paid by the trainee who then received a license worth $500 a year for his remaining working life of 40 years, we would have the $T'T'$ situation, but with the area $UT'T_1'U_1$ *below* UU strictly equal to the area $T_2'U_1UT'$ *above* UU—both equal to $20,000. Figure 10.2 is drawn approximately to scale; thus the areas $UT'T_1U_1$ and $T_2'U_1UT'$ are both $20,000. Total benefits equal total costs *if* the discount rate is zero.

But suppose the discount rate is 8 percent, and a 15-year-old is considering whether to follow the earnings trajectory UU or to follow $T'T_1'T_2'T'$. The decision is to be made now. The training costs will run $2000 a year from year 1 through year 10; the present value of this cost stream is $13,420. The stream of benefits will begin at the end of year 10 and run at the rate of $500 a year from year 11 through year 50. The present value of this benefit stream is $2761. Hence the ratio of benefit to cost is only 2761/13,420 = 0.206.

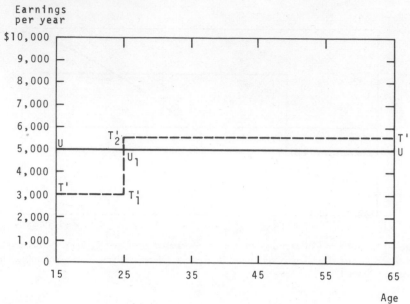

Figure 10.2.   Training costs, earnings, and age with zero discount rate.

Given the 8 percent rate of discount, the training program would be worthwhile only if the stream of benefits had a present value of $13,420 or more. This would require an increased income of at least $2430 a year running from year 11 through year 50.

Now, consider a somewhat more elaborate demonstration. We assume that the 15-year-old could start work at $5000 and hold that rate until age 65. (We assume complete retirement at 65 under each set of circumstances). Alternatively, we assume he could enroll in a one-year training program, forego the entire $5000 in year 1, and start working in year 2 at $5410, which rate would continue from age 16 to age 65. The discount rate is assumed to be 8 percent, as before. At age 16, he could elect to take another year of training, forego $5410, and start work at age 17 at $5854; the $5854 would continue until age 65.

In each successive year he could make a similar choice and raise his income by just enough to break even in terms of present value calculations at 8 percent.

Table 10.1 shows the results of a series of such calculations. We assume (1) that there is no increase in earnings for any specific level of training (i.e., no increase in the general level of money wages and salaries), and (2) that the *only* way a worker can increase his income is by taking additional training and foregoing his entire income while he takes it. (For example, he could *borrow* an amount equal to the entire income he would have earned in a given year and pay it off in equal annual installments up to age 65.)

The calculation in Table 10.1 produces a fairly plausible "equilibrium" structure of wages and salaries in relation to length of training from age 15 to age 26. Suppose a person completing his M.S. at age 24 could get a job at $10,218 (12-month basis). If his rate of discount of future income is 8 percent, and if dollar income is his only consideration, he would not be justified in taking another year of full-time training at zero income unless he was reasonably sure it would increase his annual income by

Table 10.1. Calculation of an "Equilibrium" Structure of Annual Earnings Based on Levels of Training and Costs of Income Foregone, Assuming Discount Rate of 8 Percent Annually

Age (t) (1)	Annual Income (2)	Present Value of Column 2: Income Foregone (3)	Present Value of $1000 a Year from Age (t+1) to Age 65 (4)	$1000 × Column 3 ÷ Column 4: Break-even Increase in Yearly Income (5)
15	$ 5,000	$ 4,630	$11,308	$ 410
16	5,410	5,009	11,286	444
17	5,854	5,420	11,263	481
18	6,335	5,866	11,238	522
19	6,857	6,348	11,211	566
20	7,423	6,873	11,182	615
21	8,038	7,443	11,151	667
22	8,705	8,060	11,117	725
23	9,430	8,732	11,080	788
24	10,218	9,461	11,041	857
25	11,075	10,250	10,998	932
26	12,007			
40	12,007	11,118	9,749	1,140
41	13,147			
55	13,147	12,173	5,784	2,105
56	15,252			

$857 (or more) from age 25 to age 65. He would not be justified in going on two years (from M.S. at age 24 to Ph.D. at age 26) unless he was reasonably sure this course of action would raise his annual income by $857 + $932 = $1789 (12-month basis) from age 26 through age 65. If the demand for Ph.D.s falls and/or the supply increases "too much," the realized income gain from M.S. to Ph.D. is less than $1789 and the additional training will not pay off in dollar terms.

Becker recognizes that learning can take place in informal ways. Teachers, physicians, and lawyers presumably learn a good deal by experience during their first few years of practice. A young M.D. who sees 150 patients a week may learn more per year (for a while) than one who sees 100 patients a week. The young assistant professor who works 80 hours a week (mostly on research) should learn more about research per year than his colleague who works 50 or 60 hours a week.

If one 15-year-old, by spending 60 hours a week rather than 40 on training programs, could get 1.5 normal years of training per calendar year, and if the general wage and salary structure was in equilibrium for persons willing to spend only 40 hours a week on earning or learning, the 60-hour trainee should be able to earn

Table 10.2.   Occupations Illustrating Various Scores on the Index of Occupational Status

Score Interval	Title of Occupation (Frequency per 10,000 Males in 1960 Experienced Civilian Labor Force in Parentheses)[a]
90 to 96	Architects (7); dentists (18); chemical engineers (9); lawyers and judges (45); physicians and surgeons (47)
85 to 89	Aeronautical engineers (11); industrial engineers (21); salaried managers, banking and finance (30); self-employed proprietors, banking and finance (5)
80 to 84	College presidents, professors and instructors (31); editors and reporters (14); electrical engineers (40); pharmacists (19); officials, federal public administration and postal service (13); salaried managers, business services (11)
75 to 79	Accountants and auditors (87); chemists (17); veterinarians (3); salaried managers, manufacturing (133); self-employed proprietors, insurance and real estate (9)
70 to 74	Designers (12); teachers (105); store buyers and department heads (40); credit men (8); salaried managers, wholesale trade (41); self-employed proprietors, motor vehicles and accessories retailing (12); stock and bond salesmen (6)
65 to 69	Artists and art teachers (15); draftsmen (45); salaried managers, motor vehicles and accessories retail stores (8); agents, n.e.c. (29); advertising agents and salesmen (7); salesmen, manufacturing (93); foremen, transportation equipment manufacturing (18)
60 to 64	Librarians (3); sports instructors and officials (12); postmasters (5); salaried managers, construction (31); self-employed proprietors, manufacturing (35); stenographers, typists, and secretaries (18); ticket, station, and express agents (12); real estate agents and brokers (33): salesmen, wholesale trade (106); foremen, machinery manufacturing (28); photoengravers and lithographers (5)
55 to 59	Funeral directors and embalmers (8); railroad conductors (10); self-employed proprietors, wholesale trade (28); electrotypers and stereotypers (2); foremen, communications, utilities, and sanitary services (12); locomotive engineers (13)
50 to 54	Clergymen (43); musicians and music teachers (19); officials and administrators, local public administration (15); salaried managers, food and dairy products stores (21); self-employed proprietors, construction (50); bookkeepers (33); mail carriers (43); foremen, metal industries (28); toolmakers, and die-makers and setters (41)
45 to 49	Surveyors (10); salaried managers, automobile repair services and garages (4); office machine operators (18); linemen and servicemen, telephone, telegraph and power (60); locomotive firemen (9); airplane mechanics and repairmen (26); stationary engineers (60)
40 to 44	Self-employed proprietors, transportation (8); self-employed proprietors, personal services (19); cashiers (23); clerical and kindred workers, n.e.c. (269); electricians (77); construction foremen (22); motion picture projectionists (4); photographic process workers (5); railroad switchmen (13); policemen and detectives, government (51)

$6335 at age 17, $8038 at age 19, $10,218 at age 21, and about $13,000 at age 23, when he would have accumulated the equivalent of a Ph.D. plus one year postdoctoral. However, the opportunity cost per calendar year of his 60 hours per week of training should be 1.5 times the appropriate annual income figure in column 2 of Table 10.1. Either he could have worked 60 hours a week for pay (flat rate wages, say, 40 hours for one firm and 20 hours for another), or he could have spent 20 more hours a week on activities yielding "psychic income" worth his regular hourly wage rate (or more) to him.

Table 10.2.   (*Continued*)

Score Interval	Title of Occupation (Frequency per 10,000 Males in 1960 Experienced Civilian Labor Force in Parentheses)[a]
35 to 39	Salaried and self-employed managers and proprietors, eating and drinking places (43); salesmen and sales clerks, retail trade (274); bookbinders (3); radio and television repairmen (23); firemen, fire protection (30); policemen and detectives, private (3)
30 to 34	Building managers and superintendents (7); self-employed proprietors, gasoline service stations (32); boilermakers (6); machinists (111); millwrights (15); plumbers and pipefitters (72); structural metal workers (14); tinsmiths, coppersmiths, and sheet metal workers (31); deliverymen and routemen (93); operatives, printing, publishing and allied industries (13); sheriffs and bailiffs (5)
25 to 29	Messengers and office boys (11); newsboys (41); brickmasons, stonemasons, and tile setters (45); mechanics and repairmen, n.e.c. (266); plasterers (12); operatives, drugs and medicine manufacturing (2); ushers, recreation and amusement (2); laborers, petroleum refining (3)
20 to 24	Telegraph messengers (1); shipping and receiving clerks (59); bakers (21); cabinetmakers (15); excavating, grading, and road machine operators (49); railroad and car shop mechanics and repairmen (9); tailors (7); upholsterers (12); bus drivers (36); filers, grinders, and polishers, metal (33); welders and flame-cutters (81)
15 to 19	Blacksmiths (5); carpenters (202); automobile mechanics and repairmen (153); painters (118); attendants, auto service and parking (81); laundry and dry cleaning operatives (25); truck and tractor drivers (362); stationary firemen (20); operatives, metal industries (103); operatives, wholesale and retail trade (35); barbers (38); bartenders (36); cooks, except private household (47)
10 to 14	Farmers (owners and tenants) (521); shoemakers and repairers, except factory (8); dyers (4); taxicab drivers and chauffeurs (36); attendants, hospital and other institution (24); elevator operators (11); fishermen and oystermen (9); gardeners, except farm, and groundskeepers (46); longshoremen and stevedores (13); laborers, machinery manufacturing (10)
5 to 9	Hucksters and peddlers (5); sawyers (20); weavers, textile (8); operatives, footwear, except rubber, manufacturing (16); janitors and sextons (118); farm laborers, wage workers (241); laborers, blast furnaces, steel works, and rolling mills (26); construction laborers (163)
0 to 4	Coal mine operatives and laborers (31); operatives, yarn, thread, and fabric mills (30); porters (33); laborers, sawmills, planing mills, and millwork (21)

Source.   Reproduced from Peter M. Blau and Otis Dudley Duncan, *The American Occupational Structure.* New York: John Wiley & Sons, 1967, Table 4.1, pp. 122-123.
[a] n.e.c. means "not elsewhere classified."

10.3   The American Occupational Structure

This section is based on the classic study by Peter M. Blau and Otis Dudley Duncan, *The American Occupational Structure* (1967). Blau and Duncan state (pp. 6–7) that the occupational structure is the major foundation of the social stratification system in the United States. Hence patterns of occupational mobility from one generation to the next and from first jobs to career midpoints or peaks will explain part of the dynamics of the stratification system as a whole.

Furthermore, Blau and Duncan view the occupational structure as the connecting link between the economy and the family, through which the family supplies manpower to the economy and the economy affects the family's social status. The occupational structure largely determines the hierarchies of prestige strata, economic classes, and political power in modern industrial society, as well as those of power in formal organizations; hence all these social system outputs tend to be distributed (more or less) *as though* they were rewards for the social contributions of the various occupations.

The authors base their empirical studies on data collected in 1962 from a representative sample of more than 20,000 American men between the ages of 20 and 64. The raw data with which to measure mobility consisted largely of the *names* of occupations (the respondent's present occupation, his first job, and his father's occupation). However, for their purpose, Blau and Duncan needed a measure of the *status* of each occupation.

The measure they chose was an index of occupational status developed earlier by Duncan (1961), based on "prestige ratings obtained from a sizable sample of the U.S. population in 1947" (pp. 119–120). The index of occupational status ranges from 96 to 0, based on the percentage of respondents who gave a specified occupation "excellent" or "good" prestige ratings. The authors cite a study by Hodge, Siegel, and Rossi (1964) indicating that a set of occupational prestige ratings obtained as long ago as 1925 was correlated to the extent of $r = .93$ with a set obtained in 1963. Hodge et al. concluded that there had been no substantial changes in occupational prestige in the United States over the span of nearly four decades.

Given this and other evidence of the temporal stability of occupational prestige ratings, Blau and Duncan used the following regression equation to generate values of a status index for each of 446 detailed occupation titles for which 1950 census data were available:

$$\hat{X}_1 = 0.59X_2 + 0.55X_3 - 6.0, \tag{12}$$

where X_1 is the percentage of "excellent" or "good" ratings received by an occupation in the 1947 prestige survey, X_2 the percentage of men in the occupation with 1949 incomes of \$3500 or more, and X_3 the percentage of men in the occupation with four years of high school or higher educational attainment as of March 1950. The equation was estimated on the basis of data for 45 occupations whose titles in the prestige survey closely matched those in the detailed census list; the coefficient of determination based on these 45 observations was $R^2_{1(23)} = .83$.

Values of X_2 and X_3 were inserted in this equation for each of the 446 occupations mentioned; the resulting estimated prestige scores $\hat{X}_1$ for many of these occupations appear in Table 10.2, which reproduces Blau and Duncan's Table 4.1 (1967). It will be noted that the equation (hence the status index) gives approximately equal weights to income X_2 and education X_3; for example, if X_2 and X_3 are both set at their maximum values of 100, we have

$$\hat{X}_1 = 0.59(100) + 0.55(100) - 6.0 = 59 + 55 - 6 = 108. \tag{13}$$

Having computed their status index for all census occupations, Blau and Duncan analyzed the data collected from more than 20,000 male members of the American labor force in 1962. We confine our attention here to their model of occupational

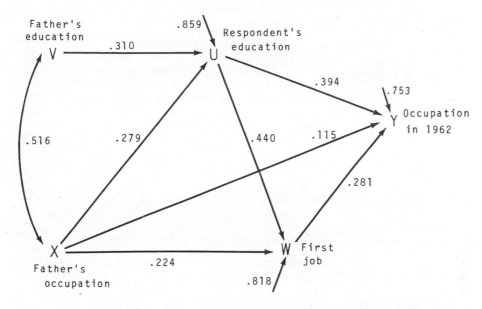

Figure 10.3.   Path coefficients in basic model of the process of stratification. *Source.* Peter M. Blau and Otis Dudley Duncan, *The American Occupational Structure.* New York: John Wiley & Sons, 1967, p. 170.

mobility from father's generation to son's, based on a highly interesting application of Sewall Wright's (1921, 1934) method of path coefficients.[1] The results are shown in Figure 10.3. The variables are placed from left to right in a causal or processual sequence, with V and X preceding U, U preceding W, and W preceding Y. The simple correlation coefficients among these five variables appear in Table 10.3.

The model "explains" 43 percent of the variation in Y, the index of occupational status of the respondents in 1962. The correlation coefficient between Y and U (1962 occupational status and education of respondent) is .596; that between X and V (occupational status and education of respondent's father) is .516.

The path coefficients in Figure 10.3 are beta coefficients obtained by expressing each variable in units of its own standard deviation and computing the following regression equations:

$$U' = .279\,X' + .310\,V', \tag{14}$$

$$W' = .224\,X' + .440\,U', \tag{15}$$

$$Y' = .115\,X' + .394\,U' + .281\,W'. \tag{16}$$

Each equation is legitimate or "structural" in terms of the causal ordering of the variables. The R^2 associated with the three equations are .26, .33, and .43, respectively. These values imply that forces "outside" the model account for 74, 67, and 57 percent of the total variation in U, W, and Y, respectively; the square roots of these percentages (stated as proportions), .859, .818, and .753, are the coefficients of alienation pertaining to U, W, and Y in Figure 10.3.

---

[1] Recent applications of this method to socioeconomic data have also been made by Sewell et al. (1970), Duncan, Featherman, and Duncan (1972), and others.

Table 10.3.   Simple Correlations for Five Status Variables

Variable	Variable				
	Y	W	U	X	V
Y: 1962 occupational status	--	.541	.596	.405	.322
W: first-job status		--	.538	.417	.332
U: education			--	.438	.453
X: father's occupational status				--	.516
V: father's education					--

Source.   Reproduced from Peter M. Blau and Otis Dudley Duncan, *The American Occupationa Structure.* New York: John Wiley & Sons, 1967, p. 169.

The model implies that the father's educational level has a direct effect on the educational level attained by the son ($\beta_{uv.x} = .310$). The father's occupation also has a direct effect on the education attained by the son ($\beta_{ux.v} = .279$).

The father's occupation has a direct effect on the son's first job ($\beta_{wx.u} = .224$) and also an indirect effect by the path $X \rightarrow U \rightarrow W$, or $\beta_{ux.v} \beta_{wu.x} = (.279)(.440) = .123$. The father's education affects the son's first job by the path $V \rightarrow U \rightarrow W$, or $\beta_{uv.x} \beta_{wu.x} = (.310)(.440) = .136$.

Finally, the paths of influence linking father's education and father's occupation to the son's 1962 occupation are as follows:

Father's education:
   Path 1: $V \rightarrow U \rightarrow Y$; $(.310)(.394) = .122$,
   Path 2: $V \rightarrow U \rightarrow W \rightarrow Y$; $(.310)(.440)(.281) = .038$.

Father's occupation:
   Path 3: $X \rightarrow U \rightarrow Y$; $(.279)(.394) = .110$,
   Path 4: $X \rightarrow W \rightarrow Y$; $(.224)(.281) = .063$,
   Path 5: $X \rightarrow Y$; $(.115) = .115$.

If we view the *respondents* as fathers of the next generation, the model can be given the following tentative policy interpretation:

1. If we increased the average educational level of respondents by one standard deviation, the result should be an increase of $.122 + .038 = .160$ standard deviations in the index of occupational status of their sons.

2. If we increased the average occupational status (index rating) of respondents by one standard deviation, the result should be an increase of $.110 + .063 + .115 = .288$ standard deviations in the index of occupational status of their sons.

Both these statements make a strong assumption of *ceteris paribus.* Of course, the paths running from the son's education and the son's first job to his own principal career occupation are more direct and the policy leverages more powerful:

Son's education:
      Path 6: $U \rightarrow Y$; (.394) = .394,
      Path 7: $U \rightarrow W \rightarrow Y$; (.440) (.281) = .124.

Son's first job:
      Path 8: $W \rightarrow Y$; (.281) = .281.

Blau and Duncan have provided important insights into the role of education for the generation receiving it and for the children of that generation. Their use of causal ordering principles means that their model lends itself to the analysis of educational and related policies.

10.4 Demographic Accounting and Model Building

Richard Stone has made distinguished contributions to several major fields of economics, including the theory and measurement of consumer demand, national income accounting, quantitative models for educational planning, and simulation models of complex economic systems. The breadth of his contributions during the early 1960s is suggested by the following title: *Mathematics in the Social Sciences and Other Essays* (Stone, 1966).

This section is based on Stone's recent technical report for the Organization for Economic Cooperation and Development (OECD), *Demographic Accounting and Model-Building* (1971). In it, Stone seeks to provide "a comprehensive and consistent basis for education and manpower research, policy, and planning" (p. 13). The system of demographic, educational, and occupational statistics he proposes would make it possible "to integrate information on human stocks and flows just as a system of national accounts statistics makes it possible to integrate information on economic and financial stocks and flows" (p. 13).

Stone gives detailed consideration in his accounting system to persons engaged in learning and earning activities (full-time formal education and gainful employment), placing the rest of the population at any given time in a few broad categories. His object (and that of OECD) is to emphasize a simple and consistent framework that could be implemented in the near future by many or all the OECD countries and would be capable of further elaboration as information and experience accumulated (p. 14).

Stone's accounting system is designed initially to classify people among an exhaustive set of categories covering the entire population of (say) a nation during a particular year. The population would be classified by age and sex. Within any age and sex class, a person would be counted in either (1) a specific category of formal educational activities, (2) a specific category of earning activities, or (3) a specific category of what Stone calls the "passive sequence." The "active sequence" includes people engaged in full-time formal education or as members of the labor force. The "passive sequence" includes the rest of the population.

The basic features of Stone's system are indicated in Table 10.4. The figures relate

Table 10.4. An Open (Year-to-Year) Demographic Matrix for Actual Residents Classified by Age and Activity

				England					
			Outside World	Age 0	Age 1	Age 2		Age 3	
				Not at School	Not at School	At School	Not at School	At School	Not at School
Outside world				443.2			0.5		0.3
England and Wales, 1964	Age 0	Not at school	8.9		442.2				
	Age 1	Not at school	1.4			1.3	426.7		
	Age 2	At school						1.5	
		Not at school	0.5					11.5	407.0
	Age 3	At school							
		Not at school	0.3						
	Age 4	At school							
		Not at school	0.2						
	Ages 5-15	At school	1.5						
		Not at school	0.2						
	Ages 16-19	At school							
		Not at school	1.5						
	Ages 20 +	At school							
		Not at school	260.3						
England and Wales, 1965	Age 0	Not at school	8.3						
	Age 1	Not at school	1.5						
	Age 2	At school							
		Not at school	0.5						
	Age 3	At school							
		Not at school	0.3						
	Age 4	At school							
		Not at school	0.3						
	Ages 5-15	At school	1.6						
		Not at school	0.2						
	Ages 16-19	At school							
		Not at school	1.6						
	Ages 20 +	At school							
		Not at school	268.0						
Total				443.2	442.2	1.3	427.2	13.0	407.3

to all male residents of England and Wales in 1965 and 1966, classified by age and activity. In this table, which emphasizes boys aged 0 to 19, only two activities are specified, "at school" and "not at school."

In the 1965 columns, males enter the system from the "outside world" *row*, mostly by birth (443,200 at age 0) but also by net immigration (500 at age 1, 300 at age 3, −700 at age 4, etc.). In the 1964 rows, males leave the system by way of the "outside world" *column*, which records deaths (8900 at age 0, 1400 at age 1, 500 at age 2, etc.). The "total" *column* indicates, for the first 1964 row, that 451,100 boys flowed out of the category "age 0 in 1964." Of these, 8900 died in 1964 (as indicated by the "outside world" entry in that row) and the 442,200 survivors entered the new category, "age 1 in 1965: not at school."

Moving down to the 1965 row for the category "age 1 in 1964: not at school," we find in the "total" column that 442,200 flowed out of that category (the same number that flowed into it), 1500 by death during 1965, 1300 by entry into the new category "age 2 in 1966: at school," and 439,400 by entry into the new category "age 2 in 1966: not at school."

Table 10.4 (*Continued*)

and Wales, 1965

Age 4		Ages 5–15		Ages 16–19		Ages 20 +	
At School	Not at School	At School	Not at School	At School	Not at School	At School	Not at School
	−0.7	−5.3	1.4		−2.1		−2.9
12.8							
101.4	292.8						
		112.5					
		273.0	8.5				
		3,327.0	122.1	106.1	116.2		
		8.9	11.9		139.7		
				90.8	104.6		2.1
					1,006.9		331.9
							15,681.2
114.2	292.1	3,716.1	143.9	196.9	1,365.3	0.0	16,037.1

For analytical purposes, a set of "transition proportions" can be calculated from Table 10.4 by dividing the elements in each row by the row total. For example, of the 3,716,100 boys who flowed out of the category "ages 5–15 in 1965: at school," 1.6/3716.1 or 0.0004 died during 1965; 3382.2/3716.1 or 0.9101 entered the category "ages 5–15 in 1966: at school"; 112.6/3716.1 or 0.0303 entered the category "ages 5–15 in 1966: not at school"; and 0.0288 and 0.0303, respectively, entered the categories "ages 16–19 in 1966: at school" and "ages 16–19 in 1966: not at school." The proportions, of course, add up to 1.0000 (except for rounding errors).

The coefficient matrix of transition proportions can in turn be converted into a matrix multiplier, similar to the inverse matrix that arises in input–output analysis.

Stone states this model and several variants and extensions of it in matrix notation (1971, p. 90–101). Thus the matrix of actual population figures in Table 10.4 is written as

$$p = Si + d, \tag{17}$$

where p is a vector of n population flows out of this year, S is an $n \times n$ matrix of

Table 10.4.   An Open (Year-to-Year) Demographic Matrix for Actual Residents Classified by Age and Activity   (*Continued*)

					England			
			Age 0 Not at School	Age 1 Not at School	Age 2 At School	Age 2 Not at School	Age 3 At School	Age 3 Not at School
Outside world			437.3	0.0		−0.2		−0.7
England and Wales, 1964	Age 0	Not at school						
	Age 1	Not at school						
	Age 2	At school						
		Not at school						
	Age 3	At school						
		Not at school						
	Age 4	At school						
		Not at school						
	Ages 5-15	At school						
		Not at school						
	Ages 16-19	At school						
		Not at school						
	Ages 20 +	At school						
		Not at school						
England and Wales, 1965	Age 0	Not at school		434.9				
	Age 1	Not at school			1.3	439.4		
	Age 2	At school					1.3	
		Not at school					14.1	412.6
	Age 3	At school						
		Not at school						
	Age 4	At school						
		Not at school						
	Ages 5-15	At school						
		Not at school						
	Ages 16-19	At school						
		Not at school						
	Ages 20 +	At school						
		Not at school						
Total			437.3	434.9	1.3	439.2	15.4	411.9

survivors into next year, i denotes a unit column vector of n elements (hence Si denotes the row sums of S), and d is a vector of deaths in the n population categories during this year. The vector of survivors into next year is defined as

$$p - d = Si. \tag{18}$$

The vector of survivors from last year is defined as

$$p - b = L^{-1}S'i, \tag{19}$$

where b is a vector of this year's births and net immigrations into the n population categories, and L^{-1} is a "lag operator" that shifts in time the variable to which it is applied; by convention $L^0 S(t) = S(t + 0)$; therefore, if S denotes this year's survivors, $L^{-1}S$ denotes last year's survivors, and LS denotes next year's survivors.

A matrix of transition coefficients C can be formed by dividing the elements in each row of $L^{-1}S$ by the corresponding element of $L^{-1}p$. Then

$$p = C'L^{-1}p + b \tag{20}$$

expresses a set of linear equations connecting this year's population flows p with

Table 10.4   (*Continued*)

and Wales, 1966

Age 4 At School	Age 4 Not at School	Ages 5-15 At School	Ages 5-15 Not at School	Ages 16-19 At School	Ages 16-19 Not at School	Ages 20 + At School	Ages 20 + Not at School	Total (thousands)
	-0.7	-0.4			1.6		13.1	
								451.1
								429.4
								1.5
								419.0
								12.8
								394.5
								112.5
								281.7
								3,672.9
								160.7
								197.5
								1,340.3
								0.0
								15,941.5
								443.2
								442.2
								1.3
								427.2
13.0								13.0
111.3	295.7							407.3
		114.2						114.2
		282.1	9.7					292.1
		3,382.2	112.6	107.0	112.7			3,716.1
		6.4	11.3		126.0			143.9
				91.5	102.5		2.9	196.9
					977.3		386.4	1,365.3
								0.0
							15,769.1	16,037.1
124.3	295.0	3,784.5	133.6	198.5	1,320.1	0.0	16,171.5	

Source. Richard Stone, *Demographic Accounting and Model-Building.* Paris: Organization for Economic Cooperation and Development, 1971, Table III.11, p. 34.

last year's population flows $L^{-1}p$ and this year's births and net immigrations b. On the assumption that C remains constant, (20) can be used to make forward projections.

In the special case of a stationary population in which $p = L^{-1}p$, (20) simplifies to

$$p = C'p + b; \tag{21}$$

hence we have

$$p(I - C') = b \tag{22}$$

and

$$p = (I - C')^{-1}b, \tag{23}$$

where $(I - C')^{-1}$ is a lower triangular matrix with ones in the major diagonal. The vector b of numbers of people flowing from the outside world (by birth and net immigration) into the n population categories is assumed to repeat itself in each successive year; the matrix multiplier $(I - C')^{-1}$ transforms these numbers entering from the outside world into the *total numbers* flowing into the n population categories. The calculation also assumes that the coefficients of C remain constant over time.

Table 10.5. A Demographic Matrix for the 1960 Vintage Based on Year-to-Year Flows (England and Wales, Male Population, 1960–1966)

		Outside World	England and Wales							Total (000)
			1960 Age 0	1961 Age 1	1962 Age 2	1963 Age 3	1964 Age 4	1965 Age 5	1966 Age 6	
Outside world			404.2	0.0	1.7	0.3	−0.8	−0.8	−0.8	
1960	Age 0	8.9		395.3						404.2
1961	Age 1	1.5			393.8					395.3
1962	Age 2	0.5				395.0				395.5
1963	Age 3	0.3					395.0			395.3
1964	Age 4	0.2						394.0		394.2
1965	Age 5	0.2							393.0	393.2
1966	Age 6	0.2								(392.2)
Total			404.2	395.3	395.5	395.3	394.2	393.2	392.2	

Source. Richard Stone, *Demographic Accounting and Model-Building.* Paris: Organization for Economic Cooperation and Development, 1971, Table III.13, p. 38.

Stone also deals with many practical questions and applications, including the problem of changing coefficients over time; we will not go into these. In three folding tables (Tables X.1, X.2, and X.3), he presents large-scale examples of the basic table $p = Si + d$, the matrix C, and the matrix multiplier $(I - C')^{-1}$. The basic table is "an educational matrix for actual residents (of England and Wales): boys ages 0 through 19," by one-year age classes, for 1964–1965. In each age class there is a category "not in full-time formal education." The younger ages include such additional categories as "nursery and primary schools" and "special schools"; at appropriate later ages other categories such as "grammar schools," "secondary modern," and "comprehensive" are added, and "nursery and primary" is deleted. For age 17, there are 12 possible categories of educational activities provided. The basic table includes 114 rows and 114 columns; so, of course, do the C and $(I - C')^{-1}$ matrices derived from it.

Stone also points out the possibility of developing demographic matrices for particular cohorts or "vintages" (i.e., all persons born in a specified year). Table 10.5 illustrates the first few years of such a table for boys born in 1960. If the rows and columns were subdivided by activity (kind of school, etc.) and extended to the year 1979, we would have the first 19 years of the educational history of the 1960 cohort displayed in a table of perhaps 114 rows and 114 columns. In principle, the history of this cohort could be continued through successions of occupation-and-industry-of-employment categories and categories of the "passive sequence"; the history would be completed when the last member of the cohort died.

Comparisons of the histories of successive cohorts would reflect rising standards of education, changes in occupational patterns, differential impacts of wars and depressions on people of different ages, and other factors.

XI

Elements of an Operational System—I: Individuals, Families, and Organizations in a Small Community

WE WILL NOW TRY TO LINK many of the concepts previously discussed into an interrelated system at the level of a small community. For illustrative data and for important insights, I will draw extensively on the pioneering work of Roger G. Barker as summarized in his book, *Ecological Psychology: Concepts and Methods for Studying the Environment of Human Behavior* (Stanford University Press, 1968).

Before proceeding, the reader should refer to Section 2.6 on Roger Barker's theory of behavior settings and Section 2.7 on a tentative integration of concepts to measure an individual's total income. In particular, the subsections entitled "Optimization for Sets of Interrelated Behavior Settings" and "Optimization for a Small Community" will serve as a prelude to this chapter.

Chapters 5 and 6 have illustrated how the Fox-Van Moeseke approach might be extended to numerical measurements of total income and its components for individuals and families. Section 2.7 had already suggested, on an abstract level, the possibility of extending this approach to a small community with a view to arriving at a scalar measure of the total income of its residents.

A great deal of empirical research would be needed to make these suggestions operational. A start could be made with Barker's data for the 198 behavior setting genotypes in his community of 830 people. Barker specifies two quantitative indexes, the *ecological resource index* (ERI) and the *general richness index* (GRI), which are combinations of his ratings on certain of the characteristics of behavior settings listed earlier. The basic ratings for any setting relate to the setting as a whole as seen by a trained observer and not to the subjective experiences of its participants. One crucial question is whether the outputs perceived by participants in various behavior settings can be translated into Parsons's media of exchange or some variant of them (as in our

Chapters 5 and 6). Another crucial question is whether participants have reasonably stable exchange rates between money and other media. Would they be willing to pay more money (as taxes, donations, or admission fees) to participate in a behavior setting if its output per participant hour were increased by specified amounts in terms of other media?

Berne (1964) evidently takes a simpler view of social system outputs than does Parsons:

> The advantages of social contact revolve around somatic and psychic equilibrium. They are related to the following factors: (1) the relief of tension (2) the avoidance of noxious situations (3) the procurement of stroking and (4) the maintenance of an established equilibrium. . . .
>
> When one is a member of a social aggregation of two or more people, there are several options for structuring time. In order of complexity, these are: (1) Rituals, (2) Pastimes, (3) Games, (4) Intimacy, and (5) Activity, which may form a matrix for any of the others. The goal of each member of the aggregation is to obtain as many satisfactions as possible from his transactions with other members . . . (pp. 18–19).

Berne provides a unit of account for at least one class of rituals, the American greeting rituals; his microunit is the "stroke." The following exchange of greetings between A and B (p. 37) would be a "two-stroke ritual":

A. "Hi!" (or Hello, or Good morning).
B. "Hi!" (or Hello, or Good morning).

If A goes on to ask "Warm enough for you?" and B responds "It certainly is," the whole transaction amounts to a "four-stroke ritual." Meanwhile, says Berne, A and B have "improved each other's health slightly"; a bit of recognition-hunger is satisfied.

For more complex exchanges, Berne uses the *transaction* as the unit of social intercourse. He then defines a behavioral entity called a "simple pastime":

> This may be defined as a series of semiritualistic, simple, complementary transactions arranged around a single field of material, whose primary object is to structure an interval of time. The beginning and end of the interval are typically signaled by procedures or rituals. The transactions are adaptively programmed so that each party will obtain the maximum gains or advantages during the interval. The better his adaptation, the more he will get out of it.
>
> Pastimes are typically played at parties ("social gatherings") or during the waiting period before a formal group meeting begins . . . (p. 41).

Since Berne refers to informal greeting transactions as consisting of a certain number of "strokes" and to pastimes as "a series of semiritualistic, simple, complementary transactions," it appears that pastimes might also be rated in terms of numbers of "strokes." If a "stroke" in this context is typically a verbal statement implying recognition, approval, agreement, or sympathy, the tempo of normal conversation under such circumstances may imply a certain average number of "strokes" per minute. A particularly pleasant or interesting conversation implies more than the average gain per minute; a dull or halting one implies less.

Berne's concept of recognition-hunger may be translated into several of the resources discussed in Chapters 5 and 6 including affect, prestige, power, income (as recognition for valued services), and perhaps others.

Zytowski's list of "work satisfactions" suggests that exchange rates between money and other reward media associated with jobs might be estimated on the basis of interviews with individual workers. Also, collective bargaining negotiations between companies and unions must involve many implicit or explicit tradeoffs between money and other media.

The concept of a time budget for a small community should be useful in discussing socioeconomic policies. Proposed changes in the performance level of any behavior setting will have some effect on the allocation of time and effort among other behavior settings in the community. Even if reward vectors and occupancy response coefficients are specified a priori, the time budget format will facilitate recognition of probable impacts and stresses on other behavior settings; the distribution of prospective gains and losses among population groups and authority systems can be anticipated approximately in quantitative terms.

11.1   Some Operational Features of Barker's System

Figure 11.1 is the data sheet for a specific behavior setting, a high school boys' basketball game. Occupancy times are recorded for each of 14 subgroups of the town's population by age, sex, socioeconomic status, and color, along with its zone of maximum penetration. Recall that zone 6 represents the single leader, and zone 5 the joint leaders, of a setting; zone 4, functionaries; zone 3, members or customers; zone 2, audience; and zone 1, onlookers. In the present case, adult referees (zone 5) control the setting, adolescent basketball players (zone 4) implement its program, younger children and the aged are in the audience (zone 2), and infants are classified as onlookers (zone 1). The sum of the 14 maximum penetration scores is 51; this is $\sum \text{PenR}$ in Barker's *general richness index* (GRI).

A rating is given for each of the 11 action patterns: aesthetics, business, professionalism, education, government, nutrition, personal appearance, physical health, recreation, religion, and social contact. The basketball game gets a very high rating, 8, on recreation, a moderately high one, 6, on social contact, and very low ratings on the other nine action patterns; the sum of these ratings, 23, is $\sum \text{ApR}$ in the GRI formula.

A rating is also given for each of the five behavior mechanisms: affective behavior, gross motor activity, manipulation, talking, and thinking. The basketball game is given ratings of 9 (the highest possible rating is 10) on affective behavior and talking, 7 on gross motor activity and manipulation, and 4 on thinking; the sum of these ratings, 36, is the $\sum \text{BmR}$ in the GRI formula, which Barker defines as follows (p. 70):

$$\text{GRI} = \frac{(\sum \text{PenR} + \sum \text{ApR} + \sum \text{BmR})cOT}{100} \tag{1}$$

In the present case we obtain

$$\text{GRI} = \frac{(51 + 23 + 36)cOT}{100} = 1.1 \, cOT, \tag{2}$$

Name:	*High School Boys Basketball Game*				
Genotype # 1-3: $O \cdot 1 \cdot 8$	Genotype Commonality # 8: 9		Locus 16: 1		
B S # 4-6: $0 \cdot 0 \cdot 5$	Authority System 13-14: $O \cdot 1$		No. of Occurr. 17-19: $0 \cdot 0 \cdot 8$		
Genotype Date 7: 3	Class of Authority Systems 15: 4		Survey # 20: 6		

Occupancy Time of Town Subgroups			Max. Penetration of Subgroups		ACTION PATTERN RATINGS
Group	No. P	Hours	OT Code	Group	
Inf	3	24	21-22: $0 \cdot 4$	Inf 21: 1	Aes: 53: 0
Presch	12	54	23-24: $0 \cdot 5$	Presch 22: 2	Bus 54: 1
Y S	10	87	25-26: $0 \cdot 6$	Y S 23: 2	Prof 55: 1
O S	18	258	27-28: $0 \cdot 9$	O S 24: 4	Educ 56: 1
Town Child	43	423	29-30: $1 \cdot 1$		Govt 57: 1
Adol	63	1720	31-32: $1 \cdot 7$	Adol 25: 4	Nutr 58: 1
Adult	72	1676	33-34: $1 \cdot 7$	Adult 26: 5	
Aged	7	81	35-36: $0 \cdot 6$	Aged 27: 2	PersAp 60: 2
Town Total	185	3900	37-38: $2 \cdot 3$	Grand Max 28: 5	
Males	97	2264	39-40: $1 \cdot 9$	Males 29: 5	PhysH 62: 2
Female	88	1636	41-42: $1 \cdot 7$	Females 30: 4	Rec 63: 8
I	35	600	43-44: $1 \cdot 2$	I 31: 4	Rel 64: 0
II	105	2236	45-46: $1 \cdot 9$	II 32: 5	Soc 65: 6
III	42	1014	47-48: $1 \cdot 4$	III 33: 4	MECHANISM RATINGS AffB 66: 9
N-G	3	50	49-50: $0 \cdot 5$	N-G 34: 4	GroMot 67: 7

POPULATION (number)		PERFORMERS (number)		Manip 68: 7
Town Child 51-53:	$0 \cdot 4 \cdot 3$	Town Child 35-36:	$0 \cdot 1$	Talk 69: 9
Out Child 54-56:	$1 \cdot 8 \cdot 7$	Out Child 37-38:	$0 \cdot 0$	Think 70: 4
Total Child 57-59:	$2 \cdot 3 \cdot 0$	Tot Child 39-40:	$0 \cdot 1$	GEN RICH 71-72: 23
Town Total 60-62:	$1 \cdot 8 \cdot 5$	Town Total 41-42:	$5 \cdot 3$	
Out Total 63-65:	$9 \cdot 3 \cdot 7$	Out Total 43-45:	$2 \cdot 4 \cdot 9$	PRESSURE RATING Children 73: 4
Grand Total 66-69:	$1 \cdot 1 \cdot 2 \cdot 2$	Grand Tot 46-48:	$3 \cdot 0 \cdot 2$	Adolesc 74: 2
Grand O.T.(code) 71-73:	70: blank $0 \cdot 3 \cdot 1$	Perf/Pop 49-50:	$2 \cdot 7$	Children 75: 0
Total Duration 74-77: $0 \cdot 0 \cdot 2 \cdot 4$		Aver. No. 51-52:	$8 \cdot 4$	WELFARE RATING Adolesc 76: 3
Average Attendance 78-80:	$3 \cdot 6 \cdot 3$			AUTONOMY RATING wtd 79: 7

Figure 11.1.   Data sheet for high school boys' basketball game. *Source.* Reproduced from Roger G. Barker, *Ecological Psychology.* Stanford: Stanford University Press, 1968, p. 99.

where cOT is the code number associated with an occupancy time OT by town residents of 3900 hours; in the present case, c is 23; and GRI is evidently $1.1(23) = 25$.[1] The code number c is a monotonically increasing transformation of OT (with OT represented by the midpoint of a range of actual OT values).

The GRI is an ingenious measure of the "offer" of a behavior setting (see Section

[1] The figure of 23 given by Barker for GEN RICH (see Figure 11.1) seems to be in error.

12.1). Zones 6, 5, and 4 in most settings offer the greatest rewards with respect to power and prestige; a setting with a high value of $\sum$ PenR permits several or many of the 14 population subgroups to be leaders and functionaries. A high value of $\sum$ ApR means that several kinds of action patterns are prominent in the setting, and a high value of $\sum$ BmR usually indicates that two or more behavior mechanisms are exercised at high levels of intensity; thus people with diverse interests can be attracted into it.

Barker uses an *ecological resources index* (ERI), which sums to 100 over all nonfamily behavior settings in the town, as a measure of the relative importances of the various segments of the town's environment. In 1963–1964 his town contained 884 specific behavior settings ($N = 884$); they occurred on an average of 60 days a year (ranging from 1 for annual celebrations to 366 for trafficways) for a total of 53,376 setting days or "occurrences" ($O = 53,376$); and they lasted an average of 5.4 hours a day for a total duration of 286,481 setting hours ($D = 286,481$).

For example, one of the town's 198 genotypes, "elementary school basic classes," showed the following values: $N = 13$, $O = 2250$, and $D = 8945$ (p. 111). The program for the genotype was:

> 58. Elementary School Basic Classes. Teacher (6) teaches reading, grammar, arithmetic, writing, elementary health, social studies, science, and engages in classroom routines; pupils (3) listen, write, recite, read, figure (p. 215).

There were 13 teachers, each with her own class ($N = 13$). Each class occurred on $O/N = 2250/13 = 173$ days, and lasted $D/O = 8945/2250 = 4$ hours (for the basic academic subjects). Hence we have

$$\mathrm{ERI} = \frac{100(13/884 + 2250/53{,}376 + 8945/286{,}481)}{3}$$

$$= \frac{1.47 + 4.22 + 3.12}{3} = 2.94; \tag{3}$$

in terms of this measure, elementary school basic classes had 2.94 percent of the ecological resources of the town's (nonfamily) environment (p. 111).

Barker uses occupancy time by the town's residents (town OT, or simply OT) as a measure of behavior output; in 1963–1964, town $OT = 1{,}125{,}134$ hours. For elementary school basic classes, town $OT = 98{,}251$ hours and town $OT/D = 98{,}251/8945 = 11.0$ *town residents* per class. (However, more than half the school's students were not residents of the town; *total* $OT = 222{,}119$ and *total* $OT/D = 222{,}119/8945 = 24.8$; thus the average number of persons in a class room was 24.8). Elementary school basic classes accounted for $98{,}251/1{,}125{,}134 = 8.73$ percent of town OT (p. 111).

Barker's Criteria for Identifying Behavior Settings and Partitioning the Town's (Nonfamily) Environment. The magnitude of Barker's achievement is perhaps masked by the simple calculations just set forth. He has partitioned the town's environment exhaustively into 198 genotype settings and he has done this in an objective, reproducible manner. It is analogous to the task of starting from scratch and classifying the GNP into a complete set of industries, commodities, and services.

There were some hard-to-judge situations. For example, is Chaco Garage a different setting from Chaco Service Station? Mr. Chaco owns and manages both, and the establishments are in adjacent buildings, but they have somewhat different programs:

> 78. Garages. Owner-manager (6) manages garage, repairs cars, services cars; mechanic (4) repairs cars; attendant (4) puts in gas, oil, washes windshields; assistant (4) carries out office routines; customers (3) have cars serviced or repaired, pay (p. 217).
>
> 177. Service Stations. Manager (6) manages business, fills tanks of cars and trucks with gasoline, checks oil, water, and tires, washes windshields, changes oil, greases cars, sells accessories; assistants (4) service cars as prescribed; customers (3) buy gasoline, oil, accessories, pay for servicing (p. 225).

Barker decided to classify two *synomorphs* (behavior-and-milieu units) A and B as parts of a single behavior setting if they had a score of $K \leq 20$, where K is the sum of scores on seven specific types of interdependence, each scaled from 1 (highest) to 7 (lowest) degree of interdependence. For example, the following measures would yield a score of $K = 14$ (pp. 40–45):

1. Some 67 to 94 percent of molar actions beginning in A are completed in B, or vice versa.[2]
2. A substantial percentage of the people who enter A also enter B, yielding a percentage overlap score of 67 to 94 from the calculation $2P_{ab}/(P_a + P_b)$, where P_a is people who enter A, P_b is people who enter B, and P_{ab} is people who enter both A and B.
3. A substantial percentage of the people who enter zones 4, 5, and 6 of A also enter zones 4, 5, and 6 of B, yielding an overlap score of 67 to 94 percent by the formula just mentioned (but confined to people in the three most central zones).
4. Some 50 to 94 percent of the space used by either A or B is common to both.
5. Some 75 to 100 percent of the occurrences of A and B take place during the same part of the same day.
6. More than half the objects used in A are also used in B.
7. Not more than two or three of the following behavior mechanisms are present in one setting but absent in the other: gross motor actions, manipulation, verbalization, singing, writing, observing, listening, thinking, eating, reading, emoting, and tactual feeling.

If these seven conditions prevail, A and B clearly belong to the same behavior setting. But if the percentages of overlap are only 33 to 66, if A and B simply use different parts of the same building, and if half (but no more) of the objects are shared, the K score rises to about 20 or 21, with $K = 20$ implying that A and B belong to the same setting and $K = 21$ implying that they do not. Barker states that in a sample of 100 synomorph pairs, three judges were unanimous in their classifications of 79 as behavior settings and 10 as not; there was initial disagreement on 11.

---

[2] "Molar actions" involve a person's moving his entire body through space—for example, walking from a workbench to a tool cabinet or a supply room.

The correlations between the ratings of pairs of judges were .93, .93, and .92 (p. 45).

Barker points out that routine application of a higher (lower) value of K as a cutting point would partition the community into a smaller (larger) number of units with a lower (higher) degree of internal interdependence:

> A cutting point between 30 and 31, for example, would place together in the same unit all the garages and service stations of the town. . . . A critical K value of 14 would separate the Fountain, Pharmacy, and Variety Department of the Drugstore into separate units; it would detach Chaco Service Station from Chaco Garage (pp. 45–46).

Having defined his 198 genotypes and accumulated data sheets like Figure 11.1 for each of them from September 1, 1963, through August 31, 1964, Barker can display the distributions of action patterns, behavior mechanisms, maximum penetration ratings, values of N, O, D, OT, GRI, ERI, and several other measures across all the settings. In effect, each behavior setting can be translated into a vector of numerical values of a common set of variables; these could be weighted, transformed, and manipulated in a variety of ways (pp. 109–136).

The Fox-Van Moeseke approach places special emphasis on the allocation of time. Barker comments as follows on town OT (p. 128):

> A behavior setting has one changeable attribute that results from the interaction of its stable, whole-entity attributes and variable properties of its actual and potential inhabitants. This is its occupancy time. Whether a Sunday school class meeting has large or small occupancy is the cumulative resultant of independent actions by separate persons. The sum of individual decisions "to go" or "not to go" and, when there, "to stay" or "not to stay" is the occupancy time.

In the next section, we adapt some of Barker's data to the requirements of other frames of reference.

11.2   Expository Model of a Small Community

Barker's town ("Midwest") was "a geographically unified community spreading over 400 acres" and surrounded by open fields in an agricultural region (p. 92). Despite its small population (830 residents on January 1, 1964), it was a county seat and had a congeries of government offices, judges, and attorneys that would not otherwise be found in a town of its size. It was 20, 35, and 45 miles, respectively, from cities of 35,000, 100,000, and 800,000 population. A large percentage of its labor force worked outside the town, and fully half the students in its schools lived on farms or in other open-country locations.

To simplify our arithmetic we will assume a town with 1000 residents; to simplify our exposition, we will assume in most of this section that the 1000 residents spend *all* their time for one year within the town limits. We assume a population distribution rather like that of the United States as a whole in 1964, with gainfully employed adults accounting for 40 percent, other adults 26 percent, adolescents and children in school 24 percent, and preschool children 10 percent of the total.

Table 11.1. Illustrative Time Allocations of Residents of a Small Town Among Behavior Setting Clusters, by Population Category

Population Category	Nonfamily Settings						Family Settings			Out-of-Town Settings	Total Time	Proportion of Town Population
	Business Places	Schools	Government Agencies	Churches	Social Life, Leisure	Traffic-ways and Hallways	Housework, Family Tasks	Personal Care	Mass Media, Leisure			
	(1)	(2)	(3)	(4)	(5)	(6)	(7)	(8)	(9)	(10)	(11)	(12)
A. Percent of Total Time of Each Population Category												
Town Residents												
Adults, employed	12.50	0.25	2.50	0.25	2.00	2.50	15.00	42.00	11.00	12.00	100.00	0.40
Adults, not employed	7.70	--	0.60	0.40	3.00	0.80	30.00	44.00	11.50	2.00	100.00	0.26
Adolescents and children in school	0.80	10.90	--	0.50	2.50	1.30	5.00	50.00	27.00	2.00	100.00	0.24
Children, preschool	1.35	--	--	--	1.35	0.60	1.40	58.30	35.00	2.00	100.00	0.10
Total population	7.33	2.72	1.16	0.32	2.34	1.56	15.14	46.07	17.36	6.00	100.00	1.00
B. Percent of Total Time of Entire Population of Town												
Town Residents												
Adults, employed	5.00	0.10	1.00	0.10	0.80	1.00	6.00	16.80	4.40	4.80	40.00	--
Adults, not employed	2.00	--	0.16	0.10	0.80	0.20	7.80	11.44	2.98	0.52	26.00	--
Adolescents and children in school	0.20	2.62	--	0.12	0.60	0.30	1.20	12.00	6.48	0.48	24.00	--
Children, preschool	0.13	--	--	--	0.14	0.06	0.14	5.83	3.50	0.20	10.00	--
Total population	7.33	2.72	1.16	0.32	2.34	1.56	15.14	46.07	17.36	6.00	100.00	--
Nonresidents	2.91	3.06	1.06	0.34	2.27	0.73						
Equivalent total occupancy time of nonfamily settings (by residents *and* nonresidents)	10.24	5.78	2.22	0.66	4.61	2.29						

Source. Columns 1 through 6 in "total population" rows and in "nonresident" row are based on data in Table 5.3, in Roger G. Barker, *Ecological Psychology*. Stanford: Stanford University Press, 1968, pp. 110–116. All other figures are inferential estimates by Karl A. Fox, although figures for adults are guided, in part, by data in Robinson and Converse (1966).

The figures in columns 1 through 6 of the "total population" rows in Table 11.1 are based on Barker's data. However, instead of dividing the town OT's by the total town OT of 1,125,134 hours *in nonfamily settings only*, we have divided them by 7,290,720, the total living time of 830 residents for 366 days (including February 29, 1964). The time allocations of each population subgroup among nonfamily settings are consistent with the weights and the "total population" figures but otherwise are simply plausible estimates made by me; the allocations for the two adult groups are based on 1966 United States time use data from Robinson and Converse (1966), some of which we reproduced in Tables 5.1 through 5.4. The two sets of data are roughly consistent if we assume that about 40 percent of the employed adults work out of town (there are three cities within commuting distance).

In the lower section of Table 11.1, the percentage time allocations for each population subgroup have been multiplied by its proportion of the population to yield percentages of the total living time of all residents. A row has been added, based on Barker's data, to show the relative importance of nonresidents (mostly nearby farm people) as customers, students, and participants in the town's nonfamily settings. Table 11.2 contains the same figures for larger aggregates of settings; Barker's nonfamily settings cover only 15.43 percent of the living time of the 830 residents. If we allow for working, shopping, and recreation outside the town to the extent of 6 percent of total time, some 78.57 percent of residents' time is spent in or just outside their own homes and in the homes of other residents.

In Table 11.3, we have taken the further step of "closing" the community by (1) adding the out-of-town shopping and recreation time to "family settings" for each of the four population groups and (2) adding the out-of-town work-related time of employed adults to "firms." Thus the proportion of time spent in family settings is placed at .700 (70 percent) for employed adults, .875 for adults not employed, .840 for adolescents and children in school, and .967 for preschool children.

In addition to time, each person has three groups of resources, the same groups as in Tables 6.7 and 6.8. Group 1 includes health, affect, and sexuality; group 2, value commitments; group 3, work-related skills and other skills; and group 4, money, power in formal organizations (including families in this usage), political power, and prestige. For employed adults, we have assumed the same relative weights of the various resources as in Table 5.7 (.2, .2, and .6, respectively, for groups 1, 2, and 3 plus 4). "Adults, not employed" include (1) married women under age 65, and (2) retired persons, the resource proportions in Table 11.3 being weighted averages of those assumed for the two subgroups. The proportions for adolescents and children in school and for preschool children are approximately in line with the "hypothetical pattern of total income and its components for an individual, by life stages" in Table 6.9. If we assume an average money income of $8000 from work related skills for employed adults, the resource figures in equivalent dollars can be displayed as follows:

Resource Group	Employed Adults	Adults, not Employed	Adolescents and Children, in School	Preschool Children
Group 1	4,000	3,000	4,000	3,000
Group 2	4,000	4,000	2,000	1,000
Groups 3 and 4	12,000	9,000	2,000	0
Total income	20,000	16,000	8,000	4,000

Table 11.2. Illustrative Time Allocations of Residents of a Small Town Among Major Aggregates of Behavior Settings, by Population Category

| Population Category | Town Settings | | Out-of-Town Settings | | Total Time | Proportion of Town Population |
	All Nonfamily Settings (1)	All Family Settings (2)	Work-Related (3)	Shopping, Recreation (4)	(5)	(6)
A. Percent of Total Time of Each Population Category						
Town residents						
Adults, employed	20.00	68.00	10.00	2.00	100.00	0.40
Adults, not employed	12.50	85.50	--	2.00	100.00	0.26
Adolescents and children in school	16.00	82.00	--	2.00	100.00	0.24
Children, preschool	3.30	94.70	--	2.00	100.00	0.10
Total population	15.43	78.57	4.00	2.00	100.00	1.00
B. Percent of Total Time of Entire Population of Town						
Town residents						
Adults, employed	8.00	27.20	4.00	0.80	40.00	--
Adults, not employed	3.26	22.22	--	0.52	26.00	--
Adolescents and children in school	3.84	19.68	--	0.48	24.00	--
Children, preschool	0.33	9.47	--	0.20	10.00	--
Total population	15.43	78.57	4.00	2.00	100.00	--
Nonresidents	10.37					
Equivalent total occupancy time of nonfamily settings (by residents and nonresidents)	25.80					

Source. Further aggregation of figures in Table 11.1.

The figures assumed for retired persons are $2000, $4000, and $4000 (total income, $10,000) and for married women not employed $4000, $4000, and $12,000 (total income, $20,000). The group 3 and 4 figures are dominated by estimates of the market values of work-related skills at different ages; the group 2 figures imply that value commitments are built up cumulatively over successive life stages; and the group 1 figures assume the same values for health and affect in each population category except the aged, but lower values of sexuality for children and the aged than for younger adults. No monetary value is assigned to time.

Tables 11.3 and 11.4 together represent an equilibrium situation. Each person who occupies a setting contributes some of his resources to it as inputs. The total value of these inputs is equal to the total value of the outputs of the setting. Within groups 3 and 4, work-related skills, money, and goods are interchangeable; we assume that the group 3 and 4 outputs are distributed in direct proportion to the group 3 and 4 inputs. We also assume that group 1 and 2 outputs are distributed in proportion to group 1 and 2 inputs. This implies that over the year as a whole people get out of behavior settings what they put into them and that inputs in each of the broad resource categories are paid for in its distinctive currencies. Recall that group 1 corresponds roughly to the Child, group 2 to the Parent, and groups 3 and 4 to the Adult in Berne's (1964) terminology or, respectively, to the id, superego and ego.

The first four rows under the "firms" column in Table 11.3 show that employed adults put into this setting the following proportions of their resources: time, .225, group 1, .225; group 2, .400; and groups 3 and 4, .850. The figures in the first four rows of the employed adults column in Table 11.4 show that the "firms" setting distributed to employed adults outputs equivalent in value to the following proportions of their total resources: time, .225, group 1, .225; group 2, .400; and groups 3 and 4, .850. The group 3 and 4 inputs consist mainly of work-related skills and the group 3 and 4 outputs mainly of wages, salaries, and proprietors' money incomes. The other three population groups enter the "firms" setting as customers and tag-alongs, making inputs as indicated below the "firms" column in Table 11.3 and receiving outputs as indicated in the first four rows of their respective columns in Table 11.4.

The inputs into the "schools" setting come, of course, mainly from the adolescents and children enrolled. Teachers constitute a very small proportion of the labor force, and their inputs make up small proportions of the total resources of employed adults. Our illustrative figures show retired persons and housewives contributing considerable fractions of their skills (work-related and other) and of their power, prestige, and value commitments to the "social settings" of the community, an extremely varied array of voluntary, occasional, and part-time unpaid activities. Adolescents and children are also shown as contributing substantial inputs to "social settings."

"Family settings" include those involving members of a single household in or just outside the home, plus a wide range of informal get-togethers in the homes of friends and relatives, plus playmates and school friends visiting in one another's homes, and the like. Barker defines family settings by exclusion:

> The data [of the behavior setting survey] . . . are concerned with the *public parts of the town*. The terms molar environment, molar behavior resources, behavior setting resources, refer in all cases to the nonfamily parts of Midwest (p. 92).

Table 11.3. Sources of Resource Inputs to Behavior Setting Aggregates in a Small Town, by Population Category, Based on Hypothetical Data

Sources of Resource Inputs, by Population Category	Behavior Setting Aggregates			
	Firms	Schools	Social Settings	Family Settings
	(Proportion of Each Resource of Each Population Category)			
	(1)	(2)	(3)	(4)
1. Adults, employed				
Time	.225	.003	.072	.700
Group 1	.225	.003	.072	.700
Group 2	.400	.015	.185	.400
Groups 3 and 4	.850	.015	.035	.100
2. Adults, not employed				
Time	.077	--	.048	.875
Group 1	.077	--	.048	.875
Group 2	.150	--	.250	.600
Groups 3 and 4	.150	--	.250	.600
3. Adolescents and children in school				
Time	.008	.109	.043	.840
Group 1	.008	.109	.043	.840
Group 2	.015	.220	.165	.600
Groups 3 and 4	.015	.220	.165	.600
4. Preschool children				
Time	.013	--	.020	.967
Group 1	.013	--	.020	.967
Group 2	.013	--	.020	.967
Groups 3 and 4	--	--	--	--
Value of resource inputs per capita of total population (dollar equivalents: money income per employed adult = $8,000)	5,674	418	1,668	6,720

In columns 5 through 10 of Table 11.3 we have made a series of illustrative calculations. Column 5 contains a value of 1.000 for each resource of each population group. Column 6 contains the proportions of the town's total population included in each group. Column 7 converts the assumed dollar values of each resource into employed adult equivalents (note that the figures for employed adults sum to 1.00 and those for the other groups to .80, .40, and .20, respectively). In column 8, each column 7 figure has been multiplied by the ratio 1.00/.40, reflecting the assumption that the market value of the work-related skills of employed adults amounts to 40

Table 11.3.   (*Continued*)

		Values of Inputs Per Person			
		Value of Each Resource per Person		Contribution of Each Resource of Each Population Category to per Capita Total Income of Town	
Total	Proportion of Total Population	Total Income of Employed Adult = 1.00	Money Income of Employed Adult = 1.00	Money Income of Employed Adult = 1.00	Money Income of Employed Adult = $8,000
(5)	(6)	(7)	(8)	(9)	(10)
1.000	.40	0	0	0	0
1.000	.40	.20	.500	.2000	1,600
1.000	.40	.20	.500	.2000	1,600
1.000	.40	.60	1.500	.6000	4,800
1.000	.26	0	0	0	0
1.000	.26	.15	.375	.0975	780
1.000	.26	.20	.500	.1300	1,040
1.000	.26	.45	1.125	.2925	2,340
1.000	.24	0	0	0	0
1.000	.24	.20	.500	.1200	960
1.000	.24	.10	.250	.0600	480
1.000	.24	.10	.250	.0600	480
1.000	.10	0	0	0	0
1.000	.10	.15	.375	.0375	300
1.000	.10	.05	.125	.0125	100
--	.10	--	--	--	--
14,480	1.00			1.8100	14,480

percent of their total incomes. Thus if we assign a value of $8000 to an employed adult's work-related skills, the product of $8000 times the first three nonzero figures in column 8 yields values of $4000, $4000, and $12,000 for the respective resources and $20,000 for total income, as in the tabulation on page 000; the total incomes of the other three groups would be calculated at $16,000, $8000 and $4000 respectively.

In column 9, the population proportions in column 6 have been multiplied by the "equivalent employed adult money income units" in column 8; the results sum to 1.8100. In column 10 each figure in column 9 has been multiplied by $8000; the

Table 11.4. Distribution of Outputs of Behavior Setting Aggregates in a Small Town to Various Population Categories, Based on Hypothetical Data

Behavior Setting Aggregates in Which Outputs Are Produced	Recipients of	
	Adults, Employed (1)	Adults, Not Employed (2)
	(Proportion of Each Resource	
1. Firms		
Time	.225	.077
Group 1	.225	.077
Group 2	.400	.150
Groups 3 and 4	.850	.150
2. Schools		
Time	.003	--
Group 1	.003	--
Group 2	.015	--
Groups 3 and 4	.015	--
3. Social Settings		
Time	.072	.048
Group 1	.072	.048
Group 2	.185	.250
Groups 3 and 4	.035	.250
4. Family Settings		
Time	.700	.875
Group 1	.700	.875
Group 2	.400	.600
Groups 3 and 4	.100	.600
Value of behavior setting outputs per capita of total population (dollar equivalents: money income per employed adult = $8,000)	8,000	4,160

sum, $14,480, is the average total income per capita. If we multiply this figure by 1000, the assumed population of the community, we obtain $14,480,000 as the aggregate total income of community residents.

Suppose that the column 10 figures are in units of $1000. If we multiply each figure in column 10 by the figure in the same row under the "firms" column, we obtain values of the inputs of each resource contributed to this setting by each population group; the sum is 5674. The corresponding sums for schools, social settings, and family settings are 418, 1668, and 6720; the total value of inputs to all four settings is 14,480.

Table 11.4.   (*Continued*)

Behavior Setting Outputs		
Adolescents and Children in School (3)	Preschool Children (4)	Total Population
of Each Population Category)		

.008	.013	0
.008	.013	432
.015	.013	804
.015	--	4,438
.109	--	0
.109	--	110
.220	--	130
.220	--	178
.043	.020	0
.043	.020	199
.165	.020	637
.165	--	832
.840	.967	0
.840	.967	2,899
.600	.967	1,649
.600	--	2,172
1,920	400	14,480

The extreme right-hand column in Table 11.4 indicates a total value of 14,480, the same as the total value of inputs. The deliveries by firms total 5674 (the same as total inputs to firms); the deliveries by schools, social settings, and family settings (at 418, 1668, and 6720) also equal the total values of their respective inputs.

Thus Tables 11.3 and 11.4 together have some of the features of an input–output table but contain no information about the interrelations between settings. Barker identified 884 nonfamily settings in Midwest; if we assume a population of 1000 comprising 250 households (based on the United States average ratio of families and unrelated individuals to total population in 1964), we can add a minimum of 250 family settings to Barker's 884 public ones. In general, community residents will try to allocate their respective resources among settings that yield the highest perceived returns. If a person's resources increase for any reason (normal growth in size and strength, improved health, learned skills), we assume that he will increase his inputs correspondingly and that the outputs of the community will increase by the same amount. For this to hold rigorously, the system of behavior settings would probably have to meet requirements similar to those for general economic equilibrium under perfect competition. For our present purpose, it is sufficient that the system of settings be flexible enough to make productive use of increases in any resource.

We could also take the view that a person whose resources have increased will claim larger amounts of behavior setting outputs; these require matching increases in the values of inputs to the settings. The sequence of detailed adjustments may be complex, but the final effect is that the settings absorb additional inputs from the individual equal in value to his increased claims on their deliveries to final demand. We recall here Berne's statements that the goal of each member of a social aggregation of two or more persons is "to obtain as many satisfactions as possible from his transactions with other members" and that (in a simple pastime) "transactions are adaptively programmed so that each party will obtain the maximum gains or advantages during the interval" (1964, pp. 19, 41).

11.3   Economic Interrelations Among Members of a Small Community

Tables 11.3 and 11.4 reflect an equilibrium situation for a single accounting period. Suppose this situation is unsatisfactory insofar as incomes of some residents of the community are below certain norms. We wish to consider whether an income payment to one resident will have any beneficial effects on other residents of the community as well.

If person 1 is given a tax-free annuity of $1000, we would expect to find some modest "multiplier effects." To simplify, suppose person 1 spends the entire $1000 at the local grocery store. The grocer takes his usual margin of $200 (the other $800 goes out of town to wholesalers) and spends it at the clothier's, who takes his margin of, say, $80 (the other $120 goes out of town to wholesalers) and gives it to his housekeeper, who spends it all at the grocer's, who takes his $16 margin and spends it at the clothier's, and so on. The second-round increases are only 8 percent as large as the first, and the third-round increases are only 8 percent as large as the second. To the nearest cent, the final score is as follows:

Individual	Increase in Annual Income
Person 1	$1000.00
Grocer	217.39
Clothier	86.96
Housekeeper	86.96
Total	$1391.31

Under the terms of our example, these increases identify the net effects of person 1's annuity (bestowed by someone outside the community) on all residents. The incomes of four individuals are increased by the amounts shown.

We can study the arithmetic of multiplier analysis with a few examples. First, suppose we have a two-person community represented by the matrix equation

$$\begin{bmatrix} y_1 \\ y_2 \end{bmatrix} = \begin{bmatrix} 0 & .5 \\ .5 & 0 \end{bmatrix} \begin{bmatrix} x_1 \\ x_2 \end{bmatrix}, \tag{4}$$

where x_i represents a change in income spent by person i and y_i represents a change in income retained in the community by person i. Whatever is retained by person i on one round as y_i is spent by him on the next round as x_i.

If person 1 receives an exogenous income increase of one unit and person 2 receives no increase, (4) becomes

$$\begin{bmatrix} y_1 \\ y_2 \end{bmatrix} = \begin{bmatrix} 0 & .5 \\ .5 & 0 \end{bmatrix} \begin{bmatrix} 1 \\ 0 \end{bmatrix}, \tag{5}$$

and the process runs on as follows:

Round	Changes in Income Spent by Person 1	Changes in Income Spent by Person 2
1	1.00000	0
2	0	0.50000
3	0.25000	0
4	0	0.12500
5	0.06250	0
6	0	0.03125
7	0.01562	0
8	0	0.00781
9 to infinity	0.00521	0.00261
Final values	1.33333	0.66667

In this example, person 2, who received no increase in his income from *outside* the community, is able to spend 0.66667 units more as a result of multiplier effects *inside* the community. Person 1, who received a one-unit increase from outside the community, gains 0.33333 more units from multiplier effects inside the community.

If the proportion p of income retained in the community out of income spent there decreased from .5 to .4, .3, .2, .1, and 0, respectively, the multiplier effects would decrease and the changes in income spent would decline as follows:

Income Retained in Community per Unit of Income Spent There, p	Change in Income Spent by		
	Person 1	Person 2	Total
0.5	1.333	0.667	2.000
0.4	1.191	0.476	1.667
0.3	1.099	0.330	1.429
0.2	1.042	0.208	1.250
0.1	1.010	0.101	1.111
0	1.000	0	1.000

The figures are calculated from the matrix equation

$$\begin{bmatrix} y_1 \\ y_2 \end{bmatrix} = \begin{bmatrix} 0 & p \\ p & 0 \end{bmatrix} \begin{bmatrix} 1 \\ 0 \end{bmatrix}. \tag{6}$$

Suppose the community is enlarged to six persons, with the following coefficient structure, and person 1 receives an exogenous one unit increase in income:

$$\begin{bmatrix} y_1 \\ y_2 \\ y_3 \\ y_4 \\ y_5 \\ y_6 \end{bmatrix} = \begin{bmatrix} 0 & .1 & .1 & .1 & .1 & .1 \\ .1 & 0 & .1 & .1 & .1 & .1 \\ .1 & .1 & 0 & .1 & .1 & .1 \\ .1 & .1 & .1 & 0 & .1 & .1 \\ .1 & .1 & .1 & .1 & 0 & .1 \\ .1 & .1 & .1 & .1 & .1 & 0 \end{bmatrix} \begin{bmatrix} 1 \\ 0 \\ 0 \\ 0 \\ 0 \\ 0 \end{bmatrix} \tag{7}$$

The successive rounds now run as follows:

Round	Change in Income Spent by Person Number						
	1	2	3	4	5	6	Total
1	1.0000	0	0	0	0	0	1.0000
2	0	0.1000	0.1000	0.1000	0.1000	0.1000	0.5000
3	0.0500	0.0400	0.0400	0.0400	0.0400	0.0400	0.2500
4	0.0200	0.0210	0.0210	0.0210	0.0210	0.0210	0.1250
5	0.0105	0.0104	0.0104	0.0104	0.0104	0.0104	0.0625
6 to infinity	0.0105	0.0104	0.0104	0.0104	0.0104	0.0104	0.0625
Total	1.0910	0.1818	0.1818	0.1818	0.1818	0.1818	2.0000

Person 1 spends his exogenous one unit, plus 0.0910 units more resulting from multiplier effects inside the community; each of the other five persons is able to spend 0.1818 units more as the result of multiplier effects. The total multiplier is 2.0000, just as in the first example. With a symmetric and equal coefficient structure as in (4) through (7), the total multiplier can be calculated as

$$k = \frac{1}{1 - \sum_{i=1}^{n} p_{ij}} , \qquad (8)$$

where $\sum_{i=1}^{n} p_{ij}$ is the sum of the "income retained" coefficients in any one column j. If the number of persons in the community increases to (say) 100 or more, the change in income spent by person 1 becomes only slightly more than 1.00 unit and the change in income spent by each other resident becomes very small—on the order of $(k - 1)/(n - 1)$ or less than 0.01 unit.

Some multipliers based on empirical data are cited in Chapter 12 in the section, "The Effects of Openness on Economic and Other Multipliers." Functional economic areas in the 1960s yielded total multiplier values on the order of 2.00, whereas smaller, more "open" communities yielded lower values. It should be noted that $\sum_{i=1}^{n} p_{ij}$ is essentially the average ratio of *value added in the community* to the value of final sales of goods and services to community residents.

11.4   Other Interrelations Among Members of a Small Community

Do multiplier effects also exist for resources other than money income? A number of cases may be considered.

1. A community resident commutes to a low-paying job in the nearby city. He takes an intensive training course (all expenses, plus his foregone earnings, paid by a grant) and moves into a job in the same company at $1000 more per year. He continues to spend the same percentage of his total earnings in the community, and the multiplier analysis applies as before.

2. The multiplier analysis would also apply if he worked in his own community in a small assembly shop that shipped its entire output to outside buyers, and if his increased skill caused the shop to produce enough additional quantity or quality to cover the $1000 increase in his earnings.

3. The analysis would continue to apply if the correction of a health problem (rather than an increase in skill) permitted him to turn out more units per day on a piece-rate system, or to take on heavier work at a higher pay scale, for the assembly shop or an outside employer.

In all these cases, improved skill or health is converted into higher earnings from outside sources, either directly by selling the improved working capacity to outside employers or indirectly by producing more local outputs for outside sale. The analysis still applies in the case of "import substitution," where the improved skill or health increases the local output of goods for sale in the community and retailers reduce their purchases from outside wholesalers by the same amount.

We are on more speculative ground with respect to resources that are not converted into money. Early in the chapter we cited Berne's statement that in the process of exchanging greetings "A and B have improved each other's health slightly. A bit of recognition-hunger has been satisfied." The Holmes and Rahe (1967) social readjustment rating scale, which we reproduced as Table 6.13, assigns numerical scores to stress experienced by a person as the result of changes in the health of a family member, changes in the number of arguments with his spouse, trouble with in-laws, or trouble with his employer. Family therapists often find that the family member brought forward as the "identified patient" is not the one with the most serious problems; the family must be seen as a transactional system.[3] In an office setting, a dour receptionist radiates gloom and a cheerful one affect.

The multiplier arithmetic of Section 11.3 could, of course, be applied formalistically to any resource or group of resources, or to total income. Without an empirical basis, however, this would not be useful. Another paragraph or two on principles may be in order.

Tables 11.3 and 11.4 can be regarded as an equilibrium situation in which the values imputed to the resources (and which sum to the value of the community's output) already embody the final effects of any multipliers resulting from complementary transactions. If person 1 receives a new honor, worth one unit of prestige according to some "objective" nationwide standard, the value imputed to it in Table 11.3 will be somewhat more than one unit as the result of a "positive reinforcement" multiplier within the community.

The existence of cliques and factions or racial and religious discrimination could be reflected in the community's transactions matrix as a series of blocks of nonzero coefficients along the major diagonal and zero (or extremely small) coefficients everywhere else. Multiplier effects would operate within blocks but not between them; the average level of such effects for the community as a whole would be reduced; and the shadow prices of its resources would fall relative to their levels if employed in a better-integrated community.

11.5   Compatibility of Barker's Framework with Other Data Systems

Occupations figure prominently in Barker's classification of 198 behavior setting genotypes. Suppose, for example, that the first three columns in Table 11.3 were disaggregated to 198 public settings (70 business, 32 school, 22 government, 9 religious, and 65 social) and the fourth to 250 households. The zone 5 and 6 leaders in most of the business, school, and government settings are full-time proprietors, managers, or professional workers; the zone 4 functionaries are craftsmen, operatives, sales people, clerks, and laborers. In principle, the occupation, earnings, and hours of work of each member of the labor force could be recorded precisely as they are in our national data systems.

Also, each employed adult is a member of a household unit. Data on age, sex, marital status, years of education completed, and the like, could be collected just as in the United States time use survey (Robinson and Converse, 1966) and/or *Productive Americans*, the study by James N. Morgan and his colleagues (1966). Regression analysis could be used to explore the relations between Barker's ratings of behavior settings (on penetration, action patterns, and behavior mechanisms) and conventional economic and demographic data on the populations of the settings.

[3] See, for example, Boszormenyi-Nagy and Framo (eds., 1965), Satir (1967), and Scherz (1971).

11.6 Measurement of Cross-Sectional Differences in Behavior Setting Quality and of Quality Changes Over Time

The variations in incomes received by zone 6 leaders in different specific settings of the same genotype (different attorneys *or* physicians *or* teachers, etc.) must to a large extent reflect differences in the values of their contributions as perceived by clients, patients, school administrators, and others. Although the offices of (say) two family physicians may be designed to satisfy the same array of patient needs, one may be perceived as satisfying them at a higher level of "quality." A detailed analysis of actual events in the two offices might permit the assignment of this "quality" difference to a number of specific attributes of the physicians and their offices, including supporting personnel.

Different genotypes are designed to serve different needs. For example, the selection of behavior settings by a particular age group might be viewed as a method of satisfying needs for the exercise of various behavior mechanisms (a homeostasis or drive-reduction model might be postulated). If there is a research basis for stating (say) "minimum," "adequate," and "desirable" levels of use of each of these mechanisms and for estimating the amounts of use per hour in various behavior settings, the adequacy of the current levels of use by particular groups could be rated and activities that would remedy deficiencies could be recommended. (In some cases deficiencies might be remedied by removal of needless restrictions on classroom or work group interactions.)

Estimates of nutritional needs have been used to compute least cost diets with or without additional stipulations that the diets not depart too far from existing preferences and habits. Similar estimates might be made of minimum time behavior setting selections to meet stipulated levels of behavior mechanism use and also limitations based on individual preferences for, and accessibility of, various settings, using a linear programming framework.

If actual time allocations among settings were sampled over a period of years, and if the behavior pattern in each setting remained constant, changes in time use could be translated into changes in levels and patterns of use of the various behavior mechanisms. In part, a historical record could be reconstructed on the basis of changes in occupational mix, hours of work, methods of transportation, types of sport and recreation, and the like.

Changes in the attributes ("quality") of genotype settings over time could also be described and evaluated in terms of behavior mechanism use. A food supermarket is at least qualitatively different from its predecessor, the neighborhood grocery, and a modern kitchen is qualitatively different from the pre-1930 version. The mixes of equipment and skills found in modern offices are different from those of previous decades. Andrew Court (1939) introduced the concept of a "hedonic index" to quantify the superiority of (say) a 1939 model automobile over the 1920 and 1930 models sold under the same name. Griliches (1961) used data on sales prices of second-hand cars with and without specific optional features (power brakes, power steering, automatic transmission, etc.) to estimate the values consumers placed on each feature. Additional studies of quality change are presented in Griliches (ed., 1971).

The view of a behavior setting as a collection of attributes is compatible with Lancaster's (1971) interpretation of commodities in the same light. It also parallels some brilliant conceptual and empirical work by Victor E. Smith (1959, 1963) who, under carefully stated assumptions, allocated the total cost of a least cost diet exhaustively among the various nutrient and food habit restrictions imposed. His data came from a survey of consumer food purchases. The shadow prices of the restrictions are translated into equivalent dollar values of their marginal utilities to a consumer who would voluntarily select the combination of products included in the optimal solution. The application of Smith's approach to behavior settings and required levels of behavior mechanism use would be straightforward.

Barker also rates each behavior setting on 11 action patterns: aesthetics, business, education, government, nutrition, personal appearance, physical health, professionalism, recreation, religion, and social contact. His numerical ratings could be used descriptively to measure changes over time in the extent of these action patterns among various groups or for cross-sectional comparisons. If certain "minimum," "adequate," or "desirable" levels were stipulated for some or all of these patterns for any population group, least time combinations of behavior settings could be selected as already described.

Barker's ratings of settings with respect to pressure on children to enter or stay out, to degree of local autonomy, and to their intended relevance to the welfare of children and adolescents could also be used descriptively or normatively. For example, the local autonomy ratings might be developed into useful measures of the extent to which residents could control the level and distribution of total income and its various components in their community. The effects on autonomy of shifts of control of government programs among federal, state, and local levels could be given a rough quantitative representation; so could the degree of autonomy of local managers of national chain stores as against that of proprietors of locally owned establishments.

If standards or goals were specified for all the variables measured by Barker and a least time selection of behavior settings computed, the total time cost could be allocated exhaustively among all the standards that were precisely met (but not exceeded) in the least time solution. The prospects of particular new types of settings displacing existing ones could also be studied in terms of their relative costs (or resource–cost vectors) in meeting the same stipulated set of output requirements.

11.7 Implications of National Goals and Activities for a Small Community

A model of a small community may shed light on the implications of national goals. We draw on Terleckyj's (1973a) pioneering work here, as we did in Section 7.1.

Assume that we have the information in Tables 11.3 and 11.4 disaggregated to the level of 1000 residents, 250 households, and 198 public behavior settings for the base year 1971, and that we also have quantitative measures of the status of the community and its residents with respect to each of Terleckyj's 22 goal output indicators. We assume the community's 1971 ratings to be identical with the national averages at that time. We then list the maximum value of each variable that Terleckyj judges to be (separately) attainable as of 1981. Our resources will not be sufficient to achieve all these maximum values by that time.

Two of the goals directly involve health. First, the average life expectancy at birth is to be increased. The principal means are to be (1) changing health-related habits and patterns, (2) increasing health services related to specific conditions, and (3) adding special health services for vulnerable population groups. Presumably, we are to record information about the health status and health habits of each resident in 1971 and again in 1981 (including, of course, the new residents under 10 years of age) and apply weights based on medical research and standard age distributions to calculate the increase in life expectancy. Second, the number of persons with major disabilities is to be reduced.

If we assume a "closed" community (no out-migration or in-migration), we could try to translate these changes in health status and habits into an annual flow of total income to residents of the community. Since total income streams will be prolonged, we could also make some present value calculations (the choice of discount rates is a problem).

Several other goals would involve changes in measurable attributes of individuals, including (1) an increased level of performance in education based on standardized tests, (2) an increased number of persons completing college, (3) a reduction in the number of persons not in the mainstream of the labor force, and (4) an increase in the median earnings of individuals in 1971 dollars. The first three items involve increases in work-related (and other) skills; their equivalent dollar values could be estimated in terms of 1971 total incomes of persons with similar test scores and skills in the community. The increase in median earnings from gainful employment would reflect the labor market value of the work related portions of the added skills.

There are three antipoverty goals: reducing the numbers of persons (1) below a specified poverty standard, (2) in near-poverty conditions, and (3) with living standard losses more than 30 percent below a stated norm. The principal means proposed are private savings, insurance and pension plans, provision of old age pensions up to 42 percent of current earnings, and a "negative income tax" or siimilar program. These programs would affect the distribution of purchasing power in the community by causing a somewhat larger share of total deliveries to final demand by firms to go to retired persons and to families with limited earning power. Those groups would probably increase their participation and influence in social settings as well.

Three goals relate to economic inequality. The adjusted family income ratio (of the 20th percentile to the 90th percentile income—20 being low and 90 high) is to be increased; the ratio of the mean family income of nonwhites to whites is to be increased; and hourly earnings of women as a percentage of hourly earnings of men are to be raised. In a community model, these modifications could result from increased skills, reduced housework and family tasks for women, increased political power, increased power in formal organizations, and changes in value commitments particularly among younger people.

Terleckyj's other goals include increased percentages of people living in adequate houses and satisfactory neighborhoods, not exposed to bothersome pollution, and regularly taking part in recreation; increased numbers of active artists and of scientists engaged in basic research; increased time free from work and chores; and an increased number of areas maintained for preservation of life and natural forms. Once methods of measuring these variables were specified, most of them could also be tried out conceptually on a small community model.

Finally, alternative sets of values of all 22 goals could be tried out simultaneously to estimate their combined implications for the community, including the redistribution of time, all other resources, and total income. If the 31 instrumental activities listed by Terleckyj were also spelled out as they would operate at the community level, they as well as the goal variables could be incorporated into a policy model of the Tinbergen type. The constraints of the model would include the initial levels and distributions of all community resources among categories of individuals and across categories of behavior settings.

11.8   Concluding Remarks

Richard Stone (1971) presented a demographic model emphasizing formal educational activities of boys aged 0 to 19 in England and Wales. The model includes a matrix of 114 rows and 114 columns to project changes in the state of the system (enrollments by age, subject matter stream, etc.) from one year to the next. Data for these age groups in Barker's small community could be incorporated in a similar model.

Stone distinguished between the "active sequence" (formal education and full-time employment) and the "passive sequence" (housewives, retired persons, pre-school children, and persons in certain institutions); for his immediate purpose, he limited his attention almost entirely to the active sequence.

It seems possible to extend Stone's models (both cross-sectional and vintage) to include all members of a small community in a single matrix and to use a behavior setting format that accounts for all uses of time. One version of the matrix might allocate numbers of persons according to their ages and primary activities (including housework, leisure, and play, in addition to full-time work or skill). A second version might be stated in terms of *man years* of the time of various age groups spent in an exhaustive set of behavior settings. The usefulness of alternative levels of aggregation could be explored.

Simulation models of universities and school systems have been used experimentally to provide insights to their administrators. Simulation models of the community served by a school system could furnish another level of insight into the impacts of the schools on the surrounding society.

XII

Elements of an Operational System–II:
Cities and Regions

TYPICALLY, COMMUNITIES of different population sizes in a country can be characterized as a hierarchy of central places—villages, towns, small cities, regional capitals, and so on, in ascending order (Berry and Harris, 1968). A village is approximately self-sufficient with respect to specified services; a town is self-sufficient with respect to village-level services and to services requiring the larger population base of a town plus several nearby villages. The successive levels can be defined in terms of the presence of certain types of retail trade, wholesale distribution, and service establishments (i.e., behavior settings in the business authority system). However, behavior settings in other authority systems—government agencies, churches, schools, and voluntary associations—could also be used in defining levels of central places.

Thus if Barker's community with its 198 behavior setting genotypes is a typical American village, a typical American town would contain all or most of these 198 genotypes plus a limited additional number. Distinctive arrays of noneconomic behavior settings would be closely associated with distinctive arrays of economic behavior settings at each level.

12.1 Interrelations Between Firms, Shopping Centers, and Communities in a Functional Economic Area

We discussed some properties of functional economic areas in Chapter 8. We now state a number of propositions about them which we believe to be approximately true for the United States in the 1960s and 1970s.[1]

 1. The United States can be subdivided approximately into 300 or more *commuting*

---

[1] The remainder of Section 12.1 is based on Sengupta and Fox (1969), pp. 429–441.

fields, each centered upon the largest city in that field. I have used the term *functional economic areas* (FEAs) to describe such areas. Berry et al. (1968), using all the home-to-work commuting data in the 1960 census, delineated 358 FEAs; these areas contained some 96 percent of the total United States population. Thus the FEA serves as a frame of reference for 96 percent of all labor market activity in the United States (probably 97 percent by 1970) and for nearly 100 percent of retail trade and service activities that normally require direct contact with consumers, citizens, taxpayers, students, patients, and so on. (Some 3 or 4 percent of the total population lives in gaps between commuting fields, often in mountainous, hilly, or desert areas with low population densities and limited transportation facilities.)

2. In nonmetropolitan areas, a typical FEA contains three levels of central places, including a *regional capital*, a few *small cities*, and a large number of *towns*, to use the terminology of Berry and Harris (1968). The trade area of the regional capital tends to be coextensive with the home-to-work commuting field, covering several counties; the trade area of a small city (often a county seat) is usually equivalent to one or two counties; and the trade area of a town is usually considerably smaller than a county. Some goods are found only in the regional capital; some are found there and also in the small cities; and some are found at all three levels (regional capital, small cities, and towns).

3. In metropolitan areas, the same three-stage hierarchy appears (Encyclopedia Britannica, 1965). The *regional*, *district*, and *neighborhood shopping plazas* or centers have facilities corresponding respectively to those of the regional capital, small cities, and towns in a nonmetropolitan FEA. (Let us call these *R*-, *D*-, and *N*-level centers for "regional," "district," and "neighborhood," respectively.) The shopping facilities of the regional plazas are in most respects as complete as those of the central business district. In terms of *minutes*, including delays at traffic lights, parking lots, and the like, the effective "distances" between shopping centers of any given level in the metropolis are not much less than those between shopping centers of the same hierarchical level in nonmetropolitan FEAs.

The nonmetropolitan FEA provides a particularly useful framework within which to analyze competition among retail stores. The partitioning of the United States into (say) 300 relatively self-contained commuting fields or labor market areas offers a useful framework for the consideration of the regionalization of national economic policies.

I have sometimes referred to the nonmetropolitan FEA, in which the trade area of the regional capital roughly coincides with the commuting field, as a "mononuclear FEA." A large metropolis containing many regional shopping plazas is equivalent to a compound or multifaceted FEA in which the different *R*-level areas may be relatively independent for shopping purposes but interdependent as suppliers of labor for the central business district (facilitated by rapid transit systems and freeways).

Firm Behavior in an FEA Framework: The Holdren Model of Monopolistic Competition Among Multiproduct Retail Firms.   Holdren (1960) has made a brilliant extension and application of monopolistic competition theory to multiproduct retail firms—specifically, food supermarkets. Holdren says in his preface that he went into a particular market asking the question, What decision variables does the entrepreneur believe to be open to him? Once the decision variables were identified, a definitive model of retail firms was developed and the nature of the relationships between firms established. The departure from previous studies lies largely in the self-conscious attempt that was made to construct a model specialized for the market in hand and including all the important decision variables objectively and subjectively open to the entrepreneur (Holdren, p. vii). Fox (1967c) and Zusman (1967) have commented on Holdren's results and extended them in several respects.

Holdren's formulation of the demand functions facing the operator of a food supermarket (one of several supermarkets in a city of 50,000 or more people) is capable of generalization to shopping centers at N, D, and R levels. It is worth noting that the product lines carried by food supermarkets in the United States can absorb approximately 30 percent of all personal consumption expenditures for goods and services other than house rents and public utilities (electricity, gas, water, telephone service) that are delivered to the home.

From a (monopolistically) competitive policy standpoint, Holdren partitions the products sold by a supermarket operator into (1) commodities with a significant effect in transferring customers' patronage from other supermarkets to his own (and vice versa), (2) commodities whose retail prices are fixed (as by retail price maintenance laws), and (3) other commodities that (for reasons he presents) have little or no impact in transferring customers (Holdren, pp. 134–153).

The prices of K-class commodities (the ones with transfer effects) are the only useful instruments available to the supermarket operator for carrying out aggressive or defensive *price competition*. In addition, Holdren gives explicit and detailed consideration to the various *nonprice offer variations* that can also be used as instruments of monopolistic competition.

Holdren formulates the basic set of demand functions confronting a supermarket operator for the n commodities he sells as

$$q_1 = f_1(p_1, p_2, \ldots, p_n, a_1, a_2, \ldots, a_m),$$

$$\vdots \tag{1}$$

$$q_n = f_n(p_1, p_2, \ldots, p_n, a_1, a_2, \ldots, a_m);$$

that is, the quantity the supermarket sells of each commodity will be (potentially) a function of the prices p_i, $i = 1, 2, \ldots, n$, of all commodities in the store, and of all the nonprice offer variations $a_j, j = 1, 2, \ldots, m$, of the store.

For a commodity with a significant transfer effect, the demand curve could be operationalized as follows:

$$q_K = \pi B_K d g_K \sum_{j=1}^{m} S_j(a_j - a_{0j}) \left[B_K w_K \alpha_K(p_{0K} - p_K) \right.$$

$$\left. + \sum_{i=1}^{K-1} \alpha_i B_i g_i w_i(p_{0i} - p_i) + \sum_{j=1}^{m} V_j(a_j - a_{0j}) + \sum_{i=1}^{n} t_i g_i \right], \tag{2}$$

where q_K is the sales level of commodity K, B_K is the average number of units of the commodity purchased per unit of time per household, d is the density of households per unit area, g_K is the percentage of households consuming the commodity, and π

is 3.1416. The appearance of π in this expression rightly suggests that the store's trade area is regarded as a circle (at least to a first approximation). However, the r^2 of the formula for the area of a circle appears in the rest of (2) in a highly disguised form (Holdren; p. 123).[2]

Without other qualifications, (2) could be written very simply as

$$q_K = B_K dg_K r^2 \pi. \tag{3}$$

Equation (3) is, however, nonlinear in the prices (r is a linear function of p, so q is a quadratic function of p), and to do away with this nonlinearity Holdren proposes the following linear substitution for r^2:

$$r^2 \approx V(a - a_0) + \alpha B(p_0 - p). \tag{4}$$

The terms in parentheses refer back to an expression

$$u = \phi[A, D, p], \tag{5}$$

in which u is the utility of the store's offer as evaluated by a consumer living a specified distance D from the store; A and p may be regarded as index numbers summarizing respectively all nonprice and price aspects of the store's offer. Holdren's substitution for r^2 makes the trading area of the store a linear function of the level of nonprice offer variation in the store ($a - a_0$) and of variations of prices charged by the store ($p_0 - p$). Both V and αB in (4) have positive signs. As Holdren observes, "so long as the range of offer variation is comparatively small (and it is), such a substitution does little violence to reality" (pp. 118–119).[3]

In (2) then, r^2 is expanded into a rather complicated expression that states that the sales of the Kth commodity are affected by the item's own price, the prices of the other $K - 1$ commodities having significant transfer effects, and the levels of the m types of nonprice offer variation in the store. Furthermore, S_j reflects the tendency of some of the nonprice offer variations adopted by supermarkets to reduce the frequency of trips by consumers to areas outside the supermarket's trading area, hence increasing the percentage of household purchases obtained by a given store within its trading area. The symbol w_i reflects the level of information on the part of consumers—if $w_i = 1$, consumers are perfectly informed. The last term on the right-hand side, $\sum_{i=1}^{n} t_i g_i$, is "an expression which is intended to cover the budget effect and the fact that, quite independently of price, a wider product line reduces the number of trips any consumer must make outside the store's trading area" (Holdren, p. 124).

Holdren then considers the nature of competition among several supermarkets, given their cost and production functions (which he describes in his third chapter) and their demand functions.

[2] In (2) p_{0K} and p_{0i} are the prices associated with zero sales of commodity K, and a_{0j} is the level of the jth type of nonprice offer variation associated with zero sales of commodity K. In effect, p_{0K}, p_{0i}, and a_{0j} are the intercepts when q_K equals zero of linearized functions describing the dependence of q_K on p_K, p_i, and a_j respectively.

[3] Holdren's original notation has been slightly modified to conform with that in (2). Equations (3), (4), and (5) apply to a single commodity and a single type of nonprice offer variation. The subscripts of p_K, p_i, and a_j in (2) recognize the dependence of q_K on prices of all commodities sold and all nonprice offer variations used by the store.

Although there are only nine or ten supermarkets in Center City (a name used to disguise a real midwestern city of 50,000 population), Holdren presents convincing arguments for his conclusion that "oligopoly agreement is virtually impossible and we are left with a market which is best described as monopolistically competitive but which is subject to many other imperfections which preclude a long-run adjustment to a zero profit equilibrium" (p. 182).

In principle, Holdren's model could be extended in a number of respects (see Fox, 1967). First, competition among the nine or ten supermarkets could be expressed as a spatial equilibrium model. This model could be constructed at various levels of aggregation with respect to (1) the number of groups of (particularly) K-class commodities whose prices are specifically recognized as policy instruments, and (2) the number of areas (hence groups of households) into which the consuming population of the city is subdivided. The basic model could probably be supplemented by stochastic elements that would allow for the fact that individual households may shop in more than one supermarket under any given constellation of price and nonprice offer variations on the parts of stores actually visited and of stores not visited in a given time period.[4]

Now suppose we think in terms of competition among *shopping centers*, each with its cluster of complementary stores, rather than among supermarkets only. We must remember that each individual store in a shopping center is presumed to be an optimizing unit, carrying out its own competitive strategies with respect to firms offering the same product line at other shopping centers. From the standpoint of consumers visiting a shopping center, the partitioning of the center's total product line into the product lines of individual firms (drug stores, men's clothing stores, shoe stores, etc.) lends itself to a "utility tree" formulation of consumer demand.

We could conceive of the entire "offer" of a shopping center in terms of a consumer demand matrix containing every individual product offered by any store in the shopping center. If there were 10 different stores in the shopping center, each offering a different nonoverlapping product line, the demand matrix for the shopping center as a whole would be very nearly block-diagonal. The proprietor of each store would carry out his own price and nonprice offer variation policies. However, the policies of one store would also influence the number of customers who visit the shopping center and *therefore* do some shopping at other stores in it. Operationally, this complementarity among stores in a shopping center could perhaps be handled on an aggregative level, as with a 10×10 matrix of coefficients indicating the percentage increase in total sales of store I resulting from an increase of 1 percent in the number of customers specifically attracted to store J by store J's price and nonprice offer variations.

If we think in terms of a group of shopping centers of roughly similar total sales volumes, it appears that an extension of Holdren's model to a collection of shopping centers would be fairly manageable. However, we would still have the problem of linking shopping centers of different hierarchical levels into a complete system.

Assume that the consumer goods and services offered in an R-level area consist of three categories: R, D, and N. The R-level goods are found only in the R-level

---

[4] Households would typically have some information about the stores not visited in a particular month based on visits to these stores in earlier months, comments by friends and neighbors, and current and past advertisements by the stores.

shopping center; D-level goods are found in R-level and D-level shopping centers; and N-level goods are found at R-, D-, and N-level shopping centers. These categories account for the great majority of consumer expenditures. The remainder (apart from tourist expenditures and other special purchases outside the area) would consist of utilities delivered directly to the home, cash or imputed rentals of dwellings, and other services for which the consumer is not required to travel within the area.

Assume further that a household living closer to the R-level center than to any center of the D or N types can acquire its three categories of goods (the three that require personal travel and inspection) without incurring any transportation costs. The household then can be regarded as attempting to maximize an objective function,

$$W = f(q_r, q_d, q_n), \tag{6}$$

subject to the demand matrix

$$
\begin{bmatrix} q_r \\ q_d \\ q_n \end{bmatrix} =
\begin{bmatrix} b_{rr} & b_{rd} & b_{rn} \\ b_{dr} & b_{dd} & b_{dn} \\ b_{nr} & b_{nd} & b_{nn} \end{bmatrix}
\begin{bmatrix} p_r \\ p_d \\ p_n \end{bmatrix} +
\begin{bmatrix} e_r \\ e_d \\ e_n \end{bmatrix} y +
\begin{bmatrix} a_r \\ a_d \\ a_n \end{bmatrix} \tag{7}
$$

and the budget constraint

$$\sum_i q_i p_i = y, \qquad i = r, d, n. \tag{8}$$

(We can include the fourth category, rents and household utilities, in the maximization process formally or, for expository purposes, we can assume that the consumer has allocated a fixed total sum to be spent on the three categories of goods that normally require him to travel and to inspect the goods.)

A household located closer to any other center than to R will incur transportation costs in acquiring one or more categories of commodities. Such a household must (at least initially) squeeze the cost of shopping travel out of its fixed income. We may think of the "brought home" price of any category of goods from any shopping center as equal to the retail store price at that center plus the (round-trip) transportation cost from the center home. In the absence of stochastic and/or irrational elements, the household may be seen as trying to maximize its utility in terms of goods and services "brought home" subject to its overall budget constraint and the vector of travel costs (round-trip) between its home and each town or shopping center within a reasonable distance that offers one or more of the three categories of goods.

Assuming that each household's demand function for each category of goods is linear over the range of probable short-run experience, each household's objective function is quadratic and the household's problem is one of maximizing a quadratic objective function that requires it to specify the particular set of centers from which it should purchase goods and services in the categories named.

Further Comments on the Holdren Model and Its Extensions.   Certain points should perhaps be emphasized.

First, Holdren's demand function should not be regarded as a consumer demand function. Suppose that our FEA is strictly self-contained, and every household in the area spends its entire disposable income at stores located in the FEA; we assume that the money income of each household is fixed. Then the weighted average income elasticity of demand for all goods and services by each household is 1 and the corresponding weighted average of own-price and cross-price elasticities of demand is

FIRMS, SHOPPING CENTERS, AND COMMUNITIES 223

-1 (see Fox 1968, pp. 517–520). Since these respective elasticities, 1 and -1, are identical for all households, we can aggregate over all households and still get an income elasticity of 1 and a price elasticity of -1 for total purchases of goods and services by all households.

This formulation implies that the total gross revenue of all consumer-oriented establishments in the area is fixed. Competition among all establishments becomes a zero-sum game. Competition might conceivably increase the total amount spent at (say) clothing stores and reduce the total amount spent at food stores; however, cross-price elasticities between such dissimilar commodities as food and clothing are likely to be considerably smaller (in absolute value) than own-price elasticities; for food purchased at stores the latter figure is in the order of -0.3 to -0.4. Own-price elasticities for nonfoods average somewhat more (in absolute value) than -1, but probably not more than -2.

The main object of competition within an FEA is to transfer customers *to* one store *from* other stores selling the same generic products. If the stores are located in different shopping centers, it will take any given consumer more minutes to reach some centers than others. Thus the disutility of distance (measured in minutes) is an important factor that must be offset by price and nonprice offer variations. Holdren (1960) comments: "In Center City in 1956, store A lowered its price level by 5 percent and doubled its sales level. Thus, A's own elasticity of demand was approximately 20. Store D adjusted to this change by reducing prices 3 percent, but still went down in volume from \$40,000 per week to \$30,000 per week" (p. 181). Holdren concludes that the remaining price differential of 2 percent is responsible for the 25 percent reduction in store D's sales, implying a cross-price elasticity of demand for store D's products of 12.5 with respect to changes in p_D/p_A.

This change in the price ratio (2 percent) would amount to \$0.40 on a grocery bill of \$20, a fairly typical weekly bill for a family of three persons in 1956. If the disutility of distance was equivalent for most consumers to \$0.10 per mile each way, a consumer would have been justified in traveling up to a mile farther than usual (each way) for a trip involving purchases of \$10 or more. A square mile of residential area even in small cities will often include more than a thousand households, representing total consumer expenditures of several million dollars.

This underscores the extreme importance of central place theory, general location theory, and spatial equilibrium models in explaining firm behavior and in choosing short-run and long-run policies for individual consumer-oriented firms in an FEA framework.

Second, Holdren gives considerable attention to nonprice offer variations. In simplified terms, he states that

$$q = f(p, a), \tag{9}$$

where q is a vector of quantities sold by a store, p is a vector of prices, and a is a vector of nonprice offer variations or amenities (such as good parking facilities, air conditioning, automatic doors, facilities for paying utility bills, a lunch counter, and other features not directly related to the store's product line). The equation implies that both price and nonprice offer variations can be evaluated in terms of their effects on quantities sold; for example,

$$\frac{\partial q}{\partial p_i} = \lambda_{ij} \left(\frac{\partial q}{\partial a_j} \right), \tag{10}$$

where λ_{ij} is the effect on sales of a unit change in the ith price *relative to* that of a unit change in the jth amenity (which is in some cases a zero-one variable). Since the firm's gross revenue is

$$W = p'q, \tag{11}$$

it also follows that

$$\frac{\partial W}{\partial p_i} = \lambda_{ij} \left(\frac{\partial W}{\partial a_j} \right); \tag{12}$$

thus the price and nonprice instruments can be compared in terms of their contributions to the firm's objective function.

If we specify that total consumer expenditures in an FEA are fixed, it appears that consumers collectively must pay for all amenities in all stores; if they pay more for air conditioning, they presumably have less to spend for commodities as such. (Over time, of course, real incomes have increased, which means that consumers have been able to buy more commodities *and* to pay for more amenities; however, competition still occurs between commodities and amenities for shares of the consumers' budget.)

Third, a problem of vector versus scalar optimization is posed by the set of independent firms in a shopping center (we assume a shopping center containing only one firm of each given type, thus allowing little overlapping of product lines). Suppose that all these stores were merged into a single firm; then the objective would presumably be to maximize total net revenue for the shopping center firm. An entire store could be operated at a loss if the resulting transfer effect (attracting customers away from other shopping centers to this one) increased net revenue for the other $m - 1$ stores by a more-than-offsetting amount.

If the stores continued as private firms, it would (in principle) be possible to maintain precisely the same array of price and nonprice offer variations as before, but to pool revenues and reallocate them among firms according to their contributions to the total net revenue of the center. Strictly independent operation would require each store to (try to) at least break even; yet it would be hard not to recognize that the ability of store 1 to break even would be strongly conditioned by the policies of the other $m - 1$ stores (no doubt by some more than others).

In practice, there would be problems of communication and coordination, since one mind (or a committee) must now deal with (say) $n \cdot m$ products instead of n. We have here a version of the two-level planning problem. One possibility would be to treat a limited number of the most powerful price and nonprice instruments of each store as "central resources" to be used in a coordinated way to increase revenue for the shopping center as a whole. The remaining instruments could be left to the discretion of the proprietor of each store, who would be free to use them to maximize his own net income, *subject to* the prescribed values of the centrally coordinated instruments.

Also, the strategies of competing firms in other shopping centers would have to be countered; this would involve primarily competition between stores with similar product lines. If firms in several shopping centers are directly or indirectly involved in such competition, causes may be difficult to trace. Referring to food supermarkets, Holdren (1960) states that "the multidimensional character of response paths and the presence of consumer ignorance means that there is a long lag between the initiation of action (by one firm) and the time when the results of the action are felt by competitors. In the interim, many parameters have changed and the competitors are never sure just what caused their change in sales" (p. 182). If the firms in a given shopping center had a fairly sophisticated model of the system as a whole, of course, they might be able to unravel causes with considerably more precision than is implied in Holdren's statement, based on observations in the mid-1950s. However, sufficient uncertainty might remain to cast doubt on the optimality of any specific centrally coordinated response, so the initiative and responsibility for competition "in detail" might better be left with the individual proprietors.

Simon's (1957b) characterization of man as a creature of bounded rationality and limited computing capacity seems relevant here. It might be possible in the case of the shopping center firm to estimate the theoretical maximum revenue obtainable by optimizing at the level of $n \cdot m$ instruments and (1) to estimate the reductions of revenue involved if only the most powerful 10, 20, or 40 instruments were used in the optimization, or (2) to specify permissible reductions in revenue of (say) 1, 2, and 5 percent and to estimate the minimum numbers of instruments required to achieve each of these "satisficing" levels.

An alternative approach to the matter of price instruments might be to specify the centrally controlled variables as *price index numbers* at different levels of aggregation such as (for a supermarket) all foods, or all meats, or (all cuts of) beef. The "all foods" level would imply a single instrument; the "all meats" level would permit four or five instruments (e.g., for meats, fresh fruits and vegetables, dairy products, groceries); whereas the "beef" level might permit 20 or more instruments. The centrally controlled set might include one or a few of the total instruments available at any given level of aggregation, and instruments might be selected from different levels of aggregation.

Aggregative controls, of course, lose various degrees of precision relative to detailed controls, as suggested by the following example:

$$\begin{bmatrix} q_1 \\ q_2 \end{bmatrix} = \begin{bmatrix} -5 & 0 \\ 0 & -10 \end{bmatrix} \begin{bmatrix} p_1 \\ p_2 \end{bmatrix}, \tag{13}$$

and

$$q_T = (.5q_1 + .5q_2), \qquad p_T = (.5p_1 + .5p_2), \tag{14}$$

where q_1 and q_2 are quantity relatives, p_1 and p_2 are price relatives, the coefficients -5 and -10 represent the transfer effects of 1 percent changes in p_1 and p_2, respectively, and the coefficients .5 and .5 are weights (proportions of total dollar sales of q_1 and q_2 combined in some base period) in the index numbers q_T and p_T. Then we have

$$\frac{\partial q_T}{\partial p_1} = (.5)(-5) = -2.5 \tag{15}$$

and

$$\frac{\partial q_T}{\partial p_2} = (.5)(-10) = -5; \tag{16}$$

hence a 1 percent reduction in p_2 will have twice as much effect on q_T as will a 1 percent reduction in p_1.

If we specify only that p_T be reduced by 1 percent without stipulating anything about p_1 and/or p_2 separately, the transfer effect may range from 5 percent (if p_1 is used exclusively) to 10 percent (if p_2 is used exclusively). If both p_1 and p_2 are varied simultaneously without restrictions as to upper and lower bounds for either one, the range of transfer effects associated with $\Delta p_T = 1.00 - 0.99 = -0.01$ could include such values as 15 percent (for $p_1 = 1.02$ and $p_2 = 0.96$), no change (for $p_1 = 0.96$ and $p_2 = 1.02$), or even wider extremes. The proprietor's choice would depend on his self-interest.

Suppose that the proprietor's wholesale costs are 0.80 per unit for each commodity and that other costs do not vary with sales volume. Then his net revenue is

$$N = (p_1 - 0.80)q_1 + (p_2 - 0.80)q_2. \tag{17}$$

The first term reaches a maximum for $p_1 = 1.00$ and the second term reaches a maximum for $p_2 = 0.93$. Thus his self-interest would be best served by choosing these two prices, yielding $p_T = 0.965$ and an increase of 25 percent in q_T.

If the proprietor were required to set $p_T \leq 0.95$, his net revenue would be forced below the unrestricted maximum by about 2 percent so (in our example) a conflict of interest in this amount would exist and would have to be offset (say) by a payment from the shopping center firm. We may note in passing that if the proprietor were required to set $p_1 \leq 0.95$ *and* $p_2 \leq 0.95$, his net revenue would be forced down another 1 percent; this would be the cost to him of the additional restriction and would have to be offset to justify his cooperation.

The shopping center in general provides a good example of *external economies*. Store I's revenue is larger because the (noncompeting) store J is in the same center, and conversely. External economies will exist even if the two stores make no attempt to coordinate their policies. Additional gains through coordination (as in the shopping center firm conceptualization) would also be external economies from the standpoint of each individual store, although the costs of coordination would have to be subtracted from the increase in total gross revenue for the shopping center as a whole.

The parking area of a shopping center provides an example of *indivisibility*. Also, consider the possibility of enclosing and air conditioning a central mall onto which all stores open. This nonprice offer variation, if successful, would benefit every store; it raises the problems of (1) estimating the benefits to each store, and (2) allocating the costs among stores. The central parking lot involves the same principles and problems.

12.2   Social Indicator Problems with "Open" Communities

In Chapter 11, for expository purposes, we assumed at times that our hypothetical community of 1000 persons was "closed" to commuting and shopping travel in either direction.

In fact, Barker's (1968) town of 830 residents was the trade and service center for several hundred people in the surrounding countryside, as indicated by the following figures on occupancy times of Midwest's public behavior settings:

Occupancy Times During 1963–1964
(Thousands of Hours)

Types of Settings	Town Residents	Nonresidents	Total
Businesses	549.5	221.4	770.9
Schools	203.0	226.7	429.7
Government	88.9	79.0	167.9
Churches	26.5	27.3	53.8
Social, etc.	256.8	202.1	458.9
Total	1124.7	756.5	1881.2

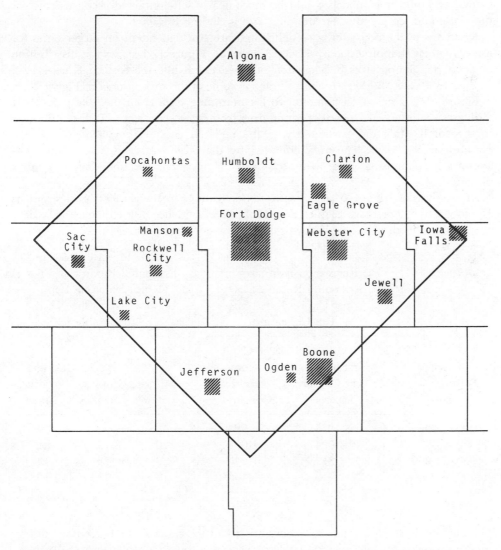

Figure 12.1.   Distribution of town population sizes in the Fort Dodge area. Areas of squares are proportional to 1960 town populations. Only towns with retail sales of $2.5 million or more for year ending June 30, 1964, are shown.

Nonresidents accounted for 29 percent of the total occupancy time in business settings, 48 percent in other settings, and 40 percent in all settings combined. It also appeared that about 40 percent of the resident labor force worked at out-of-town jobs.

Residents and nonresidents alike therefore enjoyed the advantages of larger schools, stores, and social organizations with product lines, curricula, and programs more diversified than either group could have supported on its own. As C. J. Galpin (1915) suggested long ago in his classic bulletin, *The Social Anatomy of an Agricultural Community*, the functional community includes both the town and the open country population, and the public behavior settings within the 400-acre political jurisdiction of the town provide the same goods and services to both groups. Social indicators, accounts, and models would be more nearly self-contained if constructed for the trade and service area surrounding and including the town.

Residents of the community so delineated are still dependent on larger cities for many of their shopping goods, services, and jobs. Figure 12.1 shows the distribution of town population sizes in a portion of Iowa much like the eastern Kansas area studied by Barker. Barker's town is similar to some of the smaller ones in Figure 12.1.

Figure 12.2 is based on home-to-work commuting data from the 1960 census. It indicates a substantial amount of commuting from open country townships and towns to the small cities and particularly to the regional capital (Fort Dodge), with a population of 30,000. The area bounded by the large square is a relatively self-contained commuting field, with few workers crossing the boundary in either direction.

An analysis of 1963–1964 retail sales tax collections in Iowa's 99 counties and its 450 towns of 500 or more people (Fox, 1965) gives evidence of the increasing variety of consumer goods available in towns of successively larger sizes:

Town Population Size	Regression Estimates of Annual Retail Sales per Capita Based on Tax Collections		Percentage Increases in Estimated Retail Sales per Capita from one Population Size to the Next, Attributable to		
	Not Adjusted for Effects of per Capita Income	Per Capita Income Held Constant	Total	Higher per Capita Incomes	Wider Product Lines
1,000–2,499	$ 854	$ 981	—	—	—
2,500–4,999	1,024	1,097	20	7	12
5,000–24,999	1,312	1,246	28	13	14
25,000 and over	1,640	1,405	25	11	13
$\bar{R}^2$	.57	.74			

The estimated effects of higher incomes are about the same as the percentage differences in median family incomes between successive town size categories in Iowa reported in the 1960 census—an increase of 39 percent in the latter from "rural nonfarm" to "urbanized areas" compared with 34 percent in the former from smallest

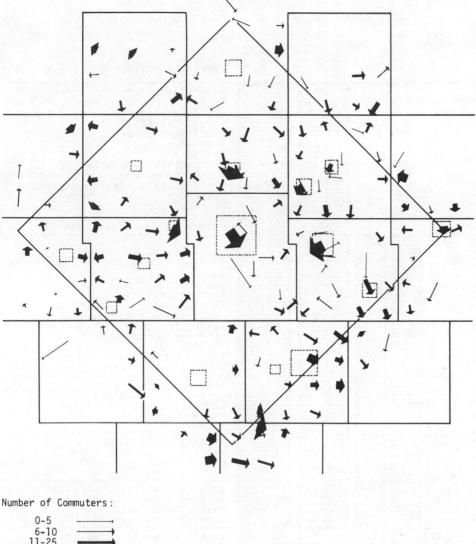

Number of Commuters:

0–5	
6–10	
11–25	
26–50	
51–100	
101–250	

Figure 12.2.   Commuting pattern in the Fort Dodge area.

to largest of the population sizes shown. This supports our interpretation of the difference between the income-adjusted and unadjusted sales tax figures as attributable to increasing widths of product line.

Figure 12.3 classifies trade center types according to the presence or absence of selected retail and wholesale business functions. This classification was based on a survey of the Upper Midwest (approximately a five-state area) in the early 1960s. Barker's town would evidently have been classified as a "full convenience center"—

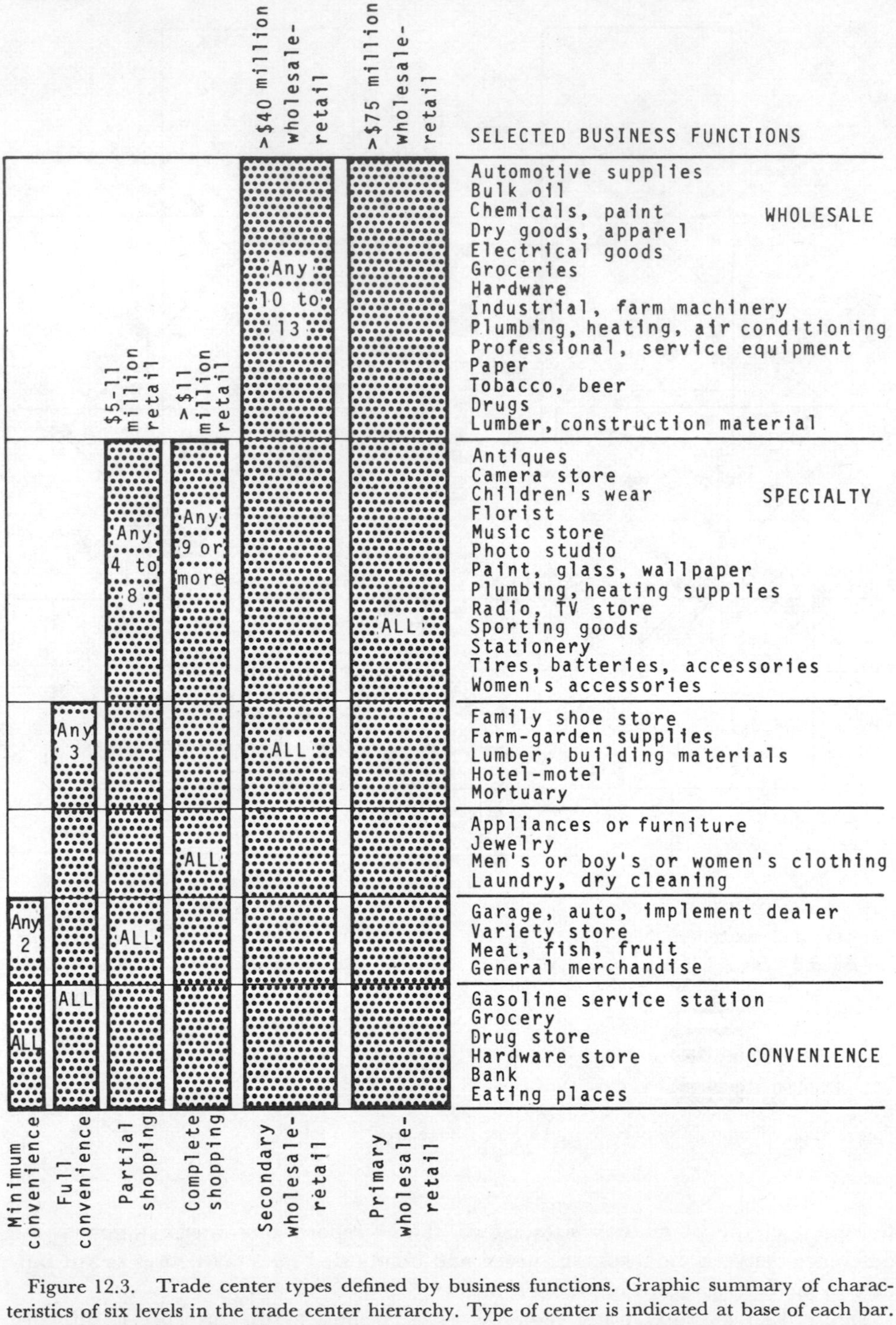
>$40 million wholesale-retail
>$75 million wholesale-retail
SELECTED BUSINESS FUNCTIONS
$5-11 million retail
>$11 million retail
Any 10 to 13
Any 4 to 8
Any 9 or more
ALL
Any 3
ALL
ALL
Any 2
ALL
ALL
ALL
ALL
Automotive supplies
Bulk oil
Chemicals, paint
WHOLESALE
Dry goods, apparel
Electrical goods
Groceries
Hardware
Industrial, farm machinery
Plumbing, heating, air conditioning
Professional, service equipment
Paper
Tobacco, beer
Drugs
Lumber, construction material
Antiques
Camera store
Children's wear
SPECIALTY
Florist
Music store
Photo studio
Paint, glass, wallpaper
Plumbing, heating supplies
Radio, TV store
Sporting goods
Stationery
Tires, batteries, accessories
Women's accessories
Family shoe store
Farm-garden supplies
Lumber, building materials
Hotel-motel
Mortuary
Appliances or furniture
Jewelry
Men's or boy's or women's clothing
Laundry, dry cleaning
Garage, auto, implement dealer
Variety store
Meat, fish, fruit
General merchandise
Gasoline service station
Grocery
Drug store
Hardware store
CONVENIENCE
Bank
Eating places
Minimum convenience
Full convenience
Partial shopping
Complete shopping
Secondary wholesale-retail
Primary wholesale-retail

Figure 12.3. Trade center types defined by business functions. Graphic summary of characteristics of six levels in the trade center hierarchy. Type of center is indicated at base of each bar. Types of business are listed in right-hand column. Businesses that were required and optional in defining each type of trade center are indicated by markings on each bar. *Source.* John R. Borchert and Russell B. Adams, *Trade Centers and Trade Areas of the Upper Midwest.* Upper Midwest Economic Study, Urban Report No. 3, Minneapolis: University of Minnesota, September 1963, p. 4.

its behavior settings included most of the "convenience" establishments listed but none of the "specialty" types; its residents would have had to buy these at larger centers.

The 1960 census data from Iowa reveal some other interesting gradients:

Town Population Size	(1) Persons 25 and Older with 4 or More Years of College, (percent)	(2) Professional, Technical, and Kindred Workers Among Employed Males (percent)	(3) Families with Incomes of $10,000 and Over (percent)	(4) Male Labor Force Aged 44 or Younger (percent)
Rural farm	2.1	0.7	6.1	62.6
Rural nonfarm	5.1	8.5	7.7	70.4
2,500–9,999	7.6	10.1	10.4	73.3
10,000–49,999	10.1	13.5	13.0	75.3
Urbanized areas (over 50,000)	8.8	10.5	16.4	76.0

The first three columns reflect well-known relationships between education, occupation, and income; the fourth reflects the consequences of increasing sizes and declining numbers of farms and consequent outmigration of younger workers to the larger centers. Columns 1, 2, and 4 suggest that the gradients with respect to college education, professional and technical occupations, and increased percentages of workers under 45 level off and perhaps change direction as population size increases beyond 50,000. The reversal in column 2 results in part from the inclusion of two university towns in the 10,000 to 49,999 population class; a few other places in this size range serve to some extent as residential suburbs for nearby urbanized areas. The gradient in percentages of families with incomes over $10,000 continues upward into the urbanized area category, reflecting a further selection of individuals within the broad classes of "professional, technical, and kindred workers" and "managers, officials, and proprietors" for higher paying specialties and for the management of larger, more complex organizations. More sensitive measures of education and occupation (percentage of professional and technical workers with advanced degrees, ratio of specialists to general practitioners among medical doctors, persons per 10,000 listed in *Who's Who in America*, etc.) should explain much of the continued rise in the percent of incomes over $10,000.

It is interesting to note (in Figure 12.3) that Borchert and Adams shifted from retail to wholesale establishments in classifying trade centers with more than $40 million annual sales at each of the two levels. In Iowa as of 1963–1964, Fort Dodge reported retail sales of $66 million; several other regional capitals with populations of 30,000 to 35,000 had retail sales of $55 to $65 million and (like Fort Dodge) would also have met the wholesale trade criteria for "secondary wholesale–retail centers." Each of these cities served an FEA population of around 150,000. The proliferation of regional shopping plazas in the suburbs of our metropolitan areas seems to indicate that economies of scale in retail trade are pretty well exhausted in serving 300,000 or so customers at a single location. This would also be the case in an FEA of the Iowa type with a regional capital of (say) 100,000 and a total population of 300,000.

The Effects of "Openness" on Economic and Other Multipliers.   Perhaps the simplest macroeconomic concept of interest in connection with FEAs and smaller areas is the so-called foreign trade multiplier. The formula for this multiplier is

$$k = \frac{1}{1 - (Y_{end}/Y_t)} \tag{18}$$

where k is the multiplier, Y_t is total value added, and Y_{end} is value added in production for the local market. This formula uses the *average* propensity to consume locally as a first approximation to the *marginal* propensity to consume locally. This assumption, which implies a linear homogeneous consumption function, was necessary in Leven's (1958) study of Elgin-Dundee, Illinois, since his data for 1956 gave him only one point on the function. Since the average propensity is generally larger than the marginal propensity, there may be an upward bias in the resulting estimate of k. On the other hand, to the extent that we were analyzing the effects of increases in activity stemming from an increase in the number of employed people rather than from an increase in the average earnings of current producers, the average propensity would be the appropriate one to use. If employment is proportional to value added, k is also an employment multiplier.

The value of k for the Elgin-Dundee area in 1956 was 1.475. The implication is that the addition of 100 jobs to the basic or export industries in the area would lead to another 47 or 48 jobs in the consumer goods, public service, and other sectors. Tiebout, quoted by Leven, computed values of 1.054 and 1.096, respectively, for Winnetka and Evanston, Illinois. The much higher value for Elgin, according to Leven, confirms the strong a priori basis for regarding trade "leakages" as being much smaller there. Evanston, though even more populous than Elgin, is literally across the street from Chicago, whereas Winnetka was primarily a domicile for upper-income people employed in Chicago.

Subsequently, Leven (Sioux City Planning Commission, 1959) computed a foreign trade multiplier of about 1.70 for the Sioux City, Iowa, metropolitan area. The population of Sioux City is larger than that of Elgin-Dundee, and its local consumer goods, public services, and construction sectors are more nearly self-sufficient as a consequence of its remoteness from any other metropolitan area of the same or larger size.

We can illustrate the effects of "import leakages" on multipliers by adapting one of our examples from Chapter 11. Four persons are given tax-free annuities of $1000 by a benefactor from outside the region, and each spends the entire amount. However, the subjects live in cities of four different sizes, and the smaller the city, the less is spent locally. In all cases, the local merchants are assumed to retain 50 percent of what is spent locally, passing the rest on to outside wholesalers. The four situations work out as follows:

	(1)	(2)	(3)	(4)	(5)
Town Population Size	Total Expenditures	Expenditures in Larger Centers	Expenditures Made Locally	Retained by Local Merchants	Multiplier
1,000–2,499	$1000	$300	$700	$350	1.54
2,500–4,999	1000	200	800	400	1.67
5,000–24,999	1000	100	900	450	1.82
25,000 and over	1000	0	1000	500	2.00

The multiplier values in column 5 are calculated from

$$k = \frac{1}{1 - 0.5(1 - m)}, \tag{19}$$

where $m = $ (expenditures in larger centers)/(total expenditures). The values of m in our example are based on the second column of per capita retail sales estimates on page 000. We assume $m = 0$ in the largest population class because a full line of retail goods is available there. But the next smaller centers would have to "import" $(1405 - 1246)/1405 = 0.11$; those in the 2500–4999 class, $(1405 - 1097)/1405 = 0.22$; and those in the 1000–2499 class, $(1405 - 981)/1405 = 0.30$, or 30 percent of their requirements by shopping at the larger centers.

If our four persons all live in the same FEA, with the city of 25,000 or more as its regional capital, the multiplier effects of their spending on income *for the FEA as a whole* will be 2.00 in each case, but the effects will be divided differently between the person's own community and the rest of the FEA:

	(1)	(2)	(3)
		Multiplier Effects	
Town Population Size	Total Multiplier Measured at FEA Level	Within Town of Residence	In Larger Centers
1,000–2,499	2.00	1.54	0.46
2,500–4,999	2.00	1.67	0.33
5,000–24,999	2.00	1.82	0.18
25,000 and over	2.00	2.00	0

Column 3 measures effects that are external to the town of residence but internal to the FEA.

The situation may be illustrated with a symmetric-equalitarian transactions matrix of the kind presented in Chapter 11:

$$
\begin{bmatrix} y_1 \\ y_2 \\ y_3 \\ y_4 \\ y_5 \\ y_6 \end{bmatrix} = \begin{bmatrix} 0 & .1 & .1 & .1 & .1 & .1 \\ .1 & 0 & .1 & .1 & .1 & .1 \\ .1 & .1 & 0 & .1 & .1 & .1 \\ .1 & .1 & .1 & 0 & .1 & .1 \\ .1 & .1 & .1 & .1 & 0 & .1 \\ .1 & .1 & .1 & .1 & .1 & 0 \end{bmatrix} \begin{bmatrix} x_1 \\ x_2 \\ x_3 \\ x_4 \\ x_5 \\ x_6 \end{bmatrix} . \tag{20}
$$

The complete matrix represents the FEA as a whole; at that level, the six coefficients in the first column sum to .5, and the multiplier is computed as

$$
k = \frac{1}{1 - \sum_{i=1}^{6} b_{i1}} = \frac{1}{1 - .5} = 2.00. \tag{21}
$$

If we compute the multiplier for a community that includes only the first five individuals, the remaining coefficients in the first column sum to .4 and the multiplier is $k = 1/(1 - .4) = 1.67$. If we compute multipliers for successively smaller communities of 4, 3, and 2 individuals, the values of k fall to 1.43, 1.25, and 1.11, respectively.

Let us consider once again the question of multiplier effects for increases in resources other than money income. If each of the four persons received training grants (funded from outside of the FEA) that increased the value he added to goods produced for export from the FEA by $1000, the effects would be the same as described previously. The sale of the increased skills *directly* to employers outside of the FEA would be inconvenient in most cases unless the person lived fairly close to the boundary between his FEA and the one in which he might consider selling his new skills. However, his residence would continue to be closer to the regional capital of his own FEA, and his time, interests, and organizational involvements would be divided between the two areas; also, his commuting time and distance would generally be increased. He could, of course, *migrate* to the other FEA, but this changes the terms of our example.

The correction of health problems (physical or emotional) and a consequent increase in productivity applied to goods for export from the FEA would have the same multiplier effects as in the case of an increase in skill. The analysis also applies if increased skill and/or health are used to provide goods for consumption in the FEA *if* merchants reduce their purchases from wholesalers outside the FEA by the same amount.

An improvement in the value commitments or "character" with respect to will power, purposefulness, integrity, responsibility, and/or wisdom in each of the four persons would have similar effects to the extent that they led to increased production of goods for export from the FEA or to be substituted for imports. If these improvements were expressed also (or alternatively) in school, government, social, and family settings they would presumably increase the value of outputs of these settings (1) as experienced by participants in the settings, and (2) perhaps as rated by an observer. A multiplier effect based on mutual reinforcement (complementary transactions) would be implicit in the increased values of the immediate settings.

Are there carryover effects from one setting to another? Evidently, values perceived in role models can be internalized and will then influence behavior in settings in which the role model is not present. The Parent (Berne, 1964) or superego consists of such internalized values; so, apparently, do the favorable outcomes of a person's successive life stages as described by Erikson (1968), as well as standards of professional conduct. Morale and *esprit de corps* in an organization evidently reflect the individual member's belief that mutual reinforcement will increase the value of output of the organization and that he will share in the associated increase in its income (prestige, support, power, visibility, and perhaps money). Community spirit and civic pride are similar phenomena.

Does the "openness" of a community have implications for the value of its multipliers in terms of these nonmonetary resources? The prestige of a small, specialized organization seems to depend largely on the prestige of its distinctive upper-echelon personnel (zone 5 and 6 leaders, in Barker's terms), who embody and symbolize the organization's central mission. The prestige of a community depends partly on the prestige of its largest and most visible organizations—in business, education, government, medicine, religion, sports, entertainment, music, art, science—which again depend on the prestige of their distinctive personnel.

On page 000 we presented some 1960 census data on percentages of families with incomes over $10,000, percentages of adults with four or more years of college, and percentages of workers in the professional, technical, and kindred occupations in Iowa communities of various population sizes. The zone 5 and 6 leaders of many highly visible settings are included in these categories, and their percentages (and absolute numbers) increase strongly with town and city size at least up to a population of 50,000. More sensitive measures would indicate that the relevant gradients continue on upward beyond the 50,000 size.

The distinctive institutions of a societal community are generally coextensive with the community itself; otherwise, there are "leakages" of prestige and the images of the various institutions do not complement one another—hence the images of the community—to a maximum extent.

The most distinctive organizations in Barker's town in 1963–1964 appear to have been the high school and the county government offices. There was no medical doctor's office among Barker's genotype settings. A considerable percentage of the town's labor force commuted daily outside its trade area, and its residents must have made frequent shopping trips to larger centers. Visits to doctors, clinics, and hospitals must have taken them successively farther afield. As of 1973, it seems likely that a large percentage of the town's high school graduates are driving daily to a community college.

These considerations lead us back to familiar ground. It appears that the commuting field, the retail business system, the medical service and health care system, and the educational system do not achieve adequate closure and complementarity below the FEA level.

12.3   The Community College and the Functional Economic Area

The Carnegie Commission on Higher Education (1970a) has recommended that by 1980 comprehensive community colleges should be located within commuting distance of at least 95 percent of our population. Residential facilities should be provided at selected community colleges for the benefit of the remaining 5 percent of the population living beyond easy commuting distance from such a facility. "Comprehensive" means that occupational, college transfer, and continuing education programs are all available; the community or "open-door" college is of central importance to the community.

The Commission recommends that community colleges, to achieve adequately varied programs at reasonable cost, have daytime enrollments of 2000 to 5000 students. It recognizes that in sparsely populated areas enrollments might have to be somewhat less than 2000. The Commission's 1980 projections of community college enrollments and total population suggest that population bases of about 120,000 and 300,000 would be required to provide daytime community college enrollments of 2000 and 5000 students, respectively.

As of 1968, the Commission indicated (1970a, p. 63) that there were 781 public 2-year institutions (community colleges) in the United States; it estimated that 226 to 280 more would be needed by 1980, bringing the total to somewhat more than 1000. The Commission's major themes with respect to community colleges include the following:

> 1. The community college has proved its great worth to American society. Community colleges should be available, within commuting distance, to all persons throughout their lives, except in sparsely populated areas which would be served by residential colleges. . . .

> 2. The Carnegie Commission favors the *comprehensive* community college with academic, occupational, and general education programs. . . .

> 3. Community colleges should remain two-year institutions and not expect to become four-year or graduate institutions. . . .

> 4. Full transfer rights should be provided qualified graduates of community colleges by comprehensive state colleges and universities. . . .

> 5. Occupational programs should be given the fullest support and status within community colleges. These programs need to be flexibly geared to the changing requirements of society. . . .

> 6. The Carnegie Commission supports open access to the "open-door" college for all high school graduates and otherwise qualified individuals. . . .

> 7. The community college should charge no tuition, or low tuition.

> 8. Guidance—occupational and personal—is a particularly important function for the community college, which serves so many students who are in the process of choosing their life-time occupations and their life styles. . . .

> 9. The community college has a special responsibility to enrich the cultural life of its neighborhood and to be an active center for art, music and drama, and intellectual discussion.

> 10. The Carnegie Commission believes that the optimum size of a community college is 2000 to 5000 students. If it is much smaller, it cannot provide a rounded program at reasonable cost. If it is much larger, it will compound unnecessarily the problems of commuting and parking, and it will be less likely to be a part of any single neighborhood. More people can be served more conveniently by several colleges of reasonable size than by one large institution.

> 11. The community college by the nature of its purposes should relate to its local community and be governed by a local board or, at least, have a local advisory board.

12. Financing should be increased and equitably shared by federal, state, and local governments . . . (pp. 1–2).

A comprehensive community college with an enrollment of 2000 to 5000 students and an implied population base of 120,000 to 300,000 fits perfectly into the FEA pattern. With its academic, occupational, and general educational programs, it can facilitate the formation and maintenance of nearly all skills (work-related and other) that do not require more than two years of training beyond high school.

In earlier chapters we referred to both kinds of skills as group 3 resources and to money income, prestige, power in formal organizations, and political power as group 4 resources. In several tables we combined these groups because the work-related skills are typically converted into money income. Blau and Duncan (1967) stress occupation as the primary source of prestige in our society and point to a coefficient of multiple determination of $R^2 = .83$ between the prestige ratings of 45 occupations and the average levels of education and earnings (income) of their members.

The community college then, is a key institution in the formation of group 3 and 4 resources; it is one of the most distinctive institutions of the FEA.

12.4   Some Reflections on the OBE Economic Areas

In Section 8.3 we expressed our approval of the OBE Economic Areas (Regional Economics Division, Office of Business Economics, 1969) and commended Olsen and Westley (1973a) for their code book facilitating the cumulation of county data from several major systems to OBE area totals. The same authors (1973b) have also published cumulations of many series from the County and City Data Book for 1967, 1962, 1956, and 1952 to OBE areas.

There are 171 OBE areas covering the continental United States, compared with 358 FEAs in the initial delineation of Berry et al. (1968). However, the 358 FEAs, which were based solely on commuting data, included 29 areas with fewer than 50,000 people each and another 35 with populations of 50,000 to 90,000. Most of these are in sparsely populated regions. It would be difficult to justify including full detail for such small population clusters in a national system of regional data. They could not individually support community colleges of adequate program breadth and quality at reasonable cost; also, a number of them have central cities of 10,000 to 15,000 population, which would leave them well below the "secondary wholesale–retail" level in Borchert and Adams's classification (Figure 12.3) and below the regional capital or R level in terms of width of product line. Berry et al. (1968), with the approval of the SSRC Committee on Areas for Social and Economic Statistics, recommended that FEAs be created for smaller regional centers of populations 25,000 to 50,000 in less densely populated parts of the country, but not for centers of 25,000 or less.

The OBE (quoted in Olsen and Westley, 1973a) followed this recommendation in nonmetropolitan regions with the further restrictions "(1) that the city [of 25,000 to 50,000] form a wholesale trade center for the area, and (2) that the area as a whole have a population minimum of about 200,000 people. (There are some exceptions to the size criteria in sparsely populated areas)" (p. 6).

The 1960 populations of the OBE areas were distributed as follows:

Population	Number of OBE Areas	Cumulative Number
Over 10,000,000	1	1
5,000,000–9,999,999	4	5
3,000,000–4,999,999	4	9
2,000,000–2,999,999	7	16
1,000,000–1,999,999	29	45
500,000–999,999	47	92
400,000–499,999	25	117
300,000–399,999	26	143
250,000–299,999	8	151
200,000–249,999	11	162
150,000–199,999	5	167
100,000–149,999	4	171
Total	171	171

The distribution of their land surfaces is also of interest:

Number of Square Miles	Number of OBE Areas	Cumulative Number
50,000–90,324	12	12
40,000–49,999	4	16
30,000–39,999	11	27
20,000–29,999	18	45
10,000–19,999	57	102
5,000–9,999	48	150
2,078–4,999	21	171

The 12 largest land areas are in the West and include wide expanses of desert, mountain, and national forest land. Most of the population is located along main highways, and the problems of commuting and shopping travel are not as difficult as the large total areas might suggest. In the Plains and Western Corn Belt states, with travel at 70 miles an hour on a rectangular grid, an area of 10,000 square miles (almost all of it in farms) can be integrated into a mononuclear FEA. Some 69 of the OBE areas contain fewer than 10,000, and another 57 fewer than 20,000, square miles. The most populous OBE areas are usually of modest geographic extent—New York 9995 square miles, Chicago 12,523, Philadelphia 10,673, and Boston 9938—except for the Los Angeles area, which is defined to include an enormous expanse of desert and mountains in addition to the commuting field of the metropolis.

Forty-five of the OBE areas had 1960 populations of a million or more. All these include more than one FEA of the R-level or regional capital class; so do many of the 98 areas with populations ranging from 300,000 to a million. The most populous areas are of the multifaceted type containing several or many subareas equivalent to FEAs. I believe that even the least populous OBE areas contain one city of the regional capital class and have sufficient population (116,324 is the very smallest) to provide 2000 aspirants for community college enrollment.

On the average, then, OBE areas are considerably larger than mononuclear FEAs. However, so far as retail trade and services requiring frequent direct contact with consumers are concerned, even the most populous OBE areas should behave like multiples of FEAs.

12.5 The Geography of Health Science, Health Education, and Health Care

In Section 12.3 we cited the Carnegie Commission's (1970a) report on community colleges and indicated that the size range and functions recommended fit perfectly into the FEA pattern. We turn now to another Commission report (1970b) entitled *Higher Education and the Nation's Health: Policies for Medical and Dental Education*; this document sheds some incidental light on the social functions performed by cities above the regional capital level.

The Geography of Health Science and Health Education. The Carnegie Commission's report (1970b) is concerned with the provision of highly skilled health manpower, which it regards as a special responsibility of higher education. The Commission emphasizes a *health care delivery* model, which involves the geographic dispersion of training centers for health manpower to locate them "where the people live."

With this in mind, and taking account of the locations of centers already in operation or being considered, the Commission recommends for the United States a total of 106 *university health science centers* and, in addition, 126 *area health education centers* "to serve localities without a health science center" (p. 6). The Commission believes that there should be a university health science center in every metropolitan area with a population of 350,000 or more, except for areas that can be served by established centers in geographically convenient communities. In the larger metropolitan areas, the Commission recommends that there should be at least one university health science center *or* area health education center for every 1.5 million persons.

Metropolitan areas (SMSAs) with 350,000 to a million residents often serve total populations much larger than this from their distinctive institutions, including medical schools and hospital complexes. Functionally, many of them serve territories intermediate in size between FEAs and NMRs (national metropolitan regions). Thus Utah, New Mexico, and Colorado, with 1970 populations of 1.1, 1.0, and 2.2 million, respectively, each had a single university health science center in that year, and several states with populations of 2.0 to 4.0 million had only two.

The Commission amplifies its rationale for the *area health education centers* as follows:[5]

> In some parts of the country the distances between university health science centers are likely to be very great, as in the sparsely populated mountain states. Elsewhere, concentration of people in congested urban areas would overwhelm the facilities of even the largest health science center. In both types of areas there should be "area health education centers," which would provide facilities for patient care, often on a referral basis from surrounding areas; educational programs for house officers and, to some extent, for M.D. candidates who could rotate through an area health educa-

[5] See also Gordon (1971).

tion center from a university health science center; clinical experience for allied health students; and continuing education programs for health manpower.

The area health education centers, in essence, would be satellites of the university health science centers with which they were affiliated. Their educational programs would be developed and supervised by the health science faculty, and their patient care functions would rely on the expertise of the health science center personnel. The area centers in turn would provide assistance and counsel to the community and neighborhood health care facilities, including the private practitioner (pp. 55–56).

Allowing for multiple facilities in the largest metropolitan areas, the Commission's maps (1970b, pp. 7–8) imply that either a university health science center or an area health education center would be located in each of 200 or more distinct cities; in all or nearly all cases these are the central cities of FEAs and (with rare exceptions) of SMSAs as well. Its suggested locations correspond quite closely to the central cities of the OBE economic areas.

John C. MacQueen and Eber Eldridge (1972), under the auspices of the Health Manpower Committee of the Iowa Comprehensive Health Planning Council, made a detailed study of the distribution of medical doctors and facilities in Iowa as of 1971 and prepared "a proposed organizational structure for providing health services and medical care in the state of Iowa" which was approved as a concept by the Health Manpower Committee.[6] The authors strongly approved of the Carnegie Commission's (1970b) concept of *area health education centers* operating as satellites of university health science centers. However, they concluded that the area health education centers should be located in the regional capitals of Iowa's 11 FEAs. Their map (1972, p. 39) of the areas to be served by the proposed 11 area health education centers is almost identical with Figure 8.2, except that the square with a dashed outline in the northwest part of the state is deleted; its central city is too small to serve as a regional capital. The authors state that each of the 11 centers would have "an educational program currently described as an Area Health Education Center (AHEC)," under which medical students and medical residents would receive part of their training, physicians practicing in the region would have access to continuing education, and allied health personnel would be trained (p. 24).

The Carnegie Commission maps (1970b, pp. 7–8) imply that Iowa should be served by two existing university health science centers plus three area health education centers, or five centers in all; MacQueen and Eldridge recommend a total of eleven.[7] The Commission believes the total number of area centers it recommends nationally to be about right, but the locations on its map are merely *suggestions*; the final selection of locations should be based on "careful regional planning" (p. 58).

The conflict between the two estimates of the desirable number of centers may not be very difficult to resolve. The Carnegie Commission may have had good reasons for believing that a few large centers provide a better educational experience for medical personnel than twice as many smaller ones. On the other hand, the

[6] The authors are, respectively, Associate Dean of the College of Medicine, University of Iowa, and Professor of Economics, Iowa State University.
[7] We assume that two FEAs would be served by the health science centers and nine by area health education centers.

MacQueen-Eldridge proposal need not imply that the same training programs would be carried out at the same level of intensity in all 11 locations—although the needs of medical personnel for continuing education would be almost identical in the 11 regions. Under both proposals, the area health education centers would be satellites of the university health science centers; the number of locations and the program mix at each should obviously be based on "careful regional planning" in either case.

The Geography of Health Care.   MacQueen and Eldridge point out that the great majority of the 1089 medical specialists in Iowa as of 1971 have chosen to practice in the central cities of "the established economic trade areas." Their map (p. 10) showing the distribution of the 1089 specialists indicates that each of the 11 regional capitals has at least 25 medical specialists; 10 of them have 35 or more. Four other cities with populations of 25,000 to 50,000 have from 22 to 41 medical specialists each; two are satellites of Des Moines, one of Cedar Rapids, and one of Davenport. There is a sharp drop to the next level in the distribution, four small cities with 10, 12, 12, and 13 specialists, respectively, and another drop to five other small cities with 5 specialists each. The 24 places enumerated are in 23 different counties; the other 76 counties in Iowa have from 0 to 4 specialists each.

The distributions of medical doctors in 1971 and population in 1970 are shown in Table 12.1: 73 percent of the medical specialists were located in the 11 FEA regional capitals, and 89 percent of the specialists were located in the 19 centers having 10 or more specialists each. Another 10 percent of the specialists were located in other places of 1000 population or larger, and less than 1 percent (5 out of 1089) were located in smaller places.

In the 19 centers with 10 or more specialists, specialists outnumbered general practitioners (family physicians, pediatricians, general internists, and some obstetricians) by nearly 4 to 1; in smaller places this ratio was reversed. General practitioners were distributed roughly in proportion to the population, when we allow for the fact that most Iowans residing in places where fewer than 1000 people live, get their medical services in nearby towns of 1000 or more. In contrast, 89 percent of the specialists are in cities having 36 percent of the population. In these cities the specialists provide *secondary health care* to residents of other places in their commuting fields who rely on nearby general practitioners for their *primary health care*; the general practitioners in the larger cities provide primary health care to the residents of the cities themselves. *Tertiary health care* is given at a university health science center at the University of Iowa (Iowa City), in Des Moines or Omaha, or at the Mayo Clinic in Rochester, Minnesota.

The number of medical doctors under age 70 in Iowa towns of fewer than 2500 people has declined drastically since 1950. Younger physicians have been joining or forming organizations for group practice, typically in places of 5000 or larger. MacQueen and Eldridge recommend that health personnel—nurses, physicians, and dentists—who are not yet operating as members of groups should at least "work under an organizational umbrella, if not in the same geographical setting" (p. 15). The proposed basic organizational unit would be an *area health care center*, typically located "in a central town with a population of 5,000 or more surrounded by a health service area with a population of 6,000 to 14,000. The greatest distance from a patient to the area health center will be 18 miles. An area health center will provide health

Table 12.1. Distributions of Medical Doctors and Population by Categories of Places, Iowa, 1970 and 1971

Categories of Places	Medical Doctors, 1971				Population, 1970	
	Specialists		General Practice			
	Number	As a Per-centage of Iowa Total	Number	As a Per-centage of Iowa Total	Number (000)	As a Percentage of Iowa Total
1. Eleven regional capitals of FEAs	797	73	194	25	848	30
2. Four other cities of 25,000 to 50,000 population	125	12	39	5	147	5
3. Four small cities with 10 to 13 specialists each	47	4	17	2	40	1
4. Five small cities with five specialists each	25	2	31	4	56	2
5. All other places of more than 1000 population	90	8	427	54	810	29
6. All other places of less than 1000 population	5	1	76	10	924	33
7. Iowa total	1,089	100	784	100	2,825	100
8. Subtotal, Categories 1, 2, and 3 (19 places)	969	89	250	32	1,035	36
9. Subtotal, Categories 4, 5, and 6 (all other places)	120	11	534	68	1,790	64

Source. Based on data from John C. MacQueen and Eber Eldridge, *A Proposed Organizational Structure for Providing Health Services and Medical Care in the State of Iowa.* Approced as a concept by the Health Manpower Committee of the Iowa Comprehensive Health Planning Council. Iowa City: College of Medicine, University of Iowa, August 1972. 199 pp. Multilith.

services for the same area that commonly uses the central town for retail trade" (pp. 19–20).

As Brian Berry (1966) observed, under Iowa conditions "counties represent good approximations to a proper functional breakdown of FEAs. Counties are the next step down in the various levels of human organization in a geographical area" (p. 64). Most Iowa towns of 5000 or more are county seats and also the centers of district or D-level trade areas covering 500 or 600 square miles (about the size of the county, but not coextensive with it). On Iowa's rectangular road grid, the 18-mile maximum distance specified by the authors leads to a trade and health service area covering 648 square miles. The authors state that this would make it possible for every Iowan to have primary medical care within 25 minutes of his home.

Hence the geography of health care delivery and area health education, as MacQueen and Eldridge perceive it, is the geography of the FEA. An area health education center, in their view, would become one of the distinctive institutions of the FEA.

12.6 Contributions of the Distinctive Institutions of a Functional Economic Area to the Resources of Its Individual Residents

In earlier chapters I sometimes characterized physical and emotional health as "group 1 resources." The organizational structure proposed by MacQueen and Eldridge for health care delivery would facilitate the formation and maintenance of these resources for all residents of an FEA.

The community college, we have noted, is also a distinctive institution of the FEA, with a key role in the formation and maintenance of skills (group 3 resources) which in turn are the primary source of money income and prestige (group 4).

We referred to the remaining group of resources, group 2, as value commitments and identified them in large part with the superego or Parent (Berne, 1964). Harris (1969) asserts that the Parent, in Berne's sense, is mostly acquired during the first 5 years of life; these are lived in the family and neighborhood (except for nursery schools and day care centers in some cases).

Mass media that depend on local advertising tend to follow trade area lines at FEA and district levels; television stations seem to require a population base on the FEA scale (or larger in metropolitan areas). To the extent that television is a purveyor of cultural values, it projects them to all in the FEA who choose to watch and listen. Bower (1973) has published the results of a recent survey of television viewing habits, to which the reader is referred.

Bell et al. (1967), in *Ecumenical Designs: Imperatives for Action in Non-Metropolitan America,* saw the FEA as a logical unit "for purposes of effective church planning":

> The churches normally have institutional strength at the FEA center and/or community center [i.e., district] levels. Their problem churches are predominantly at the neighborhood levels (which were the communities of the horse and buggy era). By using the FEA as a basis of planning by the Church, the resources of the FEA can be brought to bear on the problems of the FEA.
>
> The FEA concept makes it possible to give planning attention to an area of common concern without formal organizational restructuring. . . .

Needless to say, these [planning] procedures should be related to other area and community structures with common interests—but at the same time it should be kept in mind that the initial concern is that of adjusting existing church institutional structures so that they will be in position to engage in total ministry to total community. It is initially a matter of deployment of resources, and of logistics. Ultimately it is a matter of community and personal renewal, as the mission of the church must always be (pp. 80–82).

12.7 National Metropolitan Regions, Functional Economic Areas, and Transportation Planning

Stated objectives of planning in France since World War II have included reducing the degree of dominance of the national economy and society by Paris and fostering some eight regional *metropoles* with eventual populations of a million or more. These regional cities are often referred to as *metropoles d'equilibre*. Each of the *metropoles* is intended to become the dominant center in a region containing several million people and an area of 20,000 to 30,000 square miles.

Each *metropole* should have an outstanding university; other major cultural attractions such as orchestras, theaters, libraries, museums, and art galleries; and large numbers of capable leaders in industry, finance, and public administration. The term "growth pole" has sometimes been applied to a metropolis of this type, having a definite geographic location and a definite function in the economic and social development of the surrounding region. Indeed, similar functions are performed in the United States by 20 or so of our largest cities—certainly Boston, Chicago, Atlanta, Minneapolis-St. Paul, Los Angeles, and San Francisco are in this category. If New York (plus Washington, D.C.) is our equivalent of Paris, then the cities just named, and some others, are our equivalents of France's *metropoles*. In the Berry-Harris (1968) terminology, these cities are *national metropolises*; they are two levels above *regional capitals* in the central place hierarchy outlined by those authors, and the regions corresponding to them we call *national metropolitan* regions (NMRs). My tentative delineation made in October 1970 (shown in Figure 8.3 and described in Fox, 1973a) suggested that the United States contains about 24 such regions.

The radius of an NMR (east of the Rocky Mountains) would be about 200 miles; with few exceptions, the central cities of adjacent NMRs are spaced at least 300 miles apart. An NMR will normally contain something like 20 FEAs and metropolitan subareas (*R* level). FEAs and NMRs together provide a useful frame for the analysis and planning of passenger transportation systems.

The elements of this approach are as follows:

1. A transportation system exists to serve a community and is embedded in a community.

2. The communities relevant to transportation planning in the United States consist of a hierarchy of central places (successively larger cities) and their trade and service areas covering successively larger geographic territories.

3. Home-to-work commuting fields around cities of (typically) 25,000 or more people are the appropriate units for local transportation planning, and in nonmetropolitan areas such commuting fields often extend over several counties.

4. Larger regions for transportation planning should be made up of sets of contiguous commuting fields, and the set of larger regions itself should cover the continental United States.

This leads to the following categorization of passenger transportation planning tasks:

(*a*) *Local* transportation planning within each of some 500 multicounty FEAs and metropolitan subareas, involving motor vehicles for the most part.

(*b*) *National* transportation planning at the level of about 24 widely separated cities, mainly involving air travel.

(*c*) *Regional* transportation planning within each of some 24 NMRs, involving motor vehicles, (light) planes, and perhaps some interurban transit by rail. Mass transit systems linking *R*-level trade centers in a metropolis to the central business district and to each other would be special but important cases of interurban (inter-FEA) transit.

Comprehensive transportation planning must coordinate the movement of goods with the movement of people. The movement of goods may be viewed as involving two major components.

The NMR central cities, the regional metropolises next below them in the urban hierarchy, and the regional capitals (i.e., FEA central cities) are all involved in the wholesale distribution of finished consumers' goods to retailers. These goods usually move by truck over the same highways used for commuting and other passenger travel within an NMR; that is, finished goods and people can be accommodated by the same central-place-oriented transportation network.

For the most part, the transportation of raw products from the extractive industries (farm and forest products, coal, crude oil, iron ore, etc.) to points of first processing, as well as the transportation of semifinished goods to points of final manufacture, can be planned independently of transportation systems for passengers and finished goods. The NMR central cities are not primarily manufacturing centers, although much manufacturing takes place in them. At some point, finished *consumers' goods* must be transferred from the extractive and processing system to the wholesale and retail distribution system; the latter system is central-place-oriented. *Producers' durable goods* (heavy construction materials, machine tools, heavy equipment, etc.) in a sense never emerge from the extractive and processing system.

Hence comprehensive transportation planning might logically involve (1) a suboptimization for the central-place-oriented subsystem, (2) a suboptimization for the extractive and manufacturing subsystem, and (3) a final joint optimization that should require only moderate revisions in the initial suboptima.

We might be justified in calling the first system a *consumption system* and the second a *production system*. The first system could be viewed as aggregating the demands of final consumers and transmitting them to the manufacturers of finished consumers' goods, and we could envisage the second as a multistage transformation system culminating in a production possibilities frontier for finished consumers' goods. Equilibrium between the two systems would involve a point of tangency between the aggregate (consumer-derived) preference function of wholesalers and the aggregate production possibilities frontier of final-stage manufacturers.

XIII

Elements of an Operational System–III: National and World Models and Data

U P TO THIS POINT, we have approached problems of measurement as though the largest social system of concern was a nation. In this chapter we comment briefly on the current status of efforts to model the world economy and to compare nations in terms of political and social (as well as economic) indicators.[1]

13.1 Stabilization Models of a Hypothetical World Economy

In Section 8.4 we outlined a model of an exhaustive set of regions interacting within a closed national economy. The same model can be used to represent an exhaustive set of nations interacting within a world economy. The structure of the model is appropriate for economic stabilization policy on a year-to-year basis.

We assume to begin with a closed system consisting of two countries. The models for each country separately are:

Country 1:

$$Y_1 = C_1 + I_1 + G_1 + E_1 - M_1,$$
$$C_1 = c_1 Y_1,$$
$$I_1 = i_1 Y_1,$$
$$M_1 = m_1 Y_1.$$

Country 2:

$$Y_2 = C_2 + I_2 + G_2 + E_2 - M_2,$$
$$C_2 = c_2 Y_2,$$
$$I_2 = i_2 Y_2,$$
$$M_2 = m_2 Y_2,$$

---

[1] Economists have long been concerned with the problems of international comparison of prices and output. Some recent work on these problems is reported in Kravis and Lipsey (1969, 1970) and in Daly (ed., 1972).

where Y_1 (gross national product), C_1 (consumption), I_1 (domestic private invest-ment), and M_1 (imports) are regarded as endogenous variables from the standpoint of the policy maker in country 1, and G_1 (government expenditure) is his only policy instrument; he may (initially and naively) assume that E_1 (exports) is exogenous, depending completely on demand conditions in country 2 and not at all on his own actions in manipulating G_1. Except for the change in subscript, the same specifica-tions apply to country 2. All variables are measured in dollars.

In our two-country model, $E_1 = M_2$ and $E_2 = M_1$; thus the export variables be-come *endogenous* to the closed system, which can be written in the following form:

$$
\begin{bmatrix}
1 & -1 & -1 & & & & 1 & & -1 & \\
-c_1 & 1 & 0 & & 0 & & & & & \\
-i_1 & 0 & 1 & & & & & & & \\
& & & 1 & -1 & -1 & 1 & & -1 & \\
& 0 & & -c_2 & 1 & 0 & & & & \\
& & & -i_2 & 0 & 1 & & & & \\
-m_1 & & & & & & 1 & & & \\
& & & -m_2 & & & & 1 & & \\
& & & & & & & & -1 & 1 \\
& & & & & & -1 & & & 1
\end{bmatrix}
\begin{bmatrix}
Y_1 \\ C_1 \\ I_1 \\ Y_2 \\ C_2 \\ I_2 \\ M_1 \\ M_2 \\ E_1 \\ E_2
\end{bmatrix}
=
\begin{bmatrix}
G_1 \\ 0 \\ 0 \\ G_2 \\ 0 \\ 0 \\ 0 \\ 0 \\ 0 \\ 0
\end{bmatrix}. \quad (1)
$$

The only exogenous variables remaining are the policy instruments G_1 and G_2. The square matrix of coefficients connecting the 10 endogenous variables includes on its major diagonal a 3×3 block defining interactions among Y_1, C_1, and I_1 within country 1, a similar block defining interactions among Y_2, C_2, and I_2 within country 2, and a 4×4 block defining interactions among M_1, E_1, M_2, and E_2 in what we might call the international sector.

Since C_i and I_i are functions only of Y_i and do not appear in any of the equations involving the other country and/or the international trade sector, we can simplify the model considerably. The first equation for country 1,

$$Y_1 - C_1 - I_1 + M_1 - E_1 = G_1, \quad (2)$$

can be rewritten as

$$Y_1 - c_1 Y_1 - i_1 Y_1 + m_1 Y_1 - m_2 Y_2 = G_1 \quad (3)$$

or

$$(1 - c_1 - i_1 + m_1)Y_1 - m_2 Y_2 = G_1. \quad (4)$$

Similarly, the fourth equation can be rewritten as

$$-m_1 Y_1 + (1 - c_2 - i_2 + m_2)Y_2 = G_2. \quad (5)$$

Let $k_1 = (1 - c_1 - i_1 + m_1)$ and $k_2 = (1 - c_2 - i_2 + m_2)$; then (4) and (5) become

$$k_1 Y_1 - m_2 Y_2 = G_1, \quad (6)$$

$$-m_1 Y_1 + k_2 Y_2 = G_2, \quad (7)$$

or, in matrix form,

$$\begin{bmatrix} k_1 & -m_2 \\ -m_1 & k_2 \end{bmatrix} \begin{bmatrix} Y_1 \\ Y_2 \end{bmatrix} = \begin{bmatrix} G_1 \\ G_2 \end{bmatrix}. \tag{8}$$

We can solve (8) for the Y_i in terms of the G_i; multiplying both sides of (8) by the inverse of the coefficient matrix, we obtain

$$\begin{bmatrix} Y_1 \\ Y_2 \end{bmatrix} = \begin{bmatrix} \dfrac{k_2}{\Delta} & \dfrac{m_2}{\Delta} \\ \dfrac{m_1}{\Delta} & \dfrac{k_1}{\Delta} \end{bmatrix} \begin{bmatrix} G_1 \\ G_2 \end{bmatrix}, \tag{9}$$

where $\Delta = (k_1 k_2 - m_1 m_2)$ is the value of the determinant of the coefficient matrix. If we denote the inverse by D and its elements by $d_{11} = k_2/\Delta$, $d_{21} = m_1/\Delta$, $d_{12} = m_2/\Delta$, and $d_{22} = k_1/\Delta$, we can rewrite (9) as

$$\begin{bmatrix} Y_1 \\ Y_2 \end{bmatrix} = \begin{bmatrix} d_{11} & d_{12} \\ d_{21} & d_{22} \end{bmatrix} \begin{bmatrix} G_1 \\ G_2 \end{bmatrix}. \tag{10}$$

The policy maker in country 1 is primarily interested in knowing the effect of G_1 on Y_1; this is given by

$$\frac{\partial Y_1}{\partial G_1} = d_{11}. \tag{11}$$

However, he cannot manipulate G_1 without also affecting Y_2; this effect is given by

$$\frac{\partial Y_2}{\partial G_1} = d_{21}. \tag{12}$$

The effect of G_1 on GNP for the two-country system as a whole is

$$\frac{\partial Y_w}{\partial G_1} = d_{11} + d_{21}, \tag{13}$$

where $Y_w = Y_1 + Y_2$. We may think of d_{11} as the domestic multiplier for country 1 and $(d_{11} + d_{21})$ as the system multiplier, both with respect to G_1. Similarly, d_{22} is the domestic multiplier for country 2 and $(d_{22} + d_{12})$ is the system multiplier, both with respect to G_2.

If we let $c_1 = c_2 = .5$, $i_1 = i_2 = .2$, and $m_1 = m_2 = .3$, then $k_1 = k_2 = (1 - .5 - .2 + .3) = 0.6$; the coefficient matrix becomes

$$\begin{bmatrix} .6 & -.3 \\ -.3 & .6 \end{bmatrix}, \qquad \Delta = (.36 - .09) = .27, \tag{14}$$

and the resulting inverse is

$$D = \begin{bmatrix} \dfrac{.6}{.27} & \dfrac{.3}{.27} \\[2ex] \dfrac{.3}{.27} & \dfrac{.6}{.27} \end{bmatrix} = \begin{bmatrix} 2.222 & 1.111 \\ 1.111 & 2.222 \end{bmatrix}. \tag{15}$$

Hence the domestic multiplier in each country is 2.222 and the system multipliers with respect to G_1 and G_2 are 3.333 in each case.

In a three-country closed system, we must subdivide country 1's total imports M_1 into imports from countries 2 and 3, respectively, namely, M_{21} and M_{31}. Also, country 1's total exports E_1 must now equal the sum of M_{12} and M_{13}, these being the respective imports of country 2 and country 3 from country 1. We assume that

$$M_{21} = m_{21}Y_1, \qquad M_{31} = m_{31}Y_1,$$
$$M_{12} = m_{12}Y_2, \qquad M_{32} = m_{32}Y_2,$$
$$M_{13} = m_{13}Y_3, \qquad M_{23} = m_{23}Y_3.$$

Then (3) becomes

$$Y_1 - c_1Y_1 - i_1Y_1 + m_{21}Y_1 + m_{31}Y_1 - m_{12}Y_2 - m_{13}Y_3 = G_1; \tag{16}$$
$$k_1 = (1 - c_1 - i_1 + m_{21} + m_{31}),$$

and the system can be written as

$$\begin{bmatrix} k_1 & -m_{12} & -m_{13} \\ -m_{21} & k_2 & -m_{23} \\ -m_{31} & -m_{32} & k_3 \end{bmatrix} \begin{bmatrix} Y_1 \\ Y_2 \\ Y_3 \end{bmatrix} = \begin{bmatrix} G_1 \\ G_2 \\ G_3 \end{bmatrix}. \tag{17}$$

Solving for the Y's as functions of the G's, we have

$$\begin{bmatrix} Y_1 \\ Y_2 \\ Y_3 \end{bmatrix} = \begin{bmatrix} d_{11} & d_{12} & d_{13} \\ d_{21} & d_{22} & d_{23} \\ d_{31} & d_{32} & d_{33} \end{bmatrix} \begin{bmatrix} G_1 \\ G_2 \\ G_3 \end{bmatrix}, \tag{18}$$

where the matrix D with typical element d_{ij} $(i, j = 1, 2, 3)$ is the inverse of the coefficient matrix. If we let each of the six $m_{ij} = .15$, we obtain

$$D = \begin{bmatrix} 2.000 & 0.667 & 0.667 \\ 0.667 & 2.000 & 0.667 \\ 0.667 & 0.667 & 2.000 \end{bmatrix}. \tag{19}$$

The system multiplier with respect to G_1 is $(2.000 + 0.667 + 0.667)$ or 3.333 as before; however, the domestic multiplier $(d_{11} = 2.000)$ is somewhat smaller, and the remaining effects of G_1 are divided between the two other countries.

If we increase the number of countries n forming our closed "world" system while specifying that $c_i = .5$, $i_i = .2$, and $m_{ji} = .3/(n - 1)$ for each country i and its imports from each other country j, each domestic multiplier d_{ii} declines toward a lower limit of 1.667, the sum of the remaining $n - 1$ elements d_{ji} in the ith column increases toward an upper limit of 1.667, the system multiplier continues at 3.333, and the effect of G_i on any one of the Y_j ($j \neq i$) approaches $1.667/(n-1)$. For example, if $n = 101, \partial Y_j/\partial G_i = d_{ji} = 0.01658$.

In the foregoing, we have assumed a world system made up of countries with identical economic structures and with GNPs of approximately equal sizes. Our object has been to achieve the simplest possible exposition of the concept of short-run economic interactions between nations within a closed world system. We could achieve greater realism by calculating all the M_{ji} from international trade statistics for some recent year, obtaining the Y_i for that year from United Nations and other publications, and computing the $m_{ji} = M_{ji}/Y_i$ for all n (about 150) countries in the world and the $n(n-1)$ trade flows between pairs of countries. If country 1 is very large in GNP terms and country 2 is a very small neighboring country, m_{12} might be as large as .300 and m_{21} might be as small as .001. The inverse matrix would show values on the order of 0.5000 for $\partial Y_2/\partial G_1$ and 0.0017 for $\partial Y_1/\partial G_2$, assuming domestic multipliers of 1.667 in each country. Other steps toward realism would include disaggregation of the M_{ji} into major commodity groups and specification of detailed empirical models of the economic structures of each country.

13.2   Prospects for Empirical Models of the World Economy

Events during 1973 made it clear that a realistic model of the world economy is needed to provide policy makers in individual countries with suitable bases for economic forecasts and planning. In the United States, prices of wheat, corn, and soybeans doubled—quite unexpectedly—between August 1972 and August 1973. The causes included drought-reduced grain crops in at least four other countries and an unprecedentedly large purchase of United States wheat by one of them (the Soviet Union), synchronization of cyclical expansions in employment and income in most of the industrialized nations, devaluation of the dollar relative to most other currencies, relatively low carryover stocks of grain in the United States, rising consumer price levels in other countries, and a marked reduction in the output of fish meal in Peru. As world supplies dropped sharply and world demand increased, prices of grains and soybean meal shot up the relatively inelastic world demand curves for food and feed. In some of the less-developed countries, people ate less bread; in the industrialized nations, livestock ate less grain and protein meal and people ate less meat. Forecasts of 1973 prices of farm products, made by American economists in November 1972, missed their marks by the largest margins in the history of outlook work. Late in 1973 the curtailment of oil exports from several producing countries created serious difficulties for many of the industrialized nations—an even more dramatic illustration of the extent to which national economies have been integrated into a world system. It also exemplified the use of an economic instrument to advance (in large part) political ends.

Considerable progress has been made in modeling national economies and (since 1968) in linking such models into crude but promising world systems. We will comment briefly on these developments and give some references to the recent literature.

Models of National Economies.   Fox, Sengupta, and Thorbecke (1973) give extensive consideration to three major types of national economic model—stabilization, growth, and planning—and their applications to problems of quantitative economic policy.

The potential uses of a system of interrelated models for sectors and regions in multi-level planning for a national economy (Mexico) are illustrated in Goreux and Manne (eds., 1973). Bròdy and Carter (eds., 1972) include 32 papers on recent applications of input–output techniques; two of these deal with multiregional models of national economies.

Tinbergen (1939) published the first econometric (stabilization) model of the United States. Klein published some smaller American models of this type (3 to 12 equations) during the late 1940s and early 1950s. Klein and Goldberger (1955) made a major impact with a 20-equation model of the United States; their book was reviewed by Fox (1956), who pointed out that a much larger model, with provisions for tapping detailed information about individual sectors, would be needed to provide a useful basis for economic policy. Such a model was developed during 1961–1963 by a team of 15 or 20 distinguished economists under the joint chairmanship of Klein and Duesenberry; the resulting model of about 300 equations was published in Duesenberry et al. (eds., 1965).

Experience gained through this team effort made it possible thereafter for individuals and groups to construct smaller models and/or models emphasizing particular economic sectors or embodying improvements in certain blocks of equations. Klein (1971) describes the state of the art in 1971 and makes some prognoses about its further development in the 1970s. Hickman (ed., 1972) presents lengthy reports on simulation experiments with several major econometric models of the United States; this is a two-volume work of 1245 pages. Eckstein (ed., 1972) includes several papers on the econometrics of price and wage determination as reflected in American models and in selected models for European countries and Canada. Pindyck (1973) applies control theory to stabilization policy, using a small (10-equation) quarterly model of the United States economy.

Models of the World Economy. From a conference held in London in April 1967, Bronfenbrenner (ed., 1969) brings together 16 papers reviewing the post-1945 experience with economic fluctuations and stabilization policies in many countries. Several papers deal with the experience of the Western World and Japan, three with economic fluctuations in socialist countries, and one with the transmission of economic fluctuations from developed to developing countries. The countries discussed at the conference accounted for 75 to 80 percent of world GNP.

The success of the London conference encouraged several participants to consider the possibility of a cooperative study of the international transmission mechanism. Some of them, who were members of the Committee on Economic Stability of the Social Science Research Council, took the initiative in establishing Project LINK in 1968. In 1972 the project participants included the United Nations, the International Monetary Fund, and research institutes in 12 countries (Australia, Austria, Belgium, Canada, Finland, West Germany, Italy, Japan, Netherlands, Sweden, United Kingdom, and United States).

Progress under Project LINK through 1971 is reported in *The International Linkage of National Economic Models* (Ball, ed., 1973). The models for each of 11 developed countries included from 37 to 221 equations; simpler models were used for other countries and groups of countries. A 27×27 matrix of import shares, equivalent to m_{ji}/m_i $(i, j = 1, 2, \ldots, 27)$ in the notation of Section 13.1, was calculated for 25 individual developed countries, the centrally planned countries as a group, and the rest of the world. Imports were further classified into four major commodity groups. This project will continue at least until 1975, and further improvements in the world model are under way.

Other groups have recently published world models of food production, demand, and trade (Blakeslee, Heady, and Framingham, 1973), and of demand prospects for grain in 1980 (Mackie and Rojko, 1971). Mackie and Rojko partition the world into 22 regions (countries or groups of countries) and specify demand and supply equations for wheat, rice, and coarse grains in each region, together with equations connecting prices at different market levels. A matrix of transportation costs for grain between each pair of regions is included. Population and national income in each region are treated as exogenous variables; the world model generates estimates of prices, production, and consumption of each commodity in each region, and an interregional trade matrix for each commodity. Blakeslee, Heady, and Framingham make demand and supply projections for each of nine major food groups in each of 39 regions (99 countries), and they compute estimates of interregional trade in grains and fertilizers, taking account of transportation costs.

It would now be technically possible to develop detailed models of particular sectors of the world economy, even of individual commodities, and relate them iteratively to the world model of Project LINK. The logic of this procedure was described by Fox (1956) as a proposed basis for relating detailed models of United States agriculture (and other sectors) to more aggregative models of the country's economy as a whole. J. A. C. Brown (1969) presented a framework for integrating the agricultural and other sectors of an exhaustive set of (multinational) regional models into a consistent set of regional and world projections. In the same volume, Fox (1969b) suggested a procedure for disaggregating Brown's model by agricultural commodities and small areas (of the functional economic area type); agricultural price structures and trade linkages between the small areas within each region would be estimated by means of a set of spatial equilibrium models (Fox, 1953, 1963b), and price differentials and trade flows between the large regions would be estimated with a second set of spatial equilibrium models. One or more iterations might be required to achieve consistency between the price, production, consumption, and trade estimates at the small-area and large-region (hence, world) levels respectively.

13.3   Interstate and International Comparisons Based on Social, Political, and Economic Indicators

The economic models of Sections 13.1 and 13.2 show how events in one country can affect prices and incomes in other countries. De facto, such effects on national average prices and incomes are translated into changes in the money incomes of individuals. The Fox-Van Moeseke approach (Chapter 3) implies that a change in an individual's money income will alter the marginal utilities of his other resources relative to that of money; his total income, the proportions attributed to various resources, and the proportions allocated to various behavior settings will also be changed.

In Section 8.1, we noted that several of the Jones-Flax (1970) "quality of life" indicators for metropolitan areas were directly related to the resources of individuals— for example, measures of income, education, health, and mental health. Other indicators, such as public order, community concern, citizen participation, and social disintegration, apparently refer to properties of the metropolis as a social system—to "public goods" and "public bads." Presumably, public order and community concern are good to the extent that they increase the total incomes of individuals and/or the present values of their life plans; as research proceeds, much of the weight now assigned to "public goods" indicators may be absorbed into measures of the perceived total incomes of individuals. In the short run, however, we must also learn what we can from a heterogeneous array of published indicators, some of which appear to refer to states and nations as entities rather than as aggregates of individuals.

Social Indicator Comparisons Between States.   The problem of interpreting heterogeneous indicators can be illustrated with some interstate comparisons within a single large nation. Ben-Chieh Liu (1973) presents an array of approximately 100 statistics for each of the 50 states of the United States, plus the District of Columbia, as of 1970. After converting the raw statistics into ratios to United States averages, he combines subsets of from 7 to 22 ratios each into index numbers for 9 quality of life categories: individual status, individual equality, living conditions, agriculture, technology, economic status, education, health and welfare, and state and local governments. In most cases, he assigns equal weights to the items included in an index number; some items are included in more than one category, and an index or subindex for one category may be included as an element in the index for another.

Some of the items (e.g., mean family income per member, adjusted for the cost of living) relate directly to components of the total incomes of individuals; others do not. New York has 1.5 commercial broadcasting stations per 100,000 population, and Mississippi has 7.1; the national average is 3.4, which means that New York rates below 0.5 and Mississippi above 2.0 in terms of ratios to the national average. Obviously, these figures reflect the extreme differences in population density in the two states and do not measure the volume or variety of information available to individuals. Mississippi has 14.55 public libraries per 100,000 population, whereas New York has 4.28. However, New York has 1.88 library books per capita compared with Mississippi's 0.87; taken together, the two indicators imply that New York has about 7.3 times as many books per library as does Mississippi. (From data on state areas and 1970 populations, we can also compute that New York has about 2.4 times as many libraries as Mississippi per 1000 square miles.) As a final example, New York has 360 motor vehicle registrations per 1000 population, compared with Wyoming's 740; thus Wyoming scores twice as high as New York on "mobility," which enters into a subindex (subgoal) called "widen opportunity for individual choice." However, mass transit systems in New York City collected 2.1 billion fares during 1970 (nearly 6 million fares per day), and the relationship of passenger miles (or trips, or minutes) to the total incomes of individuals in the two states would need elucidation even if all modes of transportation were taken into account.

The standard deviations of Liu's nine major indexes (United States average equals 1.00 in each case) range from 0.15 to 0.41, with a median of 0.19; the standard deviation of his overall quality of life measure, which combines all nine indexes using equal weights, is 0.176. On the overall measure, 33 states and the District of Columbia receive scores between 0.824 and 1.176; six states are rated above 1.176 and eleven are rated below 0.824. On the single item with the clearest economic interpretation, mean family income per member adjusted for the cost of living, 6 states score above

1.10 and 11 below 0.85, with 34 in between. These variations are small compared with those we would expect to find among the nations of the world.

Political and Social Indicator Comparisons Between Nations.   Russett et al. (1964) compiled cross-sectional data for as many nations as possible on 75 items. The number of countries covered per item ranged from 12 to 133, with a median of 77. The items were grouped into nine categories: human resources, government and politics, communications, wealth, health, education, family and social relations, distribution of wealth and income, and religion. The authors also commented on the probable level of measurement error in each item and on its relevance to social and political structures and functions. They computed correlation coefficients between all pairs of indicators, published those which exceeded .20, and interpreted the most salient correlations in social system terms. They provided examples of data transformations, nonlinear relations, and multiple regression analyses based on sound theoretical considerations, as well as a suggestive classification of nations according to five "stages" of economic and political development. On the last point, they showed that nine measures (GNP per capita, percentage of population living in cities over 20,000, percentage literacy among adults, college graduates per 100,000 people, inhabitants per physician, radios per 1000 people, percentage of adult population voting, military personnel as percentage of population aged 15 to 64, and central government expenditures as percentage of GNP) were closely associated and seemed to reflect comprehensive processes of economic, political, and social development.

Thus the book is much, much more than a compendium of social and political indicators. Its authors (Russett, Alker, Deutsch, and Lasswell) are distinguished social scientists, and their work is suggestive of the advances in knowledge that might be achieved with the aid of a richer system of economic, social, and political data for all nations.

Taylor and Hudson (1972) have prepared a second edition of *World Handbook of Political and Social Indicators*, reflecting further progress in data systems relating to political structure and performance, political protest and executive change, external relations, and other fields. The total number of countries included is 136, and the number of series is slightly over 100; no variables are included unless adequate data on them are available for at least 60 countries. Time series on "political events" are presented for the years 1948–1967 both as numerical data and as computer-generated graphic displays; census-type data relate to the mid-1960s whenever possible.

Adelman and Morris (1967; paperback edition, 1971) apply more formal methods to the analysis of indicators for 74 less-developed countries. Their discussions of methodology are explicit and sophisticated. They are concerned with the relationship of various types of social, economic, and political change to the process of economic development. In particular, they seek insights into the quantitative importance of various social and political impediments to the economic performance of low-income countries. They question the universal applicability of certain generalizations about economic development, presenting evidence that supports different policy prescriptions for countries at different levels of socioeconomic development.

Where specific published data were unavailable, the authors made tentative estimates of their own and checked them with experts on particular countries or world regions. They used letter grades (running from A+ to C−, D−, E-, or F−, depending on the number of categories they deemed appropriate for each variable) and transformed them into numerical scores running from 90 for A to 10 for the lowest category (C, D, E, or F) used for each variable. The scores for intermediate grades were set at equidistant numerical intervals, and those for + or − grades were set at one-fourth the full intervals between adjacent letter grades. Thus the 74 less-developed countries were distributed among 9 to 18 numerical scores on each of 41 variables.

The variables were chosen to represent the most important aspects of economic, social, and political institutions and processes. More specifically, say the authors,

> the social variables were chosen to portray the principal social aspects of urbanization and industrialization; the political indicators were selected to represent leading characteristics of the emergence of modern states; and the economic indices were designed to summarize the changes in economic structure and institutions typical of industrialization and economic growth (pp. 15–16).

At least one of the authors (Adelman) has done extensive work on economic stabilization and planning models, in which the role of each variable is specified by economic theory. The same kind of intellectual discipline is reflected in the authors' choice of social and political indicators, although they do not attempt to construct formal models with them.

Instead, they apply factor analysis, first to data for the 74 less-developed countries as a group and then to data for each of three subsets of countries classified as low, intermediate, and high according to their scores on a factor representing level of socioeconomic development. For countries in each subset, they first derive and display rotated factor loadings for all the variables—economic, social, and political; second, they repeat the analysis with only the social and political variables included; third, they repeat it with only the economic variables; and fourth, they repeat it with only the social and economic variables. Their long-run analysis is designed to explain differences among countries in the level of per capita GNP as of 1961; their short-run analysis seeks to explain differences among countries in the rate of growth in real per capita GNP from 1950–1951 to 1963–1964.

In a subsequent article, Adelman and Morris (1968) incorporate 18 of their variables into a 14-equation model of socioeconomic and political change in less-developed countries. The authors classify five variables as economic, four as socioeconomic, five as social, and four as political; they form an additional variable (a discriminant index, D) as a weighted combination of one social, one political, and two economic variables from among the original 18. They present a causal ordering diagram linking the variables, five of which they treat as exogenous, and estimate 14 multiple regression equations required by their model to explain the endogenous variables. Each equation contains two or three independent variables, and the interpretations seem to be reasonable in all cases. The authors also present "multipliers" showing the estimated effects of a change of one standard deviation in each of the 18 other variables on the discriminant index D, which is their measure of "development." The multipliers include both direct and indirect effects of the specified variables on D, and they range from 2.309 to −0.320.

The major contribution of this article is its symmetrical treatment of economic, social, and political variables in a causal model of a type well known to economists and increasingly to other social scientists. Problems of definition, measurement, and scaling remain, of course, for some of the variables.

An article by Adelman in Bos et al. (eds., 1973) suggests that she has made further progress toward a general model of the sociopolitical process. This article cites a new book by Adelman and Morris (1973) on economic development and social equity in developing countries which evidently carries their 1967 and 1968 approaches considerably further.

It should be instructive to try to relate some of the Adelman-Morris variables to components of the total incomes of individuals. Coefficients relating other variables to real per capita GNP would provide a starting point for order-of-magnitude estimates of the equivalent dollar values of noneconomic reward streams (power, prestige) to various social classes and groups. If and when numerical estimates are made of total income and its components for samples of individuals in one or more countries, some of the Adelman-Morris variables might be evaluated as aggregates (or functions of aggregates) of such components.

Szalai et al. (1973) present data on the use of time in 12 countries as of 1966; this is the master study for which Robinson and Converse conducted the American survey we drew on so extensively for our tables in Chapters 5 and 6. The countries are as follows: the United States, the Soviet Union, West Germany, East Germany, Bulgaria, Czechoslovakia, Hungary, Poland, Yugoslavia, Belgium, France, and Peru. In addition to the statistical tables, the volume includes many interpretive chapters on particular aspects of time use in the 12 countries.

Exhibits such as those in Chapters 5 and 6 could be developed for individuals and (synthesized) households in all 12 countries. If these microdata can be linked to econometric models in one or more countries, another major step will have been taken toward an international system of social indicators, accounts, and models.

XIV

Social Indicators and Social Theory

IN THE SOCIAL INDICATORS FIELD, we face the problem of integrating theory and data with the help of quantitative methods. Theory should tell us what needs to be measured if we wish to understand certain sequences of social events, the data should measure the required variables, and the methods should yield quantitative estimates of those relationships between variables that are postulated by the theory.

Economic indicators preceded economic models. Relationships between prices, production, and consumption of some farm products were estimated successfully in the 1920s without the benefit of national income accounts. But no one had quantitative measures of the size of the American economy as a whole or of the world economy to which it was somehow vaguely related. As the Great Depression deepened from 1929 to 1933, the known effects of quantities on prices turned out to be smaller than those of the precipitous drops in national and world incomes, system variables that were as yet unmeasured. It was impossible to shield any sector from the contraction of the system as a whole.

The economic indicators and scattered demand and supply analyses of the 1920s did not add up to a system. It was inconceivable that they should span the economy when the boundaries of the economy were not known. With the publication of Kuznets's (1937) estimates of United States national income and product, Keynes's (1936) general theory, Leontief's (1936) input–output model, and Tinbergen's (1939) econometric model of the United States, it became possible to see the country's economy (or that of any other industrialized nation that prepared similar data and models) as a system. Since World War II, comparable data and models have been developed for more and more countries. By the early 1970s, work on a model of the world economy as a system of interacting national economies was well advanced, as noted in Section 13.2.

In this book I have proposed the concept of an individual's total income and have made some suggestions regarding how it might be measured. The equivalent dollar values of total incomes can be aggregated over individuals to yield estimates of total income for families, communities, regions, and nations. These total incomes are estimates of the "boundaries," so to speak, of the respective social systems.

Within such a boundary, the relationships of various social indicators to one another can be appraised and models of various subsystems can be interpreted in relation to the whole. Estimated effects on the level and distribution of total income can be used as *one* common denominator in choosing between alternative socioeconomic programs; other criteria may, of course, contradict and override this one in particular situations.

14.1   A Summary of What We Have Done and Why

If a measure of total income is to be used as the "outer envelope" of a system of accounts and indicators, it must be able to accommodate tested concepts and models from all the social sciences and from neighboring fields such as psychiatry and social philosophy. For this reason, in Chapter 2 I summarized or quoted ideas from Rawls, Cantril, Erikson, Murray, Berne, Parsons, Barker, and others. In Section 2.7, I presented a tentative integration of Talcott Parsons's (1968) concept of *generalized media of social interchange* and Roger Barker's (1967, 1968) concept of *behavior settings* at the level of one individual, and suggested its extension to a behavior setting, an organization, and a small community. An earlier version of this section appeared as Chapter 9 of Sengupta and Fox (1969).

In 1971 Paul Van Moeseke collaborated with me on a mathematical statement of my somewhat intuitive model. He confirmed most of my conjectures in the sense that my conclusions could indeed be derived rigorously from my assumptions. Sections 3.3 through 3.5 are entirely Van Moeseke's work, and Chapter 3 as a whole is based on Fox and Van Moeseke (1973). Van Moeseke's contribution expresses our joint model in the mathematical programming language that figures prominently in modern economic theory.

Chapter 4 is partly a reaching out for collateral evidence of the reasonableness of my approach. I cited Chester Barnard (1938), Oliver Williamson (1963, 1964), Walter Isard (1964, 1965a, 1965b, 1969), Gary Becker (1965), Staffan Linder (1970), and Ismail Sirageldin (1969) for formulations that I believe to be broadly convergent with my own, and independently derived.

In Chapter 5 I embarked on a course of "provocative quantification." Time budgets *have* to be important in a model that requires an exhaustive allocation of time. I rearranged some time use data from the University of Michigan's Survey Research Center (Robinson and Converse, 1966) into a behavior setting format. I then proceeded, in Tables 5.6 through 5.8, to endow a hypothetical individual with 11 resources, allocating each of these among 13 behavior setting aggregates: (1) as proportions of the amounts of each resource available, (2) as equivalent dollar amounts, and (3) as proportions of total income. These are "artist's conceptions" of the kinds of numbers that would have to be produced in an empirical implementation of the Fox-Van Moeseke approach. The list of resources I arrived at was somewhat different from that of Parsons, and I decided that the resources fell into three groups corresponding roughly to the three components of personality that Murray (1968), following Freud, calls the id, superego, and ego, and Berne (1964) calls the Child, the Parent, and the Adult. The resources I associate with the Adult or ego are work-

related skills, other skills, money, prestige, power in formal organizations, and political power. I decided also that Erikson's (1968) list of favorable outcomes of successive life stages (trust, will power, purpose, competence, fidelity, love, care, and
wisdom) could, in most cases, be subsumed under value commitments—although
competence translates into skills and love overlaps with affect and sexuality.

Chapter 6 continued the theme of provocative quantification into illustrative numerical models of individuals and of families in terms of resource groups, behavior
setting aggregates, shadow prices, and total income. Table 6.9 represents a numerical
conception of my revised list of resources and of Erikson's life-stage outcomes as flows
of total income and its components during successive segments of the life span of a
hypothetical individual. The problem of discounting in connection with Rawls's
(1971) concept of an individual's "life plan" was illustrated, though in no sense
solved. Melichar's (1968) estimates of the relations of scientists' salaries to their ages
and years of experience were cited as demonstrations that the money (and presumably skill) components of total income could be estimated from empirical data covering the complete working lives of individuals. Finally, the Holmes and Rahe (1967)
social readjustment rating scale was used to illustrate the possibility of quantifying
some of the effects of stressful "life events" on the value of a life plan.

Chapters 5 and 6 opened up the empirical implications of my approach to what I
trust will be constructive criticism from persons expert in measuring attributes of
individuals and households. In Chapter 7 I shifted to the national level, drawing
extensively on Nestor Terleckyj's (1973a) study of national goal output indicators
and resource requirements. On one hand, I considered how Terleckyj's indicators
might be related to the resources of individuals and to time budgets and behavior
settings. On the other, I discussed the structure of Terleckyj's 22 × 31 goals-and-
activities matrix as a target and instrument system of the Tinbergen type and described Tinbergen's (1952, 1954, 1956) theory of economic policy.

Tinbergen's approach involves integrating a model of a national economy with the
objective function of a policy maker. Positions of the economy that would be optimal
as viewed by a policy maker (a president or prime minister, say) might not be optimal
as measured by an aggregate of the incomes of individuals. The policy maker's deviations may be variously imputed to bias, to error in judging what state of the economy will maximize the welfare of the people, or to a correct choice of a position that
is optimal for the *society* of which the economy is only a part.

To the extent that the third explanation applies, an aggregate of the *total* incomes
of individuals should come closer to measuring the societal optimum than an aggregate of their *economic* incomes. The comparison is more nearly manageable at the
level of a city or a functional economic area.

Hence in Chapter 8 I pointed out that Tinbergen's approach could be applied to
the policy problems of cities and regions. For illustration, I drew on the set of "urban
indicators" presented by Jones and Flax (1970) in their study of the quality of life
in metropolitan Washington, D.C. I suggested that their 14 indicators could be
weighted and combined into a policy maker's objective function of the Tinbergen
type. I further proposed comparing this result with that of a direct aggregation of
the total incomes of individual residents as estimated from an appropriately designed
survey of (say) 2000 households. I suggested that the results of the survey would
provide much firmer ground for social measurement and policy than any objective
function based on existing data systems. In the short run, we must use these systems

"because they are there," and Jones and Flax have made a pioneering contribution. In the longer run, I believe a greatly improved system of "urban indicators" can be based on the total income approach.

In Chapter 8 I also stated my views on appropriate regions for social indicators and social policy models. These are the mutually exclusive *functional economic areas* (FEAs), which are by now well known and have been usefully approximated in the 171 economic areas delineated by the former Office of Business Economics (now the Bureau of Economic Analysis) of the U.S. Department of Commerce.[1] Since each area is a cluster of contiguous whole counties and the 171 constitute an exhaustive partitioning of the continental United States, the continuity of county-based data series is preserved. So, also, is the continuity of SMSA-based series, as each SMSA is contained within a single OBE area. (Some of the areas contain two or more SMSAs.)

Chapter 8 dealt with geographic areas and systems of areas; Chapter 9 was devoted to organizations and systems of organizations, the specific example being universities. These are nonmarket systems, and some mystery still surrounds the measurability of their outputs; it therefore seemed appropriate to suggest ways in which my approach might be extended to them. Chapter 9 recognizes that some of the most important communities in modern society (e.g., scientific and professional communities) are not territorially based in the usual sense.

Work is a major component of the time budgets of adults, and education and training to acquire work-related skills is a major preoccupation of young adults and teenagers. In Chapter 10 I gave a skeletal account of the economic sequence that runs from GNP (deliveries to final demand) through a Leontief input–output matrix to the production levels and labor requirements of specific industries, and thence to the demands for occupational skills and training. A reformulation of this sequence in linear or quadratic programming terms would, in principle, yield shadow prices for the various occupational skills—the earnings from current personal services that are a major component of total income. I then proceeded to expositions of Gary Becker's (1964) theory of human capital, Richard Stone's (1971) approach to demographic accounting and model building, and some elements of the Blau and Duncan (1967) study of the American occupational structure. Each of these books is a classic and will be influential in the development of accounts, indicators, and models that will span social systems.

In Chapter 11 I explored the problem of extending my approach to a hypothetical small community. To do so, I returned to the original source of the concept of behavior settings, Roger Barker (1968). I found myself going farther into his data and methods than I had originally intended, and with each step my admiration grew. Roger Barker's system is one that I believe all serious students of social indicators should understand. He partitions a community into a mutually exhaustive set of elements (behavior settings), defining these settings in a reproducible way and using them as a basis for what I would call a set of behavioral accounts and indicators. The data in his 1968 book relate to a single year, but his measures of interrelationships between settings could probably be given a dynamic formulation.

As in earlier chapters, I gave some numerical illustrations of what total income accounts might look like, this time for a small community. I also considered the

---

[1] The 171 areas cover the continental United States. Alaska and Hawaii are treated as single areas, making a total of 173 areas in all.

question of multiplier effects of exogenous increases in the resources (transfer pay-ments, skills, health, and others) of individual residents. The multiplier analysis, which is by now conventional in economics, seems to apply very well to exogenous increases in any resource that is directly or indirectly convertible into money. It is more speculative for such resources as affect, value commitments, prestige, and power; but it seemed axiomatic to Berne (1964) that most social contacts involve complementary transactions, adaptively programmed to yield maximum net gains to the participants. This view would imply near-optimal levels of output for most behavior settings, hence near-optimal returns to the resources used in them. At any rate, I presented a "complementary transactions" matrix for noneconomic resources that is a conventional multiplier in all but name. The two types of multiplier analysis permit a formal definition (and, in principle, measurement) of the influence of an exogenous change in the resources of any resident upon the level and distribution of total incomes in the community.

In Chapter 11 I also considered the compatibility of Barker's framework with other data systems, finding it to be quite straightforward. Finally, I considered how Terleckyj's (1973a) national goals and activities might be reflected in a community model.

In Chapter 12 I reexamined the problem of social system models and indicators for cities and regions, with more attention to existing data than in Chapter 8. I set forth further evidence on the relative degrees of closure of towns and trade areas of different population sizes and the effects of openness on economic and other multi-pliers. I reviewed the recommendations of the Carnegie Commission on Higher Education (1970a, 1970b) concerning comprehensive community colleges and area health education centers. My discussion of health facilities benefited from a compre-hensive report by MacQueen and Eldridge (1972) on the distribution of medical doctors in Iowa and a proposed organizational structure for improving health services throughout the state. The community college at the enrollment levels of 2000 to 5000 students recommended by the Commission implies a population base of 120,000 to 300,000 and in this and other respects fits perfectly into an FEA as one of its distinc-tive institutions. MacQueen and Eldridge found that, as of 1971, nearly three-fourths of the medical specialists in Iowa (as distinct from physicians in general practice) were concentrated in the regional capitals of Iowa's 11 FEAs and that health service areas coincided with trade areas. They proposed that area health education centers be established in each of the 11 FEA regional capitals (as satellites of the university health science center), thereby making the health education center also a distinctive institution of the FEA. I commented briefly on the contributions of these and other FEA institutions to the resources of the individual residents, on the nature of OBE economic areas, and on the significance of FEAs and national metropolitan regions for transportation planning.

Chapter 13 dealt with national and world models and data. After presenting an illustrative stabilization model of a hypothetical world economy, I reviewed recent progress toward empirical models of the world economy (Ball, ed., 1973) and of its food and agricultural sectors, toward a world system of political and social indicators (Russett et al., 1964; Taylor and Hudson, 1972), and toward empirical models in-volving the symmetrical treatment of political, social, and economic variables re-lating to 74 less-developed countries (Adelman and Morris, 1967, 1968, 1973).

In the Appendix, which I hope will be a particularly useful part of the book, I have introduced 250 references to other literatures not directly *about* social indicators; they may, however, prove basic to the full development of the field, or provide examples of rapid and turbulent social changes that our data systems should be designed to measure. The majority of these references are quite recent, and some of the works listed contain extensive bibliographies.

14.2   Some Lessons from the Development of Econometrics

The pioneers of the social indicators movement were very much aware of what has come to be the mainstream of modern aggregative or "macro" economics. However, there is an older tradition in the development of econometrics that offers constructive parallels to the present situation in social indicators. This tradition stems from the work of Henry L. Moore (1908, 1914, 1917, 1929).

In a 1908 article, "The Statistical Complement of Pure Economics," Moore outlined a program to which he devoted the rest of his professional life. He pointed out that although the great mathematical economists Cournot, Jevons, Edgeworth, and Pareto had devoted a substantial part of their work to the elaboration of the deductive phase of economics, each of them had conceived of

> an inductive statistical complement of the pure science without whose development the *a priori* instrument must lack concrete effectiveness. They have all proceeded on the assumption that the greatest need, at the time of their writing, was a correct theory of economics, in order to afford a first approximation to reality and to show what is required to solve concrete problems. But they have likewise made fundamental contributions to the inductive statistical complement of the pure science (p. 2).

Moore cites with approval passages from Jevons's *Theory of Political Economy* (3rd ed.):

> I know not when we shall have a perfect system of statistics, but the want of it is the only insuperable obstacle in the way of making Economics an exact science. In the absence of complete statistics, the science will not be less mathematical, though it will be immensely less useful than if it were, comparatively speaking, exact. A correct theory is the first step towards improvement, by showing what we need and what we might accomplish (p. 12).
>
> The deductive science of Economics must be verified and rendered useful by the purely empirical science of statistics. Theory must be invested with the reality and life of fact (p. 22).

Moore concluded his 33-page article by saying:

> If it is allowable to base an inference upon the opinion of masters of the science and upon the record of accomplished results, it is not unreasonable to say that at the point which economics has now reached further fecund scientific ideas and abiding practical results are to be found in the development of the *Statistical Complement of Pure Economics* (p. 33).

Moore was a theorist in search of data. It was self-evident to him that "the most ample and trustworthy data of economic science" then available were official statistics. And the best-developed set of data consisted of statistics on prices and production of agricultural commodities in the United States. Moore turned his attention to these data, with the somewhat unexpected result that his empirical work had its first and greatest impact on the emerging discipline of agricultural economics. His books on *Economic Cycles* (1914) and *Forecasting the Yield and Price of Cotton* (1917) furnished the inspiration for much of the work on statistical estimation of demand and supply functions that was carried on in the United States during the 1920s.

Much criticism greeted Moore's attempts in *Economic Cycles* to rationalize an apparently upward-sloping "demand curve" for pig iron and some correlations between crop yields and business cycles. However, his demand curves for agricultural commodities were well founded, and in his forecasting book three years later, he was on firm ground most of the way.

There are two main points of interest in Moore's 1917 book for the present discussion. The first is his practical resolution of the difficulties that seem to flow from the general equilibrium approach of Walras, which involves a complete simultaneous equations model of the entire economy. Moore wrote:

> One of the discouraging aspects of deductive, mathematical economics is that when a complete theoretical formulation is given of the possible relations of factors in a particular problem, one despairs of ever arriving at a concrete solution because of the multiplicity of the interrelated variables. But the attempt to give statistical form to the equations expressing the interrelations of the variables shows that many of the hypothetical relations have no significance which needs to be regarded in the practical situation (p. 161).

This was a necessary conclusion if any applied work was to be done at all.

The second point is what we would now regard as excessive faith in the efficacy of multiple correlation analysis:

> No matter what may be the number of factors in the economic problem, it is specially fitted to make a "quantitative determination" of their relative strength; and no matter how complex the functional relations between the variables, it can derive "empirical laws" which, by successive approximations, will describe the real relations with increasing accuracy. . . . When the method of multiple correlation is thus applied to economic data it invests the findings of deductive economics with "the reality and life of fact"; it is the Statistical Complement of Deductive Economics (p. 173).

One of the first men to respond to Moore's influence was not an economist, but the young editor of *Wallace's Farmer*—Henry A. Wallace—later Secretary of Agriculture and Vice-President of the United States. In *Agricultural Prices* (1920), Wallace included two alternative regression equations for forecasting the price of hogs. He decided that the number of hogs received at 11 markets (stockyards) was a more accurate indicator of hog supplies than the number of hogs received at Chicago only, and that the price of Connelsville coke was a better indicator of changes in the demand for hogs than was the volume of bank clearings outside New York City.

His primary basis for this conclusion was that the preferred variables gave a multiple correlation coefficient of .70 whereas the others yielded only .65.

Wallace's choice of demand indicators was less naive than it appears. Time series data on disposable personal income were 20 years in the future, and Wallace was not a patient man. He got encouraging results with time series that had never been conceived as forming components of an economic model (in this case, a statistical demand curve). It was at once obvious that better results could be obtained with data specifically designed to measure prices, production, market supplies, and consumer demand for hogs as an integrated system.

The American Farm Economic Association was organized in 1919 and the U.S. Bureau of Agricultural Economics (BAE) was established in 1922 under the leadership of Henry C. Taylor. The BAE immediately became the focus of quantitative economic research of unprecedented intensity. Research on statistical demand and supply functions was also carried out at many of the land grant colleges under the name of "agricultural price analysis."

Rapid progress was made in the 1920s with respect to data systems, statistical methods, and conceptual problems. Mordecai Ezekiel, Frederick V. Waugh, Holbrook Working, and Elmer J. Working made contributions to the theory, methodology, and implementation of statistical demand analysis that have stood the test of time. Sewall Wright, originator of the method of path coefficients and, in early career, a geneticist for the U.S. Department of Agriculture, also applied his approach to demand and supply analysis in a technical bulletin entitled *Corn and Hog Correlations* (1925).

None of these men was personally close to Moore, and none shared his particular grand vision (a statistical complement of deductive economics) in its entirety. This vision was shared by a single outstanding disciple, Henry Schultz. Inspired by Moore, Schultz studied intensively the works of those economists—Cournot, Walras, and Pareto—who had made the most explicit use of mathematics in formulating economic theory. Schultz also studied probability theory and statistics in considerable depth. His years in various statistical and economic research agencies in Washington (1920–1926) no doubt contributed to his sophistication in the use and interpretation of published economic data.

When Moore ceased writing in 1929, Schultz was almost the only American economist who combined a mastery of the theoretical work of Walras and Pareto with an intense interest in empirical studies of demand. He was fully abreast of the revolution in value theory associated with the names of J. R. Hicks and R. G. D. Allen (1934). Keynesian macroeconomic theory, however, was not of direct significance to Schultz's work, and the lengthy bibliography of his most important book, *The Theory and Measurement of Demand* (1938, pp. 779–803), contains no reference to Keynes.

Schultz's life work is essentially summed up in *The Theory and Measurement of Demand*. It would be difficult to point out any other econometric work of large scope written in the 1930s that achieved a better integration of economic theory and statistics with painstaking and realistic attention to institutions, markets, and data. Although Moore was the first economist in the United States to attempt a creative synthesis of economic theory and statistics as a basis for estimating economic relationships, Schultz achieved a similar synthesis at a much more sophisticated level. Unfortunately, Schultz died in 1938 at the age of 45.

However, many others built on Schultz's work. By the late 1960s, the most ambitious econometric studies of demand and supply had achieved a comprehensiveness that would have astonished the early critics of Moore. But Moore himself would not have been surprised. In his last book, *Synthetic Economics* (1929), Moore had proposed an implementation of the general equilibrium model of Walras, and its principal elements were to be comprehensive sets of empirical demand and supply functions! Kuznets, Leontief, and Tinbergen were just around the corner.

References

Adelman, Irma. 1973. Planning for social equity. In H. C. Bos, H. Linnemann, and P. de Wolff eds., *Economic structure and development: Essays in honour of Jan Tinbergen*. Amsterdam: North-Holland Publishing Company, and New York: American Elsevier.

Adelman, Irma, and Morris, Cynthia Taft. 1967 (paperback ed., 1971). *Society, politics, and economic development: A quantitative approach*. Baltimore: Johns Hopkins University Press.

————. 1968. An econometric model of socio-economic and political change in underdeveloped countries. *American Economic Review* **58**, No. 5 (December), Part 1, 1184–1218.

————. 1973. *Economic development and social equity in developing countries*. Stanford: Stanford University Press.

American Academy of Political and Social Science. 1967a. *Social goals and indicators for American society:* Volume I. *The Annals of the American Academy of Political and Social Science* **373** (September).

————. 1967b. *Social goals and indicators for American society:* Volume II. *The Annals of the American Academy of Political and Social Science* **373** (September).

Andrews, Kenneth R. 1968. Introduction. In *The functions of the executive*, by Chester I. Barnard. 30th anniversary ed. Cambridge, Mass.: Harvard University Press.

Arrow, Kenneth J., and Debreu, Gerard. 1954. Existence of an equilibrium for a competitive economy. *Econometrica* **22** (July), 265–290.

Ball, R. J., ed. 1973. *The international linkage of national economic models*. Amsterdam: North-Holland Publishing Company, and New York: American Elsevier.

Barker, Roger G. 1963. On the nature of the environment. *Journal of Sociological Issues* **19** (April), 17–38.

————. 1968. *Ecological psychology: Concepts and methods for studying the environment of human behavior* Stanford: Stanford University Press.

Barker, Roger G., Barker, Louise S., and Ragle, Dan D. M. 1967. The churches of Midwest, Kansas, and Yoredale, Yorkshire: Their contributions to the environments of the towns. In W. J. Gore and L. C. Hodapp, eds., *Change in the small community: An interdisciplinary survey*. New York: Friendship Press.

Barnard, Chester I. (1938) 1968. *The functions of the executive*. Cambridge, Mass.: Harvard University Press.

Bauer, Raymond A., ed. 1966. *Social indicators*. Cambridge, Mass.: The M.I.T. Press.

Bauer, Raymond A., and Fenn, Dan H., Jr. 1972. *The corporate social audit*. New York: Russell Sage Foundation.

Becker, Gary S. 1964. *Human capital: A theoretical and empirical analysis, with special reference to education*. New York: Columbia University Press.

266

————. 1965. A theory of the allocation of time. *Economic Journal 75*, 493–517.

Bell, Daniel. 1969. The idea of a social report. *The Public Interest* 15 (Spring), 72–84

Bell, D., Cascini, W., Kaufman, H., Kelley, A., McIntire, L., Ordway, R., Sills, H., and Williams, C. 1967. *Ecumenical designs: Imperatives for action in non-metropolitan America.* New York: The Steering Committee, National Consultation on the Church in Community Life.

Berne, Eric. 1961. *Transactional analysis in psychotherapy.* New York: Grove Press.

————. 1964. *Games people play: The psychology of human relationships.* New York: Grove Press.

Berry, Brian J. L. 1966. Reflections on the functional economic areas. In Wilbur R. Maki and Brian J. L. Berry, eds., *Research and education for regional and area development.* Ames: Iowa State University Press.

Berry, Brian J. L. 1972. Latent structure of the American urban system, with international comparisons. In Brian J. L. Berry, ed., *City classification handbook.* New York: John Wiley & Sons.

Berry, Brian J. L., et al. 1968. *Metropolitan area definition: A reevaluation of concept and statistical practice.* Working Paper 28, U.S. Department of Commerce, Bureau of the Census.

Berry, Brian J. L., and Harris, Chauncy D. 1968. Central place. In *International encyclopedia of the social sciences:* Volume 2. New York: Macmillan Company and The Free Press.

Biderman, Albert D. 1966. Social indicators and goals. In Raymond A. Bauer, ed., *Social indicators.* Cambridge, Mass.: The M.I.T. Press.

Blakeslee, Leroy L., Heady, Earl O., and Framingham, Charles F. 1973. *World food production, demand, and trade.* Ames: Iowa State University Press.

Blau, Peter, and Duncan, Otis Dudley. 1967. *The American occupational structure.* New York: John Wiley & Sons.

Borchert, John R., and Adams, Russell B. 1963. *Trade centers and trade areas of the upper midwest.* Urban Report No. 3, Upper Midwest Economic Study. Minneapolis: University of Minnesota.

Boszormenyi-Nagy, Ivan, and Framo, J. L., eds. 1965. *Intensive family therapy.* New York: Harper & Row.

Bowen, Howard R. 1967. Statement. In *Full Opportunity and Social Accounting Act* [Seminar], Part 1. Senate hearings on S. 843, June 26, 1967, 90th Congress, 1st Session.

Bower, Robert T. 1973. *Television and the public.* New York: Holt, Rinehart & Winston.

Bródy, A., and Carter, Anne P., eds. 1972. *Input–output techniques. Proceedings of the Fifth International Conference on Input–Output Techniques*, Geneva, January 1971. Amsterdam: North-Holland Publishing Company, and New York: American Elsevier.

Bronfenbrenner, Martin, ed. 1969. *Is the business cycle obsolete?* New York: Wiley-Interscience.

Brooks, Ralph M. 1972. Social planning and societal monitoring. In Leslie D. Wilcox *et al.*, eds., *Social indicators and societal monitoring: An annotated bibliography.* San Francisco: Jossey-Bass, and Amsterdam: Elsevier.

Brown, J. A. C. 1969. A regional model of agricultural development. In Erik Thorbecke, ed., *The role of agriculture in economic development.* New York: Columbia University Press.

Burkhead, Jesse. 1964. Public finance as an integral part of regional accounts. In Werner Z. Hirsch, ed., *Elements of regional accounts.* Baltimore: Johns Hopkins University Press, pp. 51–57.

Cantril, Hadley. 1965. *The pattern of human concerns.* New Brunswick, N.J.: Rutgers University Press.

Carnegie Commission on Higher Education. 1970a. *The open-door colleges: Policies for community colleges.* New York: McGraw-Hill Book Company.

————. 1970b. *Higher education and the nation's health: Policies for medical and dental education.* New York: McGraw-Hill Book Company.

Cartter, A. M. 1966. *An assessment of quality in graduate education.* Washington, D.C.: American Council on Education.

Converse, Philip E. 1968. Time budgets. In *International encyclopedia of the social sciences:* Volume 16. New York: Macmillan Company and The Free Press.

Court, Andrew T. 1939. Hedonic price indexes with automotive examples. In *The dynamics of automobile demand.* New York: General Motors Corporation.

Cowhig, James C., and Beale, Calvin L. 1965. Levels of living among whites and nonwhites. In *Indicators:* U.S. Health, Education, and Welfare Department. Washington, D.C.: Government Printing Office.

Cyert, Richard M. 1973. Book review of Karl A. Fox (ed.), *Economic analysis for educational planning: Resource allocation in nonmarket systems.* In *Journal of Economic Literature 11* (June), 592–593.

Daly, D. J., ed. 1972. *International comparisons of prices and output.* National Bureau of Economic Research, Studies in Income and Wealth, No. 37. New York: Columbia University Press.

Doeringer, Peter B., and Piore, Michael J. 1971. *Internal labor markets and manpower analysis.* Lexington, Mass.: D. C. Heath & Company.

Duesenberry, James S., Fromm, Gary, Klein, Lawrence R., and Kuh, Edwin, eds. 1965. *The Brookings quarterly econometric model of the United States.* Amsterdam: North-Holland Publishing Company, and Skokie, Ill.: Rand McNally.

Duncan, Otis Dudley. 1961a. A socioeconomic index for all occupations. In Albert J. Reiss, ed., *Occupations and social status.* New York: The Free Press.

———. 1961b. Properties and characteristics of the socioeconomic index. In Albert J. Reiss, ed., *Occupations and social status.* New York: The Free Press.

———. 1968. Social stratification and mobility: Problems in the measurement of trend. In Eleanor Bernert Sheldon and Wilbert E. Moore, eds., *Indicators of social change: Concepts and measurements.* New York: Russell Sage Foundation.

———. 1969. *Toward social reporting: Next steps.* Paper No. 2 in Social Science Frontiers Series. New York: Russell Sage Foundation.

Duncan, Otis Dudley, Featherman, David L., and Duncan, Beverly. 1972. *Socioeconomic background and achievement.* New York: Seminar Press.

Eckstein, Otto, ed. 1972. *The econometrics of price determination.* Washington, D.C.: Board of Governors of the Federal Reserve System.

Encyclopaedia Britannica. 1965. Shopping centre: Volume 20. Chicago: Encyclopaedia Britannica, Inc.

Erikson, Erik H. 1968. Life cycle. In *International encyclopedia of the social sciences:* Volume 9. New York: Macmillan Company and The Free Press.

Ezekiel, Mordecai. 1930. *Methods of correlation analysis.* New York: John Wiley & Sons. 2nd rev. ed., 1941.

Feinberg, Abraham. 1972. *An experimental investigation of an interactive approach for multi-criterion optimization, with an application to academic resource allocation.* Working Paper No. 186, Western Management Science Institute. Los Angeles: University of California.

Ferriss, Abbott L. 1969. *Indicators of trends in American education.* New York: Russell Sage Foundation.

———. 1970. *Indicators of change in the American family.* New York: Russell Sage Foundation.

———. 1971. *Indicators of trends in the status of American women.* New York: Russell Sage Foundation.

Fox, Karl A. 1938. *A critique of mortality statistics: With special reference to Utah and Mormon populations.* Unpublished M.A. thesis (Sociology), University of Utah Library, Salt Lake City.

———. 1953. A spatial equilibrium model of the livestock-feed economy in the United States. *Econometrica* **21,** 547–566.

———. 1956. Econometric models of the United States. *Journal of Political Economy* **64,** 128–142.

———. 1958. *Econometric analysis for public policy.* Ames: Iowa State University Press.

———. 1961. The concept of community development. Paper prepared for the Community Development Seminar, Iowa State University, April 18, 1961. 42 pp. Mimeograph.

———. 1962a. The study of interactions between agriculture and the nonfarm economy—local, regional, and national. *Journal of Farm Economics* **44** (February), 1–34.

———. 1962b. On the current lack of policy orientation in regional accounting. Comments stimulated by the Second Conference on Regional Accounts, Miami Beach, November 1962. 12 pp. Mimeograph. Ames: Department of Economics, Iowa State University.

———. 1963a. The concept of community development. In *Fundamentals for area progress.* Center for Agricultural and Economic Development Report No. 19. Ames: Iowa State University.

————. 1963b. Spatial price equilibrium and process analysis in the food and agricultural sector. In Alan S. Manne and Harry M. Markowitz, eds., *Studies in process analysis: Economy-wide production capabilities*. New York: John Wiley & Sons.

————. 1965. Spatial equilibrium and central place hierarchies in agricultural regions undergoing rapid changes in the mode of transport. Ames: Department of Economics, Iowa State University. Mimeograph.

————. 1967a. Functional economic areas and consolidated urban regions of the United States. *Social Science Research Council ITEMS* **21**, 45–49.

————. 1967b. Metamorphosis in America: A new synthesis of rural and urban society. In William J. Gore and Leroy C. Hodapp, eds., *Change in the small community: An interdisciplinary survey*. New York: Friendship Press.

————. 1967c. Monopolistic competition in the food and agricultural sectors. In Robert E. Kuenne, ed., *Monopolistic competition theory: Studies in impact*. Essays in Honor of Edward H. Chamberlin. New York: John Wiley & Sons.

————. 1967d. Strategies for area delimitation in a national system of regional accounts. Paper prepared at the request of Charles L. Leven, Director, Institute for Urban and Regional Studies, Washington University, St. Louis, Mo., November 1967. 48 pp., plus 17 figures. Most of this material appears in Charles L. Leven, J. B. Legler, and P. Shapiro, *An analytical framework for regional development policy*. Cambridge: The M.I.T. Press, 1970, pp. 105–125, 138–147.

————. 1968. *Intermediate economic statistics*. New York: John Wiley & Sons.

————. 1969a. Operations research and complex social systems. Chapter 9 in Jati K. Sengupta and Karl A. Fox, *Economic analysis and operations research: Optimization techniques in quantitative economic models*. Amsterdam: North-Holland Publishing Company.

————. 1969b. Toward a policy model of world economic development with special attention to the agricultural sector. In Erik Thorbecke, ed., *The role of agriculture in economic development*. New York: Columbia University Press.

————. 1969c. The new synthesis of rural and urban society in the United States. In Ugo Papi and Charles Nunn, eds., *Economic problems of agriculture in industrial societies*. London: Macmillan Company Ltd., and New York: St. Martin's Press.

————. 1969d. Decentralization or regionalization of national economic policies. Section 8.2.3 in Jati K. Sengupta and Karl A. Fox, *Economic analysis and operations research: Optimization techniques in quantitative economic models*. Amsterdam: North-Holland Publishing Company.

————. 1969e. Functional economic areas: A strategic concept for promoting civic responsibility, human dignity, and maximum employment in the United States. Ames: Department of Economics, Iowa State University.

————. 1969f. A new strategy for urban and rural America. *Appalachia* **2** (August), 10–13.

————. ed. 1972. *Economic analysis for educational planning: Resource allocation in nonmarket systems*. With contributions by Karl A. Fox, J. K. Sengupta, T. K. Kumar, and B. C. Sanyal. Baltimore: Johns Hopkins University Press.

————. 1973a. Delimitation of regions for transportation planning. In Joseph S. DeSalvo, ed., *Perspectives on regional transportation planning*. Lexington, Mass.: D. C. Heath & Company.

————. 1973b. Combining economic and noneconomic objectives in development planning: problems of concept and measurement. In Willy Sellekaerts, ed., *Economic development and planning: Essays in honor of Jan Tinbergen*. London: Macmillan Company Ltd.

————. 1973c. Economic models of academic decision-making. In *Proceedings of the Twenty-Ninth Annual Meeting, Midwestern Association of Graduate Schools*, Chicago, March 25–27, 1973.

————. 1974. Practical optimization models for university departments. In H. Correa, ed., *Analytical models in educational planning and administration*. New York: David McKay Company.

————, and Kumar, T. Krishna. 1965. The functional economic area: Delineation and implications for economic analysis and policy. *Regional Science Association Papers* **15**, 57–85.

————, and ————. 1966. Delineating functional economic areas. In Wilbur R. Maki and Brian J. L. Berry, eds., *Research and education for regional and area development*. Ames: Iowa State University Press.

————, McCamley, F. P., and Plessner, Y. 1967. Formulation of management science models for selected problems of college administration. Final report submitted to U.S. Department of Health, Education, and Welfare. Mimeographed.

————, and Van Moeseke, Paul. 1973. Derivation and implications of a scalar measure of social income. In H. C. Bos, H. Linnemann, and P. de Wolff, eds., *Economic structure and development: Essays in honor of Jan Tinbergen.* Amsterdam: North-Holland Publishing Company, and New York: American Elsevier.

————, and Sengupta, J. K. 1968. The specification of econometric models for planning educational systems: An appraisal of alternative approaches. *Kyklos* **21,** 665–694.

————, ————, and Thorbecke, Erik. 1973. *The theory of quantitative economic policy: With applications to economic growth, stabilization, and planning.* Amsterdam: North-Holland Publishing Company, and New York: American Elsevier. First ed., 1966.

————, and Taeuber, Richard C. 1955. Spatial equilibrium models of the livestock-feed economy. *American Economic Review* **45,** 584–608.

Frisch, Ragnar. 1934. *Statistical confluence analysis by means of complete regression systems.* Oslo: Universitets Økonomiske Institutet.

————. 1959. A complete scheme for computing all direct and cross demand elasticities in a model with many sectors. *Econometrica* **27** (April), 177–196.

Fullerton, Herbert H., and Prescott, James R. 1975. *An economic simulation model for regional development planning.* Ann Arbor, Mich.: Ann Arbor Science Publishers, Inc. (in press).

Galpin, C. J. 1915. *The social anatomy of an agricultural community.* Agricultural Experiment Station Research Bulletin No. 34. Madison: University of Wisconsin.

Gordon, Margaret S. 1971. Health education centers: Their role in medical education. *Journal of the American Medical Association 218* (November), 1192–1194.

Gordon, Robert A. 1961. *Business leadership in the large corporation.* Berkeley: University of California Press.

Goreux, Louis M., and Manne, Alan S., eds. 1973. *Multi-level planning: Case studies in Mexico.* Amsterdam: North-Holland Publishing Company, and New York: American Elsevier.

Gorham, William. 1967. Testimony. In *Full Opportunity and Social Accounting Act.* Part 2 of Senate Hearings on S. 843, July 19, 20, and 26, 1967, 90th Congress, 1st session.

Griliches, Zvi. 1961. Hedonic price indexes for automobiles: An Econometric analysis of quality change. In *The price statistics of the federal government*, General Series, No. 73. New York: National Bureau of Economic Research.

————, ed. 1971. *Price indexes and quality change: Studies in new methods of measurement.* Cambridge, Mass.: Harvard University Press.

Gross, Bertram M. 1966. The state of the nation: Social systems accounting. In Raymond A. Bauer, ed., *Social indicators.* Cambridge, Mass.: The M.I.T. Press.

Harris, Britton. 1964. An accounts framework for metropolitan models. In Werner Z. Hirsch, ed., *Elements of Regional Accounts.* Baltimore: Johns Hopkins Press, pp. 107–127.

Harris, Thomas A. 1969. *I'm O.K.—You're O.K.: A practical guide to transactional analysis.* New York: Harper & Row.

Hartman, Lawton M. 1969. *Graduate education: Parameters for public policy.* Washington, D.C.: National Science Foundation.

Hauser, Philip M. 1967. Social accounting. Appendix Exhibits I and II. In *Full Opportunity and Social Accounting Act.* Part 3 of Senate Hearings on S. 843, July 28, 1967, 90th Congress, 1st session.

Hickman, Bert G., ed. 1972. *Econometric models of cyclical behavior.* National Bureau of Economic Research Studies in Income and Wealth, No. 36, Volumes 1 and 2. New York: Columbia University Press.

Hicks, J. R., and Allen, R. G. D. 1934. A reconsideration of the theory of value. 2 parts. *Economica* New Series **1,** 52–76, 196–219.

Hodge, Robert W., Siegel, Paul M., and Rossi, Peter H. 1964. Occupational prestige in the United States, 1925–1963. *American Journal of Sociology* **70,** 286–302.

Holdren, Bob R.   (1960) 1968. *The structure of a retail market and the market behavior of retail firms.* Ames: Iowa State University Press.

Holmes, Thomas H. and Rahe, Richard H.   1967. The social readjustment rating scale. *Journal of Psychosomatic Research* **11**, 213–218.

Isard, Walter.   1969. *General theory: Social, political, economic, and regional.* (In association with Tony E. Smith, Peter Isard, Tze Hsiung Tung, and Michael Dacey). Cambridge, Mass.: The M.I.T. Press.

———, and Isard, Peter.   1965a. General social, political, and economic equilibrium for a system of regions: Part I. *Regional Science Association Papers* **14**, 1–33.

———, and ———.   1965b. General social, political, and economic equilibrium for a system of regions: Part II. *Regional Science Association Papers* **15**, 7–25.

———, and Ostroff, D. J.   1958. Existence of a competitive interregional equilibrium. *Regional Science Association Papers* **4**, 49–76.

———, and Tung, Tze Hsiung.   1964. Selected non-economic commodities: definitions, and speculation on supply and demand, measurement and utility. *Regional Science Association Papers* **13**, 71–92.

Jones, Martin V., and Flax, Michael I.   1970. *The quality of life in Metropolitan Washington, D.C.: Some statistical benchmarks.* Washington, D.C.: The Urban Institute.

Keynes, John Maynard.   1936. *The general theory of employment, interest and money.* New York: Harcourt Brace Jovanovich.

Klein, Lawrence R.   1971. Whither econometrics? *Journal of the American Statistical Association* **66** (June), 415–421.

———, and Goldberger, Arthur S.   1955. *An econometric model of the United States, 1929–1952.* Amsterdam: North-Holland Publishing Company.

Koenig, H. E., Keeney, M. G., and Zemach, R.   1968. *A systems model for management, planning and resource allocation in institutions of higher education.* Final report under National Science Foundation Project C-518, Division of Engineering Research. East Lansing: Michigan State University.

Koopmans, Tjalling C.   1937. *Linear regression analysis of economic time series.* Haarlem: De Erven F. Bohn N.V.

———, ed.   1951. *Activity analysis of production and allocation.* New York: John Wiley & Sons.

Kravis, Irving B., and Lipsey, Robert E.   1969. International price comparisons. *International Economic Review* **10**, 233–246.

———.   1970. *Price competitiveness in world trade.* New York: National Bureau of Economic Research.

Kuhn, H. W., and Tucker, A. W.   1951. Nonlinear programming. In Jerzy Neyman, ed., *Proceedings of the Second Berkeley symposium on mathematical statistics and probability.* Berkeley: University of California Press.

Kumar, T. Krishna.   1972a. Resource allocation processes in linear static models. In Karl A. Fox, ed., *Economic analysis for education planning.* Baltimore: Johns Hopkins University Press.

———.   1972b. Resource allocation processes in nonlinear and dynamic models. In Karl A. Fox, ed., *Economic analysis for educational planning.* Baltimore: Johns Hopkins University Press.

Kuznets, Simon.   1937. *National income and capital formation, 1919–1935.* New York: National Bureau of Economic Research.

Lancaster, Kelvin J.   1971. *Consumer demand.* New York: Columbia University Press.

Land, Kenneth C.   1970. Social indicators. In Robert B. Smith, ed., *Social science methods.* New York: The Free Press.

———.   1971. On the definition of social indicators. *The American Sociologist* **6** (November), 322–325.

———.   1974. Social indicator models: An overview. In Kenneth C. Land and Seymour Spilerman, eds., *Social indicator models.* New York: Russell Sage Foundation.

———, and Spilerman, Seymour, eds.   1974. *Social indicator models.* New York: Russell Sage Foundation.

Lecht, Leonard A.   1966. *Goods, priorities and dollars: The next decade.* New York: The Free Press.

Leontief, Wassily W.   1936. Quantitative input and output relations in the economic system of the United States. *Review of Economics and Statistics* **18** (August), 105–125.

———.   1951. *The structure of American economy, 1919–1939.* 2nd edition. New York: Oxford University Press.

Leven, Charles L.   1958. *Theory and method of income and product accounts for metropolitan areas.* Ames: Department of Economics, Iowa State University. Multilith.

Leven, Charles L., Legler, J. B., and Shapiro, P.   1970. *An analytical framework for regional development policy.* Cambridge, Mass.: The M.I.T. Press.

Levinson, Harry.   1968. *The exceptional executive: A psychological conception.* Cambridge, Mass.: Harvard University Press.

Linder, Staffan Burenstam.   1970. *The harried leisure class.* New York: Columbia University Press.

Liu, Ben-Chieh.   1973. *The quality of life in the United States, 1970.* Kansas City, Mo.: Midwest Research Institute.

Mackie, Arthur B., and Rojko, Anthony S.   1971. *World demand prospects for grain in 1980.* Economic Research Service, Foreign Agricultural Economic Report No. 75. Washington, D.C.: U.S. Department of Agriculture.

MacQueen, John C., and Eldridge, Eber.   1972. *A proposed organizational structure for providing health services and medical care in the state of Iowa.* Iowa City: College of Medicine, University of Iowa. Multilith.

March, James G., ed.   1965. *Handbook of organizations.* Skokie, Ill.: Rand McNally.

March, James G., and Simon, Herbert A.   1958. *Organizations.* New York: John Wiley & Sons.

Marshall, Alfred.   (1890) 1948. *Principles of economics.* 8th edition. New York: Macmillan Company.

Maslow, Abraham H.   (1954) 1970. *Motivation and personality.* 2nd edition. New York: Harper & Row.

Masuda, Minoru, and Holmes, Thomas H.   1967a. Magnitude estimations of social readjustments. *Journal of Psychosomatic Research* **11,** 219–225.

———, and ———.   1967b. The social readjustment rating scale: A cross-cultural study of Japanese and Americans. *Journal of Psychosomatic Research* **11,** 227–237.

McCamley, F. P.   1967. Activity analysis models of educational institutions. Unpublished Ph.D. dissertation. Ames: Iowa State University Library.

Meier, Richard L.   1972. Communications stress. In Richard F. Johnston, ed., and Peter W. Frank and Charles D. Michener, assoc. eds., *Annual Review of Ecology and Systematics:* Volume III, pp. 289–314, Palo Alto, California: Annual Reviews, Inc.

Melichar, Emanuel.   1968. Factors affecting 1966 basic salaries in the National Register professions: Study II. In *Studies of the structure of economists' salaries and income.* Supplement, Part 2. *American Economic Review* **58** (December), 56–69.

Mondale, Walter F.   1969. S-5—Introduction of Bill—Full Opportunity Act of 1969. *Congressional Record* **115,** No. 9, January 15, 1969, pp. 780–786.

Moore, Henry L.   1908. The statistical complement of pure economics. *Quarterly Journal of Economics* **22,** 1–33.

———.   1914. *Economic cycles: Their law and cause.* New York: Macmillan Company.

———.   1917. *Forecasting the yield and price of cotton.* New York: Macmillan Company.

———.   1929. *Synthetic economics.* New York: Macmillan Company.

Moore, Wilbert E, and Sheldon, Eleanor Bernert.   1965. Monitoring social change: A conceptual and programmatic statement. In American Statistical Association, *Proceedings of the Social Statistics Section,* Washington, D.C.: American Statistical Association.

Morgan, James N., Sirageldin, Ismail, and Baerwaldt, Nancy.   1966. *Productive Americans: A study of how individuals contribute to economic progress.* Survey Research Center Monograph 43. Ann Arbor: University of Michigan.

———, Sonquist, John A., and Andrews, Frank M.   1967. *Multiple classification analysis.* Ann Arbor: Survey Research Center, University of Michigan.

Murray, Henry A.   1968. Personality: Contemporary viewpoints. II. Components of an evolving personological system. In *International encyclopedia of the social sciences:* Volume 12. New York: Macmillan Company and The Free Press.

National Commission on Technology, Automation, and Economic Progress.   1966. *Technology and the American economy.* Washington, D.C.: Government Printing Office.

National Goals Research Staff.   1970. *Toward balanced growth: Quantity with quality.* Washington, D.C.: The White House.

Niskanen, William A.   1964. The use of intrametropolitan data. In Werner Z. Hirsch, ed., *Elements of Regional Accounts.* Baltimore: Johns Hopkins Press, pp. 131–142.

Office of Research and Statistics, Social Security Administration.   1969. *Geographic codes used to classify records of employers, workers, and self-employed persons.* Washington, D.C.: Government Printing Office.

Olsen, Richard J., and Westley, G. W.   1973a. *County code equivalents for regional economic analysis.* Oak Ridge, Tenn.: Oak Ridge National Laboratory. Multilith.

————, 1973b.   *1967 County and city data book: Cumulations to OBE areas.* Oak Ridge, Tenn.: Oak Ridge National Laboratory. Multilith.

Olson, Mancur.   1969. The plan and purpose of the social report. *The Public Interest* **15** (Spring), 85–97.

Parsons, Talcott.   1968. Systems analysis: Social systems. In *International encyclopedia of the social sciences:* Volume 15. New York: Macmillan Company and The Free Press.

Penfield, Wilder.   1952. Memory mechanisms. *American Medical Association Archives of Neurology and Psychiatry* **67,** 178–198.

Pindyck, Robert S.   1973. *Optimal planning for economic stabilization.* Amsterdam: North-Holland Publishing Company, and New York: American Elsevier.

Plessner, Y., Fox, K. A., and Sanyal, B. C.   1968. On the allocation of resources in a university department. *Metroeconomica* **20** (September–December), 256–271.

President's Commission on National Goals.   1960. *Goals for Americans.* Englewood Cliffs, N.J.: Prentice-Hall.

President's Research Committee on Social Trends.   1933. *Recent social trends.* New York: McGraw-Hill Book Company.

Rawls, John.   1971. *A theory of justice.* Cambridge, Mass.: Harvard University Press.

Regional Economics Division, Office of Business Economics, U.S. Department of Commerce.   1967. OBE economic areas of the United States. Unpublished paper, revised January 1969.

Reiss, Albert J., ed.   1961. *Occupations and social status.* New York: The Free Press.

Robinson, John P., and Converse, Philip E.   1966. *66 Basic tables on time-budget data for the United States.* Ann Arbor: Institute for Social Research, University of Michigan.

Roethlisberger, T. J.   1968. Barnard, Chester I. In *International encyclopedia of the social sciences:* Volume 2. New York: Macmillan Company and The Free Press.

Roose, K. D., and Andersen, C. J.   1970. *A rating of graduate programs.* Washington, D.C.: American Council on Education.

Russett, Bruce M., Alker, Hayward R., Jr., Deutsch, Karl W., and Lasswell, Harold D.   1964. *World handbook of political and social indicators.* New Haven, Conn.: Yale University Press.

Samuelson, Paul A.   1947. *Foundations of economic analysis.* Cambridge, Mass.: Harvard University Press.

Sanyal, Bikas C.   1972. The systems approach to resource allocation in educational planning. In Karl A. Fox, ed., *Economic analysis for educational planning.* Baltimore: Johns Hopkins University Press.

Satir, Virginia.   (1964) 1967. *Conjoint family therapy.* Revised edition. Palo Alto, Calif.: Science and Behavior Books.

Scherz, Frances H.   1971. Family services: Family therapy. In *Encyclopedia of social work:* 16th issue, Volume 1. New York: National Association of Social Workers.

Schultz, Henry.   1938. *The theory and measurement of demand.* Chicago: University of Chicago Press.

Schultz, Theodore W.   1960. The formation of human capital by education. *Journal of Political Economy* **68**, 571–583.

———.   1962. Reflections on investment in man. *Journal of Political Economy* 70, Part 2 (October), 1–8.

Sengupta, Jati K.   1972. Economic problems of resource allocation in nonmarket systems. In Karl A. Fox, ed., *Economic analysis for educational planning*. Baltimore: Johns Hopkins University Press.

———, and Fox, Karl A.   1969. *Economic analysis and operations research: Optimization techniques in quantitative economic models*. Amsterdam: North-Holland Publishing Company.

———, and ———.   1970. A computable approach to optimal growth for an academic department. *Zeitschrift für die gesamte Staatswissenschaft* (January), 97–125.

Sewell, William H., et al.   1970. The educational and early occupational status attainment process: Replication and revision. *American Sociological Review* **35** (December), 1014–1027.

Sheldon, Eleanor Bernert.   1971. Social reporting for the 1970's. In *Federal statistics: Report of the President's Commission:* Volume II. Washington, D.C.: Government Printing Office.

———, and Land, Kenneth C.   1972. Social reporting for the 1970's: A review and programmatic statement. *Policy Sciences* **3** (July), 137–151.

———, and Moore, Wilbert E., eds.   1968. *Indicators of social change: Concepts and measurements*. New York: Russell Sage Foundation.

Simon, Herbert A.   (1947) 1957a. *Administrative behavior: A study of decision-making processes in administrative organization*. 2nd edition. New York: The Free Press.

———.   1957b. *Models of man: Social and rational*. New York: John Wiley & Sons.

Sioux City, Iowa, City Planning Commission.   1959. *Economic report*. (Includes regional accounts and multiplier analysis prepared by Charles L. Leven.)

Sirageldin, Ismail Abdel-Hamid.   1969. *Non-market components of national income*. Ann Arbor: Survey Research Center, University of Michigan.

Smith, Adam.   (1776) 1950. *Wealth of nations*. Edited by Edwin Cannan. London: Methuen. (A two-volume paperback edition was published by Richard D. Irwin, Homewood, Ill., in 1963.)

Smith, Victor E.   1959. Linear programming models for the determination of palatable human diets. *Journal of Farm Economics* **41** (May), 272–283.

———.   1963. *Electronic computation of human diets*. East Lansing: Bureau of Business and Economic Research, Michigan State University. (Plus a detached supplement of 105 pages containing tabular material.)

Social Science Research Council.   1973. *Social Indicators Newsletter*, No. 1, March.

Sonquist, John A., and Morgan, James N.   1964. *The detection of interaction effects*. Monograph No. 35. Ann Arbor: Survey Research Center, University of Michigan.

Stone, Richard.   1966. *Mathematics in the social sciences and other essays*. Cambridge, Mass.: The M.I.T. Press.

———.   1971. *Demographic accounting and model-building*. Paris: Organization for Economic Co-operation and Development.

Szalai, Alexander, ed. (in collaboration with Philip E. Converse, Pierre Feldheim, Erwin K. Scheuch, and Philip J. Stone).   1973. *The use of time*. Publications of the European Coordination Centre for Research and Documentation in the Social Sciences. Volume 5. The Hague, Netherlands: Mouton.

Takayama, T., and Judge, G. G.   1971. *Spatial and temporal price and allocation models*. Amsterdam: North-Holland Publishing Company.

Taylor, Charles Lewis, and Hudson, Michael C.   1972. *World handbook of political and social indicators*. 2nd edition. New Haven, Conn.: Yale University Press.

Terleckyj, Nestor E.   1970. Measuring progress towards social goals: Some possibilities at national and local levels. *Management Science* **16** (August), B765–B778.

———.   1971. Measuring output of government activities. Paper presented at the International

Conference on Income and Wealth, Ronneby, Sweden, August 29, 1971. Washington, D.C.: National Planning Association. 28 pp. Mimeograph.

———. 1973a. Estimating possibilities for improvement in the quality of life in the United States, 1972–1981. *Looking Ahead* **20** (January), 1–12.

———. 1973b. *Estimates of possibilities for improvements in the quality of life in the United States, 1971–1981*. Washington, D.C.: National Planning Association. (Discussion draft No. 2, May 1973.)

Theil, Henri. 1956. On the theory of economic policy. *American Economic Review* **45** (May), 360–366.

———. 1958. *Economic forecasts and policy*. Amsterdam: North-Holland Publishing Company. 2nd edition, 1961.

———. 1964. *Optimal decision rules for government and industry*. Amsterdam: North-Holland Publishing Company.

Tinbergen, Jan. 1939. *Statistical testing of business cycle theories:* Volume I. *A method and its application to investment activity:* Volume II. *Business cycles in the United States of America, 1919–1932*. Geneva: League of Nations Economic Intelligence Service.

———. 1952. *On the theory of economic policy*. Amsterdam: North-Holland Publishing Company.

———. 1954. *Centralization and decentralization in economic policy*. Amsterdam: North-Holland Publishing Company.

———. 1956. *Economic policy: Principles and design*. Amsterdam: North-Holland Publishing Company.

Tunstall, Daniel B. 1971. Developing a social statistics publication. In *Social statistics proceedings of the American Statistical Association, 1970*. Washington, D.C.: American Statistical Association.

U.S. Bureau of the Census. 1968. *County and city data book, 1967* (A Statistical Abstract Supplement). Washington, D.C.: Government Printing Office.

———. 1972. *Public use sample of basic records from the 1970 census: Description and technical documentation*. Washington, D.C.: Government Printing Office.

U.S. Department of Health, Education, and Welfare. 1969. *Toward a social report*. Washington, D.C.: Government Printing Office.

U.S. Senate, 90th Congress, 1st session. 1967. *Hearings before the Subcommittee on Government Research of the Committee on Government Operations on S.B. S.843, the Full Opportunity and Social Accounting Act*. Part 1 (June 26, 1967), Part 2 (July 19, 20, and 26, 1967), and Part 3 (July 28, 1967).

Uzawa, Hirofumi. 1958. The Kuhn-Tucker theorem in concave programming. In Kenneth J. Arrow, Leonid Hurwicz, and Hirofumi Uzawa, eds., *Studies in linear and nonlinear programming*. Stanford: Stanford University Press.

Van Eijk, C. J., and Sandee, J. 1959. Quantitative determination of an optimum economic policy. *Econometrica* **27** (January), 1–13.

Van Moeseke, Paul. 1965. A general duality theorem of convex programming. *Metroeconomica* **17**, 161–170.

———. 1968. Towards a theory of efficiency. In A. Zarley and J. Quirk, eds., *Papers in quantitative economics*. Lawrence: University of Kansas Press.

Wagner, W. G., and Weathersby, G. B. 1971. Optimality in college planning: A control theoretic approach. Paper P-22. Berkeley: Ford Foundation Program for Research in University Administration, University of California.

Wallace, Henry A. 1920. *Agricultural prices*. Des Moines, Iowa: Wallace Publishing Company.

Washburn, S. L., and Avis, Virginia. 1958. Evolution of human behavior. In Anne Roe and George Gaylord Simpson, eds., *Behavior and evolution*. New Haven, Conn.: Yale University Press.

Waugh, Frederick V. 1935a. A simplified method of determining multiple regression constants. *Journal of the American Statistical Association* **30**, 694–700.

———. 1935b. The marginal utility of money in the United States from 1917 to 1921 and from 1922 to 1932. *Econometrica* **3**, 376–399.

———. 1942. Regressions between sets of variables. *Econometrica* **10**, 290–310.

———. 1951. The minimum-cost dairy feed (an application of "linear programming"). *Journal of Farm Economics* **33** (August), 299–310.

————. 1956. A partial indifference surface for beef and pork. *Journal of Farm Economics* **38** (February), 102–112.

White, Robert W., ed. 1963. *The study of lives: Essays on personality in honor of Henry A. Murray.* New York: Atherton Press.

Wilcox, Leslie D., Brooks, Ralph M., Beal, George M., and Klonglan, Gerald E. 1972. *Social indicators and societal monitoring: An annotated bibliography.* San Francisco: Jossey-Bass, and Amsterdam: Elsevier.

Williamson, Oliver E. 1963. Managerial discretion and business behavior. *American Economic Review* **53** (December), 1032–1057.

————. 1964. *The economics of discretionary behavior: Managerial objectives in a theory of the firm.* Englewood Cliffs, N.J.: Prentice-Hall.

Wold, Herman O. 1938. *A study in the analysis of stationary time series.* Uppsala: Almquist & Wiksells.

Wold, Herman O. 1956. Causal inference from observational data: A review of ends and means. *Journal of the Royal Statistical Society*, Series A.119, 28–60.

Wright, Sewall. 1921. Correlation and causation. *Journal of Agricultural Research* **20**, 557–585.

————. 1925. *Corn and hog correlations.* Bulletin 1300. Washington, D.C.: U.S. Department of Agriculture.

————. 1934. The method of path coefficients. *Annals of Mathematical Statistics* **5**, 161–215.

Zusman, P. 1967. The role of retail trade in the competitive system. In D. C. Hague, ed., *Price formation in various economies.* London: Macmillan Company Ltd., and New York: St. Martin's Press.

Zytowski, Donald G. 1970. The concept of work values. *Vocational Guidance Quarterly* **18** (March), 176–186.

Appendix

Some Comments on Related Literatures

THIS APPENDIX is a bibliographic essay. It introduces many references that are not directed specifically to social indicators, although they may prove useful—in some cases, basic—to the further development of the field. Most of these references are recent and some contain extensive bibliographies.

Section A.7 on disequilibrium, discontinuous social change, and comparisons over space and time contains many references to historical periods and situations marked by rapid—even abrupt—social transitions. These can be viewed as examples of periods in which social indicators would be most needed in principle, although they would be subjected at these times to the most severe dangers of conceptual erosion. Measurement problems are easiest when only quantities—not qualities—are changing. The section concludes with a very recent statement by a committee of the American Agricultural Economics Association that the data systems for agriculture and rural life are now in serious crisis.

The major categories in the appendix as a whole are (1) theories of measurement, aggregation, and utility, measurement of quality change, and mathematical social science; (2) statistical demand analysis and the analysis of causal relations; (3) theories of competitive equilibrium, lifetime income and choice, economic growth, optimal control, and human capital; (4) social learning theories, entitivity, and fuzzy sets; (5) hierarchies, decentralization, resource allocation, information theory, and the theory of teams; (6) welfare economics, public choice, and policy sciences; and (7) disequilibrium, discontinuous social change, and the obsolescence of social data systems.

A.1   Theories of Measurement, Aggregation, and Utility, Measurement of Quality Change, and Mathematical Social Science

The theory of measurement has become a subject of active inquiry among behavioral scientists in recent years. The most impressive contribution is the joint work of four authors, Krantz, Luce, Suppes, and Tversky (1).[1] Pfanzagl (2) is also concerned with the methodological foundation of measurement. Ijiri (3) is concerned with accounting measurement primarily in the context of business firms, but many of his concepts would be applicable to social accounts, as well. He also introduces such novel concepts as causal double-entry bookkeeping, multidimensional bookkeeping, and a *linear aggregation coefficient.*

Ijiri (4) reviews the recent literature on aggregation theory and provides a succinct description (p. 766) of the scope of the field, which is the study of *aggregation structures.* An aggregation structure consists of a *microsystem*, a *macrosystem*, and an *aggregation function*; the aggregation function relates the elements in the microsystem to those in the macrosystem. Theil (5) considered the possibility of a "perfect aggregation" of linear microeconomic equations that would agree precisely with the corresponding macroequation (which might appear in a model of a national economy). He found that perfect aggregation was possible under restricted conditions if, for example, national income is not taken as an exogenous aggregate but rather as a fixed-weight index of the individual incomes, each weighted "proportionally to the microparameters that are attached to them in the microequations." Expositions of Theil's approach are given by Allen (6, pp. 694–724) and at a less advanced level by Fox (7, pp. 495–536). Fisher (8) gives a recent and advanced treatment of clustering and aggregation in economics.

Fishburn (9) presents an excellent review of utility theory with more than 300 recent references. In a later book (10), he provides "a unifying upper-level text and a research-reference work" on utility theory at about the same mathematical level as Pfanzagl (2) and Krantz et al. (1). Von Neumann and Morgenstern (11) and Luce and Raiffa (12) treat utility theory in relation to the theory of games. Georgescu-Roegen's (13) encyclopedia article reviews utility theory as it developed historically within economics. Arrow (14) and Chipman (15) give modern treatments by economists. Fisher (16) was one of the first economists to propose "a statistical method for measuring marginal utility." Frisch (17, 18) made a similar proposal in more rigorous form and his method was applied to some United States national income data by Waugh (19). Fellner (20) makes a modern contribution in the Fisherian tradition.

Strotz (21, 22) considers the empirical implications of a *utility tree*—that is, a utility function that can be partitioned or separated into M mutually exclusive and exhaustive subsets or branches. This corresponds to the logic of making a family budget (so much for clothing, so much for food, etc.) and adhering to it strictly, or, alternatively, the logic of making budget allocations to the various divisions of a firm or departments of a university. Strotz's "strong" definition of separability (Ref. 22, p. 482) is as follows:

A utility function

(1) $$U = U(q_1, \ldots, q_N)$$

is separable in the branches $A, B, \ldots, M$ if it can be written as

(2) $$U = U[V^A(q_{a_1}, \ldots, q_{a_\alpha}), V^B(q_{b_1}, \ldots, q_{b_\beta}), \ldots, V^M(q_{m_1}, \ldots, q_{m_\mu})];$$

... (the V's are called branch utilities) ... and such that the value of any q

---

[1] Numbers in parentheses designate Appendix bibliography references.

in a given branch cannot affect the marginal rate of substitution between any two commodities not in that branch. Thus, for example,

$$
(4) \qquad \partial \left(\frac{\partial U / \partial q_a}{\partial U / \partial q_b} \right) \Big/ \partial q_m = 0, \qquad q_m \in M; \qquad q_b, \; q_b \notin M.
$$

Strong separability has important implications for decentralization and aggregation. Strotz's 1959 article, from which this definition is quoted, corrects an error in his 1957 article that had been pointed out by Gorman (23). Frisch (24) and Brandow (25) used the same assumption of strong separability to synthesize complete systems of elasticities and cross-elasticities of demand (by a consumer) for all goods and services. George and King (26) assume strong separability between commodity groups but estimate cross elasticities empirically for commodities within a group; they also furnish an excellent review of the literature on theory and measurement of consumer demand through 1968.

Cochrane and Zeleny (27) include 59 papers presented at an October 1972 conference on multiple-criteria decision making. One of these, by MacCrimmon (28), gives an overview of methods available to a decision maker who values several objectives in connection with a single choice (e.g., the purchase of an automobile, in which appearance, prestige, economy, comfort, and dependability are desired). Possibilities include at least the following: (a) lexicographic ordering, in which one objective (say, economy) dominates the rest and will be met in full, after which a second (say, dependability) is met so far as possible, and a third is considered only if, or after, the second has been met in full; (b) goal programming, in which one or more targets must be met in full, after which an objective function containing the rest of the desired qualities is optimized; and (c) optimization of a function which includes all the desired objectives simultaneously, as in Theil's (*1958*) specification of the utility function of a policy maker.[2] Most of the other papers in the volume are also of high quality. One of the outstanding early treatments of goal programming is that by Ijiri (29).

Griliches (30) edited a volume of recent studies on the measurement of quality change and the adjustments in price indexes logically required to allow for it; the volume includes an extensive bibliography. Griliches (31) and Adelman and Griliches (32) also deal with the quality problem. Court (33) raised the question in connection with automobiles and constructed a "hedonic price index" to allow for the improved performance and comfort built into successive models of "the same car" (a Chevrolet, say) over a period of 20 or 30 years.

Griliches (31) viewed passenger cars as clusters of attributes and used multiple regression analysis to estimate the prices consumers were implicitly willing to pay for each feature. Lancaster's (34–36) new approach to consumer demand consists "in viewing goods as intermediaries which can produce the properties or characteristics in which the consumer is actually interested. People buy goods to obtain a particular collection of characteristics." Smith (37–39) had used the same concept in a more specialized connection—interpreting consumer demand for food as a demand for specified food nutrients. Waugh (40) treated various feedstuffs as sources of stipulated nutrients in his linear programming analysis of the "minimum-cost dairy feed."

---

[2] When the date of a reference is shown in italics, the reference will be found in the alphabetical listing of *text* references beginning on page 266 but not in the bibliography for this appendix.

Earlier, Waugh (41) had used canonical correlation to relate several measurable attributes of wheat to desired attributes of flour.

A few standard works of a mathematical nature are also listed in this section. Three of these are directly concerned with the social sciences: James S. Coleman, *Introduction to Mathematical Sociology* (42); Nathan Keyfitz, *Introduction to the Mathematics of Population* (43); and Paul F. Lazarsfeld and Neil W. Henry, editors, *Readings in Mathematical Social Science* (44). Alfred J. Lotka's classic, *Elements of Mathematical Biology* (45), is amazingly insightful and relevant to present concerns over the impacts of human population growth on the environment.

A.2   Statistical Demand Analysis and the Analysis of Causal Relations

The first successes in applied econometrics were statistical analyses of demand, supply, and price interrelationships for farm products. The leading academic figures in this development were Henry L. Moore and Henry Schultz (see Section 14.2). However, the center of empirical work in this field in the 1920s and 1930s and of much practically oriented work on methodology was the U.S. Bureau of Agricultural Economics.[3] The empirical work of Henry Schultz and a few economists in the land grant colleges was also noteworthy.

The new method of multiple regression analysis was adapted for clerical pools using desk calculators by Tolley and Ezekiel (46) and Ezekiel (47). Bean (48) developed a simplified method of graphic curvilinear regression analysis. In the following year, Ezekiel published his *Methods of Correlation Analysis* (49) which, according to Waugh (50), "for many years was the bible of those using least squares methods." Frisch and Waugh (51) demonstrated that the addition of time as a variable in a linear multiple regression equation yielded the same partial regression coefficients between the substantive variables as if a linear trend had been removed from each variable separately and an equation had been fitted to the deviations from the trends. Waugh (52) published a simplified method of determining multiple regression constants using the inverse correlation matrix. B. B. Smith (53) of the BAE produced a manual on the use of punched card tabulating equipment in multiple correlation problems; Wallace and Snedecor (54) of Iowa State College published a manual on correlation and machine calculation two years later.

Some of the earliest empirical demand studies were made by Holbrook Working (55), Waugh (56), Schultz (57), Wright (58), and Haas and Ezekiel (59). A trilogy of excellent methodological articles was written for the *Quarterly Journal of Economics* by Holbrook Working (60), E. J. Working (61), and Ezekiel (62). Schultz (63) made perhaps the first use of "weighted regressions" in economics, and Warren and

[3] In this section, I shall mean by "the BAE economists" of the 1920s and 1930s primarily the following people: Howard R. Tolley, Mordecai Ezekiel, Bradford B. Smith, Louis H. Bean, Frederick V. Waugh, and Foster F. Elliott. Many others were involved in the development of statistical demand and supply analysis in BAE, but usually for limited times or in particular commodity areas. Ezekiel and Waugh made the most numerous and influential contributions to scientific publications such as the *Journal of the American Statistical Association*, *Quarterly Journal of Economics*, *Econometrica*, and *American Economic Review*, but the others were also able and gifted men.

After 1945, by "the BAE economists" I shall mean primarily Richard J. Foote, Frederick V. Waugh, and Karl A. Fox. Richard C. Taeuber, Marc Nerlove, and Richard H. Day were also employed by BAE's successor agency for brief periods, when they wrote the publications cited.

Pearson (64) published empirical demand curves for a number of farm products. Elliott (65) wrote a scholarly article on the nature and measurement of the elasticity of supply of farm products, and Bean (66) contributed an ingenious one on the farmer's response to price, showing evidence of lagged effects of prices both two years and one year in advance of the current season.

More sophisticated topics were handled in the 1930s. Ezekiel (67) contributed an article on the analysis of prices of competing or substitute commodities to Volume 1 of *Econometrica*; the same volume contained an article by Schultz (68) on a comparison of elasticities of demand obtained by different methods and the article by Frisch and Waugh (51) already mentioned. Ezekiel and Bean (69) applied their expertise to a report on the economic bases for the Agricultural Adjustment Act on behalf of the new Secretary of Agriculture, Henry A. Wallace. Waugh, Burtis, and Wolf (70) combined economic theory with empirical demand functions in a paper on the controlled distribution of a crop among independent markets, and Ezekiel (71) published a classic paper on the "cobweb theorem."

The economic emergency of the Great Depression drew Ezekiel, Bean, and others out of research and into policy. World War II and its aftermath dispersed the former BAE economists among a number of national and international agencies.

After 1945 the tradition of empirical demand analysis in BAE was resumed by a younger group, later reinforced by the return of F. V. Waugh from the Council of Economic Advisers in 1952. Reports by Foote and Fox (72) on seasonal adjustment, by Fox and Cooney (73) on the effects of intercorrelation, by Foote and Fox (74) on analytical tools for measuring demand, by Foote (75) on the same subject, and by Nerlove (76) on distributed lags and demand analysis continued the tradition of work on new techniques. Substantive work on demand analysis was represented by Fox (77–82).

Waugh (*1951*) introduced linear programming to agricultural economists in an article on the minimum-cost dairy feed. Fox and Norcross (83) displayed the major relationships between agriculture and the rest of the economy in an input–output context. Fox (84, 85) and Fox and Taeuber (86) published empirical models of spatial price equilibrium and interregional trade, and Fox (87) illustrated the same model in connection with international trade. Waugh (88) estimated a community indifference surface for pork and beef. Richard H. Day's classic study, *Recursive Programming and Production Response* (89), was also written under the auspices of BAE's successor agency.

Systems of empirical demand and supply functions underlay publications by Fox (90–92) and Fox and Wells (93) on the measurement of price support costs, interactions between agriculture and the rest of the economy, and appropriate reserve levels for storable farm products. The same bases were used in reports by Fox (94–98) on guiding agricultural adjustments, agricultural income, economic instability and agricultural adjustment, prospects for commercial agriculture, and a submodel of the agricultural sector for an econometric model of the United States. Input–output analysis was applied to the food and agricultural sectors of the United States by Fox (99).

Some of the most useful surveys of the history and contributions of statistical demand analysis are to be found in Fox (100), Ezekiel and Fox (101), Waugh (52, 102), Fox (103), and Fox and Johnson (104). Fox (7) may be considered as an extension of the tradition established by Ezekiel's *Methods of Correlation Analysis* (*1930*).

The works by Victor E. Smith (37–39), George Brandow (25), and George and King (26) mentioned in Section A.1, were done in universities, but in my judgment, they reflect the same spirit that characterized the BAE tradition—an effort to make the best possible integration of theory, methods, and data.

The Analysis of Causal Relations.   The BAE (and other) demand and supply analysts of the 1920s listed previously were quite clear about problems of identification and causal ordering so far as they affected the appropriateness of their estimation techniques. For many farm products, time lags were clearly marked by the seasonality of production inputs and the perishability of marketable outputs under the technologies then available. The easy cases from a methodological standpoint were also those of the greatest practical importance. The trilogy by H. Working (60), E. J. Working (61), and Ezekiel (62) indicates that all three investigators knew *why* their methods were appropriate in these cases. Ezekiel (67) used causal ordering principles correctly in estimating demand functions for two competing commodities, and, according to Waugh (102), Ezekiel's 1938 article (71) on the cobweb theorem "still stands as a landmark in the theory of prices and production."

Sewall Wright (105) was well acquainted with the BAE group and was mentioned in the preface to Ezekiel (49) as one of those who had contributed to the development of the new multiple regression methods; mentioned in the same sentence were Donald Bruce, Fred Waugh, Louis Bean, and Andrew Court. Bradford B. Smith is mentioned in the preceding sentence in essentially the same context.

Trained as a geneticist, Wright went on to achieve international distinction in that field. On three occasions, Wright (58, 106, and in Ref. 107) applied his method of path coefficients to the empirical estimation of demand and supply relations in multiple equation systems. In principle, Wright's method could be generalized to any number of equations and any number of causal orders.

In recent years, Wright's brilliant and powerful approach has been exceedingly fruitful in the hands of sociologists and has spread rapidly in educational research and to some extent in political science; economists and sociologists have collaborated on some recent applications, including Hauser and Goldberger (108) and Griliches and Mason (109). Goldberger (110) chides his fellow economists for their almost complete neglect of Wright's work.

I believe that the multiple regression approach of the BAE economists was perfectly appropriate and quite adequate for the simple econometric structures that were important to them in the 1920s and 1930s. Also, the data system for food and agriculture still had important gaps, and data for the rest of the country's economy were pitifully inadequate; in no sense did they form a *system* until Kuznets (*1937*) began to publish his time series on the national income and its components, Tinbergen (*1939*) constructed his econometric model of the United States, and Leontief (*1936, 1951*) gained support for his work on input–output models.

Ezekiel (111) used the new income data for a major article on statistical investigations of saving, consumption and investment, which led to an exchange with Klein (112, 113; see, also Ezekiel, Ref. 114). For expository purposes, Koopmans (115) later showed that Ezekiel's six-equation model was formally identifiable and that Ezekiel had chosen predetermined variables in such a pattern that the model could indeed be estimated by least squares.

It is one of the minor ironies in the development of econometrics that World War

II, which made it possible to bring together at the Cowles Commission a brilliant constellation of European economists, completed the dispersal of the BAE economists into action agencies and administrative positions here and abroad. In particular, Ezekiel moved permanently to Rome in 1946, where he helped his early mentor, H. R. Tolley, establish the Economics Division of the Food and Agricultural Organization. Much earlier, others had moved into private industry, universities, and action agencies. Henry Schultz of the University of Chicago, a personal friend of Sewall Wright, had died in 1938. The new econometricians knew almost nothing of the earlier BAE tradition; moreover, they were primarily interested in macroeconomic models and saw little to gain by reading old bulletins and articles about demand and supply structures for farm products. They might reasonably have been criticized for ignoring Wright's 1934 article in the *Annals of Mathematical Statistics* but not for neglecting his 1925 U.S. Department of Agriculture bulletin, *Corn and Hog Correlations*, or his contribution to the appendix of his father's 1928 book, *The Tariff on Animal and Vegetable Oils* (107). As a final touch of irony, we should note that during the height of the Cowles Commission's activity at the University of Chicago, Sewall Wright held the title of Ernest D. Burton Distinguished Service Professor of Zoology at that institution!

I read and admired Wright's 1921 article in 1941. In 1947 I began drawing arrow diagrams like Figure A.1 as a prelude to statistical estimation of demand functions for a large number of farm and food products. These causal ordering diagrams were used to determine whether the relationships of interest to me were logically identifiable. I included 15 such diagrams in a doctoral dissertation (Fox, 116) and subsequently published them (Fox, 80, 100). A BAE staff member from 1945 to 1954, I found Wright's work quite compatible with the BAE tradition, as well as a source of insight into the new simultaneous equations approach, and in 1958 I wrote:

> In view of the turn that demand analysis has taken since 1943, with its emphasis on causal or structural relationships, I believe the work of Sewall Wright deserves increased attention.
>
> In his 1921 article, "Correlation and causation," Wright was also dealing with the problem of estimating causal relationships under circumstances in which it was impossible to eliminate other sources of variation in order to isolate the direct effects of one variable upon another. His diagram on page 560 of that article is a logical forerunner both of the diagrams I use in Chapters 4 and 5 and of the diagrams and equations used by Simon in his 1953 paper on "Causal ordering and identifiability." In the same sense, his "method of path coefficients" may be considered a forerunner of the whole simultaneous equations approach (Ref. 100, p. 17.)

Herman Wold, who had published an article on demand analysis (in Swedish) in 1940, had by far the greatest influence from 1946 on in demonstrating to econometricians the continued usefulness of single equation methods in recursive or "causal chain" models (117–124). A classic paper by Simon (125) also had a major impact. Publications by Fox (77, 116, 80, 81, 91, 100) and by Foote and Fox (74) probably had some influence in the same direction among agricultural economists. Richard Stone (126, 127), who had begun work on demand analysis by 1940, also used single equation methods for appropriate reasons. Hence continuity of a tradition in econometric analysis that began with Moore and was elaborated by the BAE economists,

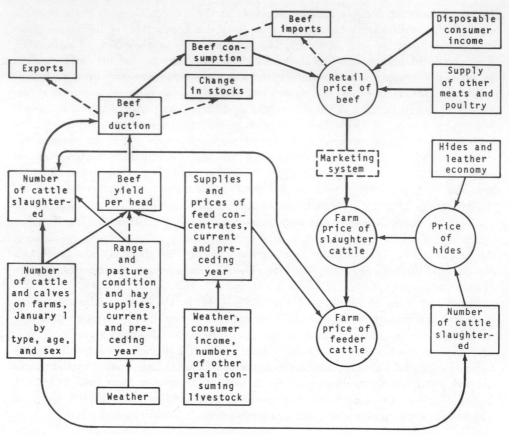

Figure A.1.   The demand and supply structure for beef. Arrows show direction of influence. Heavy arrows indicate major paths of influence that account for the bulk of variation in current prices. Light solid arrows indicate definite but less important paths. Dashed arrows indicate paths of negligible, doubtful, or occasional importance. *Source.* Karl A. Fox, *The Analysis of Demand for Farm Products*, Technical Bulletin No. 1081. Washington, D. C.: U.S. Department of Agriculture, September 1953, p. 34.

Schultz, and a few others—and by Sewall Wright in his very distinctive fashion—was provided by a new generation of demand analysts.

References to classic books and articles on the causal analysis of economic models based on time series include Frisch (128), Haavelmo (129, 130), Koopmans (131), and Hood and Koopmans (132). Waugh (50, 102) supplies valuable perspective on the history of demand analysis and of cobweb or recursive models from the 1920s into the 1960s.

More recent expositions and discussions of path analysis are contained in Wright (133–135), Tukey (136), Duncan (137), and Goldberger (110). Alker (138) makes illustrative applications of path analysis to examples from political science, and Sewell and Hauser (139) apply the method to data on the further educations, incomes, and occupations of a cohort of graduates from Wisconsin high schools. Collections of expository articles on causal and structural equation models in the social sciences are contained in volumes edited by Blalock (140) and Goldberger and Duncan (141).

A.3   Theories of Competitive Equilibrium, Lifetime Income and Choice, Economic Growth, Optimal Control, and Human Capital

Theories of equilibrium or homeostasis are important in many fields of science and have been highly developed in economics. Arrow and Hahn (142) is the standard work currently on general competitive analysis and has a substantial bibliography. There are, of course, many other expositions on many different levels in economics texts and monographs. Malinvaud (143) gives an excellent treatment with somewhat less use of formal mathematics.

Kornai (144) calls for the reconstruction of economic theory on a broader and more realistic, but no less mathematical, base to include concepts drawn from organization theory, the behavioral theory of the firm, and systems analysis. Hahn (145) responds to Kornai's critique of general equilibrium (GE) theory in a substantial and constructive review article, stating that extensions of GE theory are now being made to include dynamic and stochastic elements and alternative information structures (i.e., Kornai had underestimated the capacity of GE theory to deal with these problems), but that some of Kornai's ideas for broadening the scope of economic theory were "very good indeed" (p. 330).

In Chapter 6, we discussed briefly the notion of a "life plan." Samuelson (146) and Merton (147) have considered this problem, as have Yaari (148, 149) and Meade (150). Some of their papers view a life plan as a special kind of "portfolio selection" problem. The pioneer work on portfolio selection is Markowitz (151). I have included later references by Lintner (152) and Mossin (153). Koopmans (154) gives an advanced theoretical treatment of "stationary ordinal utility and impatience."

The choice of appropriate discount rates for evaluating alternative investments is a difficult one. Cohn (155) gives a clear, nontechnical exposition of various alternatives and their limitations. Eckstein's (156) survey of the theory of public expenditure criteria is still an excellent introduction to this problem area. Arrow and Kurz (157) offer a new formulation of the problem of public expenditures in the context of modern growth theory. They pose the issues by regarding them "as the dynamic analogue of Tinbergen's theory of economic policy," indicating that under certain assumptions "it is possible to calculate what may be termed the *publicly optimal policy*."

A number of originally separate literatures converge around modern economic growth theory (158–160), the mathematical theory of optimal processes (161), stochastic control theory (162, 163), and some aspects of systems theory (164). Fox, Sengupta, and Thorbecke included a chapter on "the control theory approach to the theory of economic policy with applications to optimal growth and stabilization policies" in their first edition, published in 1966; this chapter has been expanded and brought up to date in Fox, Sengupta, and Thorbecke (165).

By 1972 several young economists had noted that when Tinbergen's theory of economic policy is applied to a sequence of time periods in the presence of random disturbances, it becomes formally equivalent to what Athans (162) calls the "linear-quadratic-Gaussian" model of stochastic control theory. Van den Bogaard and Theil (166) had applied a similar model in their illustrative study of macrodynamic policy making for a national economy. Åström and Eykhoff (167) give an extensive survey of identification problems encountered in control systems engineering and note their similarities to the identification problems in econometrics; they list 230 references, mostly from the engineering literature. Athans (162) also provides an extensive bibliography.

Tintner and Sengupta, in *Stochastic Economics* (163), present a major chapter (93 pages) on stochastic control theory, as well as extensive references, primarily to works by economists. I have also included a reference to a basic paper by Kalman (168).

A life plan involves many choices between alternative investments—of time and other resources as well as money. Systematic study of these investments in "human capital" was stimulated by T. W. Schultz (169–173) and Gary Becker (174) and has been pursued by many other economists with initial emphasis on the economic value of education but later extending into health, welfare, and other fields. The *Journal of Human Resources* was founded in 1966 to serve as a forum for the analysis of this extended range of problems. Logically, some of these problems should be studied from the standpoint of portfolio selection and optimal control theory, in addition to what are now—thanks to Schultz and Becker—more conventional approaches.

A.4   Social Learning Theories, Entitivity, and Fuzzy Sets

Some rather heterogeneous references are mentioned in connection with social learning theories, entitivity, and fuzzy sets.

Estes (175) surveys recent research and theories about how individuals form estimates of the probabilities of events as a basis for action and supplies a bibliography of 85 items, primarily from the work of psychologists. Arrow (176) makes a very simple suggestion that people "learn by doing." In an economic development context, we learn by producing GNP, and the cumulative record of a country's GNP over a recent period of years is the best evidence of what has been learned (both at the individual level and at the level of organizations and institutions) that is economically relevant.

Dunn has written a stimulating book, *Economic and Social Development: A Process of Social Learning* (177), in which he concludes that social science must begin to apply learning models to the analysis and control of social processes:

> When we are faced with the reality of the social learning process . . . it becomes evident that since social systems are frequently temporary systems, less emphasis needs to be given to the nature and design of optimum transfer networks and more to the design of adaptable networks—systems that can be more easily adapted to the requirements of new social goals and controls (p. 247).

Dunn gives considerable attention to the concept of *entitivity* in social systems, noting the impossibility of identifying or defining many such systems in terms of observable physical boundaries. Entitivity, he says, "is the ratio of the endogenous linkages mediated directly by the boundary conditions of a system and the exogenous linkages that link subsystems directly with external systems not subject to the direct control of the given system boundary" (Ref. 177, pp. 196–197). Formal hierarchies are based on a different perception of reality that makes little allowance for overlapping boundaries.

Zadeh (178–182) has proposed the concept of *fuzzy sets* as "a natural way of dealing with problems in which the source of imprecision is the absence of sharply defined criteria of class membership rather than the presence of random variables" (178, p. 339). He has published many papers since 1965 extending his approach. The 1973 article (181) is a lucid exposition of his system as it then stood, and it summarizes many of the results reported in his earlier papers.

In 1973 Zadeh's approach had three main distinguishing features: (1) the use of so-called linguistic variables (e.g., *tall, not tall, very tall*) whose values are statements in a natural or artificial language, in place of or in addition to numerical variables; (2) characterization of relations between such variables by "fuzzy conditional statements" (e.g., if *x* is *small*, then *y* is *large*, where *small* and *large* are viewed as labels of fuzzy sets); and (3) characterization of complex relations by "fuzzy algorithms." Zadeh describes the potential of his system as follows:

> By relying on the use of linguistic variables and fuzzy algorithms, the approach provides an approximate and yet effective means of describing the behavior of systems which are too complex or too ill-defined to admit of precise mathematical analysis. Its main applications lie in economics, management science, artificial intelligence, psychology, linguistics, information retrieval, medicine, biology, and other fields in which the dominant role is played by the animate rather than the inanimate behavior of system constituents. (Ref. 181, p. 688.)

Zadeh (178, pp. 338–339) stated that a fuzzy set is characterized by a *membership function* that associates with each point in a space of points (objects) a real number in the interval [0, 1], with the value of this number representing the "grade of membership" of the point in the set; the closer to unity, the higher the grade of membership. In ordinary set theory, this value would be either 1 or 0, according to whether the point did or did not belong to the set. Zadeh extended the notions of inclusion, union, intersection, complement, and convexity to fuzzy sets and proved "a separation theorem for convex fuzzy sets . . . without requiring that the fuzzy sets be disjoint." Zadeh's approach may hold considerable promise for dealing with the entitivity problem posed by Dunn, including the representation of transitions from one authority system to another (e.g., from church to state control, in the Middle Ages) or from community organization based on the horse and buggy to community organization based on the automobile.

Roberts and Holdren, in *Theory of Social Process: An Economic Analysis* (183), have attempted to incorporate learning theory into a revised version of utility theory. They state that received utility theory assumes preferences as given, whereas it is clear that "all preferences are learned." They have written that "Current utility theory views the process of going from the knowledge set to the action set as utility maximization. [Our] objective . . . is to generalize the process of going from the knowledge set to the action set and to specify the process of going from experiences to the knowledge set" (pp. 13–14).

A.5 Hierarchies, Decentralization, Resource Allocation, Information Theory, and the Theory of Teams

There are vast literatures on hierarchies and some of the related topics. I will mention only a few examples out of many that are relevant to the context of this book.

Some classic works on administrative behavior (Barnard, *1938*; Simon, *1947*) and organizations (March and Simon, *1958*; March, *1965*) were mentioned in Chapter 4. To these I would add Downs's *Inside Bureaucracy* (184), which is widely known among social scientists, and a very different kind of book by Chandler (185).

Chandler made intensive studies of the histories of four very large corporations: General Motors, DuPont, Standard Oil of New Jersey, and Sears, Roebuck. He states:

> The comparison emphasizes that a company's strategy in time determined its structure and that the common denominator of structure and strategy has been the application of the enterprise's resources to market demand. Structure has been the design for integrating the enterprise's existing resources to current demand; strategy has been the plan for the allocation of resources to anticipated demand. (Ref. 190, p. 383.)

Chandler surveyed 70 other large corporations in a more cursory fashion. He concluded that in most cases, as corporations grew in size and in product diversity, the following situation developed:

> Each major product line came to be administered through a separate, integrated autonomous division. Its manager became responsible for the major operating decisions involved in the coordination of functional activities to changing demand and taste. Expansion into new regions encouraged the formation of comparable divisions for comparable reasons. Yet, as the different geographical markets became more homogeneous (and this occurred as all parts of the United States became more industrial and more urbanized and suburbanized), the regionally defined divisions in petroleum, dairy products, and container enterprises tended to combine into a single unit for one line of products. (Ref. 185, p. 393.)

Strategic decisions were systematized through the building of a general office, and "the formation of a research department . . . institutionalized the strategy of diversification" (p. 394).

Simon (186) gives a broad philosophical discussion of hierarchy in biological and social systems as "the architecture of complexity." Mesarovic, Macko, and Takahara (187) present a theory of hierarchical, multilevel systems in mathematical form, drawing on the literatures of economics, organization theory, and control systems engineering. Kornai and Liptak (188) discuss two-level planning in a mathematical programming format; their objective is to allocate centrally controlled flexible resources in an optimal manner among sectors or divisions, each one having some fixed or specialized resources that cannot be transferred. McCamley (189) applied this approach to a hypothetical model of the optimal allocation of college-level resources among academic departments.

Kumar (190, 191) reviews the theory of resource allocation in linear static and in nonlinear and dynamic models in the context of universities and other nonmarket systems. In the same volume, Sengupta (192) considers a number of problems of resource allocation in nonmarket systems, including those of decentralization and aggregation.

Some fundamental contributions to the economic literature on decentralization have been made by Arrow and Hurwicz (193), Hurwicz (194), and Malinvaud (195).

Gruver (196) discusses linear methods of decentralization in economic decision models. Heal (197) systematically treats the theory of economic planning, giving considerable attention to decentralized planning procedures. Tinbergen's (198) theory of the optimum regime is a classic statement of the aspects of economic systems that must be dealt with in both capitalist and socialist nations; by providing a terminology and a conceptual framework with operational content, he attempted to encourage scientific and objective discussion among economists from countries of both types, and his hopes have been realized to a considerable extent in recent years.

Jacob Marschak has made pioneering contributions to several successive phases of the development of econometrics. In Marschak (199), he summarizes recent work by himself and others on the economics of information systems, including, but not limited to, the information and decision systems of organizations; a reference list of 56 items is provided. Important related papers were included by McGuire and Radner in *Decision and Organization: A Volume in Honor of Jacob Marschak* (200), which they edited.

Marschak and Radner (201) have published the basic work on the economic theory of *teams*. This is intended as a step toward a broader and more complex economic theory of organization:

> First, the kind of information on the basis of which each member of an organization decides about his actions may differ from one member to another. . . .
>
> Second, the interests and beliefs of each member of an organization may differ from the interests and beliefs of his fellow members.
>
> A team is defined as an organization in which the first but not the second characteristic is present. . . .
>
> Accordingly, the bulk of the book is concerned with economic, that is, optimal, efficient ways of providing information and of allocating it among the decision-makers who constitute a team: optimal, that is, with respect to common interests and beliefs. (Ref. 206, p. ix.)

To this list we should add Theil's *Economics and Information Theory* (202), also a highly original work. The author points out that the problem of allocating scarce resources to alternative ends can be formulated in terms of the *share* of the total quantity of each resource that is to be allocated to each end. Such shares are nonnegative and add up to unity; in this respect they are formally equivalent to probabilities. Theil pursues this topic by means of concepts derived from information theory, a branch of probability theory developed by communications engineers.

A.6 Welfare Economics, Public Choice, and Policy Sciences

Welfare economics penetrates many areas of interest relevant to social indicators and social accounts. Arrow and Scitovsky's (203) *Readings in Welfare Economics* provides a wide range of selections from the modern literature in this field. To this we may add *Economic Theories of International Politics* (204), a book edited by Russett and containing 29 readings from areas of overlap between economics, political science, and (in some cases) sociology. Dorfman and Dorfman (205) present 26 readings on the economics of the environment; several of these apply or elucidate concepts associated with welfare economics, such as divergence between social cost and private cost, externalities, neighborhood effects, and public goods.

One starting point for the social indicators movement was Bauer's (*1966*) observation that "*for many of the important topics . . . on which policies are made, there are no yardsticks by which to know if things are getting better or worse*" (p. 20). Much of the current interest in social measurement is based on the expectation that the results will clarify problems of social policy, legislation, and the allocation of public expenditures—in a word, problems of public choice. In a democracy, public choice involves electoral politics, voting rules in legislative committees, and other elements of prime interest to political scientists. However, economists are also interested in public choice from the standpoint of translating the preferences of individuals into patterns of taxation and public expenditure that are "good," "better," or even "optimal" (according to certain criteria) in implementing those preferences. Economists are also acutely aware that a large fraction of the GNP (more than 20 percent in the United States during the early 1970s) goes for purchases of goods and services by federal, state, and local governments. Hence the actual allocation of economic resources involves voting mechanisms as well as market mechanisms.

Arrow (206) makes a fundamental contribution to the theory of public choice, using relatively advanced mathematical demonstrations. Downs (207) avoids mathematics and formulates "a generalized yet realistic behavior rule for a rational government similar to the rules traditionally used for rational consumers and producers." He seeks to integrate government "with private decision makers in a general equilibrium theory" (p. 3).

Buchanan and Tullock (208) are the leading contributors to what is sometimes called the new public finance. They apply the conceptual apparatus of economics to an investigation of the logical foundations of constitutional democracy in their 1962 book, and they are the coauthors of a number of articles. Buchanan (209) is concerned with analyzing the effects of various fiscal institutions on individual behavior in collective choice situations. In addition he has written (210) the standard work on the demand and supply of public goods (i.e., goods and services supplied and demanded through political institutions).

Olson (211) presents a remarkably well-balanced synthesis of concepts from economics, sociology, and political science in his classic analysis of the logic of collective action. He points out that a large organization of any kind that achieves a common goal or satisfies a common interest of its members has ipso facto provided a public or collective good for them: "A state is first of all an organization that provides public goods for its members, the citizens; and other types of organizations similarly provide collective goods for their members" (p. 15).

Almond (212) takes a major step forward in the conceptual framework and vocabulary of political science with his "functional approach to comparative politics." Such conventional terms as "state," "powers," and "offices" had legal and institutional connotations stemming from the political culture of Western Europe but inappropriate for the developing areas; Almond substituted "political systems," "functions," and "roles," respectively. Similarly, for the terms "institutions," "public opinion," and "citizenship training" he substitutes "structures," "political culture," and "political socialization." The new concepts, he says, lend themselves to the development of "a probabilistic theory of the polity" (p. 58) and "a formal theory of political modernization . . . which would improve our capacity to predict the trend of political development in modernizing states from carefully selected indicators" (p. 63); the polities of all nations could be compared in empirically testable ways and the regional divisions of the study of politics (e.g., Latin American or African "area studies") would become obsolete.

Easton (213) describes his book as the third work in a long-range project on empirically oriented political theory. He regards political life as an open and adaptive system surrounded by a variety of environments and subject to stresses from them. He uses concepts from general systems theory (e.g., inputs, outputs, and feedback) to link potentially measurable indicators of inputs (demands and support) and outputs (policies, decisions, and actions) of a political system. The resulting theory seems to be sufficiently general to apply to all types of political system.

Almond and Easton were major contributors to a scientific revolution in the study of political systems that gathered momentum during the 1960s and early 1970s. Harold Lasswell's contributions to political science began in the 1920s and his influence subsequently extended to many other fields. We have noted in Chapter 4 that Isard et al. (*1969*) based their list of "noneconomic commodities" primarily on Lasswell's work. Lasswell also conceptualized the field of "policy sciences," which is attracting considerable interest (in the United States, at least) as of 1974. The term was first given currency in Lerner and Lasswell (214).

Lasswell (215) states that the policy sciences "study the process of deciding or choosing and evaluate the relevance of available knowledge for the solution of particular problems" (p. 181). Lasswell (216) presents a more extended discussion of the field. The policy sciences "are concerned with knowledge *of* and *in* the decision processes of the public and civic order" (p. 2). *Public order* decisions are those made by formal agencies of government; *civic order* decisions are those made by semiofficial or nonofficial processes. For example, decisions nominally made by government often register determinations made outside government in various organizations and pressure groups.

Dror (217, 218) is the most energetic protagonist of the policy sciences approach, which, he says, is "a new supradiscipline based on novel scientific paradigms. . . . Policy sciences is concerned with the contribution of systematic knowledge, structured rationality and organized creativity to better policymaking" (217, preface). Dror (218) presents many applications of his approach under such major headings as "a policy sciences view of planning" and policy sciences views of (respectively) futures studies, behavioral sciences, law, and modernization.

A.7 Disequilibrium, Discontinuous Social Change, and the Obsolescence of Social Data Systems

Richard L. Meier (219) presents a sweeping review of the present state of knowledge concerning *communications stress*:

> The central problem that underlies the phenomena associated with communications stress is posed by the rapid and unprecedented transitions now under way in the ecosystem of this planet. Much attention has been paid recently to critical situations arising out of the expansion of human

population size . . . but little effort has been expended in investigating the effects of a much greater growth rate, that of communications—or meaningful interaction. Communications seem to be required for humans to make all the needed adaptations to a continuously modified environment . . . (p. 289).

The conventions of biology and the sociobehavioral sciences identify seven hierarchic *levels* of discourse concerning the organization of living systems: cells, organs or tissues, organisms, groups, organizations, societies, and supranational systems . . . (p. 292).

Meier proceeds to discuss communications stress at each level in turn; he includes a substantial list of references and concludes that:

The risk of communications stress can be regarded as a price to be paid for enhanced social integration, increased levels of cooperation, and reduced costs of conflict. . . .

Perhaps equally important is the observation that violent conflict can be evaded much more easily when the principal parties are well informed . . . (p. 311).

The purpose of this section is to stimulate thinking about the robustness of prospective systems of social accounts and indicators with respect to the changes that are and will be taking place over time and to the comparisons that must be made across nations and political systems as guides to international cooperation in promoting human well-being.

Some of the references listed below are, in my judgment, the best that might be cited to illustrate my points; others may be more or less random drawings from a class of relevant works.

E. A. J. Johnson, in his distinctive and distinguished book, *The Organization of Space in Developing Countries* (220), describes five types of *landscape* in human geography that reflect five different dominant principles or underlying purposes: military, sacerdotal, juridical, administrative, and "a hierarchy of markets." (In Barker's sense, these reflect different authority systems.)

If military control of an area is the principal object of policy, the landscape "will be studded with forts, castles, cantonments, and other military or paramilitary institutions strategically located" (p. 1). If a priestly group controls the people living in a given area, its chief concern will be "to propagate some ethical doctrine," and the landscape will be divided into units appropriate to this objective (e.g., the network of dioceses and parishes established in Christianized Europe), "each with its complement of clergy" (p. 1).

Another type of landscape results when juridical institutions are the organizing principle:

If justice is to be administered in a territory, a network of courts, assizes, and other adjudicative agencies must be created and sustained to assure an operative set of procedures. This juridical structure will perforce require provisional or permanent political jurisdictions within which courts can function and wherein, if appeals are permitted, a hierarchy of appellate jurisdictions will link the whole complex into a juridical system (p. 2).

Administrative control over both land and people in a dependent area is a fourth organizing principle, although it must obviously be based on power, which may have been achieved by military force or sacerdotal persuasion in the applicable contexts. In either case, if the population is reasonably acquiescent, the landscape will be under the influence of "collectors" (e.g., tax farmers or tithe gatherers). The incidence of the taxes and contributions and the character of the administrative procedures will strongly condition the structure of the landscape and the capacity of the area for economic and social development (p. 2).

The fifth means for organizing a landscape, and by far the most important according to Johnson, is "a hierarchy of markets that interlinks the economic activities of the people of an area into some meaningful arrangement" (p. 3).

Johnson illustrates each type of landscape. The bulk of his book is concerned with policies for the fifth type of spatial organization in developing countries. The book is unique, or nearly so, in its scholarly discussion of the interpenetration of authority systems and territorially based communities.

Godfrey and Monica Wilson's book (221) is a pioneering study of social change based on observations in Central Africa of the impact of European civilization on traditional African societies. Their most striking concept is that of social change as a *change in scale*. The various elements of a traditional society formed a coherent whole; so did those of the civilized society into which Africans were being drawn. The transition involves changes in all elements: economic, political, technical and scientific, and religious. From a small territorially based society with oral traditions covering a few generations, Africans were moving into a society that was worldwide in its contemporary relationships and at least 2500 years deep in terms of religion, philosophy, literature, and science.

Robert Redfield's essay, *The Little Community: Viewpoints for the Study of a Human Whole* (222), is an idealized and generalized interpretation of the social organization and culture of a small, self-contained preliterate community. Although transitions are not discussed, by implication the work dramatizes the profound nature of the differences between "the little community" and modern society.

Jan Myrdal's *Report from a Chinese Village* (223) is of direct contemporary interest. The village is small but shares, of course, a cultural tradition of great time depth and geographic extent. Fox and Wang (224) present some ideas for the measurement of the effects of institutional and technological changes during China's successive reorganizations of agriculture and rural society from 1948 to the late 1960s.

V. Gordon Childe's classic, *What Happened in History* (225), is an interpretive study, based mainly on archaeological findings, with a time depth of many thousand years. Childe emphasizes major technological revolutions and their consequences for social organization; his chapter headings include "Paleolithic Savagery," "Neolithic Barbarism," "The Higher Barbarism of the Copper Age," "The Urban Revolution in Mesopotamia," "The Culmination of Bronze Age Civilization," "The Early Iron Age," and "The Decline and Fall of the Ancient World." The successive transformations were profound; the rate of technological change in our own time and its potential consequences have been dramatized by Toffler (226) in his concept of "future shock."

On a more modest time scale are Carl Stephenson's (227, 228) works on medieval feudalism, the nature of its military, political, economic, and social organization, and the reasons for its decline "as one phase of the economic revolution experienced by western Europe between the eleventh and thirteenth centuries." Pirenne (229, 230) discusses medieval cities, their origins, and the revival of trade, with primary emphasis on the tenth, eleventh, and twelfth centuries. From E. A. J. Johnson's viewpoint, the emergence of medieval cities involved a fascinating interplay of military (feudal), sacerdotal, and market-hierarchical systems of authority and spatial organization. Haskins writes in the literary-historical tradition of "the renaissance of the twelfth century":

> The epoch of the Crusades, of the rise of towns, and of the earliest bureaucratic states of the West, [the twelfth century] saw the culmination of Romanesque art and the beginnings of Gothic; the emergence of the vernacular literatures; the revival of the Latin classics and of Latin poetry and Roman law; the recovery of Greek science, with its Arabic additions, and of much of Greek philosophy; and the origin of the first European universities. (Ref. 231, p. vi.)

Rice writes of the foundations of early modern Europe, 1460–1559:

> The century of European history between 1460 and 1559 was a period of rapid, comprehensive change. Like all periods of transition from one firmly contoured civilization to another, its most obvious characteristic is an intricate counterpoint of tradition and innovation, catastrophe and promise. (Ref. 232, p. ix.)

This century witnessed the formation of the "early modern state" in England, France, and Spain and "revolution and reformation in the church," ending with "the triumph of the territorial church":

> ... The Church, which in the high Middle Ages had been a European corporation, broke apart into a congeries of local territorial churches, their boundaries determined by the geography of political power; there were national churches, princely churches, provincial churches, even churches confined to the population of a single city or, as in Poland, to the population of a single aristocratic estate. ... [The essential character of the new system was] the concentration of ecclesiastical appointments, taxation, jurisdiction, administration, and discipline in the hands of secular authorities. In this context the Reformation is another aspect of the emergence of the sovereign state. (Ref. 232, pp. 165–167.)

R. H. Tawney's (233) classic study, *Religion and the Rise of Capitalism*, was an effort "to trace some strands in the development of religious thought on social and economic questions in the period which saw the transition from medieval to modern theories of social organization." In his preface to the 1937 edition, he wrote:

> The economic theories propounded by Schoolmen; the fulminations by the left wing of the Reformers against usury, landgrabbing, and extortionate prices; the appeal of hard-headed Tudor statesmen to traditional religious sanctions; the attempt of Calvin and his followers to establish an economic discipline more rigorous than that which they had overthrown ... all rest on the assumption that the institution of property, the transactions of the

> market-place, the whole fabric of society and the whole range of its activi-
> ties . . . must justify themselves at the bar of religion. All insist that Chris-
> tianity has no more deadly foe than . . . the unbridled indulgence of the
> acquisitive appetite. Hence the claim that religion should keep its hands off
> business encountered, when first formulated, a great body of antithetic
> doctrine, embodied not only in literature and teaching, but in custom and
> law. It was only gradually, and after a warfare not confined to paper, that
> it effected the transition from the status of an odious paradox to that of an
> unquestioned truth (pp. 4–5).

Barraclough (234) felt in 1944 that it was essential to provide a broad perspective
on German history from 800 to 1939 as a basis for the major decisions about boundaries and political institutions for Germany that would be made at the end of World
War II. He remarks that in contrast to the continuity of development of France and
England from medieval times to the twentieth century,

> German history . . . is a story of discontinuity, of development cut short . . .,
> the consolidation of the early monarchy was cut short in 1076, the estab-
> lishment of national unity was fatally checked after 1250, the growth of
> representative estates withered after the Reformation, the expansion of the
> middle classes was halted as a result of the Thirty Years War, the settle-
> ment of 1815 prolonged particularism, the growth of self-government was
> stunted by the constitution of 1871, the transfer of social and economic
> power was sidetracked in 1918 and 1919. (Ref. 234, p. 456.)

The first 250 pages are a detailed and fascinating account of attempts by able mon-
archs (at various periods from 919 to 1250) to establish a power base sufficiently
stable and broad in an "open" geographic situation. For various reasons, these attempts failed, and political power devolved to a large number of territorial princes.

Eisenstadt (235) gives an impressive sociological analysis of the rise and fall of
"historical bureaucratic empires." He makes some of the same points in his introduction to *The Decline of Empires* (236), which contains a number of readings on the characteristics of specific empires. Ehrenberg presents a classic study of the Greek city-
state:

> Out of this twofold inheritance—the preponderance of urban settlement
> and the geographical conditions—the new immigrants, hitherto bound to
> one another by the personal and social relationships of the tribe, created
> those new political forms of which the Polis, the Greek city-state, was the
> crown. (Ref. 237, p. 3.)

Ehrenberg also discusses at some length the Hellenistic states that were created from
the short-lived empire of Alexander the Great.

Kuznets (238) puts modern economic growth in global and historical perspective.
To some extent, his book is a continuation of the story of the modern nation-state,
capitalism, industrialism, and imperialism. Marx's (239) interpretation of history is
familiar to all. Morishima (240) reviews Marx's economic thought "in the light of
the present-day advanced level of economic theory." He confines himself to discussing only the core of Marx's theory, "that is, his general equilibrium model,
which has two main constituents: the theory of value and the theory of reproduction."

Schumpeter (241) presents his well-known disequilibrium theory of economic development, with waves of innovation as the main elements in the so-called Juglar type of business cycle and also in growth. Borchert (242) and Borchert and Lukermann (243) give what might be called a Schumpeterian account of waves of innovation in transportation systems in the United States from 1790 to the 1960s and their consequences for waves of growth in American cities at particular kinds of locations.

Finally, we list three works that dramatize, as by-products, the rapidity of the transitions that must be measured, anticipated, and dealt with in the decades ahead. Toffler's *Future Shock* (226) is widely known. Incidentally, Toffler's concept of "the flow of situations" would be equivalent to "the flow of behavior settings" in Roger Barker's terminology. According to Toffler (pp. 32–33 of 1971 Bantam Books edition), every situation has a certain "wholeness" and can be analyzed in terms of five components: things, places, people, organizational locus, and a context of information or ideas. His formulation is evidently independent of Barker's, since his 19-page bibliography contains no reference to Barker.

Limits to Growth (244) is also widely known; less so is the somewhat more sober work by Forrester (245) on which it is largely based. Although the specific simulations of Meadows et al. (244) may be alarmist, the social function of alarmism is to avert catastrophe—its prophesies are successful to the extent that they are self-defeating.

Richard L. Meier's *Science and Economic Development: New Patterns of Living* (246) shows an amazing grasp of the relevant literature across the physical, biological, and behavioral sciences. It is a much more optimistic book than *Limits to Growth*, because Meier matter of factly assumes that sweeping changes in patterns of resource use will occur in response to specific shortages.

In his preface to the 1956 edition (reprinted on pages ix–xiii of the 1966 edition), Meier states:

> It is curious that . . . the scientific fraternity has not in recent times sought to create tentative models for world development. . . .
>
> Perhaps this is because the concepts of the working natural scientist do not mix well with those from the social scientist. The same term will have different meanings, and using the same methods will have different hazards. . . .
>
> In the last chapter, entitled "New Patterns of Living," the first- and second-order effects of the new technologies upon the course of development are considered. This takes one quite a long way from the substantial foundation of laboratory investigation and ends up well within the study of society. . . .
>
> Thus the invasion of the social studies was carefully considered; it was intended to establish a continuity of analysis that overlaps the experience of social scientists. Only by such means (i.e., the penetration of each other's domain) can the various specialists communicate with each other to solve the problems of society. The problems, of course, hardly ever respect academic boundaries. . . .

Meier estimates that the world *could* support 50 billion people at biologically adequate standards. In a recent (July 1973) television presentation, he expressed the belief that world population will level off in the neighborhood of 12 to 15 billion. In the most densely populated regions, much of the relatively flat land now used for agriculture will be occupied by metropolitan areas (networks of relatively self-contained cities) ranging up to 20 million in population. A large proportion of food requirements in such regions may be met, directly and indirectly, by hydroponic gardening and the mass culture of algae. Meier consistently stresses the importance of using "every channel of communications likely to change family values so that adults would feel impelled to avail themselves of contraceptive services. . . ."

All three formulations of man's future (226, 244, 246) imply that social data systems will be exposed to severe stresses and must incorporate whatever flexibility is necessary to cope with them. Social change also entails the obsolescence of data systems. The recent report of the American Agricultural Economics Association Committee on Economic Statistics (247) underscores this problem.

In its report (p. 867), the Committee refers to a presidential address to the American Economic Association in which Wassily Leontief (248) indicted the economics profession for its failure to create an adequate empirical foundation for the highly articulated economic analytics and theory developed over the last several decades. Leontief specifically excepted agricultural economists from his indictment:

> "An exceptional example of a healthy balance between theoretical and empirical analysis, and of the readiness of professional economists to cooperate with experts in the neighboring disciplines, is offered by agricultural economics as it developed in this country over the last 50 years. . . . Official agricultural statistics are more complete, reliable and systematic than those pertaining to any other major sector of our economy . . . agricultural economists demonstrated the effectiveness of a systematic combination of theoretical approach and detailed factual analysis. They also were the first among economists to make use of the advanced methods of mathematical statistics. However, in their hands, statistical inference became a complement to, not a substitute for, empirical research" (p. 5).

The Committee (1972) continues:

> Professor Leontief does us great honor, but the honor properly belongs to an earlier generation, for the specialization of the last several decades has brought similar ills to agricultural economics. Among these ills is a growing lack of interest in the data systems that make good empirical work possible. Individually there are many distinguished and honorable exceptions, but as a profession we are vulnerable to this criticism.

> Problems of formulating and selecting concepts around which data are gathered seem to be perceived today by most economists as the responsibility of statisticians. Statisticians more correctly see the problem of "what is to be measured" as something that should best be answered by people who use the numbers and the discipline whose theoretical concepts are being quantified by the data system. We are falling into a chasm between these two postures. Consequently, we have been failing to renew our early investment in the conceptualization of agricultural data systems and to develop the entirely new systems of data needed to contend with a rapidly changing economy and way of life.

> The Committee on Economic Statistics concludes that the data systems upon which we depend are in serious crisis. With each passing year, fundamental structural change transforms agriculture and rural life. Thus theoretical concepts around which we have constructed our data systems grow progressively more obsolete—so obsolete that minor tinkering with each

census or survey no longer serves to bridge the basic inadequacy of the
ideas being quantified. Predictive analyses built upon these concepts perform less and less well despite great efforts at statistical manipulation of
data, refinement of technique, and elaborate economic modeling. In addition, we have never really succeeded in conceptualizing theoretical systems
that will allow us to understand, measure, and deal effectively with development and various aspects of human welfare. This Committee believes
the profession must begin to devote major resources and some of its best
minds to the solution of these problems, or see the profession itself decline
in intellectual capacity and social utility. (Ref. 247, pp. 867–868.)

In its conclusion the Committee states:

We have described some major problems. Yet rapid technological and
social change creates an even more important problem. Extremely fast
societal change produces situations in which data systems are faced with
the necessity of frequent redefinition of what is being measured as well as
the necessity to adjust statistical measurement procedures to those changes.
Have we not reached the point where the overpowering problem is not so
much the difficulties described above but rather the question of how to design a statistical data system with the capability of continued adjustment to
social change?

We should not imagine that the kind of progressive conceptual erosion described in this report is limited to the data systems upon which rural social
scientists depend. It is a problem which all social scientists must face soon
and seriously. (Ref. 247, p. 874.)

In his discussion, Edgar Dunn (249) commended the AAEA Committee on
Economic Statistics for a report of "major significance":

I have read almost every report and article written in the last 10 years related to the issues of statistical reform. Insofar as official reports go, this one
is in a class by itself. In the report the Committee modestly declined credit
for the Leontief accolade on behalf of the current generation of agricultural
economists. But if this report is an indication, that current generation may
be positioning itself to take the vanguard of social science once again in
this domain. (Ref. 249, p. 878.)

Dunn further commends the report for its "sense of shock"

in recognizing that our data problems create a crisis so fundamental as to
raise serious questions about the meaningfulness of current social science.
This alone makes the report worthwhile, for what bothers me most about
the current state of social science is that *it should be in a state of shock about
these matters and is not.* But I will go one step further. I have become con-
vinced that these problems are not only bigger than we thought, they are,
for the time being, "bigger than we are." (Ref. 249, p. 878.)

Although Dunn's last statement may seem unduly dramatic, it is clearly intended
as a challenge, not only to the agricultural economists who heard his address, but
to all social scientists concerned with data systems, indicators, and accounts. Dunn's
1974 book, *Social Information Processing and Statistical Systems—Change and Reform* (250),
is a major contribution to the conceptualization and design of social data systems.

Appendix Bibliography

1. *Theories of Measurement, Aggregation and Utility, Measurement of Quality Change, and Mathematical Social Science*

   1. Krantz, D. H., Luce, R. D., Suppes, P., and Tversky, A. 1971. *Foundations of measurement:* Volume I. *Additive and polynomial representations.* New York: Academic Press.
   2. Pfanzagl, J. 1968. *Theory of measurement.* New York: John Wiley & Sons.
   3. Ijiri, Yuji. 1967. *The foundations of accounting measurement: A mathematical, economic and behavioral inquiry.* Englewood Cliffs, N.J.: Prentice-Hall.
   4. ———. 1971. Fundamental queries in aggregation theory. *Journal of the American Statistical Association* **66** (December), 766–782.
   5. Theil, Henri. 1954. *Linear aggregation of economic relations.* Amsterdam: North-Holland Publishing Company.
   6. Allen, R. G. D. 1959. *Mathematical economics.* 2nd edition. London: Macmillan & Company Ltd.
   7. Fox, Karl A. 1968. *Intermediate economic statistics.* New York: John Wiley & Sons.
   8. Fisher, Walter D. 1969. *Clustering and aggregation in economics.* Baltimore: Johns Hopkins University Press.
   9. Fishburn, Peter C. 1968. Utility theory. *Management Science* **14** (January), 335–378.
   10. ———. 1970. *Utility theory for decision making.* New York: John Wiley & Sons.
   11. Von Neumann, John, and Morgenstern, Oskar. (1944) 1964. *Theory of games and economic behavior.* New York: John Wiley & Sons.
   12. Luce, R. Duncan, and Raiffa, Howard. 1957. *Games and decisions.* New York: John Wiley & Sons.
   13. Georgescu-Roegen, Nicholas. 1968. Utility. In *International encyclopedia of the social sciences:* Volume 16. New York: Macmillan Company and The Free Press.
   14. Arrow, Kenneth J. 1958. Utilities, attitudes, choices: A review note. *Econometrica* **26** (January), 1–23.
   15. Chipman, John S. 1960. The foundations of utility. *Econometrica* **28,** 193–224.
   16. Fisher, Irving. 1927. A statistical method for measuring "marginal utility" and testing the justice of a progressive income tax. In Jacob H. Hollander, ed., *Economic essays: Contributed in honor of John Bates Clark.* New York: Macmillan Company.
   17. Frisch, Ragnar. 1926. Sur un problème d'économie pure. *Norsk Matematisk Forenings Skrifter* **1,** 1–40.
   18. ———. 1932. New methods of measuring marginal utility. *Beiträge zur ökonomischen Theorie.* Tübingen: J. C. B. Mohr (Paul Siebeck).

19. Waugh, Frederick V. 1935. The marginal utility of money in the United States from 1917 to 1921 and from 1922 to 1932. *Econometrica* **3**, 376–399.

20. Fellner, William. 1967. Operational utility: The theoretical background and a measurement. In W. Fellner *et al.*, eds., *Ten economic studies in the tradition of Irving Fisher*. New York: John Wiley & Sons.

21. Strotz, Robert H. 1957. The empirical implications of a utility tree. *Econometrica* **25**, 269–280.

22. ———. 1959. The utility tree—A correction and further appraisal. *Econometrica* **27** (July), 482–488.

23. Gorman, W. M. 1959. Separable utility and aggregation. *Econometrica* **27** (July), 469–481.

24. Frisch, Ragnar. 1959. A complete scheme for computing all direct and cross demand elasticities in a model with many sectors. *Econometrica* **27** (April), 177–196.

25. Brandow, George E. 1961. *Interrelations among demands for farm products and implications for control of market supplies*. Pennsylvania Agricultural Experimental Station Bulletin 680. University Park: Pennsylvania State University.

26. George, P. S., and King, Gordon A. 1971. *Consumer demand for food commodities in the United States with projections for 1980*. Giannini Foundation Monograph Number 76. Berkeley: University of California Division of Agricultural Sciences.

27. Cochrane, James L., and Zeleny, Milan, eds. 1973. *Multiple criteria decision making*. Columbia: University of South Carolina Press.

28. MacCrimmon, Kenneth R. 1973. In James L. Cochrane and Milan Zeleny, eds., *Multiple criteria decision making*. Columbia: University of South Carolina Press.

29. Ijiri, Yuji. 1965. *Management goals and accounting for control*. Amsterdam: North-Holland Publishing Company.

30. Griliches, Zvi, ed. 1971. *Price indexes and quality change: Studies in new methods of measurement*. Cambridge, Mass.: Harvard University Press.

31. Griliches, Zvi. 1961. Hedonic price indexes for automobiles: An econometric analysis of quality change. In *The price statistics of the federal government*, General Series, No. 73. New York: National Bureau of Economic Research.

32. Adelman, Irma, and Griliches, Zvi. 1961. On an index of quality change. *Journal of the American Statistical Association* **56**, 535–548.

33. Court, Andrew T. 1939. Hedonic price indexes with automotive examples. In *The dynamics of automobile demand*. New York: General Motors Corporation.

34. Lancaster, Kelvin J. 1966. A new approach to consumer theory. *The Journal of Political Economy* **74** (April), 132–157.

35. ———. 1966. Change and innovation in the technology of consumption. *American Economic Review* **56** (May), 14–23.

36. ———. 1971. *Consumer demand*. New York: Columbia University Press.

37. Smith, Victor E. 1959. Linear programming models for the determination of palatable human diets. *Journal of Farm Economics* **41** (May), 272–283.

38. ———. 1960. Measurement of product attributes recognized by consumers. CAEA Report 5, Seminar on Consumer Preferences and Market Development for Farm Products. Ames: Center for Agriculture and Economic Adjustment, Iowa State University (Winter Quarter). Mimeograph.

39. ———. 1963. *Electronic computation of human diets*. East Lansing: Bureau of Business and Economic Research, Michigan State University. (Plus a detached supplement of 105 pages containing tabular material.)

40. Waugh, Frederick V. (1951) 1969. The minimum-cost dairy feed (an application of "linear programming"). *Journal of Farm Economics* **33** (August 1951), 299–310. Reprinted as Chapter 8 in Karl A. Fox and D. Gale Johnson (eds.), *Readings in the economics of agriculture*. Homewood, Ill.: Richard D. Irwin, 1969.

41. ———. 1942. Regressions between sets of variables. *Econometrica* **10**, 290–310.

42. Coleman, James S. 1964. *Introduction to mathematical sociology*. New York: Free Press of Glencoe.

43. Keyfitz, Nathan. 1968. *Introduction to the mathematics of population*. Reading, Mass.: Addison-Wesley

44. Lazarsfeld, Paul F., and Henry, Neil W. 1966. *Readings in mathematical social science*. Cambridge, Mass.: The M.I.T. Press.

45. Lotka, Alfred J. (1925) 1956. *Elements of mathematical biology*. New York: Dover Publications.

2. *Statistical Demand Analysis and the Analysis of Causal Relations*
   Statistical demand analysis, 1920–1939

46. Tolley, Howard R., and Ezekiel, Mordecai. 1923. A method of handling multiple correlation problems. *Journal of the American Statistical Association* **18** (December), 994–1003.

47. Ezekiel, Mordecai. 1924. A method of handling curvilinear correlation for any number of variables. *Journal of the American Statistical Association* **19**, pp. 431–453.

48. Bean, Louis H. 1929. A simplified method of graphic curvilinear correlation. *Journal of the American Statistical Association* **24** (December), 386–397.

49. Ezekiel, Mordecai. 1930. *Methods of correlation analysis*. New York: John Wiley & Sons. 2nd revised edition, 1941.

50. Waugh, Frederick V. 1964. *Demand and price analysis: Some examples from agriculture*. Technical Bulletin No. 1316, Economic and Statistical Analysis Division, Economic Research Service, U.S. Department of Agriculture. Washington, D.C.: Government Printing Office.

51. Frisch, Ragnar, and Waugh, Frederick V. 1933. Partial time regressions as compared with individual trends. *Econometrica* **1** (October), 387–401.

52. Waugh, Frederick V. 1935. A simplified method of determining multiple regression constants. *Journal of the American Statistical Association* **30**, 694–700.

53. Smith, Bradford B. 1923. The use of punched card tabulating equipment in multiple correlation problems. U.S. Department of Agriculture, Bureau of Agricultural Economics. Mimeograph.

54. Wallace, Henry A., and Snedecor, George W. 1925. Correlation and machine calculation. Bulletin 35. Ames: Iowa State College.

55. Working, Holbrook. 1922. Factors determining the price of potatoes in St. Paul and Minneapolis. Agricultural Experiment Station Technical Bulletin 10. St. Paul: University of Minnesota.

56. Waugh, Frederick V. 1923. Factors influencing the price of New Jersey potatoes on the New York market. Circular 66. Trenton: New Jersey Department of Agriculture.

57. Schultz, Henry. 1924. The statistical measurement of the elasticity of demand for beef. *Journal of Farm Economics* **6** (July), 254–278.

58. Wright, Sewall. 1925. *Corn and hog correlations*. Bulletin 1300. Washington, D.C.: U.S. Department of Agriculture.

59. Haas, George C., and Ezekiel, Mordecai. 1926. Factors affecting the price of hogs. Bulletin 1440. Washington, D.C.: U.S. Department of Agriculture.

60. Working, Holbrook. 1925. The statistical determination of demand curves. *Quarterly Journal of Economics* **39** (August), 503–543.

61. Working, Elmer J. 1927. What do statistical "demand curves" show? *Quarterly Journal of Economics* **41** (February), 212–235.

62. Ezekiel, Mordecai. 1928. Statistical analyses and the "laws" of price. *Quarterly Journal of Economics* **42** (February), 199–227.

63. Schultz, Henry. 1928. *Statistical laws of demand and supply*. Chicago: University of Chicago Press.

64. Warren, George F., and Pearson, Frank A. 1928. Interrelations of supply and price. Agricultural Experiment Station Bulletin 466. Ithaca, N.Y.: Cornell University.

65. Elliott, Foster F. 1927. The nature and measurement of the elasticity of supply of farm products. *Journal of Farm Economics* **9** (July), 288–302.

66. Bean, Louis H. 1929. The farmers' response to price. *Journal of Farm Economics* **11**, 368–385.

67. Ezekiel, Mordecai. 1933. Some considerations on the analysis of the prices of competing or substitute commodities. *Econometrica* 1 (April), 172–180.

68. Schultz, Henry. 1933. A comparison of elasticities of demand obtained by different methods. *Econometrica* 1 (July), 274–308.

69. Ezekiel, Mordecai, and Bean, Louis H. 1933. Economic bases for the Agriculture Adjustment Act. Washington, D.C.: U.S. Department of Agriculture.

70. Waugh, Frederick V., Burtis, E. L., and Wolf, A. F. 1936. The controlled distribution of a crop among independent markets. *Quarterly Journal of Economics* 51 (November), 1–41.

71. Ezekiel, Mordecai. 1938. The cobweb theorem. *Quarterly Journal of Economics* 52 (February), 255–280.

Statistical demand analysis, 1950–1969

72. Foote, Richard J., and Fox, Karl A. 1952. *Seasonal variation: Methods of measurement and tests of significance.* U.S. Department of Agriculture. Agriculture Handbook No. 48. Washington, D.C.: Government Printing Office.

73. Fox, Karl A., and Cooney, James F., Jr. 1954. Effects of intercorrelation upon multiple correlation and regression measures. Agricultural Marketing Service Bulletin (reissued October 1959). Washington, D.C.: U.S. Department of Agriculture.

74. Foote, Richard J., and Fox, Karl A. 1954. *Analytical tools for measuring demand.* U.S. Department of Agriculture. Agriculture Handbook No. 64. Washington, D.C.: Government Printing Office.

75. Foote, Richard J. 1958. *Analytical tools for studying demand and price structures.* U.S. Department of Agriculture. Agriculture Handbook No. 146. Washington, D.C.: Government Printing Office.

76. Nerlove, Marc. 1958. *Distributed lags and demand analysis for agricultural and other commodities.* Agriculture Handbook No. 141. Washington, D.C.: U.S. Department of Agriculture.

77. Fox, Karl A. 1951. Factors affecting farm income, farm prices, and food consumption. *Agricultural Economics Research* 3 (July), 65–82.

78. ———. 1951. Relations between prices, consumption, and production. *Journal of the American Statistical Association* 46, 323–333.

79. ———. 1953. Factors affecting the accuracy of price forecasts. *Journal of Farm Economics* 35, 323–340.

80. ———. 1953. *The analysis of demand for farm products.* U.S. Department of Agriculture, Technical Bulletin No. 1081. Washington, D.C.: Government Printing Office.

81. ———. 1954. Structural analysis and the measurement of demand for farm products. *Review of Economics and Statistics* 37, 57–66.

82. ———. 1955. Changes in the structure of demand for farm products. *Journal of Farm Economics* 37, 411–428.

83. Fox, Karl A., and Norcross, Harry C. 1952. Some relationships between agriculture and the general economy. *Agricultural Economics Research* 4, 13–21.

84. ———. 1953. A spatial equilibrium model of the livestock-feed economy in the United States. *Econometrica* 21, 547–566.

85. ———. 1963. Spatial price equilibrium and process analysis in the food and agricultural sector. In Alan S. Manne and Harry M. Markowitz, eds., *Studies in process analysis: Economy-wide production capabilities.* New York: John Wiley & Sons.

86. ———, and Taeuber, Richard C. 1955. Spatial equilibrium models of the livestock-feed economy. *American Economic Review* 45, 584–608.

87. ———. 1954. The use of economic models in appraising foreign trade policies. *Journal of Farm Economics* 36, 944–958.

88. Waugh, Frederick V. 1956. A partial indifference surface for beef and pork. *Journal of Farm Economics* 38 (February), 102–112.

89. Day, Richard H. 1963. *Recursive programming and production response.* Amsterdam: North-Holland Publishing Company.

90. Fox, Karl A. 1951. The measurement of price support costs. *Journal of Farm Economics* **33,** 470–484.

91. ———. 1956. The contribution of farm price support programs to general economic stability. In National Bureau of Economic Research, *Policies to combat depression.* Princeton, N.J.: Princeton University Press.

92. ———. 1956. The interdependence between an effective stabilization policy and agriculture. In Gerhard Colm, ed., *The Employment Act past and future.* National Planning Association Special Report 41. Washington, D.C.: National Planning Association.

93. ———, and Wells, Oris V. 1952. *Reserve levels for storable farm products.* U.S. 82nd Congress, 2nd Session, Senate Document 130. Washington, D.C.: Government Printing Office.

94. ———. 1957. Guiding agricultural adjustments. *Journal of Farm Economics* **39** (December), 1090–1107.

95. ———. 1958. Agricultural income. In National Bureau of Economic Research, *A critique of the United States income and product accounts: Studies in income and wealth.* Volume 22. Princeton, N.J.: Princeton University Press.

96. ———. 1959. Economic instability and agricultural adjustment. In Center for Agricultural and Economic Development, *Problems and policies of American agriculture.* Ames: Iowa State University Press.

97. ———. 1962. Commercial agriculture: Perspectives and prospects. In *Farming, farmers and markets for farm goods.* Essays on the Problems and Potentials of American Agriculture, Supplementary Paper No. 15. New York: Committee for Economic Development.

98. ———. 1965. A submodel of the agricultural sector. In J. S. Duesenberry et al., eds., *The Brookings quarterly econometric model of the United States.* Skokie, Ill.: Rand McNally; and Amsterdam: North-Holland Publishing Company.

99. ———. 1963. The food and agricultural sectors in advanced economies. In T. Barna, ed., *Structural interdependence and economic development.* London and New York: Macmillan Company.

100. ———. 1958. *Econometric analysis for public policy.* Ames: Iowa State University Press.

101. Ezekiel, Mordecai, and Fox, Karl A. 1959. *Methods of correlation and regression analysis.* 3rd ed. New York: John Wiley & Sons.

102. Waugh, Frederick V. 1964. Cobweb models. *Journal of Farm Economics* 46 (November), 732–750. Reprinted as Chapter 6 in Karl A. Fox and D. Gale Johnson (eds.), *Readings in the economics of agriculture.* Homewood, Ill.: Richard D. Iwrin, 1969.

103. Fox, Karl A. 1968. Demand and supply: II. Econometric studies. In *International encyclopedia of the social sciences:* Volume 4. New York: Macmillan Company and The Free Press.

104. ———, and Johnson, D. Gale, eds. 1969. *Readings in the economics of agriculture.* Homewood, Ill.: Richard D. Irwin.

The analysis of causal relations

105. Wright, Sewall. 1921. Correlation and causation. *Journal of Agricultural Research* **20,** 557–585.

106. ———. 1934. The method of path coefficients. *Annals of Mathematical Statistics.* **5,** 161–215.

107. Wright, Philip G. 1928. *The tariff on animal and vegetable oils.* New York: Macmillan Company. (See Appendix, prepared in collaboration with Sewall Wright.)

108. Hauser, Robert M., and Goldberger, Arthur S. 1971. The treatment of unobservable variables in path analysis. In H. L. Costner, ed., *Sociological methodology.* San Francisco: Jossey-Bass.

109. Griliches, Zvi, and Mason, W. 1972. Education, income, and ability. *Journal of Political Economy* **80** (May–June), S74–S103.

110. Goldberger, Arthur S. 1972. Structural equation methods in the social sciences. *Econometrica* **40,** No. 6 (November), 979–1001.

111. Ezekiel, Mordecai. 1942. Statistical investigations of savings, consumption and investment, I and II. *American Economic Review* **32** (March), 22–49; (June), 272–307.

112. Klein, Lawrence R. 1943. Pitfalls in the statistical determination of the investment schedule. *Econometrica* **11** (July–October), 246–258.

113. ———. 1944. The statistical determination of the investment schedule: A reply. *Econometrica* **12** (January), 91–92.

114. Ezekiel, Mordecai. 1944. The statistical determination of the investment schedule. *Econometrica* **12** (January), 89–90.

115. Koopmans, Tjalling C. 1953. Identification problems in econometric model construction. In William C. Hood and Tjalling C. Koopmans, eds., *Studies in econometric method.* New York: John Wiley & Sons.

116. Fox, Karl A. 1952. *The demand for farm products: An appraisal of the applicability of single equation methods to statistical demand analysis for agricultural commodities.* Unpublished doctoral dissertation (Economics), University of California Library, Berkeley.

117. Bentzel, R., and Wold, Herman O. 1946. On statistical demand analysis from the viewpoint of simultaneous equations. *Skandinavisk Aktuarietidskrift* **29**, 95–114.

118. Wold, Herman O. 1949. Statistical estimation of economic relationships. *Econometrica* **17** (Supp., July), 1–22.

119. ———. 1956. Causal inference from observational data: A review of ends and means. *Journal of the Royal Statistical Society*, Series A. **119**, 28–60.

120. ———. 1959. Ends and means in econometric model building. In U. Grenander, ed., *Probability and statistics: The Harold Cramer volume.* Stockholm: Almquist & Wiksell.

121. ———. 1960. A generalization of causal chain models. *Econometrica* **28** (April), 443–463.

122. ———. 1969. Econometrics as pioneering in nonexperimental model building. *Econometrica* **37** (July), 369–381.

123. ———, and Juréen, Lars. 1953. *Demand analysis.* New York: John Wiley & Sons.

124. Strotz, Robert H., and Wold, Herman O. 1960. Recursive vs. nonrecursive systems: An attempt at synthesis. *Econometrica* **28** (April), 417–427.

125. Simon, Herbert A. 1953. Causal ordering and identifiability. In William C. Hood and Tjalling C. Koopmans, eds., *Studies in econometric method.* New York: John Wiley & Sons.

126. Stone, Richard. 1945. The analysis of market demand. *Journal of the Royal Statistical Society* **107**, 1–98.

127. ———, et al. 1954. *The measurement of consumers' expenditures and behaviour in the United Kingdom, 1920–1938:* Volume I. Cambridge: Cambridge University Press.

128. Frisch, Ragnar. 1934. *Statistical confluence analysis by means of complete regression systems.* Oslo: Universitets Økonomiske Institutet.

129. Haavelmo, Trygve. 1943. The statistical implications of a system of simultaneous equations. *Econometrica* **11**, 1–12.

130. ———. 1944. The probability approach in econometrics. *Econometrica* (Suppl.) **12**.

131. Koopmans, Tjalling, ed. 1950. *Statistical inference in dynamic economic models.* New York: John Wiley & Sons.

132. Hood, William C., and Koopmans, Tjalling C., eds. 1953. *Studies in econometric method.* New York: John Wiley & Sons.

133. Wright, Sewall. 1954. The interpretation of multivariate systems. In Oscar Kempthorne et al., eds., *Statistics and mathematics in biology.* Ames: Iowa State University Press.

134. ———. 1960. Path cofficients and path regressions. *Biometrics* **16**, 189–202.

135. ———. 1960. The treatment of reciprocal interaction, with or without lag, in path analysis. *Biometrics* **16** (September), 423–445.

136. Tukey, John W. 1954. Causation, regression, and path analysis. In Oscar Kempthorne et al., eds., *Statistics and mathematics in biology.* Ames: Iowa State University Press.

137. Duncan, Otis Dudley. 1966. Path analysis: Sociological examples. *American Journal of Sociology* **72** (July), 1–16.

138. Alker, Hayward R., Jr. 1966. Causal inference and political analysis. In Joseph L. Bernd, ed., *Mathematical applications in political science:* Volume II. Dallas, Tex.: Southern Methodist University Press.

139. Sewell, William H., and Hauser, Robert M. 1972. Causes and consequences of higher edu-

cation: Models of the status attainment process. *American Journal of Agricultural Economics* **54,** 5 (December), 851–861.

140. Blalock, H. M., Jr., ed. 1971. *Causal models in the social sciences.* Chicago: Aldine-Atherton.

141. Goldberger, Arthur S., and Duncan, Otis Dudley, eds. 1973. *Structural equation models in the social sciences.* New York: Seminar Press.

3. *Theories of Competitive Equilibrium, Lifetime Income and Choice, Economic Growth, Optimal Control, and Human Capital*

142. Arrow, Kenneth J., and Hahn, F. H. 1971. *General competitive analysis.* San Francisco: Holden-Day, and Edinburgh: Oliver & Boyd.

143. Malinvaud, E. 1972. *Lectures on microeconomic theory.* Amsterdam: North-Holland Publishing Company, and New York: American Elsevier.

144. Kornai, Janos. 1971. *Anti-equilibrium: On economic systems theory and the tasks of research.* Amsterdam: North-Holland Publishing Company.

145. Hahn, F. H. 1973. The winter of our discontent. *Economica,* New Series. **40,** No. 159 (August), 322–330.

146. Samuelson, Paul A. 1969. Lifetime portfolio selection by dynamic stochastic programming. *Review of Economics and Statistics* **51,** 239–246.

147. Merton, Robert C. 1969. Lifetime portfolio selection under uncertainty: The continuous-time case. *Review of Economics and Statistics* **51,** 247–257.

148. Yaari, M. E. 1964. On the consumer's lifetime allocation process. *International Economic Review* **5,** 304–317.

149. ———. 1965. Uncertain lifetime, life insurance and the theory of the consumer. *Review of Economic Studies* **32,** 137–150.

150. Meade, J. E. 1966. Life-cycle savings, inheritance and economic growth. *Review of Economic Studies* **33,** 61–78.

151. Markowitz, H. M. 1959. *Portfolio selection.* New York: John Wiley & Sons.

152. Lintner, J. 1965. Security prices, risk, and maximum gains from diversification. *Journal of Finance* **20,** 587–615.

153. Mossin, J. 1966. Equilibrium in a capital asset market. *Econometrica* **34,** 768–783.

154. Koopmans, Tjalling C. 1960. Stationary ordinal utility and impatience. *Econometrica* **28,** 287–309.

155. Cohn, Elchanan. 1972. *Public expenditure analysis: With special reference to human resources.* Lexington, Mass.: D. C. Heath & Company.

156. Eckstein, Otto. 1961. A survey of the theory of public expenditure criteria. In James M. Buchanan, ed., *Public finances: Needs, sources and utilization.* Princeton, N.J.: Princeton University Press.

157. Arrow, Kenneth J., and Kurz, Mordecai. 1970. *Public investment, the rate of return, and optimal fiscal policy.* Baltimore: Johns Hopkins Press.

158. Stiglitz, Joseph E., and Uzawa, Hirofumi, eds. 1969. *Readings in the modern theory of economic growth.* Cambridge, Mass.: The M.I.T. Press.

159. Koopmans, Tjalling C. 1965. On the concept of optimal economic growth. In *The econometric approach to development planning.* Study Week on the Econometric Approach to Development Planning, Vatican City, 1963. Amsterdam: North-Holland Publishing Company.

160. ———. 1967. Objectives, constraints, and outcomes in optimal growth models. *Econometrica* **35** (January), 1–15.

161. Pontryagin, L. S., Boltyanskii, V. G., Gamkrelidze, R. V., and Mishchenko, E. F. 1962. *The mathematical theory of optimal processes.* New York: Wiley-Interscience.

162. Athans, Michael. 1971. The role and use of the stochastic linear-quadratic-Gaussian problem in control system design. *IEEE Transactions on Automatic Control* **AC-16** (December), 529–552.

163. Tintner, Gerhard, and Sengupta, Jati K. 1972. *Stochastic economics: Stochastic processes, control, and programming.* New York: Academic Press.

164. Zadeh, L. A., and Polak, E., eds. 1969. *System theory*. New York: McGraw-Hill Book Company.

165. Fox, Karl A., Sengupta, Jati K., and Thorbecke, Erik. 1973. *The theory of quantitative economic policy: With applications to economic growth, stabilization, and planning*. Amsterdam: North-Holland Publishing Company, and New York: American Elsevier. 1st edition, 1966.

166. Van den Bogaard, P. J., and Theil, Henri. 1959. Macro-dynamic policymaking: An application of strategy and certainty equivalence concepts to the economy of the United States, 1933–1936. *Metroeconomica* 11 (December), 151–154.

167. Åström, K. J., and Eykhoff, P. 1971. System identification—A survey. *Automatica* 7, 123–162.

168. Kalman, R. E. 1961. On the general theory of control systems. *Proceedings of the International Congress on Automatic Control:* Volume 1. London: Butterworths Scientific Publishers.

169. Schultz, Theodore W. 1960. The formation of human capital by education. *Journal of Political Economy* 68, 571–583.

170. ———. 1962. Reflections on investment in man. *Journal of Political Economy* 70, Part 2 (October), 1–8.

171. ———. 1963. *The economic value of education*. New York: Columbia University Press.

172. ———. 1971. *Investment in human capital: The role of education and of research*. New York: The Free Press.

173. ———. 1972. Human capital: Policy issues and research opportunities. In National Bureau of Economic Research, *Human resources*. Fiftieth Anniversary Colloquium VI. New York: Columbia University Press.

174. Becker, Gary S. 1964. *Human capital: A theoretical and empirical analysis, with special reference to education*. New York: Columbia University Press.

4. *Social Learning Theories, Entitivity, and Fuzzy Sets*

175. Estes, William K. 1972. Research and theory on the learning of probabilities. *Journal of the American Statistical Association* 67 (March), 81–102.

176. Arrow, Kenneth J. 1962. The economic implications of learning by doing. *Review of Economic Studies* 29 (June), 155–173.

177. Dunn, Edgar S., Jr. 1971. *Economic and social development: A process of social learning*. Baltimore: Johns Hopkins University Press.

178. Zadeh, L. A. 1965. Fuzzy sets. *Information and Control* 8 (June), 338–353.

179. ———. 1968. Fuzzy algorithms. *Information and Control* 12 (February), 94–102.

180. ———. 1971. Toward a theory of fuzzy systems. In R. E. Kalman and N. DeClaris, eds., *Aspects of network and systems theory*. New York: Holt, Rinehart & Winston.

181. Zadeh, L. A. 1973. Outline of a new approach to the analysis of complex systems and decision processes. In James L. Cochrane and Milan Zeleny, eds., *Multiple criteria decision making*. Columbia: University of South Carolina Press. (Ref. 186 has also been published in the *IEEE Transactions on Systems, Man, and Cybernetics*, SMC-3, No. 1, January 1973.)

182. Bellman, R. E., and Zadeh, L. A. 1970. Decision-making in a fuzzy environment. *Management Science* 17 (December), B141–B164.

183. Roberts, Blaine, and Holdren, Bob R. 1972. *Theory of social process: An economic analysis*. Ames: Iowa State University Press.

5. *Hierarchies, Decentralization, Resource Allocation, Information Theory, and the Theory of Teams*

184. Downs, Anthony. 1967. *Inside bureaucracy*. Boston: Little, Brown & Company.

185. Chandler, Alfred D., Jr. 1962. *Strategy and structure: Chapters in the history of the American industrial enterprise*. Cambridge, Mass.: The M.I.T. Press.

186. Simon, Herbert A. 1962. The architecture of complexity. *Proceedings of the American Philosophical Society* 106 (December), 467–482.

187. Mesarovic, M. D., Macko, D., and Takahara, Y. 1970. *Theory of hierarchical, multilevel systems*. New York: Academic Press.

188. Kornai, J., and Liptak, T. L. 1965. Two-level planning. *Econometrica* **33,** 141–169.

189. McCamley, F. P. 1967. Activity analysis models of educational institutions. Unpublished Ph.D. dissertation. Ames: Iowa State University Library.

190. Kumar, T. Krishna. 1972. Resource allocation processes in linear static models. In Karl A. Fox, ed., *Economic analysis for educational planning.* Baltimore: Johns Hopkins University Press.

191. ———. 1972. Resource allocation processes in nonlinear and dynamic models. In Karl A. Fox, ed., *Economic analysis for educational planning.* Baltimore: Johns Hopkins University Press.

192. Sengupta, Jati K. 1972. Economic problems of resource allocation in nonmarket systems. In Karl A. Fox, ed., *Economic analysis for educational planning.* Baltimore; Johns Hopkins University Press.

193. Arrow, Kenneth J., and Hurwicz, L. 1960. Decentralization and computation in resource allocation. In R. W. Pfouts, ed., *Essays in economics and econometrics.* Chapel Hill: University of North Carolina Press.

194. Hurwicz, Leonid. 1969. On the concept and possibility of informational decentralization. *American Economic Review* **59** (May), 513–524.

195. Malinvaud, E. 1967. Decentralized procedures for planning. In E. Malinvaud and M. O. L. Bacharach, eds., *Activity analysis in the theory of economic growth and planning.* London: Macmillan & Company, Ltd., and New York: St. Martin's Press.

196. Gruver, Gene W. 1972. Economic decision models under linear methods of decentralization. Unpublished Ph.D. dissertation. Ames: Iowa State University Library.

197. Heal, G. M. 1973. *The theory of economic planning.* Amsterdam: North-Holland Publishing Company, and New York: American Elsevier.

198. Tinbergen, Jan. (1959) 1969. The theory of the optimum regime. In Karl A. Fox, Jati K. Sengupta, and G. V. L. Narasimham, eds., *Economic models, estimation and risk programming: Essays in honor of Gerhard Tintner.* Berlin and New York: Springer-Verlag.

199. Marschak, Jacob. 1971. Economics of information systems. *Journal of the American Statistical Association* **66** (March), 192–219.

200. McGuire, C. B., and Radner, Roy, eds. 1972. *Decision and Organization: A volume in honor of Jacob Marschak.* Amsterdam: North-Holland Publishing Company, and New York: American Elsevier.

201. Marschak, Jacob, and Radner, Roy. 1972. *Economic theory of teams.* Cowles Foundation Monograph 22. New Haven, Conn.: Yale University Press.

202. Theil, Henri. 1967. *Economics and information theory.* Amsterdam: North-Holland Publishing Company.

6. *Welfare Economics, Public Choice, and Policy Sciences*

203. Arrow, Kenneth J., and Scitovsky, Tibor, eds. 1969. *Readings in welfare economics.* Homewood, Ill.: Richard D. Irwin.

204. Russett, Bruce M., ed. 1968. *Economic theories of international politics.* Chicago: Markham Publishing Company.

205. Dorfman, Robert, and Dorfman, Nancy S., eds. 1972. *Economics of the environment: Selected readings.* New York: W. W. Norton & Company.

206. Arrow, Kenneth J. (1951) 1963. *Social choice and individual values.* New York: John Wiley & Sons.

207. Downs, Anthony. 1957. *An economic theory of democracy.* New York: Harper & Row.

208. Buchanan, James M., and Tullock, Gordon. (1962) 1965. *The calculus of consent: Logical foundations of constitutional democracy.* Ann Arbor: University of Michigan Press.

209. Buchanan, James M. 1967. *Public finance in democratic process: Fiscal institutions and individual choice.* Chapel Hill: University of North Carolina Press.

210. ———. 1968. *The demand and supply of public goods.* Skokie, Ill.: Rand McNally.

211. Olson, Mancur. (1965) 1971. *The logic of collective action: Public goods and the theory of groups.* Cambridge, Mass.: Harvard University Press.

212. Almond, Gabriel A. 1960. Introduction: A functional approach to comparative politics. In Gabriel A. Almond and James S. Coleman, eds., *The politics of the developing areas*. Princeton, N.J.: Princeton University Press.

213. Easton, David. 1965. *A systems analysis of political life*. New York: John Wiley & Sons.

214. Lerner, Daniel, and Lasswell, Harold D., eds. 1951. *The policy sciences: Recent developments in scope and method*. Stanford: Stanford University Press.

215. Lasswell, Harold D. 1968. Policy sciences. In *International encyclopedia of the social sciences: Volume 12*. New York: Macmillan Company and The Free Press.

216. ———. 1971. *A pre-view of policy sciences*. Amsterdam: Elsevier, and New York: American Elsevier.

217. Dror, Yehezkel. 1971. *Design for policy sciences*. Amsterdam: Elsevier, and New York: American Elsevier.

218. ———. 1971. *Ventures in policy sciences*. Amsterdam: Elsevier, and New York: American Elsevier.

7. *Disequilibrium, Discontinuous Social Change, and the Obsolescence of Social Data Systems*

219. Meier, Richard L. 1972. Communications stress. In Richard F. Johnston, ed.; Peter W. Frank and Charles D. Michener, assoc. eds., *Annual Review of Ecology and Systematics*. Volume III, 289–314. Palo Alto, California: Annual Reviews Inc.

220. Johnson, E. A. J. 1970. *The organization of space in developing countries*. Cambridge, Mass.: Harvard University Press.

221. Wilson, Godfrey, and Wilson, Monica. (1945) 1968. *The analysis of social change: Based on observations in Central Africa*. Cambridge: Cambridge University Press.

222. Redfield, Robert. (1955) 1960. *The little community: Viewpoints for the study of a human whole*. Chicago: University of Chicago Press.

223. Myrdal, Jan. 1965. *Report from a Chinese village*. New York: Signet Books (New American Library).

224. Fox, Karl A., and Wang, Tong-eng. 1969. Estimating the effects of institutional and technological changes upon agricultural development: A comparison of multiple regression and programming approaches. In Karl A. Fox, Jati K. Sengupta, and G. V. L. Narasimham, eds., *Economic models, estimation, and risk programming: Essays in honor of Gerhard Tintner*. Berlin: Springer-Verlag.

225. Childe, V. Gordon. (1942) 1960. *What happened in history*. Revised edition. Baltimore: Penguin Books.

226. Toffler, Alvin. 1970. *Future shock*. New York: Random House. Bantam Books edition, 1971.

227. Stephenson, Carl. (1942) 1956. *Medieval feudalism*. Ithaca, N.Y.: Cornell University Press.

228. ———. 1954. *Medieval institutions*. Ithaca, N.Y.: Cornell University Press.

229. Pirenne, Henri. (1925) 1969. *Medieval cities: Their origins and the revival of trade*. Princeton, N.J.: Princeton University Press.

230. ———. (1933) 1937. *Economic and social history of medieval Europe*. New York: Harcourt Brace Jovanovich.

231. Haskins, Charles Homer. (1927) 1957. *The renaissance of the twelfth century*. Cleveland, Ohio: Meridian Books.

232. Rice, Eugene T., Jr. 1970. *The foundations of early modern Europe, 1460–1559*. New York: W. W. Norton & Company.

233. Tawney, R. H. (1926) 1937. *Religion and the rise of capitalism*. New York: Mentor Books.

234. Barraclough, Geoffrey. 1946. *The origins of modern Germany*. New York: Capricorn Books.

235. Eisenstadt, Shmuel N. 1968. Empires. In *International encyclopedia of the social sciences: Volume 5*. New York: Macmillan Company and The Free Press.

236. Eisenstadt, Shmuel N., ed. 1967. *The decline of empires*. Englewood Cliffs, N.J.: Prentice-Hall.

237. Ehrenberg, Victor. (1960) 1964. *The Greek state*. New York: W. W. Norton & Company.

238. Kuznets, Simon. 1966. *Modern economic growth: Rate, structure, and spread.* New Haven, Conn.: Yale University Press.

239. Marx, Karl. (1867–1879) 1925–1926. *Capital: A critique of political economy.* 3 volumes. Chicago: Kerr.

240. Morishima, Michio. 1973. *Marx's economics: A dual theory of value and growth.* Cambridge: Cambridge University Press.

241. Schumpeter, Joseph A. (1934) 1961. *The theory of economic development.* New York: Oxford University Press.

242. Borchert, John R. 1967. American metropolitan evolution. *Geographical Review* (July), 301–332.

243. ———, and Lukermann, Fred. 1969. A cautionary tale: The setting of anomalous places. In *Minnesota experimental city*, Volume II. *Economic and physical aspects.* Minneapolis: University of Minnesota.

244. Meadows, D. H., Meadows, D. L., Randers, R., and Behrens, W. W. 1972. *The limits to growth.* New York: Universe Books.

245. Forrester, Jay W. 1971. *World dynamics.* Cambridge: Wright-Allen Press.

246. Meier, Richard L. (1956) 1966. *Science and economic development: New patterns of living.* 2nd edition. Cambridge, Mass.: The M.I.T. Press.

247. American Agricultural Economics Association Committee on Economic Statistics. 1972. Our obsolete data systems: New directions and opportunities. *American Journal of Agricultural Economics* **54** (December), 867–875.

248. Leontief, Wassily W. 1971. Theoretical assumptions and non-observed facts. *American Economic Review* **61** (March), 1–7.

249. Dunn, Edgar S., Jr. 1972. Discussion. *American Journal of Agricultural Economics* **54** (December), 878–879.

250. ———. 1974. *Social information processing and statistical systems—change and reform.* New York: John Wiley & Sons.

Author Index

Subject Index